A CALIFORNIA COMPANION

FOR THE COURSE IN WILLS, TRUSTS, AND ESTATES

Selected Cases and Statutes
Including All Statutes Required
for the California Bar Exam

A CALIFORNIA COMPANION FOR THE COURSE IN WILLS, TRUSTS, AND ESTATES

Selected Cases and Statutes
Including All Statutes Required
for the California Bar Exam
2019-2020

Susan F. French

Professor of Law, Emerita
UCLA School of Law

Printed in the United States of America.

1 2 3 4 5 6 7 8 9 0

ISBN 978-1-4548-9485-8

About Wolters Kluwer Legal & Regulatory U.S.

Wolters Kluwer Legal & Regulatory U.S. delivers expert content and solutions in the areas of law, corporate compliance, health compliance, reimbursement, and legal education. Its practical solutions help customers successfully navigate the demands of a changing environment to drive their daily activities, enhance decision quality and inspire confident outcomes.

Serving customers worldwide, its legal and regulatory portfolio includes products under the Aspen Publishers, CCH Incorporated, Kluwer Law International, ftwilliam.com and MediRegs names. They are regarded as exceptional and trusted resources for general legal and practice-specific knowledge, compliance and risk management, dynamic workflow solutions, and expert commentary.

For Tom, Sarah, Ellie, and Dylan, the lights of my life

Summary of Contents

NOTE: *California Companion chapters track the chapters in Dukeminier & Sitkoff, Wills, Trusts, & Estates (10th Ed. 2017). There are no California Companion materials for Chapter 11, Charitable Trusts, or Chapter 15, Wealth Transfer Taxation.*

Table of Contents

Table of Contents

Table of Contents

Table of Contents

Table of Contents

Table of Contents

Preface to the 2019-2020 Edition

California teachers of Wills, Trusts & Estates always face the question of how much California law to include in their courses. In addition to the bar statutes, there are a number of areas in which California law is different from the Uniform Probate Code or the "national" law presented in casebooks. Inheritance rights of parents and children in adoption and nonmarital situations, disqualified transferees, consequences of financial elder abuse, rights of creditors in trust assets, extension of wills rules to nonprobate transfers, and rights of beneficiaries to information about trusts are just some of the areas in which California law has distinct rules that students should be aware of. This book is my answer to the question of how much to include. I found it an interesting and manageable set of supplemental materials that fit well into a 4-hour course, and I think it can easily be adapted for a 3-hour course.

In addition to the bar statutes—clearly marked with ❖ in the title—the book includes a variety of nonbar statutes that give context to the bar statutes, reflect recent legislative changes, or illustrate areas where California law is different from "national" law. Bills introduced in the 2019-2020 session of the legislature that would affect included statutes if enacted are noted. Chapter 1 begins with a broad outline of the California Probate Code to give students an idea about the breadth and location of subjects covered.

The book is designed for ease of use. I have given the statutes captions that are more informative than those found in the code books and I have edited the cases, often severely, to allow for easier classroom use. I have also included some Notes about recent cases and the dates on which statutes were adopted and amended.

The detailed Table of Contents lists all the included statutes, with identifying captions, and all the principal cases, which are preceded by a short description that identifies the subject matter. At the end of the book there is a Table of Cases, which includes note cases as well as principal cases, and a Table of Statutes. The Table of Statutes groups the statutes into Bar Statutes, other sections of the Probate Code, sections of the Family Code, the Civil Code, the Code of Civil Procedure, and the Welfare and Institutions Code. Instructions for the California Bar Exam listing the Bar Statutes may be found immediately following this Preface.

Two principal cases and twenty-seven note cases are new to this edition. The new principal cases are: *Aviles v. Swearingen,* which addressed the requirements for a "protected instrument" for purposes of the no-contest clause statutes; and *Orange Catholic Foundation v. Arvizu,* which found there was no abuse of discretion in excusing the trustee from liability for failure to evict the destitute and ailing life beneficiary for failure to pay maintenance expenses as required by the trust, and for a two-year delay in sale of residence after he died. The trustee believed she was carrying out the wishes of the settlor and the value of the house appreciated substantially during the two-year delay.

New note cases, which can be found through the Table of Cases, are: *Barefoot v. Jennings* (review granted on Dec. 12, 2018), *Bellows v. Bellows, Blech v. Blech, County Line Holdings, LLC v. McClanahan, Dent v. Wolf, Ebree v. Embree, Estate of Betty Lou O'Connor, Estate of John O'Connor, Estate of Obata, Estate of Powell, Gaynor v. Bulen, Kasperbauer v. Fairfield, Kerley v. Weber, Morgan v. Superior Court, People ex rel. Harris v. Shine, Powell v. Tagami, Pratt v. Ferguso, Rumbaugh v. Harley, Schwan v. Permann, Smith v. Szeyller, Sveen v. Melin, Trolan v. Trolan, United States v. Harris, Urick v. Urick, Williamson v. Brooks,* and *Yeh v. Tai.*

All cases are listed in the Table of Cases. Principal cases are shown in upper case, note cases in lower case. The sequence of these materials tracks the Dukeminier & Sitkoff casebook (Wills, Trusts, and Estates, 10th ed. 2017), but the materials can easily be used with other casebooks because the Table of Contents clearly shows the subject matter of each section.

Footnotes in cases retain their original numbers. Footnotes I have added are indicated by "—Ed." The materials are up-to-date as of February 15, 2019.

Susan F. French
March 2019

Scope of the California Bar Examination

INSTRUCTIONS REGARDING WILLS AND SUCCESSION

Applicants should be familiar with the following provisions of the California Probate Code and understand California law in the specific areas noted:

Division 2. General Provisions

Part 1. Effect of Death of Married Person on Community and Quasi-Community Property, Sections 100-103

Part 3. Contractual Arrangements Relating to Rights at Death, Sections 140-147

Part 5. Simultaneous Death, Sections 220, 222-224

Part 6. Distribution Among Heirs or Beneficiaries, Section 240

Division 6. Wills and Intestate Succession

Part 1. Wills

Chapter 1. General Provisions, Sections 6100, 6101, 6104, 6105

Chapter 2. Execution of Wills, Sections 6110-6113

Chapter 3. Revocation and Revival, Sections 6120, 6121, 6123

Part 2. Intestate Succession, Sections 6400-6402

Division 11. Construction of Wills, Trusts and Other Instruments

Part 1. Rules of Interpretation of Instruments, Sections 21105, 21109, 21110

Part 6. Family Protection: Omitted Spouses and Children [for decedents dying on or after January 1, 1998]

Chapter 2. Omitted Spouses, Sections 21610-21612

Chapter 3. Omitted Children, Sections 21620-21623

From _http://www.calbar.ca.gov/Admissions/Examinations/California-Bar-Examination/California-Bar-Examination-Scope._ Site visited Feb. 14, 2019.

Chapter 1. Introduction: Freedom of Disposition

Section B. The Mechanics of Succession

Outline of California Probate Code

The California Probate Code is organized into Divisions, which are divided into Parts, and then into Chapters. There are 13 Divisions:

Division 1   Preliminary Provisions & Definitions, §§ 1-88

Division 2   General Provisions, §§ 100-883

Division 3   General Provisions of Procedural Nature, §§ 1000-1312

Division 4   Guardianship, Conservatorship, and Other Protective Proceedings, §§ 1400-3925

Division 4.5 Powers of Attorney, §§ 4000-4545

Division 4.7 Health Care Decisions, §§ 4600-4806

Division 5   Nonprobate Transfers, §§ 5000-5705

Division 6   Wills & Intestate Succession, §§ 6100-6806

Division 7   Administration of Estates of Decedents, §§ 7000-12591

Division 8   Disposition of Estate Without Administration, §§ 13000-13660

Division 9   Trust Law, §§ 15000-19530

Division 10 Proration of Taxes, §§ 20100-20225

Division 11 Construction of Wills, Trusts, and Other Instruments, §§ 21101-21700

Probate in the Digital Age: What of Digital Assets?

California adopted the Revised Uniform Fiduciary Access to Digital Assets Act effective Jan. 1, 2017. The Act is codified at CPC §§ 870-883.

Probate Administration

California provides for both fully supervised and independent administration of decedents' estates in Division 7. There are 13 Parts in Division 7:

1. General Provisions, §§ 7000 *et seq.*

2. Opening Estate Administration, §§ 8000 *et seq.*

3. Inventory and Appraisal, §§ 8800 *et seq.*

4. Creditor Claims, §§ 9000 *et seq.*

5. Estate Management, §§ 9600 *et seq.*

6. Independent Administration, §§ 10400 *et seq.*

7. Compensation of Personal Representative and Attorney, §§ 10800 *et seq.*

8. Accounts, §§ 10900 *et seq.*

9. Payment of Debts, §§ 11400 *et seq.*

10. Distribution of Estate, §§ 11600 *et seq.*

11. Closing Estate Administration, §§ 12200 *et seq.*

12. Administration of Estates of Missing Persons Presumed Dead, §§ 12400 *et seq.*

13. Nondomiciliary Decedents, §§ 12500 *et seq.*

Probating a Will

CPC § 8200. Custodian of Will; Duties upon Testator's Death; Liability; Copies of Delivered Will to be Released by Clerk; Fees

(a) Unless a petition for probate of the will is earlier filed, the custodian of a will shall, within 30 days after having knowledge of the death of the testator, do both of the following:

(1) Deliver the will, personally or by registered or certified mail, to the clerk of the superior court of the county in which the estate of the decedent may be administered.

(2) Deliver a copy of the will pursuant to Section 1215 to the person named in the will as executor, if the person's whereabouts is known to the custodian, or if not, to a person named in the will as a beneficiary, if the person's whereabouts is known to the custodian.

(b) A custodian of a will who fails to comply with the requirements of this section shall be liable for all damages sustained by any person injured by the failure.

(c) The clerk shall release a copy of a will delivered under this section for attachment to a petition for probate of the will or otherwise on receipt of payment of the required fee and either a court order for production of the will or a certified copy of a death certificate of the decedent.

***

(Stats. 1990, 1994, 2012, 2013, 2017)

NOTE: The process for proving a will for admission to probate is governed by CPC §§ 8220-8226.

CPC § 8226. Conclusiveness of Probate of Will; Time Limits for Petitioning for Probate of Will

(a) If no person contests the validity of a will or petitions for revocation of probate of the will within the time provided in this chapter, admission of the will to probate is conclusive, subject to Section 8007.[1]

(b) Subject to subdivision (c), a will may be admitted to probate notwithstanding prior admission to probate of another will or prior distribution of property in the proceeding. The will may not affect property previously distributed, but the court may determine how any provision of the will affects property not yet distributed and how any provision of the will affects provisions of another will.

(c) If the proponent of a will has received notice of a petition for probate or a petition for letters of administration for a general personal representative, the proponent of the will may petition for probate of the will only within the later of either of the following time periods:

(1) One hundred twenty days after issuance of the order admitting the first will to probate or determining the decedent to be intestate.

(2) Sixty days after the proponent of the will first obtains knowledge of the will.

(Stats 1990, 1997)

⤙⤚

Will Not Admitted to Probate: Not Filed Within Later of 120 Days After Determination of Intestacy or 60 Days After Obtaining Knowledge of Will

ESTATE of EARLEY

California Court of Appeal, Second District, Division 1
173 Cal. App. 4th 369, 92 Cal. Rptr. 3d 577 (2009)

MALLANO, P.J. . . . On May 8, 2007, James Peter Earley died, leaving an estate valued at around $1.25 million. On July 31, 2007, Kathleen Anderson, Earley's first cousin, filed a petition . . . , seeking letters of administration. Anderson also filed an heirship declaration, stating she was the sole beneficiary of the estate. . . .

On August 17, 2007, Anderson filed a notice of the petition to administer the estate. The notice was addressed to all heirs and beneficiaries, among others, and was served on the Los Angeles Public Administrator and Anderson herself. No one else was served.

By order dated September 5, 2007, the trial court appointed Anderson as the administrator of the estate with limited authority under the Independent Administration of Estates Act (Prob. Code, § 10400 *et seq.*; all statutory references are to that code). The court also determined that

---

[1] Extrinsic fraud or jurisdictional defect.—Ed.

Earley had died intestate. On September 7, 2007, the trial court issued letters of administration to Anderson.

On September 28, 2007, Vicky Breeden ... filed a request for special notice (see § 1250) .... Breeden was a first cousin once removed of Earley.

On October 22, 2007, Anderson discovered a holographic will of Earley dated June 14, 1954, and two codicils, dated August 2, 1954, and March 13, 1967. The will and first codicil named Earley's brother, Thomas, as sole beneficiary. Under the second codicil, if Thomas predeceased Earley, Anderson would become the sole beneficiary. Thomas died before Earley.

Anderson had the holographic will and codicils examined by a handwriting expert to determine their authenticity. After the expert confirmed that the documents were written by Earley, Anderson took steps to have them admitted to probate. ...

On February 19, 2008, Anderson filed a petition for probate of the will and for letters of administration with will annexed. ... Breeden filed an objection to the petition, stating that she was ... entitled to an intestate share of his estate. Breeden asserted that the [petition for probate of the will was not timely filed under Section 8226.—Ed.]

... Anderson discovered the will ... on October 22, 2007. Under the 60-day rule of section 8226, subdivision (c)(2), she had until December 21, 2007, to file the petition to probate the will. In the alternative, the trial court "determin[ed] the decedent to be intestate" by order dated September 5, 2007. Under the 120-day rule of section 8226, subdivision (c)(1), Anderson had until January 3, 2008, to file the petition. Section 8226, subdivision (c), gave her the benefit of waiting until the later of these two deadlines. But she filed the petition on February 19, 2008, more than a month late.

Anderson argues that section 8226 is limited to situations in which petitions to probate *successive wills* are filed and thus does not apply where a petition to probate a single will is filed after a determination that the decedent died intestate. We disagree. ...

[S]ection 8226 provides filing deadlines for admitting a will to probate regardless of whether another will has already been admitted to probate or whether estate proceedings have already commenced based on a determination of intestacy. This interpretation "facilitate[s] the prompt administration of estates." ... Anderson's construction does just the opposite.

Thus, the trial court properly found that the petition to admit the holographic will to probate was untimely under section 8226, subdivision (c). ...

NOTE: Estate of Kelly, 172 Cal. App. 4th 1367, 91 Cal. Rptr. 3d 674, rev. den. (2009) held that the period of § 8226(c) does not begin to run until the proponent of the will receives notice of the petition for probate or of the petition for letters of administration for a general personal representative. That the proponent is generally aware of the probate proceedings is not sufficient.

Barring Creditors

The period for filing creditors' claims is the later of 4 months after letters of administration are first issued to a general personal representative or 60 days after the date notice of administration is mailed or personally delivered to the creditor, CPC § 9100. Generally, a claimant has 90 days after rejection of a claim to file suit. See, CPC § 9353.

Disposition of Estates Without Probate

Small Estates: Probate Code Division 8, Part 1, §§ 13000-13210, provides for the collection or transfer of property, including real estate, in small estates (less than $150,000) by successors to the decedent without probate after 40 days have elapsed from the date of death. Nonprobate assets, property passing to a surviving spouse under § 13500, motor vehicles, boats, mobile homes, up to $15,000 in unpaid salary, and some other assets are excluded by CPC § 13050 in determining whether the estate is less than $150,000.

NOTE: AB 473 introduced in the 2019-2020 session of the legislature, if adopted, would increase these amounts to $166,250 and $16,625 and provide for adjustment every three years beginning in 2022.

Property Passing to Surviving Spouse: Part 2, §§ 13500-13660, allows property to pass from the decedent to the surviving spouse without probate under most circumstances. However, the surviving spouse may elect to have the property pass through administration, CPC §13502, and, if there is no administration, is personally liable for debts of the deceased spouse chargeable against the property as provided in CPC § 13550. If administration proceedings are commenced within three years after the decedent's death, the surviving spouse is liable to restore to the estate decedent's property or its value, CPC § 13562.

CPC § 13500. Spouse Dying Intestate; Surviving Spouse; Administration Not Necessary

Except as provided in this chapter, when a spouse dies intestate leaving property that passes to the surviving spouse under Section 6401, or dies testate and by his or her will devises all or a part of his or her property to the surviving spouse, the property passes to the survivor subject to the provisions of Chapter 2 (commencing with Section 13540) and Chapter 3 (commencing with Section 13550), and no administration is necessary.

(Stats. 1990, 2016)

CPC § 7250. Release of Beneficiaries' Claims Against Personal Representative and Sureties

(a) When a judgment or order made pursuant to the provisions of this code concerning the administration of the decedent's estate becomes final, it releases the personal representative and the sureties from all claims of the heirs or devisees and of any persons affected thereby based upon any act or omission directly authorized, approved, or confirmed in the judgment or order. For the purposes of this section, "order" includes an order settling an account of the personal representative, whether an interim or final account.

(b) . . .

(c) This section shall not apply where the judgment or order is obtained by fraud or conspiracy or by misrepresentation contained in the petition or account or in the judgment as to any material fact. For purposes of this subdivision, misrepresentation includes, but shall not be limited to, the omission of a material fact.

(Stats.1990, 1993)

NOTE: Graham-Sult v. Clainos, 756 F.3d 724 (9th Cir. 2014) held that plaintiffs' allegations of executor's fraud were sufficient to overcome executor's res judicata defense so as to establish plaintiffs' reasonable probability of prevailing and defeat executor's anti-SLAPP motion.

Section C. Professional Responsibility

California has long recognized that lack of privity is not a defense to a suit by a beneficiary whose gift fails because of negligence by the attorney. See **Lucas v. Hamm**, 56 Cal. 2d 583, 364 P.2d 685 (1961); **Heyer v. Flaig**, 70 Cal. 2d 223, 449 P.2d 161 (1969). In **Chang v. Lederman**, 172 Cal. App. 4th 67, 90 Cal. Rptr. 3d 758 (2d Dist. 2009), the court refused to extend the attorney's duty of care to a beneficiary who claimed that she was intended to receive a larger gift than that provided in the executed trust instrument.

Ch. 1. Introduction: Freedom of Disposition

The attorney's duty of care is further explored in *Moore v. Anderson*, Chapter 4.

Chapter 2. Intestacy: An Estate Plan by Default

Some Definitions

CPC § 13. Lineal and Collateral Kinship; Calculating Degree

(a) The degree of kinship or consanguinity between two persons is determined by counting the number of generations separating those persons, pursuant to subdivision (b) or (c). Each generation is called a degree.

(b) Lineal kinship or consanguinity is the relationship between two persons, one of whom is a direct descendant of the other. The degree of kinship between those persons is determined by counting the generations separating the first person from the second person. In counting the generations, the first person is excluded and the second person is included. For example, parent and child are related in the first degree of lineal kinship or consanguinity, grandchild and grandparent are related in the second degree, and great-grandchild and great-grandparent are related in the third degree.

(c) Collateral kinship or consanguinity is the relationship between two people who spring from a common ancestor, but neither person is the direct descendent of the other. The degree of kinship is determined by counting the generations from the first person up to the common ancestor and from the common ancestor down to the second person. In counting the generations, the first person is excluded, the second person is included, and the common ancestor is counted only once. For example, siblings are related in the second degree of collateral kinship or consanguinity, an aunt or uncle and a niece or nephew are related in the third degree, and first cousins are related in the fourth degree.

(Stats. 2009)

CPC § 28. Community Property

"Community property" means:

(a) Community property heretofore or hereafter acquired during marriage by a married person while domiciled in this state.

(b) All personal property wherever situated, and all real property situated in this state, heretofore or hereafter acquired during the marriage by a married person while domiciled elsewhere, that is community property, or a substantially equivalent type of marital property, under the laws of the place where the acquiring spouse was domiciled at the time of its acquisition.

(c) All personal property wherever situated, and all real property situated in this state, heretofore or hereafter acquired during the marriage by a married person in exchange for real or personal property, wherever situated, that is community property, or a substantially equivalent type of marital property, under the laws of the place where the acquiring spouse was domiciled at the time the property so exchanged was acquired.

(Stats. 1990)

CPC § 37. Domestic Partner

(a) "Domestic partner" means one of two persons who have filed a Declaration of Domestic Partnership with the Secretary of State pursuant to Division 2.5 (commencing with Section 297) of the Family Code, provided that the domestic partnership has not been terminated pursuant to Section 299 of the Family Code.

(b) Notwithstanding Section 299 of the Family Code, if a domestic partnership is terminated by the death of one of the parties and Notice of Termination was not filed by either party prior to the date of death of the decedent, the domestic partner who survives the deceased is a surviving domestic partner, and shall be entitled to the rights of a surviving domestic partner as provided in this code.

(Stats. 2001)

CPC § 44. Heir

"Heir" means any person, including the surviving spouse, who is entitled to take property of the decedent by intestate succession under this code.

(Stats. 1990)

CPC § 66. Quasi-Community Property

"Quasi-community property" means the following property, other than community property as defined in Section 28:

(a) All personal property wherever situated, and all real property situated in this state, heretofore or hereafter acquired by a decedent while domiciled elsewhere that would have been the community property of the decedent and the surviving spouse if the decedent had been domiciled in this state at the time of its acquisition.

(b) All personal property wherever situated, and all real property situated in this state, heretofore or hereafter acquired in exchange for real or personal property, wherever situated, that would have been the community property of the decedent and the surviving spouse if the decedent had been domiciled in this state at the time the property so exchanged was acquired.

(Stats. 1990)

CPC § 72. Spouse Includes Domestic Partner

"Spouse" includes domestic partner, as defined in Section 37 of this code, as required by Section 297.5 of the Family Code.

(Stats. 2016)

CPC § 78. Surviving Spouse

"Surviving spouse" does not include any of the following:

(a) A person whose marriage to, or registered domestic partnership with, the decedent has been dissolved or annulled, unless, by virtue of a subsequent marriage or registered domestic partnership, the person is married to, or in a registered domestic partnership with, the decedent at the time of death.

(b) A person who obtains or consents to a final decree or judgment of dissolution of marriage or termination of registered domestic partnership from the decedent or a final decree or judgment of annulment of their marriage or termination of registered domestic partnership, which decree or judgment is not recognized as valid in this state, unless they (1) subsequently participate in a marriage ceremony purporting to marry each to the other or (2) subsequently live together as spouses.

(c) A person who, following a decree or judgment of dissolution or annulment of marriage or registered domestic partnership obtained by the decedent, participates in a marriage ceremony with a third person.

(d) A person who was a party to a valid proceeding concluded by an order purporting to terminate all marital or registered domestic partnership property rights.

(Stats. 1990, 2016)

Section B. The Structure of Intestate Succession

❖ CPC § 6400. Property Subject to Intestacy Provisions

Any part of the estate of a decedent not effectively disposed of by will passes to the decedent's heirs as prescribed in this part.

(Stats. 1990)

Share of Surviving Spouse

❖ CPC § 100. Community Property

(a) Upon the death of a person who is married or in a registered domestic partnership, one-half of the community property belongs to the surviving spouse and the other half belongs to the decedent.

(b) Notwithstanding subdivision (a), spouses may agree in writing to divide their community property on the basis of a non pro rata division of the aggregate value of the community property or on the basis of a division of each individual item or asset of community property, or partly on each basis. Nothing in this subdivision shall be construed to require this written agreement in order to permit or recognize a non pro rata division of community property.

(Stats. 1990, 1998, 2016)

❖ CPC § 101. Quasi-Community Property

(a) Upon the death of a person who is married or in a registered domestic partnership, and is domiciled in this state, one-half of the decedent's quasi-community property belongs to the surviving spouse and the other half belongs to the decedent.

(b) Notwithstanding subdivision (a), spouses may agree in writing to divide their quasi-community property on the basis of a non pro rata division of the aggregate value of the quasi-community property, or on the basis of a division of each individual item or asset of quasi-community property, or partly on each basis. Nothing in this subdivision shall be construed to require this written agreement in order to permit or recognize a non pro rata division of quasi-community property.

(Stats. 1990, 1998, 2016)

Family Code § 297. Domestic Partners & Partnership Defined

(a) Domestic partners are two adults who have chosen to share one another's lives in an intimate and committed relationship of mutual caring.

(b) A domestic partnership shall be established in California when both persons file a Declaration of Domestic Partnership with the Secretary of State pursuant to this division, and, at the time of filing, all of the following requirements are met:

(1) Neither person is married to someone else or is a member of another domestic partnership with someone else that has not been terminated, dissolved, or adjudged a nullity.

(2) The two persons are not related by blood in a way that would prevent them from being married to each other in this state.

(3) Both persons are at least 18 years of age, except as provided in Section 297.1.

(4) Either of the following:

(A) Both persons are members of the same sex.

(B) One or both of the persons meet the eligibility criteria under Title II of the Social Security Act as defined in 42 U.S.C. Section 402(a) for old-age insurance benefits or Title XVI of the Social Security Act as defined in Section 1381 of Title 42 of the United States Code for aged individuals. Notwithstanding any other provision of this section, persons of opposite sexes may not constitute a domestic partnership unless one or both of the persons are over the age of 62.

(5) Both persons are capable of consenting to the domestic partnership.

(Stats. 1999, 2001, 2003, 2011)

NOTE: SB 30 introduced in the 2019-2020 session of the legislature would, if enacted, remove the requirement that domestic partners be either of the same sex or of the opposite sex and over the age of 62.

Family Code § 297.5. Rights of Domestic Partners

(a) Registered domestic partners shall have the same rights, protections, and benefits, and shall be subject to the same responsibilities, obligations, and duties under law, whether they derive from statutes, administrative regulations, court rules, government policies, common law, or any other provisions or sources of law, as are granted to and imposed upon spouses.

* * *

(c) A surviving registered domestic partner, following the death of the other partner, shall have the same rights, protections, and benefits, and shall be subject to the same responsibilities, obligations, and duties under law, whether they derive from statutes, administrative regulations, court rules, government policies, common law, or any other provisions or sources of law, as are granted to and imposed upon a widow or a widower.

(d) The rights and obligations of registered domestic partners with respect to a child of either of them shall be the same as those of spouses. The rights and obligations of former or surviving registered domestic partners with respect to a child of either of them shall be the same as those of former or surviving spouses.

* * *

(j) Where necessary to implement the rights of registered domestic partners under this act, gender-specific terms referring to spouses shall be construed to include domestic partners.

* * *

(Stats. 2003, 2004, 2006)

❖ *CPC § 6401. Intestate Share of Surviving Spouse*

(a) As to community property, the intestate share of the surviving spouse is the one-half of the community property that belongs to the decedent under Section 100.

(b) As to quasi-community property, the intestate share of the surviving spouse is the one-half of the quasi-community property that belongs to the decedent under Section 101.

(c) As to separate property, the intestate share of the surviving spouse is as follows:

(1) The entire intestate estate if the decedent did not leave any surviving issue, parent, brother, sister, or issue of a deceased brother or sister.

(2) One-half of the intestate estate in the following cases:

(A) Where the decedent leaves only one child or the issue of one deceased child.

(B) Where the decedent leaves no issue but leaves a parent or parents or their issue or the issue of either of them.

(3) One-third of the intestate estate in the following cases:

(A) Where the decedent leaves more than one child.

(B) Where the decedent leaves one child and the issue of one or more deceased children.

(C) Where the decedent leaves issue of two or more deceased children.

(Stats. 1990, 2002, 2014)

NOTE: Rights of Putative Spouse and Domestic Partner

1. Estate of Leslie, 37 Cal. 3d 186, 689 P.2d 133, 207 Cal. Rptr. 561 (1984) held that a putative spouse (one who believed, contrary to fact, they were validly married) is entitled to surviving spouse's share and to priority of appointment as administrator under the probate code.

2. In re Domestic Partnership of Ellis & Arraiga, 162 Cal. App. 4th 1000, 76 Cal. Rptr. 3d 401 (2008) held that the putative spouse doctrine applies to domestic partners.

3. Burnham v. California Public Employees' Retirement System, 208 Cal. App. 4th, 146 Cal. Rptr. 3d 607 (2012), held that a domestic partnership can be established only by filing the required declaration, which must be done before the death of either partner, and that the putative spouse doctrine applies only to partners who have accumulated property after entering into what one or both believed was a valid domestic partnership.

Simultaneous Death and 120-Hour Survival Requirement

❖ CPC § 103. *Community and Quasi-Community Property*

Except as provided by Section 224, if spouses die leaving community or quasi-community property and it cannot be established by clear and convincing evidence that one spouse survived the other:

(a) One-half of the community property and one-half of the quasi-community property shall be administered or distributed, or otherwise dealt with, as if one spouse had survived and as if that half belonged to that spouse.

(b) The other half of the community property and the other half of the quasi-community property shall be administered or distributed, or otherwise dealt with, as if the other spouse had survived and as if that half belonged to that spouse.

(Stats. 1990, 2016)

❖ CPC § 220. *Simultaneous Death: In General*

Except as otherwise provided in this chapter [§§ 220-226], if the title to property or the devolution of property depends upon priority of death and it cannot be established by clear and convincing evidence that one of the persons survived the other, the property of each person shall be administered or distributed, or otherwise dealt with, as if that person had survived the other.

(Stats. 1990)

CPC § 221. Exceptions: When §§ 220-224 Do Not Apply

(a) This chapter does not apply in any case where Section 103, 6211,[1] or 6403 applies.

(b) This chapter does not apply in the case of a trust, deed, or contract of insurance, or any other situation, where (1) provision is made dealing explicitly with simultaneous deaths or deaths in a common disaster or otherwise providing for distribution of property different from the provisions of this chapter or (2) provision is made requiring one person to survive another for a stated period in order to take property or providing for a presumption as to survivorship that results in a distribution of property different from that provided by this chapter.
(Stats. 1990, 2002)

❖ CPC § 222. Gift Conditioned on Survival of Another

(a) If property is so disposed of that the right of a beneficiary to succeed to any interest in the property is conditional upon surviving another person and it cannot be established by clear and convincing evidence that the beneficiary survived the other person, the beneficiary is deemed not to have survived the other person.

(b) If property is so disposed of that one of two or more beneficiaries would have been entitled to the property if he or she had survived the others, and it cannot be established by clear and convincing evidence that any beneficiary survived any other beneficiary, the property shall be divided into as many equal portions as there are beneficiaries and the portion of each beneficiary shall be administered or distributed, or otherwise dealt with, as if that beneficiary had survived the other beneficiaries.
(Stats. 1990)

❖ CPC § 223. Joint Tenants

(a) As used in this section, "joint tenants" includes owners of property held under circumstances that entitled one or more to the whole of the property on the death of the other or others.

(b) If property is held by two joint tenants and both of them have died and it cannot be established by clear and convincing evidence that one survived the other, the property held in joint tenancy shall be administered or distributed, or otherwise dealt with, one-half as if one joint tenant had survived and one-half as if the other joint tenant had survived.

(c) If property is held by more than two joint tenants and all of them have died and it cannot be established by clear and convincing evidence that any of them survived the others, the property held in joint tenancy shall be divided into as many portions as there are joint tenants and the share of each joint tenant shall be administered or distributed, or otherwise dealt with, as if that joint tenant had survived the other joint tenants.
(Stats. 1990)

---

[1] § 6211 imposes a 120-hour survival requirement on beneficiaries named in a California Statutory Will.—Ed.

❖ *CPC § 224. Life Insurance*

If the insured and a beneficiary under a policy of life or accident insurance have died and it cannot be established by clear and convincing evidence that the beneficiary survived the insured, the proceeds of the policy shall be administered or distributed, or otherwise dealt with, as if the insured had survived the beneficiary, except if the policy is community or quasi-community property of the insured and the spouse of the insured and there is no alternative beneficiary except the estate or personal representative of the insured, the proceeds shall be distributed as community property under Section 103.

(Stats. 1990)

CPC § 6403. 120-Hour Survival Requirement for Intestate Succession

(a) A person who fails to survive the decedent by 120 hours is deemed to have predeceased the decedent for the purpose of intestate succession, and the heirs are determined accordingly. If it cannot be established by clear and convincing evidence that a person who would otherwise be an heir has survived the decedent by 120 hours, it is deemed that the person failed to survive for the required period. The requirement of this section that a person who survives the decedent must survive the decedent by 120 hours does not apply if the application of the 120-hour survival requirement would result in the escheat of property to the state.

(b) This section does not apply to the case where any of the persons upon whose time of death the disposition of property depends died before January 1, 1990, and such case continues to be governed by the law applicable before January 1, 1990.

(Stats. 1990)

LAW REVISION COMMISSION COMMENT on CPC § 6403:

. . . Where Section 6403 applies, the 120-hour survival requirement is used to determine whether one person survived another for the purposes of Sections 103 (simultaneous death of husband and wife) and 234 (proceedings to determine survival). . . .

Shares of Descendants, Ancestors, Collaterals & Others

❖ *CPC § 6402. Share Not Passing to Surviving Spouse*

Except as provided in Section 6402.5,[2] the part of the intestate estate not passing to the surviving spouse under Section 6401, or the entire intestate estate if there is no surviving spouse, passes as follows:

---

[2] § 6402.5 provides special rules for succession to property of the decedent attributable to a predeceased spouse, but applies only to a decedent who is not survived by either spouse or issue. —Ed.

(a) To the issue of the decedent, the issue taking equally if they are all of the same degree of kinship to the decedent, but if of unequal degree those of more remote degree take in the manner provided in Section 240.

(b) If there is no surviving issue, to the decedent's parent or parents equally.

(c) If there is no surviving issue or parent, to the issue of the parents or either of them, the issue taking equally if they are all of the same degree of kinship to the decedent, but if of unequal degree those of more remote degree take in the manner provided in Section 240.

(d) If there is no surviving issue, parent or issue of a parent, but the decedent is survived by one or more grandparents or issue of grandparents, to the grandparent or grandparents equally, or to the issue of those grandparents if there is no surviving grandparent, the issue taking equally if they are all of the same degree of kinship to the decedent, but if of unequal degree those of more remote degree take in the manner provided in Section 240.

(e) If there is no surviving issue, parent or issue of a parent, grandparent or issue of a grandparent, but the decedent is survived by the issue of a predeceased spouse, to that issue, the issue taking equally if they are all of the same degree of kinship to the predeceased spouse, but if of unequal degree those of more remote degree take in the manner provided in Section 240.

(f) If there is no surviving issue, parent or issue of a parent, grandparent or issue of a grandparent, or issue of a predeceased spouse, but the decedent is survived by next of kin, to the next of kin in equal degree, but where there are two or more collateral kindred in equal degree who claim through different ancestors, those who claim through the nearest ancestor are preferred to those claiming through an ancestor more remote.

(g) If there is no surviving next of kin of the decedent and no surviving issue of a predeceased spouse of the decedent, but the decedent is survived by the parents of a predeceased spouse or the issue of those parents, to the parent or parents equally, or to the issue of those parents if both are deceased, the issue taking equally if they are all of the same degree of kinship to the predeceased spouse, but if of unequal degree those of more remote degree take in the manner provided in Section 240.

(Stats. 1990, 2014)

CPC § 50. Meaning of Issue

"Issue" of a person means all his or her lineal descendants of all generations, with the relationship of parent and child at each generation being determined by the definitions of child and parent.

(Stats. 1990)

NOTE: The court does not have power to limit generational level at which issue are entitled to take. **Estate of Beckel**, 174 Cal. App. 4th 34, 93 Cal. Rptr. 3d 890 (2009).

❖ CPC § 240. Distributions to Issue (Modern Per Stirpes)

If a statute calls for property to be distributed or taken in the manner provided in this section, the property shall be divided into as many equal shares as there are living members of the nearest generation of issue then living and deceased members of that generation who leave issue then living, each living member of the nearest generation of issue then living receiving one share and the share of each deceased member of that generation who leaves issue then living being divided in the same manner among his or her then living issue.
(Stats. 1990)

Distributions to Issue or Descendants in Wills and Trusts

CPC § 245. Modern Per Stirpes Distribution

(a) Where a will, trust, or other instrument calls for property to be distributed or taken "in the manner provided in Section 240 of the Probate Code," or where a will, trust, or other instrument that expresses no contrary intention provides for issue or descendants to take without specifying the manner, the property to be distributed shall be distributed in the manner provided in Section 240.

(b) Use of the following words without more, as applied to issue or descendants, is not an expression of contrary intention:

(1) "Per capita" when living members of the designated class are not all of the same generation.

(2) Contradictory wording, such as "per capita and per stirpes" or "equally and by right of representation."

(Stats. 1990)

CPC § 246. "Per Stirpes" Means Strict Per Stirpes Distribution

(a) Where a will, trust, or other instrument calls for property to be distributed or taken "in the manner provided in Section 246 of the Probate Code," the property to be distributed shall be divided into as many equal shares as there are living children of the designated ancestor, if any, and deceased children who leave issue then living. Each living child of the designated ancestor is allocated one share, and the share of each deceased child who leaves issue then living is divided in the same manner.

(b) Unless the will, trust, or other instrument expressly provides otherwise, if an instrument executed on or after January 1, 1986, calls for property to be distributed or taken "per stirpes," "by representation," or "by right of representation," the property shall be distributed in the manner provided in subdivision (a).

(c) If a will, trust, or other instrument executed before January 1, 1986, calls for property to be distributed or taken "per stirpes," "by representation," or by "right of representation," the property shall be distributed in the manner provided in subdivision (a), absent a contrary intent of the transferor.

(Stats. 1990)

CPC § 247. Per Capita at Each Generation Distribution

(a) Where a will, trust, or other instrument calls for property to be distributed or taken "in the manner provided in Section 247 of the Probate Code," the property to be distributed shall be divided into as many equal shares as there are living members of the nearest generation of issue then living and deceased members of that generation who leave issue then living. Each living member of the nearest generation of issue then living is allocated one share, and the remaining shares, if any, are combined and then divided and allocated in the same manner among the remaining issue as if the issue already allocated a share and their descendants were then deceased.

(b) Unless the will, trust, or other instrument expressly provides otherwise, if an instrument executed on or after January 1, 1986, calls for property to be distributed or taken "per capita at each generation," the property shall be distributed in the manner provided in subdivision (a).

(c) If a will, trust, or other instrument executed before January 1, 1986, calls for property to be distributed or taken "per capita at each generation," the property shall be distributed in the manner provided in subdivision (a), absent a contrary intent of the transferor.

(Stats. 1990)

CPC § 11604. Distribution to Heir Hunters & Other Transferees

(a) This section applies where distribution is to be made to any of the following persons:

    (1) The transferee of a beneficiary.

    (2) Any person other than a beneficiary under an agreement, request, or instructions of a beneficiary or the attorney in fact of a beneficiary.

(b) The court on its own motion, or on motion of the personal representative or other interested person or of the public administrator, may inquire into the circumstances surrounding the execution of, and the consideration for, the transfer, agreement, request, or instructions, and the amount of any fees, charges, or consideration paid or agreed to be paid by the beneficiary.

(c) The court may refuse to order distribution, or may order distribution on any terms that the court deems just and equitable, if the court finds either of the following:

    (1) The fees, charges, or consideration paid or agreed to be paid by a beneficiary are grossly unreasonable.

(2) The transfer, agreement, request, or instructions were obtained by duress, fraud, or undue influence.

(d) . . .

(Stats. 1990)

NOTES:

1. CPC § 11604.5 sets forth requirements governing validity of transfers of interests in a decedent's estate to a person who purchases a beneficiary's interest pursuant to a written agreement and who regularly engages in the purchase of beneficial interests in estates for consideration. It also provides that the court may inquire into the circumstances surrounding execution of the agreement and may refuse to order distribution or order distribution to the transferee on any terms the court considers equitable under circumstances specified in the statute. Section 11604.5 does not apply to a transferee engaged in the business of locating missing or unknown heirs who acquires an interest from a beneficiary solely in exchange for providing information or services associated with locating the beneficiary.

2. Legatees' "heir-hunting" agreements with a private investigator were held invalid assignments of their interests in **Estate of Molino**, 165 Cal. App. 4th 913, 81 Cal. Rptr. 3d 512 (2008). The agreements were void as against public policy because they authorized the heir hunter to retain an attorney and control litigation over rights in the estate.

Halfbloods

CPC § 6406. Relatives of the Halfblood

Except as provided in Section 6451, relatives of the halfblood inherit the same share they would inherit if they were of the whole blood.

(Stats. 1990, 1993)

Inclusion and Exclusion of Halfbloods, Adopted Persons, Nonmarital Children, Stepchildren, Foster Children and Their Issue in Gifts Made in Wills and Trusts

CPC § 21115. When Class Gift Includes Halfbloods, Adopted Persons, Nonmarital Children, Stepchildren, Foster Children and Their Issue

(a) Except as provided in subdivision (b), halfbloods, adopted persons, persons born out of wedlock, stepchildren, foster children, and the issue of these persons when appropriate to the class, are included in terms of class gift or relationship in accordance with the rules for determining relationship and inheritance rights for purposes of intestate succession.

(b) In construing a transfer by a transferor who is not the natural parent, a person born to the natural parent shall not be considered the child of that parent unless the person lived while a minor as a regular member of the household of the natural parent or of that parent's parent, brother, sister, spouse, or surviving spouse. In construing a transfer by a transferor who is not the adoptive parent, a person adopted by the adoptive parent shall not be considered the child of that parent unless the person lived while a minor (either before or after the adoption) as a regular member of the household of the adopting parent or of that parent's parent, brother, sister, or surviving spouse.

(c) Subdivisions (a) and (b) shall also apply in determining:

(1) Persons who would be kindred of the transferor or kindred of a surviving, deceased, or former spouse of the transferor under Section 21110.

(2) Persons to be included as issue of a deceased transferee under Section 21110.

(3) Persons who would be the transferor's or other designated person's heirs under Section 21114.

(d) The rules for determining intestate succession under this section are those in effect at the time the transfer is to take effect in enjoyment.

(Stats. 1994, 2002)

Escheat

CPC § 6404. Escheat

Part 4 (commencing with Section 6800) (escheat) applies if there is no taker of the intestate estate under the provisions of this part.

(Stats. 1990)

Section C. Transfers to Children

CPC § 6450. Adopted & Non-Marital Children

Subject to the provisions of this chapter, a relationship of parent and child exists for the purpose of determining intestate succession by, through, or from a person in the following circumstances:

(a) The relationship of parent and child exists between a person and the person's natural parents, regardless of the marital status of the natural parents.

(b) The relationship of parent and child exists between an adopted person and the person's adopting parent or parents.

(Stats. 1993)

Adopted Children

CPC § 6451. When Adoption Does & Does Not Sever Relationship with Natural Family

(a) An adoption severs the relationship of parent and child between an adopted person and a natural parent of the adopted person unless both of the following requirements are satisfied:

> (1) The natural parent and the adopted person lived together at any time as parent and child, or the natural parent was married to or cohabiting with the other natural parent at the time the person was conceived and died before the person's birth.

> (2) The adoption was by the spouse of either of the natural parents or after the death of either of the natural parents.

(b) Neither a natural parent nor a relative of a natural parent, except for a wholeblood brother or sister of the adopted person or the issue of that brother or sister, inherits from or through the adopted person on the basis of a parent and child relationship between the adopted person and the natural parent that satisfies the requirements of paragraphs (1) and (2) of subdivision (a), unless the adoption is by the spouse or surviving spouse of that parent.

(c) For the purpose of this section, a prior adoptive parent and child relationship is treated as a natural parent and child relationship.

(Stats. 1993)

NOTE: Estate of Obata, 27 Cal. App. 5th 730, 238 Cal. Rptr. 3d 545 (2018), held that California law recognizes the Japanese practice called yoshi-engumi as an adoption within the meaning of CPC §§ 6450 and 6451. The status of adoption is determined by the laws of the jurisdicdtion where the adoption took place as of the date of the adoption. Whether decedent's 1911 adoption in Japan would have severed the relationship with his natural parents is irrelevant. The law of decedent's domicile at the time of death (California) determines inheritance rights. Decedent's heirs are the adoptive family, not the biological family.

NOTE: Gift to Issue Does Not Include Adult Adoptee

A person adopted as an adult does not take as issue of the adopting parent under a class gift made by anyone other than the adopting parent. See CPC § 21115, *supra*.

Adopted-Out Children Inherit from Natural Parent; Statute in Effect at Time of Death Controls

ESTATE of DYE

California Court of Appeal, Third District
92 Cal. App. 4th 966, 112 Cal. Rptr. 2d 362 (2001)

MORRISON, J. This case illustrates the danger of using preprinted wills. Decedent Haskell J. Dye had two natural sons who were adopted away (with his consent) by his first wife's new husband (Arthur Battles) in 1959. Under the law at that time, this cut off their right to inherit from him. The law was changed, effective 1985, to permit some adopted-out children to inherit from their natural parents. In 1989 decedent and his second wife Eleanor signed reciprocal form wills, leaving their property to each other. Eleanor died in January, 1999. Decedent died on June 17, 1999. [Neither will provided for disposition on the death of the survivor.—Ed.]

Scott Dye, Eleanor's son who had been adopted by decedent, petitioned to probate decedent's estate. Phillip Joe Battles, one of decedent's adopted away natural sons, and some of the issue of the deceased adopted away son (Jimmie Dean Battles) filed an objection, seeking to share in decedent's estate. The trial court granted their heirship petition and Scott filed a notice of appeal. . . .

DISCUSSION

. . . In 1993 the language of the present section 6451 was adopted. . . . Now an adoption severs the blood relationship "unless both of the following requirements are satisfied: . . . (1) The natural parent and the adopted person lived together at any time as parent and child . . . (2) The adoption was by the spouse of either of the natural parents. . . ". . . .

Before Jimmie Dean and Phillip Joe were adopted out, decedent lived with them, and their adoption was by the new husband of their mother, decedent's former wife. They satisfy the new exception to the statute. . . .

Where, as here, the decedent has no surviving spouse, the estate passes "To the issue of the decedent, the issue taking equally if they are all of the same degree of kinship to the decedent, but if of unequal degree those of more remote degree take in the manner provided in Section 240." . . .

II.

Scott asserts in his brief that decedent and Eleanor did not consult a lawyer and thought he was their only lawful heir, and that decedent never intended to benefit objectors, "some of whom he never even met." Scott urges the case should be remanded so he can introduce evidence to establish decedent's intention regarding the adopted-out children.

A.

Assuming Scott accurately sets forth decedent's wishes, decedent could have expressed such intention by inserting into the will "I disinherit Phillip Joe and Jimmie Dean," or he could have given them each "one dollar." On Eleanor's death he could have written a new will or a codicil naming Scott as sole beneficiary. Decedent did none of these things.

. . . It is presumed citizens know the law, including the intestacy laws, and it is up to any person who does not want those laws applied to his or her estate to opt out by preparing a will setting forth other dispositions. Decedent did not so provide and therefore is presumed to endorse application of the default intestacy laws. This accords with the general rule that the law governing a will is measured as of the date of death, under the fiction that until then, the decedent is presumed to know the law and has the power to change his will. . . . Here both the drafting of the will and death occurred after the critical revision to the probate laws. . . .

B. . . .

Scott concludes in part: "It would be a manifest injustice if Haskell's estate were distributed in any part to the Battles when he truly intended the exact opposite." The intestacy laws by their nature will defeat many "true" intentions. Decedent could have prevented such "injustice," if any, by making a new will, or by including in the first will language stating his wishes if Eleanor died first. The objectors have not caused an injustice by invoking applicable law. . . . [Held: the three sons are equally entitled to the estate.—Ed.]

CPC § 6454. *Right to Inherit from Foster or Stepparent*

For the purpose of determining intestate succession by a person or the person's issue from or through a foster parent or stepparent, the relationship of parent and child exists between that person and the person's foster parent or stepparent if both of the following requirements are satisfied:

(a) The relationship began during the person's minority and continued throughout the joint lifetimes of the person and the person's foster parent or stepparent.

(b) It is established by clear and convincing evidence that the foster parent or stepparent would have adopted the person but for a legal barrier.

(Stats. 1993)

CPC § 6455. *Equitable Adoption*

Nothing in this chapter affects or limits application of the judicial doctrine of equitable adoption for the benefit of the child or the child's issue.

(Stats. 1993)

Theoretical Basis for Equitable Adoption Doctrine

ESTATE of FORD

Supreme Court of California
32 Cal. 4th 160, 82 P.3d 747, 8 Cal. Rptr. 3d 541
as Modified on Denial of Rehearing (2004)

WERDEGAR, J. Terrold Bean claims the right to inherit the intestate estate of Arthur Patrick Ford as Ford's equitably adopted son. The superior court denied the claim, and the Court of Appeal affirmed the denial, for lack of clear and convincing evidence that Ford intended to adopt Bean. We . . . affirm the judgment of the Court of Appeal. . . .

Born in 1953, Bean was declared a ward of the court and placed in the home of Ford and his wife, Kathleen Ford, as a foster child in 1955. Bean never knew his natural father, whose identity is uncertain, and he was declared free of his mother's control in 1958, at the age of four. Bean lived continuously with Mr. and Mrs. Ford and their natural daughter, Mary Catherine, for about 18 years, until Mrs. Ford's death in 1973, then with Ford and Mary Catherine for another two years, until 1975.

During part of the time Bean lived with the Fords, they cared for other foster children and received a county stipend for doing so. Although the Fords stopped taking in foster children after Mrs. Ford became ill with cancer, they retained custody of Bean. The last two other foster children left the home around the time of Mrs. Ford's death, but Bean, who at 18 years of age could have left, stayed with Ford and Mary Catherine.

Bean knew the Fords were not his natural parents, but as a child he called them "Mommy" and "Daddy," and later "Mom" and "Dad." Joan Malpassi, Mary Catherine's friend since childhood and later administrator of Ford's estate, testified that Bean's relationship with Mary Catherine was "as two siblings" and that the Fords treated Bean "more like Mary rather than a foster son, like a real son was my observation." Mary Catherine later listed Bean as her brother on a life insurance application.

Bean remained involved with Ford and Mary Catherine even after leaving the Ford home and marrying. . . . When Ford suffered a disabling stroke in 1989, Mary Catherine conferred with Bean and Malpassi over Ford's care; Ford was placed in a board and care facility where Bean continued to visit him regularly until his death in 2000.

Mary Catherine died in 1999. Bean and Malpassi arranged her funeral. Bean petitioned for Malpassi to be appointed Ford's conservator, and with Malpassi's agreement Bean obtained a power of attorney to take care of Ford's affairs pending establishment of the conservatorship. Bean also administered Mary Catherine's estate, which was distributed to the Ford conservatorship. When a decision was needed as to whether Ford should receive medical life support, Malpassi consulted with Bean in deciding he should. When Ford died, Bean and Malpassi arranged the funeral.

The Fords never petitioned to adopt Bean. Mrs. Ford told Barbara Carter, a family friend, that "they wanted to adopt Terry," but she was "under the impression that she could not put in for adoption while he was in the home." She worried that if Bean was removed during the adoption process he might be put in "a foster home that wasn't safe."

Ford's nearest relatives at the time of his death were the two children of his predeceased brother, nephew John J. Ford III and niece Veronica Newbeck. Neither had had any contact with Ford for about 15 years before his death, and neither attended his funeral. John J. Ford III filed a petition to determine entitlement to distribution (Prob. Code, § 11700), listing both himself and Newbeck as heirs. Bean filed a statement of interest claiming entitlement to Ford's entire estate under Probate Code sections 6454 . . . (foster child heirship) and 6455 (equitable adoption) as well as sections 6402, subdivision (a) and 6450.

After trial, the superior court ruled against Bean. Probate Code section 6454's requirement of a legal barrier to adoption was unmet, since the Fords could have adopted Bean after his mother's parental rights were terminated in 1958. [(See generally *Estate of Joseph* (1998) 17 Cal. 4th 203, 208-212, 70 Cal. Rptr. 2d 619, 949 P.2d 472.)] The doctrine of equitable adoption, the trial court found, was inapplicable because "there is no evidence that [Ford] ever told [Bean] or anyone else that he wanted to adopt him nor publicly told anyone that [Bean] was his adopted son." There was thus no clear and convincing evidence of "an intent to adopt."

Bean appealed only on the equitable adoption issue. The Court of Appeal affirmed . . . . We granted Bean's petition for review.

Discussion

. . . [S]ection 6455 provides in full: "Nothing in this chapter affects or limits application of the judicial doctrine of equitable adoption for the benefit of the child or the child's issue." We therefore look to decisional law, rather than statute, for guidance on the equitable adoption doctrine's proper scope and application.

I. Criteria for Equitable Adoption

In its essence, the doctrine of equitable adoption allows a person who was accepted and treated as a natural or adopted child, and as to whom adoption typically was promised or contemplated but never performed, to share in inheritance of the foster parents' property. "The parents of a child turn him over to foster parents who agree to care for him as if he were their own child. Perhaps they also agree to adopt him. They do care for him, support him, educate him, and treat him in all respects as if he were their child, but they never adopt him. Upon their death he seeks to inherit their property on the theory that he should be treated as if he had been adopted. . . . The doctrine is widely applied to allow inheritance from the adoptive parent: at least 27 jurisdictions have so applied the doctrine, while only 10 have declined to recognize it in that context. (Annot., Modern Status of Law as to Equitable Adoption or Adoption by Estoppel (1980) 97 A.L.R.3d 347, § 3.)[2]

---

[2] In California, at least, adoption itself is "purely statutory in origin and nature." (*Estate of Radovich* (1957)

A California court first recognized the doctrine, albeit in the atypical context of inheritance *through* the adoptive parent, in *Estate of Grace* (1948) 88 Cal. App. 2d 956, 200 P.2d 189. . . . [Discussion of California cases omitted.—Ed.]

As reflected in this summary, California decisions have explained equitable adoption as the specific enforcement of a contract to adopt. Yet it has long been clear that the doctrine, even in California, rested less on ordinary rules of contract law than on considerations of fairness and intent for, as Justice Schauer put it, the child "should have been" adopted and would have been but for the decedent's "inadvertence or fault."[3] . . . In the earliest case, *Estate of Grace*, the court quoted a New Mexico case explaining why specific performance was an unrealistic description of equitable adoption: "A specific performance of a contract to adopt is impossible after the death of the parties who gave the promise. Equity was driven to the fiction that there had been an adoption. That fiction being indulged, the case was not one of specific performance." . . . In both *Estate of Rivolo* [15 Cal. Rptr. 268 (Cal. Ct. App. 1961)] . . . and *Estate of Wilson*, [168 Cal. Rptr. 533 (Cal. Ct. App. 1980)] . . . moreover, the contracts purportedly being enforced were made between foster parents and their minor charges, yet neither court addressed the children's capacity to contract, suggesting, again, that the contract served mainly as evidence of the parties' intent, rather than as an enforceable legal basis for transmission of property.[4]

Bean urges that equitable adoption be viewed not as specific enforcement of a contract to adopt, but as application of an equitable, restitutionary remedy he has identified as quasi-contract or, as his counsel emphasized at oral argument, as an application of equitable estoppel principles. While we have found no decisions articulating a quasi-contract theory, courts in several states have, instead of or in addition to the contract rationale, analyzed equitable adoption as arising from "a broader and vaguer equitable principle of estoppel." (Clark, The Law of Domestic Relations in the United States, . . . [(2d ed. 1988) § 20.9] at p. 926.) . . . Bean argues Mr. Ford's conduct toward him during their long and close relationship estops Ford's estate or heirs at law from denying his status as an equitably adopted child.

For several reasons, we conclude the California law of equitable adoption, which has rested on contract principles, does not recognize an estoppel arising merely from the existence of a familial relationship between the decedent and the claimant. The law of intestate succession is intended to carry out "'the intent a decedent without a will is most likely to have had.'" (*Estate of Griswold* (2001) 25 Cal. 4th 904, 912, 108 Cal. Rptr. 2d 165, 24 P.3d 1191.) The existence of a mutually affectionate relationship, without any direct expression by the decedent of an intent

---

48 Cal. 2d 116, 128, 308 P.2d 14 (dis. opn. of Schauer, J.).) The effect of an equitable adoption finding, therefore, is limited to the child's inheritance rights and does not in other respects equate the child's rights with those of a statutorily adopted child.

[3] *Estate of Radovich, supra* at 308 P.2d 24, 26 (CA 1957).—Ed.

[4] The difficulty of applying ordinary contract law to equitable adoption has also been recognized by commentators and by courts in other states. (See, *e.g.,* . . . ; Rein, *Relatives by Blood, Adoption, and Association: Who Should Get What and Why* (1984) 37 Vand. L. Rev. 711, 772-775 . . . .

to adopt the child or to have him or her treated as a legally adopted child, sheds little light on the decedent's likely intent regarding distribution of property. While a person with whom the decedent had a close, caring and enduring relationship may often be seen as more deserving of inheritance than the heir or heirs at law, whose personal relationships with the decedent may have been, as they were here, attenuated, equitable adoption in California is neither a means of compensating the child for services rendered to the parent nor a device to avoid the unjust enrichment of other, more distant relatives who will succeed to the estate under the intestacy statutes. Absent proof of an intent to adopt, we must follow the statutory law of intestate succession.

In addition, a rule looking to the parties' overall relationship in order to do equity in a given case, rather than to particular expressions of intent to adopt, would necessarily be a vague and subjective one, inconsistently applied, in an area of law where "consistent, bright-line rules" . . . are greatly needed. Such a broad scope for equitable adoption would leave open to competing claims the estate of *any* foster parent or stepparent who treats a foster child or stepchild lovingly and on an equal basis with his or her natural or legally adopted children. A broad doctrine of equitable adoption would also render section 6454, in practice, a virtual nullity, since children meeting the familial-relationship criteria of that statute would necessarily be equitable adoptees as well.

While a California equitable adoption claimant need not prove all the elements of an enforceable contract to adopt, therefore, we conclude the claimant must demonstrate the existence of some direct expression, on the decedent's part, of an intent to adopt the claimant. This intent may be shown, of course, by proof of an unperformed express agreement or promise to adopt. But it may also be demonstrated by proof of other acts or statements directly showing that the decedent intended the child to be, or to be treated as, a legally adopted child, such as an invalid or unconsummated attempt to adopt, the decedent's statement of his or her intent to adopt the child, or the decedent's representation to the claimant or to the community at large that the claimant was the decedent's natural or legally adopted child. (See, *e.g.*, *Estate of Rivolo,* [parents who orally promised child she would "be their little girl" later told her and others they had adopted her]; *Estate of Wilson,* [petition to adopt filed but dismissed for lack of natural mother's consent]; *Estate of Reid* (1978) 80 Cal. App. 3d 185, 188, 145 Cal. Rptr. 451 [written agreement with adult child].)

Thus, in California the doctrine of equitable adoption is a relatively narrow one . . . . In addition to a statement or act by the decedent unequivocally evincing the decedent's intent to adopt, the claimant must show the decedent acted consistently with that intent by forming with the claimant a close and enduring familial relationship.[6] That is, in addition to a contract or other direct evidence of the intent to adopt, the evidence must show "objective conduct indicating mutual recognition of an adoptive parent and child relationship to such an extent that in equity and good conscience an adoption should be deemed to have taken place." . . .

---

[6] A close familial relationship sufficient to support the decedent's intent to adopt must persist up to, or at least not be repudiated by the decedent before, the decedent's death.

II. Standard of Proof of Equitable Adoption

Bean also contends the lower courts erred in applying a standard of clear and convincing proof to the equitable adoption question. We disagree. Most courts that have considered the question require at least clear and convincing evidence in order to prove an equitable adoption. . . . Several good reasons support the rule. . . . Finally, too relaxed a standard could create the danger that "a person could not help out a needy child without having a de facto adoption foisted upon him after death." . . . As pointed out in an early Missouri decision, if the evidentiary burden is lowered too far, "then couples, childless or not, will be reluctant to take into their homes orphan children, and for the welfare of such children, as well as for other reasons, the rule should be kept and observed. . . . ". . .

Conclusion

Although the evidence showed the Fords and Bean enjoyed a close and enduring familial relationship, evidence was totally lacking that the Fords ever made an attempt to adopt Bean or promised or stated their intent to do so; they neither held Bean out to the world as their natural or adopted child (Bean, for example, did not take the Ford name) nor represented to Bean that he was their child. Mrs. Ford's single statement to Barbara Carter was not clear and convincing evidence that Mr. Ford intended Bean to be, or be treated as, his adopted son. . . .

WE CONCUR: GEORGE, C.J., KENNARD, BAXTER, CHIN, BROWN, and MORENO, JJ.

Posthumous Children

CPC § 6407. Posthumous Heirs

Relatives of the decedent conceived before the decedent's death but born thereafter inherit as if they had been born in the lifetime of the decedent.

(Stats. 1990)

Nonmarital Children

CPC § 6453. Determining Who Is a Natural Parent

For the purpose of determining whether a person is a "natural parent" as that term is used in this chapter:

(a) A natural parent and child relationship is established where that relationship is presumed and not rebutted pursuant to the Uniform Parentage Act (Part 3 (commencing with Section 7600) of Division 12 of the Family Code).

(b) A natural parent and child relationship may be established pursuant to any other provisions of the Uniform Parentage Act, except that the relationship may not be established by an action under subdivision (c) of Section 7630 of the Family Code unless any of the following conditions exist:

(1) A court order was entered during the parent's lifetime declaring parentage.[4]

(2) Parentage is established by clear and convincing evidence that the parent has openly held out the child as that parent's own.

(3) It was impossible for the parent to hold out the child as that parent's own and parentage is established by clear and convincing evidence, which may include genetic DNA evience acquired during the parent's lifetime.

(c) A natural parent and child relationship may be established pursuant to Section 249.5.[5]

(Stats. 1993, 2004, 2018)

Family Code § 7610. Establishing Parent-Child Relationship

The parent and child relationship may be established as follows:

(a) Between a child and the natural parent, it may be established by proof of having given birth to the child, or under this part.

(b) Between a child and an adoptive parent, it may be established by proof of adoption.

(Stats. 1992, 2013)

Family Code § 7611. Presumed Natural Parent

A man is presumed to be the natural parent of a child if the person meets the conditions provided in Chapter 1 (commencing with Section 7540) or Chapter 3 (commencing with Section 7570) of Part 2 or in any of the following subdivisions:

(a) The presumed parent and the child's natural mother are or have been married to each other and the child is born during the marriage, or within 300 days after the marriage is terminated by death, annulment, declaration of invalidity, or divorce, or after a judgment of separation is entered by a court.

(b) Before the child's birth, the presumed parent and the child's natural mother have attempted to marry each other by a marriage solemnized in apparent compliance with law, although the attempted marriage is or could be declared invalid, and either of the following is true:

(1) If the attempted marriage could be declared invalid only by a court, the child is born during the attempted marriage, or within 300 days after its termination by death, annulment, declaration of invalidity, or divorce.

---

[4] Before the 2018 amendment, subsections (1)-(3) applied only to the father. The requirement that a paternity order be entered in father's lifetime did not violate child's right to equal protection. Hardy v. Colvin, 930 F. Supp. 2d 1196 (C.D. Calif. 2013).—Ed.

[5] Section 249.5 is set out below in the section on Reproductive Technology and New Forms of Parentage.—Ed.

(2) If the attempted marriage is invalid without a court order, the child is born within 300 days after the termination of cohabitation.

(c) After the child's birth, the presumed parent and the child's natural mother have married, or attempted to marry, each other by a marriage solemnized in apparent compliance with law, although the attempted marriage is or could be declared invalid, and either of the following is true:

(1) With his or her consent, the presumed parent is named as the child's parent on the child's birth certificate.

(2) The presumed parent is obligated to support the child under a written voluntary promise or by court order.

(d) The presumed parent receives the child into his or her home and openly holds out the child as his or her natural child. . . .

(f) The child is in utero after the death of the decedent and the conditions set forth in Section 249.5 of the Probate Code are satisfied.

(Stats. 1992, 1993, 1994, 2004, 2013)

Family Code § 7612. Presumption Under § 7611 Rebuttable; Conflicting Presumptions

(a) Except as provided in Chapter 1 (commencing with Section 7540)[6] and Chapter 3 (commencing with Section 7570)[7] of Part 2 or in Section 20102, a presumption under Section 7611 is a rebuttable presumption affecting the burden of proof and may be rebutted in an appropriate action only by clear and convincing evidence.

(b) If two or more presumptions arise under Section 7611 that conflict with each other, or if one or more presumptions under Section 7611 conflict with a claim by a person identified as a genetic parent pursuant to Section 7555, the presumption that on the facts is founded on the weightier considerations of policy and logic controls. If one of the presumed parents is also a presumed parent under section 7540, the presumption arising under Section 7540 may only be rebutted pursuant to Section 7541.

(c) In an appropriate action, a court may find that more than two persons with a claim to parentage under this division are parents if the court finds that recognizing only two parents would be detrimental to the child. In determining detriment to the child, the court shall consider all relevant factors, including, but not limited to, the harm of removing the child from a stable placement with a parent who has fulfilled the child's physical needs and the child's psychological needs for care and affection, and who has assumed that role for a substantial period of time. A finding of detriment to the child does not require a finding of unfitness of any of the parents or persons with a claim to parentage.

---

[6] Child of wife cohabiting with husband who is not impotent or sterile is conclusively presumed child of the marriage unless experts in blood test procedure under Family Code § 7550 et seq. conclude husband is not the father.—Ed.

[7] Voluntary declaration of paternity.—Ed.

(d) Unless a court orders otherwise after making the determination specified in subdivision (c), a presumption under Section 7611 is rebutted by a judgment establishing parentage of the child by another person.

(e) Within two years of the execution of a voluntary declaration of paternity, a person who is presumed to be a parent under Section 7611 may file a petition pursuant to Section 7630 to set aside a voluntary declaration of paternity. The court's ruling on the petition to set aside the voluntary declaration of paternity shall be made taking into account the validity of the voluntary declaration of paternity, and the best interests of the child based upon the court's consideration of the factors set forth in subdivision (b) of Section 7575, and the best interests of the child based upon the nature, duration, and quality of the petitioning party's relationship with the child and the benefit or detriment to the child of continuing that relationship. In the event of a conflict between the presumption under Section 7611 and the voluntary declaration of paternity, the weightier considerations of policy and logic shall control.

(f) A voluntary declaration of paternity is invalid if, at the time the declaration was signed, any of the following conditions exist:

> (1) The child already had a presumed parent under Section 7540.

> (2) The child already had a presumed parent under subdivision (a), (b), or (c) of Section 7611.

> (3) The man signing the declaration is a sperm donor, consistent with subdivision (b) of Section 7613.

(g) A person's offer or refusal to sign a voluntary declaration of paternity may be considered as a factor, but shall not be determinative, as to the issue of legal parentage in any proceedings regarding the establishment or termination of parental rights.

(h) This section shall remain in effect only until January 1, 2020, and as of that date is repealed. (Stats. 1992, 1993, 1994, 2008, 2013, 2015, 2016, 2018)

NOTE: Section 7612, which becomes effective on January 1, 2020, is the same as the previous section except that subsections (e) and (f) are deleted, subsection (g) becomes subsection (e) with the word "paternity" changed to "parentage" and "any proceedings" changed to "a proceeding." Subsection (h) becomes subsection (f) and provides that the section becomes operative on Jan. 1, 2020.

Family Code § 7630. Bringing Action to Determine Parentage

***

(c) Except as to cases coming within Chapter 1 (commencing with Section 7540) of Part 2, or when paragraph (2) of subdivision (a) applies,[6] an action to determine parentage may be

---

[6] Section 7630(a)(2) provides: "For the purpose of declaring the nonexistence of the parent and child relationship presumed under subdivision (a), (b), or (c) of Section 7611 only if the action is brought within a reasonable time after obtaining knowledge of relevant facts. After the presumption has been rebutted, parentage of the child by another person may be determined in the same action, if that person has been made a party."—Ed.

brought by the child, a personal representative of the child, the Department of Child Support Services, a presumed parent or the personal representative or a parent of that presumed parent if that parent has died or is a minor, or, in cases in which the natural mother is the only presumed parent or an action under Section 300 of the Welfare and Institutions Code or adoption is pending, a man alleged or alleging himself to be the father or the personal representative or a parent of the alleged father if the alleged father has died or is a minor. (Stats. 1992, 2000, 2001, 2003, 2004, 2005, 2006, 2007, 2008, 2010, 2012, 2013, 2014, 2018)

NOTE: Dent v. Wolf, 15 Cal. App. 5th 230, 222 Cal. Rptr. 3d 846 (2017) held that a person who claims to be a child has standing to bring a parentage action under § 7630 without making any claim for monetary relief.

Nonmarital Children & Forensic Genealogist Inherit from Natural Father Who Paid Child Support

ESTATE of GRISWOLD

Supreme Court of California
25 Cal. 4th 904, 24 P.3d 1191, 108 Cal. Rptr. 2d 165 (2001)

BAXTER, J. . . . Denis H. Griswold died intestate in 1996, survived by his wife, Norma B. Doner-Griswold. Doner-Griswold petitioned for and received letters of administration and authority to administer Griswold's modest estate, consisting entirely of separate property.

In 1998, Doner-Griswold filed a petition for final distribution, proposing a distribution of estate property, after payment of attorney's fees and costs, to herself as the surviving spouse and sole heir. Francis V. See, a self-described "forensic genealogist" (heir hunter) who had obtained an assignment of partial interest in the Griswold estate from Margaret Loera and Daniel Draves,[1] objected . . . and filed a petition to determine entitlement to distribution. . . . See and Doner-Griswold stipulated to the following background facts . . . .

Griswold was born out of wedlock to Betty Jane Morris on July 12, 1941 in Ashland, Ohio. The birth certificate listed his name as Denis Howard Morris and identified John Edward Draves of New London, Ohio as the father. A week after the birth, Morris filed a "bastardy complaint"[2] in the juvenile court in Huron County, Ohio and swore under oath that Draves was the child's father. In September of 1941, Draves appeared in the bastardy proceeding and "confessed in Court that the charge of the plaintiff herein is true." The court adjudged Draves to be the "reputed father" of the child, and ordered Draves to pay medical expenses related to Morris's pregnancy as well as $5 per week for child support and maintenance. Draves

---

[1] California permits heirs to assign their interests in an estate, but such assignments are subject to court scrutiny. (See [CPC] §11604).

[2] A "bastardy proceeding" is an archaic term for a paternity suit. (Black's Law Dict. (7th ed. 1999) pp. 146, 1148.)

complied, and for 18 years paid the court-ordered support to the clerk of the Huron County court.

Morris married Fred Griswold in 1942 and moved to California. She began to refer to her son as "Denis Howard Griswold," a name he used for the rest of his life. For many years, Griswold believed Fred Griswold was his father. At some point in time, either after his mother and Fred Griswold divorced in 1978 or after his mother died in 1983, Griswold learned that Draves was listed as his father on his birth certificate. So far as is known, Griswold made no attempt to contact Draves or other members of the Draves family.

Meanwhile, at some point after Griswold's birth, Draves married in Ohio and had two children, Margaret and Daniel. Neither Draves nor these two children had any communication with Griswold, and the children did not know of Griswold's existence until after Griswold's death in 1996. Draves died in 1993. His last will and testament, dated July 22, 1991, made no mention of Griswold by name or other reference. Huron County probate documents identified Draves's surviving spouse and two children—Margaret and Daniel—as the only heirs.

. . . [T]he probate court denied See's petition. . . [finding that] . . . See had not demonstrated that Draves was Griswold's "natural parent" or that Draves "acknowledged" Griswold as his child as required by section 6452. The Court of Appeal . . . reversed . . . . We granted Doner-Griswold's petition for review.

Discussion
. . . Griswold's mother (Betty Jane Morris) and father (John Draves) both predeceased him. Morris had no issue other than Griswold and Griswold himself left no issue. . . . See contends that Doner-Griswold is entitled to one-half of Griswold's estate and that Draves's issue (See's assignors, Margaret and Daniel) are entitled to the other half pursuant to . . . [CPC §§] 6401 and 6402. . . .

It is undisputed . . . that Draves contributed court-ordered child support for 18 years, thus satisfying subdivision (b) [of section 6452] . . . . At issue . . . is whether the record establishes . . . the remaining requirements of section 6452 as a matter of law. First, did Draves acknowledge Griswold. . . ? Second, did the Ohio judgment of reputed paternity establish Draves as the natural parent of Griswold. . . ? . . .

A. Acknowledgement
. . . Section 6452 does not define the word "acknowledged." Nor does any other provision of the Probate Code. . . . [H]owever, we may logically infer that the word refers to conduct other than . . . contributing to the child's support or care; otherwise, subdivision (a) of the statute would be surplusage and unnecessary.

. . . [T]he common meaning of "acknowledge" is "to admit to be true or as stated; confess." (Webster's New World Dict. (2d ed. 1982) . . . . Were we to ascribe this common meaning to the statutory language, there could be no doubt that section 6452's acknowledgement requirement is met here. . . . Griswold's natural mother initiated a bastardy proceeding . . . in which she alleged that Draves was the child's father. Draves appeared in that proceeding and publicly "confessed" that the allegation was true. There is no evidence indicating that Draves did not confess knowingly and voluntarily, or that he later denied paternity or knowledge of Griswold to those who were aware of the circumstances.[3] Although the record establishes that Draves did not speak of Griswold to Margaret and Daniel, there is no evidence suggesting he sought to actively conceal the facts from them or anyone else. Under the plain terms of section 6452, the only sustainable conclusion on this record is that Draves acknowledged Griswold. . . .

There is a dearth of case law pertaining to section 6452 or its predecessor statutes, but what little there is supports the foregoing construction. Notably, *Lozano v. Scalier* (1996) 51 Cal. App. 4th 843, 59 Cal. Rptr. 2d 346 (*Lozano*), the only prior decision directly addressing section 6452's acknowledgement requirement, declined to read the statute as necessitating more than what its plain terms call for. . . .

Significantly, *Lozano* rejected arguments that an acknowledgement under Probate Code section 6452 must be (1) a witnessed writing and (2) made after the child was born so that the child is identified. In doing so, *Lozano* initially noted there were no such requirements on the face of the statute. . . . *Lozano* next looked to the history of the statute and made two observations in declining to read such terms into the statutory language. First, even though the Legislature had previously required a witnessed writing in cases where an illegitimate child sought to inherit from the father's estate, it repealed such requirement in 1975 in an apparent effort to ease the evidentiary proof of the parent-child relationship. . . . Second, other statutes that required a parent-child relationship expressly contained more formal acknowledgement requirements for the assertion of certain other rights or privileges. . . . Had the Legislature wanted to impose more stringent requirements for an acknowledgement . . . it certainly had precedent for doing so. . . .

Doner-Griswold disputes whether the acknowledgement required . . . may be met by a father's single act of acknowledging a child in court. In her view, the requirement contemplates a situation where the father establishes an ongoing parental relationship with the child or otherwise acknowledges the child's existence to his subsequent wife and children. To support this contention, she relies on three other authorities addressing acknowledgement under former section 230 of the Civil Code: *Blythe v. Ayres,* . . . 96 Cal. 532, 31 P. 915, *Estate of Wilson,* . . . 164 Cal. App. 2d 385, 330 P.2d 452, and *Estate of Maxey* (1967) 257 Cal. App. 2d 391, 64 Cal. Rptr. 837. . . . [discussion of cases omitted]

Doner-Griswold correctly points out that the foregoing decisions illustrate the principle that the existence of acknowledgement must be decided on the circumstances of each case. . . . In those decisions, however, the respective fathers had not confessed to paternity in a legal action. . . . That those decisions recognized the validity of different forms of acknowledgement should

---

[3] Huron County court documents indicate that at least two people other than Morris, one of whom appears to have been a relative of Draves, had knowledge of the bastardy proceeding.

not detract from the weightiness of a father's in-court acknowledgement of a child in an action seeking to establish the existence of a parent and child relationship. . . . [S]uch an acknowledgement is a critical one that typically leads to a paternity judgment and a legally enforceable obligation of support. Accordingly, such acknowledgements carry as much, if not greater, significance than those made to certain select persons. . . .

Doner-Griswold's authorities do not persuade us that section 6452 should be read to require that a father have personal contact with his out-of-wedlock child, that he make purchases for the child, that he receive the child into his home and other family, or that he treat the child as he does his other children. First and foremost, the language of section 6452 does not support such requirements . . . . We may not, under the guise of interpretation, insert qualifying provisions not included in the statute. . . .

Finally, Doner-Griswold contends that a 1996 amendment of section 6452 evinces the Legislature's unmistakable intent that a decedent's estate may not pass to siblings who had no contact with, or were totally unknown to, the decedent. . . . [T]hat contention proves too much.

Prior to 1996, section 6452 and a predecessor statute, former section 6408, expressly provided that their terms did not apply to "a natural brother or a sister of the child" born out of wedlock . . . . In construing former section 6408, *Estate of Corcoran* (1992) 7 Cal. App. 4th 1099, 9 Cal. Rptr. 2d 475 held that a half sibling was a "natural brother or sister" within the meaning of such exception. That holding effectively allowed a half sibling and the issue of another half sibling to inherit from a decedent's estate where there had been no parental acknowledgement or support of the decedent as ordinarily required. In direct response to *Estate of Corcoran,* the Legislature amended section 6452 by eliminating the exception for natural siblings and their issue. . . . According to legislative documents, the Commission had recommended deletion of the statutory exception because it "creates an undesirable risk that the estate of the deceased out-of-wedlock child will be claimed by siblings with whom the decedent had no contact during lifetime, and of whose existence the decedent was unaware." . . .

This legislative history does not compel Doner-Griswold's construction of section 6452. Reasonably read, the comments of the Commission merely indicate its concern over the "undesirable risk" that unknown siblings could rely on the statutory exception to make claims against estates. Neither the language nor the history of the statute, however, evinces a clear intent to make inheritance contingent upon the decedent's awareness of or contact with such relatives. . . . Indeed, had the Legislature intended to categorically preclude intestate succession by a natural parent or a relative of that parent who had no contact with or was unknown to the deceased child, it could easily have so stated. Instead, by deleting the statutory exception for natural siblings, thereby subjecting siblings to section 6452's dual requirements of acknowledgement and support, the Legislature acted to prevent sibling inheritance under the type of circumstances presented in *Estate of Corcoran* . . . and to substantially reduce the risk noted by the Commission.[8]

B. Requirement of a Natural Parent and Child Relationship

. . . Under section 6453, subdivision (a), a natural parent and child relationship is established where the relationship is presumed under the Uniform Parentage Act and not rebutted. . . . It is undisputed, however, that none of those presumptions applies in this case. . . .

Although Griswold's mother was not acting pursuant to the Uniform Parentage Act when she filed the bastardy complaint in 1941, neither that legislation nor the Probate Code provision should be construed to ignore the force and effect of the judgment she obtained. . . . [T]hat all procedural requirements of an action under Family Code section 7630 may not have been followed, should not detract from its binding effect in this probate proceeding where the issue adjudicated was identical with the issue that would have been presented in a Uniform Parentage Act action. . . . [W]e find that the 1941 Ohio judgment was a court order "entered during the father's lifetime declaring paternity" . . . and that it establishes Draves as the natural parent of Griswold for purposes of intestate succession under section 6452.

Disposition

. . . We do not disagree that a natural parent who does no more than openly acknowledge a child in court and pay court-ordered child support may not reflect a particularly worthy predicate for inheritance by that parent's issue, but section 6452 provides in unmistakable language that it shall be so. While the Legislature remains free to reconsider the matter and may choose to change the rules of succession at any time, this court will not do so under the pretense of interpretation.

The judgment of the Court of Appeal is affirmed.

GEORGE, C.J., KENNARD, J., WERDEGAR, J., CHIN, J., concur.

Concurring Opinion by BROWN, J. I reluctantly concur. . . . I doubt most children born out of wedlock would have wanted to bequeath a share of their estate to a "father" who never contacted them, never mentioned their existence to his family and friends, and only paid court-ordered child support. I doubt even more that these children would have wanted to bequeath a share of their estate to that father's other offspring. Finally, I have *no* doubt that most, if not all, children born out of wedlock would have balked at bequeathing a share of their estate to a "forensic genealogist."

---

[8] . . . Doner-Griswold does not dispute that the right of the succession claimants to succeed to Griswold's property is governed by the law of Griswold's domicile, *i.e.*, California law, not the law of the claimants' domicile or the law of the place where Draves's acknowledgement occurred. (Civ. Code, §§ 755, 946; see *Estate of Lund* (1945) 26 Cal. 2d 472, 493-496, 159 P.2d 643 [where father died domiciled in California, his out-of-wedlock son could inherit where all the legitimation requirements of former § 230 of the Civ. Code were met, even though the acts of legitimation occurred while the father and son were domiciled in two other states wherein such acts were not legally sufficient].)

To avoid such a dubious outcome in the future, I believe our laws of intestate succession should allow a parent to inherit from a child born out of wedlock only if the parent has some sort of parental connection to that child. . . . [S]uch a requirement would comport with the stated purpose behind our laws of succession because that child likely would have wanted to give a share of his estate to a parent that treated him as the parent's own.

Of course, this court may not remedy this apparent defect in our intestate succession statutes. Only the Legislature may make the appropriate revisions. I urge it to do so here.

NOTE: Establishing Parent-Child Relationship

1. Estate of Britel, 236 Cal. App. 4th 127, 186 Cal. Rptr. 3d 321, rev. denied (2015) held that "openly held out" in § 6453(b)(2) requires alleged father to have made an unconcealed affirmative representation of his paternity in open view, and that child who can prove paternity by DNA test is not denied equal protection by denial of inheritance rights under § 6453. A lineal descendant must also be in a parent-child relationship to inherit. The *Britel* court disagreed with the conclusion in **Estate of Burden**, 146 Cal. App. 4th 1021, 53 Cal. Rptr. 3d 390, rev. den. (2007), that acknowledgment of a child meets the requirement of openly holding out.

2. In Estate of Sanders, 2 Cal. App. 4th 462, 3 Cal. Rptr. 2d 536 (1992), the court denied the request of a nonmarital child to order that DNA samples be taken to establish his claim to a share of his putative father's estate, holding that the methods set out in the predecessor of CPC § 6453 for establishing paternity for inheritance purposes are exclusive.

3. Estate of Chambers, 175 Cal. App. 4th 891, 96 Cal. Rptr. 3d 651 (2 Dist. 2009) held that when the presumed father under Family Code § 7611(d) is deceased, Probate Code § 6453 (b) requires proof of paternity by clear and convincing evidence.

Reproductive Technology and New Forms of Parentage

CPC § 249.5. Child Conceived After Death of Genetic Parent

For purposes of determining rights to property to be distributed upon the death of a decedent, a child of the decedent conceived and born after the death of the decedent shall be deemed to have been born in the lifetime of the decedent, and after the execution of all of the decedent's testamentary instruments, if the child or his or her representative proves by clear and convincing evidence that all of the following conditions are satisfied:

(a) The decedent, in writing, specifies that his or her genetic material shall be used for the posthumous conception of a child of the decedent, subject to the following:

(1) The specification shall be signed by the decedent and dated.

(2) The specification may be revoked or amended only by a writing, signed by the decedent and dated.

(3) A person is designated by the decedent to control the use of the genetic material.

(b) The person designated by the decedent to control the use of the genetic material has given written notice by certified mail, return receipt requested, that the decedent's genetic material was available for the purpose of posthumous conception. The notice shall have been given to a person who has the power to control the distribution of either the decedent's property or death benefits payable by reason of the decedent's death, within four months of the date of issuance of a certificate of the decedent's death or entry of a judgment determining the fact of the decedent's death, whichever event occurs first.

(c) The child was in utero using the decedent's genetic material and was in utero within two years of the date of issuance of a certificate of the decedent's death or entry of a judgment determining the fact of the decedent's death, whichever event occurs first. This subdivision does not apply to a child who shares all of his or her nuclear genes with the person donating the implanted nucleus as a result of the application of somatic nuclear transfer technology commonly known as human cloning.

(Stats. 2004, 2005)

Family Code § 7650. Determining Mother-Child Relationship

(a) Any interested person may bring an action to determine the existence or nonexistence of a mother and child relationship.

Insofar as practicable, the provisions of this division applicable to the father and child relationship apply.

(b) A woman is presumed to be the natural mother of a child if the child is in utero after the death of the decedent and the conditions set forth in Section 249.5 of the Probate Code are satisfied.

(Stats. 1992, 2004, 2018)

Family Code § 7613. Paternity of Child Conceived by Artificial Insemination

(a)

(1) If a woman conceives through assisted reproduction with semen or ova or both donated by a donor, not her spouse, with the consent of another intended parent, that intended parent is treated in law as if he or she were the natural parent of a child thereby conceived. The other intended parent's consent shall be in writing and signed by the other intended parent and the woman conceiving through assisted reproduction.

(2) Failure to consent in writing, as required by paragraph (1), does not preclude the court from finding that the intended parent consented if the court finds by clear and convincing evidence that, prior to the conception of the child, the woman and the intended parent had an oral agreement that the woman and the intended parent would both be parents of the child.

(b)

(1) The donor of semen provided to a licensed physician and surgeon or to a licensed sperm bank for use in assisted reproduction by a woman other than the donor's spouse is treated in law as if he were not the natural father of a child thereby conceived, unless otherwise agreed to in a writing signed by the donor and the woman prior to the conception of the child.

(2) If the semen is not provided to a licensed physician and surgeon or a licensed sperm bank . . . the donor of semen for use in assisted reproduction by a woman other than the donor's spouse is treated in law as if he were not the natural parent of a child thereby conceived if either of the following are met:

(A) The donor and the woman agreed in a writing signed prior to conception that the donor would not be a parent.

(B) A court finds by clear and convincing evidence that the child was conceived through assisted reproduction and that, prior to the conception of the child, the woman and the donor had an oral agreement that the donor would not be a parent.

(3) Paragraphs (1) and (2) do not apply to a man who provided semen for use in assisted reproduction by a woman other than the man's spouse pursuant to a written agreement signed by the man and the woman prior to conception of the child stating that they intended for the man to be a parent.

(c) The donor of ova for use in assisted reproduction by a person other than the donor's spouse or nonmarital partner is treated in law as if the donor were not the natural parent of a child thereby conceived unless the court finds satisfactory evidence that the person providing ova and the person intended for the person providing ova to be a parent.

(Stats. 1992, 2008, 2011, 2013, 2015, 2016, 2018)

NOTE: Social Security Benefits for Posthumously-Conceived Children in the 9th Circuit

In **Gillett-Netting v. Barnhart**, 371 F.3d 593 (9th Cir. 2004), the court held that posthumously-conceived twins, whose father delayed cancer treatment to deposit semen for later use by his wife, were natural children of the father under Arizona law and thus qualified for social security benefits as a dependent of the deceased father, without also having to show that they were entitled to inherit from him under Arizona law. Section 402(d)(3) of the Social Security Act provides that a child shall be deemed a dependent of its father even if the father was not living with or contributing to the support of the child at the time of the father's death if the child is the legitimate or adopted child of the father.

The court noted that in all states in the Ninth Circuit, the characterization of children as legitimate or illegitimate has been replaced by a determination whether a parent and child relationship exists. It held that if a parent and child relationship is established under state law, the social security dependency requirement is satisfied. The Social Security Administration acquiesced to this interpretation of the law, but for the Ninth Circuit only.

In **Vernoff v. Astrue**, 568 F.3d 1102 (9th Cir. 2009), the court held that a California child conceived three years after her father's death from sperm collected after his accidental death, and without any agreement on his part, was not entitled to Social Security benefits as a dependent child of her father. The court held that the child could not establish that her biological father was her natural parent under Family Code § 7611, and thus there was no parent and child relationship. It also rejected her argument that she was entitled to inherit from him under CPC § 7453(b)(3) ("it was impossible for the father to hold out the child as his own . . . ") because she would have had to prevail in a paternity action brought under Family Code 7630(c), which she had not done.

Even if CPC § 249.5 had been in effect when the child was conceived or born, she would not have met its requirements for establishing that her biological father was her natural parent.

Advancements and Hotchpot

CPC § 6409. Advancement Requires Writing; Not Charged Against Issue of Predeceased Advancee

(a) If a person dies intestate as to all or part of his or her estate, property the decedent gave during lifetime to an heir is treated as an advancement against that heir's share of the intestate estate only if one of the following conditions is satisfied:

(1) The decedent declares in a contemporaneous writing that the gift is an advancement against the heir's share of the estate or that its value is to be deducted from the value of the heir's share of the estate.

(2) The heir acknowledges in writing that the gift is to be so deducted or is an advancement or that its value is to be deducted from the value of the heir's share of the estate.

(b) Subject to subdivision (c), the property advanced is to be valued as of the time the heir came into possession or enjoyment of the property or as of the time of death of the decedent, whichever occurs first.

(c) If the value of the property advanced is expressed in the contemporaneous writing of the decedent, or in an acknowledgment of the heir made contemporaneously with the advancement, that value is conclusive in the division and distribution of the intestate estate.

(d) If the recipient of the property advanced fails to survive the decedent, the property is not taken into account in computing the intestate share to be received by the recipient's issue unless the declaration or acknowledgment provides otherwise.

(Stats. 1990, 2002)

CPC § 6410. Debt Owed to Decedent Chargeable Only Against Debtor's Intestate Share

(a) A debt owed to the decedent is not charged against the intestate share of any person except the debtor.

(b) If the debtor fails to survive the decedent, the debt is not taken into account in computing the intestate share of the debtor's issue.

(Stats. 1990)

Guardianship and Conservatorship of Minors

California law provides for guardianship of the persons and estates of minors in Probate Code Division 4, Part 2, §§ 1500-1611 and for conservatorship for of the person of a minor who is married or whose marriage has been dissolved in Part 3, §§ 1800-1898. Management of guardianships and conservatorships is governed by Part 4, §§ 2100-2893. California's Uniform Transfers to Minors Act is in Part 9, §§ 3900-3925.

Section D. Bars to Succession

The Slayer Rule

CPC § 250. Slayer Not Entitled

(a) A person who feloniously and intentionally kills the decedent is not entitled to any of the following:

> (1) Any property, interest, or benefit under a will of the decedent, or a trust created by or for the benefit of the decedent or in which the decedent has an interest, including any general or special power of appointment conferred by the will or trust on the killer and any nomination of the killer as executor, trustee, guardian, or conservator or custodian made by the will or trust.

> (2) Any property of the decedent by intestate succession.

> (3) Any of the decedent's quasi-community property the killer would otherwise acquire under Section 101 or 102 upon the death of the decedent.

> (4) Any property of the decedent under Division 5 (commencing with Section 5000).

> (5) Any property of the decedent under Part 3 (commencing with Section 6500) of Division 6.

(b) In the cases covered by subdivision (a):

(1) The property interest or benefit referred to in paragraph (1) of subdivision (a) passes as if the killer had predeceased the decedent and Section 21110 does not apply.

(2) Any property interest or benefit referred to in paragraph (1) of subdivision (a) which passes under a power of appointment and by reason of the death of the decedent passes as if the killer had predeceased the decedent, and Section 673 does not apply.

(3) Any nomination in a will or trust of the killer as executor, trustee, guardian, conservator, or custodian which becomes effective as a result of the death of the decedent shall be interpreted as if the killer had predeceased the decedent.

(Stats. 1990, 1991, 1992, 1997, 2002, 2015)

CPC § 251. *Killing by Joint Tenant*

A joint tenant who feloniously and intentionally kills another joint tenant thereby effects a severance of the interest of the decedent so that the share of the decedent passes as the decedent's property and the killer has no rights by survivorship. This section applies to joint tenancies in real and personal property, joint and multiple-party accounts in financial institutions, and any other form of coownership with survivorship incidents.

(Stats. 1990)

CPC § 252. *Killing by Beneficiary of Life Insurance or Other Contract*

A named beneficiary of a bond, life insurance policy, or other contractual arrangement who feloniously and intentionally kills the principal obligee or the person upon whose life the policy is issued is not entitled to any benefit under the bond, policy, or other contractual arrangement, and it becomes payable as though the killer had predeceased the decedent.

(Stats. 1990)

CPC § 253. *Other Slayer Cases*

In any case not described in Section 250, 251, or 252 in which one person feloniously and intentionally kills another, any acquisition of property, interest, or benefit by the killer as a result of the killing of the decedent shall be treated in accordance with the principles of this part.

(Stats. 1990)

CPC § 254. *Effect of Judgment; Burden of Proof*

(a) A final judgment of conviction of felonious and intentional killing is conclusive for purposes of this part.

(b) In the absence of a final judgment of conviction of felonious and intentional killing, the court may determine by a preponderance of evidence whether the killing was felonious and intentional for purposes of this part. The burden of proof is on the party seeking to establish that the killing was felonious and intentional for the purposes of this part.

(Stats. 1990)

NOTE: **Peterson v. Peterson**, 156 Cal. App. 4th 676, 67 Cal. Rptr. 3d 584 (2007) held a murder conviction on appeal was not a final judgment of conviction, but was prima facie evidence that killing was felonious and intentional under § 254(b).

The Unworthy Heir

Abandonment, Failure to Acknowledge, Termination of Parental Rights

CPC § 6452. Conditions Preventing Parent from Inheriting from or through a Child

(a) A parent does not inherit from or through a child on the basis of the parent and child relationship if any of the following apply:

(1) The parent's parental rights were terminated and the parent-child relationship was not judicially reestablished.

(2) The parent did not acknowledge the child.

(3) The parent left the child during the child's minority without an effort to provide for the child's support or without communication from the parent for at least seven consecutive years that continued until the end of the child's minority, with the intent on the part of the parent to abandon the child. The failure to provide support or to communicate for the prescribed period is presumptive evidence of an intent to abandon.

(b) A parent who does not inherit from or through the child as provided in subdivision (a) shall be deemed to have predeceased the child, and the intestate estate shall pass as otherwise required under Section 6402.

(Stats. 2013)

NOTE: Former § 6452 was repealed and replaced with this section to reverse the result in **Estate of Shellenbarger**, 169 Cal. App. 4th 894, 86 Cal. Rptr. 3d 862 (2008) (review denied 2009), which held that a father's failure to pay child support and lack of meaningful parent-child relationship did not affect his rights as an intestate heir.

Elder Abuse & Bad Faith Taking of Property

CPC § 259. Abuser Deemed to Predecease

(a) Any person shall be deemed to have predeceased a decedent to the extent provided in subdivision (c) where all of the following apply:

(1) It has been proven by clear and convincing evidence that the person is liable for physical abuse, neglect, or financial abuse of the decedent, who was an elder or dependent adult.

(2) The person is found to have acted in bad faith.

(3) The person has been found to have been reckless, oppressive, fraudulent, or malicious in the commission of any of these acts upon the decedent.

(4) The decedent, at the time those acts occurred and thereafter until the time of his or her death, has been found to have been substantially unable to manage his or her financial resources or to resist fraud or undue influence.

(b) Any person shall be deemed to have predeceased a decedent to the extent provided in subdivision (c) if that person has been convicted of a violation of Section 236 of the Penal Code or any offense described in Section 368 of the Penal Code.

(c) Any person found liable under subdivision (a) or convicted under subdivision (b) shall not (1) receive any property, damages, or costs that are awarded to the decedent's estate in an action described in subdivision (a) or (b), whether that person's entitlement is under a will, a trust, or the laws of intestacy; or (2) serve as a fiduciary as defined in Section 39,[8] if the instrument nominating or appointing that person was executed during the period when the decedent was substantially unable to manage his or her financial resources or resist fraud or undue influence. This section shall not apply to a decedent who, at any time following the act or acts described in paragraph (1) of subdivision (a), or the act or acts described in subdivision (b), was substantially able to manage his or her financial resources and to resist fraud or undue influence within the meaning of subdivision (b) of Section 1801[9] of the Probate Code and subdivision (b) of Section 39 of the Civil Code.

(d) For purposes of this section, the following definitions shall apply:

(1) "Physical abuse" as defined in Section 15610.63 of the Welfare and Institutions Code.

(2) "Neglect" as defined in Section 15610.57 of the Welfare and Institutions Code.

(3) "False imprisonment" as defined in Section 368 of the Penal Code.

(4) "Financial abuse" as defined in Section 15610.30 of the Welfare and Institutions Code.

(e) Nothing in this section shall be construed to prohibit the severance and transfer of an action or proceeding to a separate civil action pursuant to Section 801.

(Stats. 1998, 2011)

CPC § 859. *Remedy for Bad Faith Taking of Property*

If a court finds that a person has in bad faith wrongfully taken, concealed, or disposed of property belonging to a conservatee, a minor, an elder, a dependent adult, a trust, or the estate

---

[8] CPC § 39 defines fiduciary to include a "personal representative, trustee, guardian, conservator, attorney-in-fact under a power of attorney, custodian under the California Uniform Transfers to Minors Act . . . , or other legal representative subject to this code."—Ed.

[9] CPC § 1801 spells out the circumstances under which a conservator may be appointed for an adult or minor who has been married.—Ed.

of a decedent, or has taken, concealed, or disposed of the property by the use of undue influence in bad faith or through the commission of elder or dependent adult financial abuse, as defined in Section 15610.30 of the Welfare and Institutions Code, the person shall be liable for twice the value of the property recovered by an action under this part. In addition, except as otherwise required by law, including Section 15657.5 of the Welfare and Institutions Code, the person may, in the court's discretion, be liable for reasonable attorney's fees and costs. The remedies provided in this section shall be in addition to any other remedies available in law to a person authorized to bring an action pursuant to this part.

(Stats. 2001, 2011 2013)

NOTES:

1. Liability for double the value of property under § 859 is a statutory penalty not damages and is available against a successor to the person who misappropriated the property, **Hill v. Superior Court**, 244 Cal. App. 4th 1281, 198 Cal. Rptr. 3d 831 (2016); ability to pay is not relevant in awarding double recovery, **Estate of Kraus**, 184 Cal. App. 4th 103, 108 Cal. Rptr. 3d 760 (2010).

2. Kerley v. Weber, 27 Cal. App. 5th 1187, 238 Cal. Rptr. 3d 781 (2018) held that defendant convicted of theft from an elder was collaterally estopped from contesting amount of victim's loss in conservator's civil action; restitution award in criminal case did not preclude conservator from seeking damages; no separate finding of bad faith was required to support award of double damages under § 859; damages were properly awarded on basis of total amount stolen rather than difference between amount stolen and amount defendant had already paid in restitution.

Welfare & Institutions Code § 15610.30. Financial Abuse of an Elder

(a) "Financial abuse" of an elder or dependent adult occurs when a person or entity does any of the following:

(1) Takes, secretes, appropriates, obtains, or retains real or personal property of an elder or dependent adult for a wrongful use or with intent to defraud, or both.

(2) Assists in taking, secreting, appropriating, obtaining, or retaining real or personal property of an elder or dependent adult for a wrongful use or with intent to defraud, or both.

(3) Takes, secretes, appropriates, obtains, or retains, or assists in taking, secreting, appropriating, obtaining, or retaining, real or personal property of an elder or dependent adult by undue influence, as defined in Section 15610.70.

(b) A person or entity shall be deemed to have taken, secreted, appropriated, obtained, or retained property for a wrongful use if, among other things, the person or entity takes, secretes, appropriates, obtains, or retains the property and the person or entity knew or should have known that this conduct is likely to be harmful to the elder or dependent adult.

(c) For purposes of this section, a person or entity takes, secretes, appropriates, obtains, or retains real or personal property when an elder or dependent adult is deprived of any property right, including by means of an agreement, donative transfer, or testamentary bequest, regardless of whether the property is held directly or by a representative of an elder or dependent adult.

(d) For purposes of this section, "representative" means a person or entity that is either of the following:

(1) A conservator, trustee, or other representative of the estate of an elder or dependent adult.

(2) An attorney-in-fact of an elder or dependent adult who acts within the authority of the power of attorney.

(Stats. 1994, 1997, 1998, 2000, 2008, 2013)

NOTES:

1. Bounds v. Superior Court, 229 Cal. App. 4th 468, 177 Cal. Rptr. 3d 320 (2014), held that getting elder suffering from Alzheimer's to sign escrow instructions authorizing sale of real property was a "taking" for a "wrongful use" even though sale was not consummated. Existence of escrow instructions impaired the right to use and sell the property.

2. Mahan v. Charles W. Chan Insurance Agency, Inc., 14 Cal. App. 5th 841, 222 Cal. Rptr. 3d 360 (2017) reversed grant of demurrers holding that complaint adequately alleged facts sufficient to bring action for financial abuse of an elder. Plaintiff insureds claimed that insurance advisors wrongfully caused changes in life insurance policies held in revocable living trust that dramatically increased premiums and reduced coverage. Even though policies were owned by the trust, elderly insureds were deprived of property because the value of the assets they intended to convey to their children by their estate plan was destroyed.

Standing to Bring Claim for Elder Abuse

ESTATE of LOWRIE

California Court of Appeal, Second District
118 Cal. App. 4th 220, 12 Cal. Rptr. 3d 828 (2004)

ALDRICH, J. . . . In this case, a granddaughter accuses her uncle of financial abuse, isolation, and neglect constituting elder abuse of her grandmother. In the published parts of this opinion . . . we hold that the granddaughter has standing to bring this elder abuse civil lawsuit. . . . In unpublished portions of this opinion . . . we hold there is substantial evidence to support the findings of elder abuse, there is substantial evidence to support the damages awarded, and there is no procedural impediment to the imposition of punitive damages.

II. FACTUAL AND PROCEDURAL BACKGROUND

A. The parties and decedent's estate plan.

Laura Marie Lowrie (decedent) had three children, all of whom are still living: Norma Goodreau, Alan Lowrie, and appellant Sheldon Lawrence Lowrie (Sheldon). Decedent had six grandchildren, including respondent Lynelle L. Goodreau (Lynelle) who is the eldest daughter of Norma Goodreau. ...

Decedent's husband died in 1986, leaving to decedent gold coins, cash in bank accounts, a number of pieces of commercial property, and two single family residences located in Burbank, California. Decedent's husband also left to decedent an airplane parts business, SAL Instruments (SAL), located in Burbank. Decedent lived in the residence located on Kenwood Street. The second residence, on Edison Boulevard, was the house where Lynelle had lived with her grandparents when Lynelle was an infant. During this time, Lynelle and decedent developed a special bond.

After his father died, Sheldon started to run SAL. Alan assisted by doing the bookkeeping.

... On March 20, 1989, decedent reformulated her estate plan and executed a will (pour over) and a trust, the effect of which placed most of her real and personal property in trust. On March 19, 1992, decedent, amended the trust.

In the March 1989, estate documents, Sheldon was named as the executor, Lynelle was designated as the successor executor, decedent was designated as the trustee, Sheldon was designated as the first successor trustee, and Lynelle was designated as the second successor trustee. Additionally, Alan Lowrie and Norma Goodreau each were bequeathed the sum of $10,000 and Lynelle was to receive the Edison Boulevard residence. Sheldon was bequeathed the remainder of the estate (which would be the bulk of the property), and if Sheldon did not survive decedent, Lynelle was to receive the remainder. ... The 1992 trust amendment was a one-page document which deleted the bequest to Lynelle of the house and replaced it with a monetary bequest of $10,000.

Unbeknown to others, decedent transferred the Edison Boulevard residence and the Kenwood Street residence to Sheldon in 1993 and 1995, respectively. In 1993, decedent transferred all of her personal property to Sheldon.

In August 1997, decedent resigned as trustee of her trust and Sheldon became trustee. Decedent died on August 13, 1999, at the age of 89. At the time of her death, decedent's estate was worth approximately $1 million.

B. Procedure.

1. The petition.

On November 1, 2000, Lynelle filed a multiple-part petition ... Lynelle contended ... that Sheldon exploited his relationship with decedent, and through manipulation, fraud and undue influence enticed decedent to gift him property and to change her estate plan so Sheldon would receive substantially all of decedent's assets. Further, Sheldon abused decedent physically and financially, and intentionally isolated decedent. Lynelle alleged that over the years, "Sheldon isolated Decedent from her two other children, her five grandchildren and from most of the

48

outside world. Sheldon intentionally prevented Decedent from seeing or speaking with family members and other people and denied family members and others access to Decedent's house by among others: duct taping her telephones so that she could not receive or make telephone calls; by locking her metal security door from the outside so that decedent could not open her front door to leave the house and so that she could not allow in visitors such as family members; and by affixing a sign to her door which stated: 'DAY SLEEPER, DO NOT DISTURB!! NO SOCIAL WORKERS. NO PEDDLERS. WILL NOT ANSWER DOOR.'" The complaint also alleged that Sheldon denied and delayed medical care to decedent and failed to assist her with personal hygiene.

Among other relief, Lynelle sought to void the 1992 trust amendment, to set aside the transfer of real property, compensatory and punitive damages, a finding pursuant to Probate Code section 259 that Sheldon was deemed to have predeceased decedent and thus was not entitled to inherit the remainder of decedent's estate, imposition of a constructive trust, attorney fees, and costs.

2. The trial, the judgment, and the appeal.
. . . [T]he trial court rejected Sheldon's argument that Lynelle had no standing to bring this case for elder abuse.

A bifurcated trial was held before the court. At the end of the first phase . . . the court found, by clear and convincing evidence, that Sheldon was guilty of elder abuse by reason of neglect, isolation, and financial abuse . . . [and] that Sheldon was disinherited from decedent's estate . . . . . The trial court made a specific finding that Sheldon acted with recklessness, oppression, fraud and malice, entitling Lynelle to attorney fees and punitive damages. . . .

Thereafter, a hearing before the court was held on the issues of attorney fees, costs, and punitive damages. The trial court found that "during the pendency of this action, [Sheldon] intentionally and systematically liquidated virtually all of his assets and the assets of the trust (of which [Sheldon] was the sole beneficiary) prior to completion of this trial . . . so that his assets would be unavailable for execution by [Lynelle] as a potential judgment creditor of [Sheldon]." . . .

A judgment was entered awarding [Lynelle] $665,623 for financial abuse, $250,000 for pain and suffering, $392,621.20 in attorney fees, $32,406.37 in costs, and $50,000 for punitive damages, disinheriting Sheldon from decedent's trust, . . . and other relief. Sheldon appeals.

III. DISCUSSION

A. Lynelle has standing to pursue this elder abuse case.

Sheldon asserts that Lynelle has no standing to bring this elder abuse case. . . .

1. The Elder Abuse Act and the Standing Provision, Welfare and Institutions Code section 15657.3, subdivision (d).

"The purpose of the [Elder Abuse Act, (Welf. & Inst. Code, §§ 15600 *et seq.*)] is essentially to protect a particularly vulnerable portion of the population from gross mistreatment in the form of abuse and custodial neglect." . . . [citations omitted]

Originally, the Elder Abuse Act was designed to encourage the reporting of abuse and neglect of elders and dependent adults. . . . It also provided for criminal prosecution of such cases. . . . However, elder abuse lawsuits were seldom pursued as few attorneys would handle the cases, partially because survival statutes did not permit compensation if the elder died before a verdict was rendered.[3] Then, the Legislature shifted the focus. The statutory scheme was modified to provide incentives for private, civil enforcement through lawsuits against elder abuse and neglect. . . .

Subject to statutory criteria and limitations, the statutory scheme now permits heightened remedies. These include pain and suffering damages even after the abused elder dies, punitive damages, and attorney fee awards. . . .

Welfare and Institutions Code section 15657.3, subdivision (d), delineates who has standing to bring an elder abuse lawsuit *after the death* of an elder or dependent adult . . . : "Upon petition, after the death of the elder or dependent adult, the right to maintain an action shall be transferred to the personal representative of the decedent, or if none, to the person or persons entitled to succeed to the decedent's estate."

The Legislature did not define the operative words . . . . However, when . . . section 15657.3 was added to the statutory scheme . . . the Legislature specified that the Elder Abuse Act was intended to "enable *interested persons* to engage attorneys to take up the cause of abused elderly persons and dependent adults." . . . This statement of legislative intent suggests the Legislature intended a broad definition of standing in the context of elder abuse cases.[5]

2. Lynelle has standing.
Sheldon argues Lynelle does not have standing because: (1) under the trust he is the named trustee and thus, decedent's "personal representative" . . . and, (2) Lynelle is not a person "entitled to succeed to the decedent's estate" because she does not succeed to decedent's estate under the laws of intestate succession . . . , but rather, Lynelle is simply a beneficiary who was bequeathed $10,000. Sheldon points to provisions of the survival statutes . . . and the

---

[3] Survival statutes (Code Civ. Proc., § 377.20 *et seq.*) seek damages for a decedent's injuries and harm sustained prior to the death of the decedent. Recovery becomes an asset of the decedent's estate. (Cal. Elder Law Litigation: An Advocate's Guide (Cont. Ed. Bar 2003) § 6.46, p. 411; Ross, Cal. Practice Guide, Probate (The Rutter Group 2003) [¶] 15:280, p. 15-78 *et seq.*) In general, survival statutes do not provide recovery of pain and suffering if the plaintiff dies. . . .

Survival statutes are not to be confused with wrongful death statutes . . . that prescribe actions that belong to the "decedent's heirs and other specified relations and [are] meant to compensate them for their own losses resulting from the decedent's death." . . .

[5] There are a number of definitions of "interested person" in the Probate Code . . . , but none is contained in the Elder Abuse Act.

wrongful death statutes . . . as well as the definition of "decedent's successor in interest" prescribed for those purposes. . . . These statutes use language similar to that in Welfare and Institutions Code section 15657.3. According to Sheldon, only Norma and Alan, decedent's other surviving children, have standing to bring this elder abuse case. . . . However, establishing a uniform definition of terms throughout the codified laws is less important than effectuating the purpose of the legislative scheme . . . .

. . . The purpose of Probate Code section 259 was to deter the abuse of elders by prohibiting abusers from benefiting from the abuse. (Note, *Extinguishing Inheritance Rights: California Breaks New Ground in the Fight Against Elder Abuse But Fails to Build an Effective Foundation* (2001), 52 Hastings L.J. 537, 569; Civ. Code, §3517 . . . .) . . . [T]he Legislature hoped that the threat of extinguishing inheritance rights, and the financial incentive to others to report abuse, would deter abuse. (Moskowitz, *Golden Age in the Golden State: Contemporary Legal Developments in Elder Abuse and Neglect,* . . . 36 Loyola L.A. L. Rev. at pp. 653-656; . . . .)

According to decedent's estate plan, if Sheldon predeceased decedent, Lynelle would become the successor trustee and the successor beneficiary to the remainder. Thus, Lynelle would become the person entitled to succeed to decedent's estate and Lynelle would have standing to bring this case. . . . Standing, for purposes of the Elder Abuse Act, must be analyzed in a manner that induces interested persons to report elder abuse and to file lawsuits against elder abuse and neglect. In this way, the victimized will be protected. Here, Lynelle's expectancy, *i.e.,* her contingent interest, provides her with a strong incentive to pursue this action and gives her standing.

Sheldon argues Probate Code section 259 is irrelevant because disinheritance under the statute occurs only *after* a person is found to have been guilty of elder abuse, but standing must exist *at the time* the action is filed. . . . Were we to accept this rigid view, the purposes of the Elder Abuse Act could be eviscerated. . . .

"Elders are uniquely vulnerable to abuse because . . . they face advancing frailty, deterioration of mental capacity, and increasing reliance for assistance upon the families they raised." (Note, *A New Approach to Fighting Elder Abuse in America,* . . . 2 Hastings L.J. at pp. 571-572. . . .) Elders frequently relinquish control to those who have gained their trust, becoming emotionally and financially dependent. In such circumstances, abusers become the elder or dependent adult's trustee or executor and primary beneficiary. For example, most financial abuse is perpetrated by one person, usually a family member, or other trusted person. (Finberg, *Financial Abuse of the Elderly in California* (2003) 36 Loyola L.A. L. Rev. 667.)

Courts must interpret the standing provision . . . to deter, not encourage such abuse. If abusers gain control of an estate, they may not use a restrictive interpretation of standing as an escape hatch. . . . [T]o effectuate the purposes of the Elder Abuse Act and Probate Code section 259, standing must be given to Lynelle, who is the successor representative of decedent's estate. Any other conclusion would discourage interested persons from bringing elder abuse lawsuits and would ignore the legislative scheme. . . .

The judgment is affirmed. Sheldon Lowrie is to pay all costs on appeal.

NOTE: Lichter v. Lichter, 189 Cal. App. 4th 712, 118 Cal. Rptr. 3d 123 (2010), review denied (2011), held that grandchildren lacked standing to bring elder abuse action because they were not interested persons. Even though they were beneficiaries of $10,000 each under grandmother's trust, and would take the balance if all three of named beneficiaries of the residue predeceased the grandmother, they had been paid their $10,000 bequests, and there was no evidence that at least one of the prior beneficiaries had committed elder abuse. To be an interested person, the person's beneficial interest in the trust must be affected by the elder abuse action.

Remedy under §259 for Elder Abuse is Limited

ESTATE of DITO

Court of Appeal, First District, Division 3
198 Cal. App. 4th 791, 130 Cal. Rptr. 3d 279 (2011)
Certified for Partial Publication*

McGUINESS, P.J. In an earlier appeal arising out of this probate matter, we affirmed the trial court's ruling that respondent Elenice S. Dito is the surviving spouse of decedent Frank P. Dito and is entitled to receive a share of his estate as an omitted spouse . . . . After the earlier appeal had been decided, appellants Barbara and George Merritt filed a petition alleging that Elenice is liable for financial elder abuse committed against Frank. The trial court sustained a demurrer to the petition without leave to amend on the ground the claim was barred by the doctrine of res judicata.

We conclude the trial court erred. Because the primary right at issue in appellants' petition is different from the one at issue in the earlier appeal, the petition is not barred as a matter of law on the basis of res judicata. Nevertheless, we conclude the demurrer should have been sustained on other grounds, albeit with leave to amend.

FACTUAL AND PROCEDURAL HISTORY

. . .

Summary of Prior Appeal
Elenice was born in Brazil. She came to the United States in the early 1990's to work as a housekeeper for a Brazilian family. Elenice began working as a live-in housekeeper for

---

* Pursuant to California Rules of Court, rules 8.1105(b) and 8.1110, this opinion is certified for publication with the exception of parts 4, 5 and 6 of the Discussion.

decedent Frank Dito and his wife, Rosana . . . in late 1994 or early 1995. The couple were elderly and physically impaired when Elenice began working for them. Elenice's visa did not permit her to work legally for the Ditos.

Rosana died in December 1995. Elenice continued to live with Frank and care for him after Rosana's death. At some point in 1997, Frank and Elenice began discussing marriage as an option. They were married in August 1997. At the time of their marriage, Frank was 94 years old and Elenice was 28 years old. Before they were married, Frank and Elenice entered into a prenuptial agreement. The agreement provided that both parties waived their right to alimony, maintenance, or spousal support in the event of divorce, death, or dissolution of marriage.

Frank and Rosana had one child, appellant Barbara Merritt, who is married to appellant George Merritt. Barbara was the trustee of her parents' living trust. [Barbara "played a key role in the marriage. She drove Elenice and Frank to Redwood City to get a marriage license, and she hosted the wedding in her home. . . . Terrence Merritt, Frank's grandson, served in the wedding as Frank's best man and signed the marriage license as a witness."][10]

Frank died in December 2004. In early 2005, Elenice filed a petition for letters of administration. Barbara filed a competing petition to administer Frank's estate and to admit his will to probate. Barbara attached to her petition a pour-over will executed by Frank in 1994 that identified Rosana as his wife. The will did not mention Elenice. In July 2005, Frank's grandson, Terrence, filed a petition to administer the estate. Barbara withdrew her petition to administer Frank's estate in favor of her son, Terrence.

In October 2005, Elenice filed a petition seeking, among other things, her share of Frank's estate as an omitted spouse, a determination that the prenuptial agreement is unenforceable, and a determination that the surviving spouse's waiver in the prenuptial agreement is unenforceable. She also sought an accounting and a reconveyance of trust assets allegedly transferred to Barbara. She further alleged that Barbara was liable for financial elder abuse and should be deemed to have predeceased Frank pursuant to section 259 as a result of the elder abuse.

Upon stipulation of the parties, the trial court ordered the issues . . . bifurcated so that the following issues could be tried before all other issues . . . : (1) whether Elenice is the surviving spouse of Frank and is entitled to receive a share of his estate . . . ; (2) whether the prenuptial agreement is enforceable; and (3) whether the surviving spouse's waiver contained in the prenuptial agreement is enforceable. . . .

The court conducted a bench trial on the three issues . . . [and] ruled that Elenice is the surviving spouse of Frank and is entitled to receive a share of his estate . . . . The court further ruled that the prenuptial agreement was invalid and unenforceable. For the same reasons it found the prenuptial agreement invalid, the court ruled that the spousal waiver contained in

---

[10] These and additional facts may be found in the unpublished opinion in the prior appeal in this case at 2008 WL 821694.—Ed.

the agreement was . . . invalid.

Terrence appealed. He claimed the marriage between Frank and Elenice was void because it was entered into for the sole purpose of allowing an illegal immigrant to remain in the United States. He also contended the prenuptial agreement was valid and that the surviving spouse's waiver should be given effect. In an unpublished opinion filed March 28, 2008, we affirmed the trial court's order. We concluded Terrence lacked standing to challenge the validity of his grandfather's marriage on the grounds he raised. We also concluded the prenuptial agreement was unenforceable because it was both procedurally and substantively unconscionable.[11] Terrence sought review in the Supreme Court, which denied his petition.

Post-Appeal Procedural History

. . . [A]ppellants Barbara and George Merritt filed the petition that is the subject of this appeal, entitled "Petition to Determine Entitlement to Receive Omitted Spousal Share." In the petition, appellants allege that Elenice committed financial elder abuse against Frank . . . and, as a consequence, that Elenice should be deemed to have predeceased Frank pursuant to section 259. As support for the petition, appellants allege that Elenice paid her friends amounts totaling at least $19,357 from her joint account with Frank. . . . Because Elenice did not have paid employment outside the marital home, it is alleged the funds paid to Elenice's friends necessarily belonged to Frank and were not used for his benefit. It is further alleged that Frank suffered from dementia as of April 2002, and that many of the checks were written after that date. . . . Appellants seek a determination that Elenice is deemed to have predeceased Frank pursuant to section 259 as a result of the elder abuse. Further, they allege that by operation of law Elenice would "not be the 'surviving spouse' under the Probate Code irrespective of the validity of the marriage." Appellants also seek compensatory damages, punitive damages, and attorney fees and costs.

Elenice demurred to the petition. She argued the elder abuse claim fails as a matter of law because (1) it is barred by the four-year statute of limitations, (2) it is barred by the doctrine of res judicata in that the court had already determined Elenice's entitlement to receive a share of the estate or trust, (3) appellants lack the capacity to sue for elder abuse because only the personal representative—i.e., Elenice—could pursue such a claim, and (4) the petition fails to state facts sufficient to state a cause of action because there were no allegations that Elenice acted with oppression, fraud, or malice when making the purportedly abusive distributions. As

---

[11] Elenice "testified that she signed a document she believed was a tax document. She stated that she and Frank accompanied Barbara to an office in downtown Burlingame. The notary refused to notarize the prenuptial agreement out of concern for Elenice's lack of English-speaking ability. They were directed to a second notary, Lori Horn, in a nearby office, where the document was signed and notarized. Elenice testified that the signature on the prenuptial agreement is hers but that she had not been given any of the other pages of the document before being presented with the signature page to sign. She also claims she did not speak with a lawyer or anyone else about the agreement before signing it. Elenice claimed she was not given a copy of the prenuptial agreement after she signed it." 2008 WL 821694. Other problems with the agreement were that it did not include Frank's substantial brokerage account in the disclosure of assets, allowed Elenice to live in the family home for only 6 months after Frank died, and provided that all community property would go to Barbara.—Ed.

to the claim that Elenice should be deemed to have predeceased Frank under section 259, Elenice demurred on the ground that the claim necessarily fails if the court grants the demurrer to the elder abuse claim. She also contended the petition fails to state a cause of action under section 259 because there are no factual allegations that she acted in bad faith or that the decedent was substantially unable to manage his finance resources or resist fraud or undue influence at the time the alleged abuse occurred.

In an order filed May 4, 2010, the trial court sustained the demurrer without leave to amend. The court based its decision solely on res judicata grounds, reasoning as follows: "Here the spousal share was explicitly determined in the trial . . . . That decision was ultimately appealed to the Supreme Court and is now final. . . . The court reasoned as follows: "The primary right in both the action tried and that before the court today is the entitlement of Elenice Dito to receive a share of the estate and trust of Frank Dito as a surviving spouse. The same interest was litigated by both [Terrence] at trial and the [appellants] here." . . . [T]he court did not reach any of the other grounds for the demurrer. Appellants appealed from the order sustaining the demurrer without leave to amend.

DISCUSSION . . .

3. Res Judicata
. . . As we explain, we agree with appellants that the claims raised in their petition are not identical to the issues litigated in the prior proceeding. . . .

[T]he trial court reasoned that the primary right at issue in both the prior judgment and the petition filed by appellants is Elenice's right to receive a share of the estate and trust as a surviving spouse. Likewise, Elenice argues on appeal . . . that the primary right at issue in both proceedings is her entitlement to the decedent's estate and trust.

The primary right at issue in the former proceeding was Elenice's own right under [Probate Code] section 21610 to receive a share of the decedent's estate as an omitted spouse. Section 21610 provides that, except as set forth in section 21611, if a decedent fails to provide for a surviving spouse in a testamentary instrument executed before the marriage to the surviving spouse, the omitted spouse is entitled to receive a share of the decedent's estate as provided in the statute. Specifically, the omitted spouse is entitled to one-half of the decedent's community and quasi-community property plus a share of the decedent's separate property as specified in the statute. . . . Section 21611 provides in general that an omitted spouse is *not* entitled to a share of the estate under section 21610 if *any* of three circumstances are established: (1) the decedent intended to omit the surviving spouse from the testamentary instrument; (2) the decedent provided for the surviving spouse by transfer outside the testamentary instrument and intended that such transfer was in lieu a provision for the surviving spouse in the testamentary instrument; or (3) the surviving spouse made a valid agreement waiving the right to a share of the decedent's estate.

Among the issues the parties contested in the prior proceeding were the validity of Elenice's marriage to Frank and the validity of the spousal waiver contained in the prenuptial agreement. It was necessary to resolve these issues to determine the primary right asserted by Elenice—

i.e., her status as an omitted spouse entitled to receive a share of Frank's estate under section 21610 et seq.

The primary right at issue in appellants' petition is different from that considered in the prior proceeding. As stated in the petition, appellants seek a finding that Elenice committed financial elder abuse against Frank. . . . " 'The purpose of the [Elder Abuse Act . . .] is essentially to protect a particularly vulnerable portion of the population from gross mistreatment in the form of abuse and custodial neglect.' . . . " (*Estate of Lowrie* (2004) 118 Cal. App. 4th 220, 226, 12 Cal. Rptr. 3d 828.) Thus, the primary right addressed by the petition is that of Frank not to be abused or defrauded. This primary right belongs to Frank and interested persons entitled to assert that right on his behalf. . . .

The financial elder abuse allegations have no bearing upon the determination whether Elenice is an omitted spouse entitled to receive a share of Frank's estate . . . . Section 21610 specifies that an omitted spouse shall be entitled to a share of the estate unless one or more of the exceptions in section 21611 applies. A finding of elder abuse is not one of the listed exceptions. Thus, even if the elder abuse issue had been raised in the prior proceeding, it would have been improper for the court to rely on a determination that Elenice committed financial elder abuse as the basis for denying her entitlement to a share of the estate under section 21610 et seq.

Appellants' petition also seeks a determination that Elenice is deemed to have predeceased Frank pursuant to section 259 as a result of the elder abuse. . . . [T]he claim under section 259 presents a closer issue than the elder abuse claim on which it is predicated because it appears to seek a result directly at odds with the court's previous determination that Elenice is entitled to a share of the estate as an omitted spouse. As we explain, a section 259 claim is distinct from, and unrelated to, a claim that an omitted spouse is entitled to a share of the estate.

The parties and the court below appear to be operating under the assumption that a person found liable for elder abuse is deemed to have predeceased the decedent for purposes of *any* entitlement to property, interests, and benefits the abuser would otherwise receive by reason of the decedent's death. While that may be the practical effect of section 259 in some cases, the statute does not necessarily disinherit an abuser entirely but rather restricts the abuser's right to benefit from his or her abusive conduct.[6] . . . Section 259, subdivision (a) provides in pertinent part that "[a]ny person shall be deemed to have predeceased a decedent *to the extent provided in subdivision (c)* " where it is proven that the person is liable for elder abuse of the decedent, acted in bad faith, and was reckless, oppressive, fraudulent, or malicious in the commission of the abuse. (Italics added.) Subdivision (c), in turn, provides in relevant part that "[a]ny person found liable under subdivision (a) . . . shall not (1) receive any property, damages, or costs that are awarded to the decedent's estate in an action described in subdivision (a) . . .

---

[6] By contrast, in the case of a person who intentionally and feloniously kills the decedent, that person is deemed to have predeceased the decedent for purposes of any property, interests, or benefits the person would otherwise be entitled to receive by reason of the decedent's death. (§ 250, (a) & (b); see 2 Ross, Cal. Practice Guide: Probate (2010 ed.) ¶ 14.525, at p. 14–103.)

whether that person's entitlement is under a will, a trust, or the laws of intestacy . . . ."[7]

Thus, a person found liable under subdivision (a) of section 259 is deemed to have predeceased the decedent only to the extent the person would have been entitled through a will, trust, or laws of intestacy to receive a distribution of the damages and costs the person is found to be liable to pay to the estate as a result of the abuse.[8] Section 259 does not necessarily eliminate the abuser's entitlement to a share of the estate; it simply restricts the value of the estate to which the abuser's percentage share is applied and prevents that person from benefiting from his or her own wrongful conduct.

In this case, the section 259 claim advanced by appellants does not affect or threaten the prior determination that Elenice is a surviving omitted spouse . . . . Elenice retains that status and is entitled to her share of the estate as specified in section 21610, although she is not allowed to share in any damages and costs she could be liable to pay to the estate as a result of the alleged elder abuse. It is conceivable that any damages and costs Elenice might be liable to pay to the estate would exceed her share of the estate, resulting in a situation in which she pays more to the estate in damages and costs than she receives as an omitted spouse under section 21610. However, the mere fact that application of section 259 *might* reduce or even effectively eliminate Elenice's inheritance does not mean that it concerns the same primary right as a claim she is an omitted spouse with an entitlement to a share of the estate. . . .

We conclude the court erred in sustaining the demurrer on the ground of res judicata. . . .

Disclaimer

CPC § 282. *Effect of Disclaimer*

(a) Unless the creator of the interest provides for a specific disposition of the interest in the event of a disclaimer, the interest disclaimed shall descend, go, be distributed, or continue to be held (1) as to a present interest, as if the disclaimant had predeceased the creator of the

---

[7] In addition, subdivision (c)(2) of section 259 prevents any person found liable under section (a) or convicted of criminal elder abuse from serving as a personal representative or other fiduciary if the instrument nominating or appointing the abuser was executed during the period when the decedent was "substantially unable to manage his or her financial resources or resist fraud or undue influence."

[8] We observe that in *Estate of Lowrie,* . . . the court referred to the trial court "disinherit[ing]" the abuser entirely "from [the] decedent's estate." The court also described section 259 as a "forfeiture statute that deems abusers of elders . . . to have predeceased a deceased, abused elder," without specifying that an abuser is deemed to have predeceased the decedent only to the extent provided in subdivision (c) of section 259. . . . The court in *Estate of Lowrie* did not address the scope of the remedy under section 259 but instead focused on the issue of standing. Therefore, the court's general description of the statute's effect is not authority for the proposition that section 259 operates to completely disinherit a person found liable for elder abuse. . . .

interest or (2) as to a future interest, as if the disclaimant had died before the event determining that the taker of the interest had become finally ascertained and the taker's interest indefeasibly vested. A disclaimer relates back for all purposes to the date of the death of the creator of the disclaimed interest or the determinative event, as the case may be.

(b) Notwithstanding subdivision (a), where the disclaimer is filed on or after January 1, 1985:

(1) The beneficiary is not treated as having predeceased the decedent for the purpose of determining the generation at which the division of the estate is to be made under Part 6 (commencing with Section 240) or other provision of a will, trust, or other instrument.

(2) The beneficiary of a disclaimed interest is not treated as having predeceased the decedent for the purpose of applying subdivision (d) of Section 6409[12] or subdivision (b) of Section 6410.[13]

(Stats. 1990)

CPC § 283. Disclaimer Not Fraudulent Transfer

A disclaimer is not a voidable transfer by the beneficiary under the Uniform Voidable Transactions Act (Chapter 1 (commencing with Section 3439)) of Title 2 of Part 2 of Division 4 of the Civil Code.

(Stats. 1990, 2015)

NOTE: Vance v. Bizek, 228 Cal. App. 4th 1155, 177 Cal. Rptr. 3d 167 (2014) held that a contingent interest may be accepted before it vests, that a creditor claiming a disclaimer invalid because of acceptance by the beneficiary has the burden of proof to show acceptance, and that a creditor cannot invoke the § 16004 presumption that a self-dealing transaction by a trustee is presumed to violate the trustee's fiduciary duties. The trustee's commingling of trust funds that resulted in transfers to a trust of which she was the contingent remainderman and use of those funds to pay the life beneficiary did not prove acceptance of her remainder interest, even if the life beneficiary then transferred some of the funds to the trustee.

---

[12] CPC § 6409 is the advancements statute.—Ed.

[13] CPC § 6410 provides that advancements are not counted against share of person who takes in place of recipient of advancement who predeceases the decedent.—Ed.

Chapter 3. Wills: Formalities and Forms

❖ CPC § 6101. Property Which May Be Disposed of by Will

A will may dispose of the following property:

(a) The testator's separate property.

(b) The one-half of the community property that belongs to the testator under Section 100.

(c) The one-half of the testator's quasi-community property that belongs to the testator under Section 101.

(Stats. 1990)

CPC § 88. Will

"Will" includes codicil and any testamentary instrument which merely appoints an executor or revokes or revises another will.

(Stats. 1990)

Section A. Execution of Wills

Attested Wills

Writing, Signature, and Attestation: Strict Compliance

❖ CPC § 6110. Requirements for Formal Will

(a) Except as provided in this part, a will shall be in writing and satisfy the requirements of this section.

(b) The will shall be signed[14] by one of the following:

> (1) By the testator.

> (2) In the testator's name by some other person in the testator's presence and by the testator's direction.

> (3) By a conservator pursuant to a court order to make a will under Section 2580.

---

[14] Both the California Civil Code (§ 14) and the California Code of Civil Procedure (§ 17) state that for purposes of those codes "signature or subscription includes mark, when the person cannot write, his or her name being written near it by a person who writes his or her own name as a witness." They also state that "writing includes printing and typewriting" and that "the word 'will' includes codicil."—Ed.

(c)

(1) Except as provided in paragraph (2), the will shall be witnessed by being signed, during the testator's lifetime, by at least two persons each of whom (A) being present at the same time, witnessed either the signing of the will or the testator's acknowledgment of the signature or of the will and (B) understand that the instrument they sign is the testator's will.

(2) If a will was not executed in compliance with paragraph (1), the will shall be treated as if it was executed in compliance with that paragraph if the proponent of the will establishes by clear and convincing evidence that, at the time the testator signed the will, the testator intended the will to constitute the testator's will.

(Stats. 1990, 1996, 2008)

NOTES:

1. Subsection (c)(2) was added to § 6110 in 2008 after the California Supreme Court's decision in **Estate of Saueressig**, 38 Cal. 4th 1045, 136 P.3d 201, 44 Cal. Rptr. 3d 672 (2006), which held that a notarized, typewritten, will could not be admitted to probate because the second witness (the notary's husband who saw testator sign the will) did not sign the will until after the testator had died.

2. Estate of Stoker, 193 Cal. App. 4th 236, 122 Cal. Rptr. 3d 529 (2011) upheld the admission of a will to probate that lacked any witness signatures because the court found by clear and convincing evidence that the testator, who signed it, intended it to be his will.

3. Estate of Ben-Ali, 216 Cal. App. 4th 1026, 157 Cal. Rptr. 3d 353, review denied (2013), held that no presumption of due execution arises from the presence of an attestation clause unless there is proof of the genuineness of the signatures of the testator and both witnesses. Proof of the testator's signature and that of one of the witnesses is not sufficient.

CPC § 6112. Witnesses

(a) Any person generally competent to be a witness may act as a witness to a will.

(b) A will or any provision thereof is not invalid because the will is signed by an interested witness.

(c) Unless there are at least two other subscribing witnesses to the will who are disinterested witnesses, the fact that the will makes a devise to a subscribing witness creates a presumption that the witness procured the devise by duress, menace, fraud, or undue influence. This presumption is a presumption affecting the burden of proof. This presumption does not apply where the witness is a person to whom the devise is made solely in a fiduciary capacity.

(d) If a devise made by the will to an interested witness fails because the presumption established by subdivision (c) applies to the devise and the witness fails to rebut the presumption, the interested witness shall take such proportion of the devise made to the witness in the will as does not exceed the share of the estate which would be distributed to the witness if the will were not established. Nothing in this subdivision affects the law that applies where it is established that the witness procured a devise by duress, menace, fraud, or undue influence.

(Stats. 1990)

❖ CPC § 6113. Laws Determining Validity of Will

A written will is validly executed if its execution complies with any of the following:

(a) The will is executed in compliance with Section 6110 or 6111 or Chapter 6 (commencing with Section 6200) (California statutory will) or Chapter 11 (commencing with Section 6380) (Uniform International Wills Act).

(b) The execution of the will complies with the law at the time of execution of the place where the will is executed.

(c) The execution of the will complies with the law of the place where at the time of execution or at the time of death the testator is domiciled, has a place of abode, or is a national.

(Stats. 1990)

❖ CPC § 6105. Conditional Will

A will, the validity of which is made conditional by its own terms, shall be admitted to probate or rejected, or denied effect after admission to probate, in conformity with the condition.

(Stats. 1990)

❖ CPC § 6111.5. Determining Whether Document Is a Will

Extrinsic evidence is admissible to determine whether a document constitutes a will pursuant to Section 6110 or 6111, or to determine the meaning of a will or a portion of a will if the meaning is unclear.

(Stats. 1990)

Holographic Wills

❖ CPC § 6111. Requirements for Holographic Will

(a) A will that does not comply with Section 6110 is valid as a holographic will, whether or not witnessed, if the signature and the material provisions are in the handwriting of the testator.

(b) If a holographic will does not contain a statement as to the date of its execution and:

(1) If the omission results in doubt as to whether its provisions or the inconsistent provisions of another will are controlling, the holographic will is invalid to the extent of the inconsistency unless the time of its execution is established to be after the date of execution of the other will.

(2) If it is established that the testator lacked testamentary capacity at any time during which the will might have been executed, the will is invalid unless it is established that it was executed at a time when the testator had testamentary capacity.

(c) Any statement of testamentary intent contained in a holographic will may be set forth either in the testator's own handwriting or as part of a commercially printed form will.

(Stats. 1990)

Document Titled "Last Will Etc. or What? Of Homer Eugene Williams" and Not Otherwise Signed a Valid Holographic Will

ESTATE of WILLIAMS

California Court of Appeal, Sixth District
155 Cal. App. 4th 197, 66 Cal. Rptr. 3d 34, review denied (2007)

BAMATTRE-MANOUKIAN, Acting P.J. In this probate case, Eric Williams Towle, the biological son of the decedent, Homer Eugene Williams, appeals from orders admitting to probate a holographic will offered by the decedent's stepdaughter, Deborah Ann Cox, and appointing Cox executor. . . .

Evidence

. . . After the decedent's death, Towle was unable to locate a will in the decedent's belongings and thus began probate proceedings based on the understanding that no will existed. About a week after the decedent's death, Cox found what appeared to be a holographic will in "the center drawer of [decedent's] desk" and later brought this to the attention of Towle's attorney. The desk contained other important documents such as bank statements and tax returns. The center drawer did not appear to contain any important documents other than a checkbook.

The document found by Cox was handwritten on the front and back of the first page of a note pad. The entire text was written in block-style capital letters. The next two sheets of the note pad were blank. After the blank pages, the next page of the note pad contained what appeared to be a list of movies, in the same block printing. The remaining pages were blank. . . .

Cox testified that the name written at the top of this document appeared to be written by the decedent. She explained that the decedent often left her notes to do things for him that were in block letters, with his name also written in block letters, similar to that on the holographic will. Cox had never seen the decedent write in cursive, although she had come across checks where he had signed his name. Cox explained that her stepfather was aware of the value of properties in the neighborhood because he would talk to people on the block when properties were for sale. Therefore, she believed that his estimate of the value of the house at $225,000 to $350,000 likely reflected values at the time he wrote the document. Cox estimated that the current value of the house is approximately $700,000, which she believed indicated that the document was written some years ago. Where she found the notepad, in the decedent's desk drawer, he would have had easy access to it.

Cox testified that the decedent had told her that "he put [her and his sister-in law] both down as the executor for his will." He was aware that Cox had previously been the executor for her grandmother's estate and he knew that the probate had gone smoothly. . . . Cox also testified that "on two occasions" her stepfather had promised her the house. He had told her "if I stayed there with him, I would get the house if he died, and then also when the house was paid off and he showed me the paper from the bank and says now, you don't have anything to worry about." The decedent had two life insurance policies. One was payable to Cox, and her niece was the beneficiary of the other one.

The decedent and Virginia Towle divorced when their two children, Eric and Gayle, were three and seven respectively. Virginia Towle remarried four years later and subsequently began using Towle as her last name and the last name for her children. The decedent also remarried and began living with his second wife and her children, including Cox. In the 1970's, they moved as a family to 1945 Serge Avenue, San Jose, where the decedent lived until his death in 2005. Cox left home while in college, but moved back into the home at 1945 Serge Avenue for good in 1988, at her stepfather's request after her mother had died. She provided companionship and care for her stepfather for the last 17 years of his life. She did things such as fixing his dinner, cleaning, shopping, doing laundry, running errands, picking up medications, and taking him to the doctor. When he became ill, she continued to take care of him. The night before he died, she went to the hospital with him and stayed with him until he died. The Towle family decided not to have a funeral because the family had plans for Virginia Towle's birthday. Cox later learned that the cremation had taken place and that the ashes had been sent back to Nebraska. She and her niece were very upset by this.

APPENDIX 1

ATTACHMENT 4e(2)

LAST Will ETC. or WHAT?

of

HOMER Eugene Williams
1945 SERGE AVE,
SAN JOSE, CA 95130~1850

EXECUTORS:
STEP   DEBORAH COX
DAUGHTER / 1945 SERGE AVE. SJ.

SISTER   LORNA WILLIAMS
IN LAW.   6731 Mt. LENEVE DR. SS

POWER OF ATTORNEY: NOW
DEBORAH COX

ALL MY COLLICTABLES: EVERY THING
INCLUDING two PISTOLS & two
RIFLES, NONE FIRED: to NEPHEW
KIRK BELL
2504 No. 56 th St. Apt. #1
LINCOLN, NE 68504

ATTA   1ENT 4e(2)

IN THE EVENT OF A SERIOUS SICK-
NESS OR ACCIDENT; I DO NOT WANT
TO BE KEPT ALIVE BY LIFE SUPPORT
MEANS. AND I NAME MY EXECUTORS
TO SEE TO MY WISHES ARE CARRIED
OUT.

MY ESTATE:

HOUSE, PRESENT MARKET VALUE
$225,000 TO $350,000.00
BANK ACCOUNT: CHECKING
AND SAVINGS.

I WOULD LIKE MY STEP
DAUGHTER, DEBRA COX TO BE
ABLE TO LIVE IN THE HOUSE
AS LONG AS SHE WANTS BEFORE
PUTTING IT UP FOR SALE.

Cox testified that she and her stepfather had a close, loving, familial relationship. She called him "dad." He had mentioned to her that he wanted to adopt her. In contrast, she testified that the decedent had a "distant" relationship with his biological children. She said that Eric

Towle only visited his father "five times" in thirty years, although he lived in Scotts Valley and worked in San Jose. His father's home was only approximately 15 minutes off of the route Towle would take back and forth to work. Cox thought Towle called his father "two or three times a year." Cox remembered four occasions when the decedent's daughter visited him in thirty years. She did not remember the decedent's daughter calling. Cox felt that the families were completely separate after the divorce and that the decedent essentially became part of his second wife's family. She said her stepfather had been "very upset" when he found out that his biological children were no longer using his name.

Towle and Virginia Towle provided testimony that conflicted with Cox's testimony regarding family relationships and the way the decedent wrote documents. Virginia Towle testified that the decedent loved his biological children and that she and her children socialized with the decedent "constantly." . . . Virginia Towle explained that Cox "never" attended those events and that the decedent never discussed Cox. Virginia Towle continues her relationship with the decedent's remaining siblings. She testified that the funeral was not held for the decedent because "no one was interested and it seemed why, there was no one to go to it." . . .

Towle testified that he "had a very good relationship with [his] father." He did not see him regularly because "I was in a very busy phase of my life, and he basically, like many elderly people, became much more bound to his routines, and the list of things he would do got shorter and shorter." According to Towle, the relationship was not "estranged" and the decedent sent Towle and his sister "birthday and Christmas cards every year." The cards to Towle were signed, "love, dad." He also sent his grandchildren "cards and gifts." Towle testified that Cox's relationship with the decedent was not close. . . .

Towle testified that he had never seen his father write any documents in block letters similar to that in the purported holographic will. He introduced credit cards, checks, and identification cards, all of which the decedent had signed in cursive. Towle identified the signatures on those documents as his father's. . . .

The primary purpose of the holographic will statute is to prevent fraud by requiring that the material provisions be in the testator's writing. . . . As the Supreme Court observed in *Estate of Black* . . . [(1982) 30 Cal. 3d 880, 883, 181 Cal. Rptr. 222, 641 P.2d 754] "'[t]he policy of the law is toward "a construction favoring validity, in determining whether a will has been executed in conformity with statutory requirements." . . . The high court affirmed "the tendency of both the courts and the Legislature . . . toward greater liberality in accepting a writing as an holographic will . . . . *Substantial compliance with the statute, and not absolute precision is all that is required* . . . ."

Appellant's primary argument is that the will was not a holographic will because it did not contain a valid signature. . . . Two components of the signature requirement are relevant here: the location of the name in the document, and whether the testator's use of block letters constituted his signature.

Ch. 3. Wills: Formalities and Forms

A. Location of the Signature

There is no requirement that the signature on a holographic will must be at the end of the document, so long as it appears from the document itself that the signature was intended to authenticate the document. . . . (*Estate of Bloch* (1952), 39 Cal. 2d 570, 572-573, 248 P.2d 21.) Several cases illustrate this rule. . . . [Discussion of cases omitted.—Ed.]

In the holographic will before us, . . . the testator did not include his name at the end of the document. However, the evidence on the face of the document as a whole supports a finding that the name was placed with the intention of authenticating the document. The phrase "Last Will . . . of Homer Eugene Williams" located at the top of the document is almost identical to the title of the holographic will in *Morgan* [Estate of Morgan, 200 Cal. 400, 402, 253 P. 702 (1927)]. . . . Cases have shown that completeness is highly relevant in determining if the name was written with an intent to authenticate the document. . . .

The document before us has . . . indicia of completeness. First, the decedent took the time . . . to list the addresses of those people included in the will: Cox, his sister-in-law, and his nephew. . . . He also wrote down his own address. Second, . . . there was sufficient room at the end of the document for the decedent to write more if he had wanted to do so. Another characteristic indicating completeness was the age of the document. Here the inference could be drawn from the property values stated in the document that it was written a number of years ago. Cox testified that she found it in the decedent's center desk drawer, where it was readily available had he wanted to change or add to it. All of this evidence reasonably supports the conclusion that "the writer *had done everything* that he intended to do." . . .

The case before us differs from *Estate of Bernard* (1925), 197 Cal. 36, 239 P. 404, in which the document clearly appeared to be unfinished. There the court wrote: "The abrupt termination of the document near the middle of the last page is a strong indication of decedent's intent to do something more in order to make it a complete will." . . . In contrast, here the decedent appointed an executor, disposed of his collectables, listed assets for reference, and then indicated his intention for the house. Unlike the will in *Brooks* [Estate of Brooks, 214 Cal. 138, 4 P.2d 148 (1931)] . . . the document ended with a period. . . .

From an evaluation of the whole document in the case before us, it appears that the name at the top of the document was intended as a mark of execution. . . .

B. Form of the Signature

Appellant contends that the decedent's name at the top of the document is written in block letters, and therefore, cannot be considered a signature. This argument is based upon the decision in *Estate of Twohig* (1986) 178 Cal. App. 3d 555, 223 Cal. Rptr. 352 . . . . *Twohig* concerned a handwritten codicil to an executed formal will. However, the testator failed to sign the codicil. The court reasoned that the unsigned codicil could not incorporate the formal will by reference because it was not itself a complete testamentary document since it lacked a signature. The court explained that "[w]hile the courts have been liberal with regard to the form and location of the signature within the holograph . . . they have not condoned its absence." . . . The court further found that the two documents could not be deemed integrated because one was holographic and one was not, and the holographic document altered the provisions of the formal document. The court concluded that the codicil could not be admitted into probate because it was unsigned.

Our case is distinguishable . . . . In *Twohig*, the codicil did not include the testator's name at all. There was therefore no authenticating mark from which an intent to execute the document could be inferred. Further, it appeared that the testator had intended to sign it because he wrote "signed" on a particular date. Thus, unlike our case, the document on its face tended to show that there was something else the testator intended to add before the document was complete, namely his signature. Finally, there was no issue in our case that the document attempted to modify a valid will. The holographic will in our case was the testator's only expression of his testamentary wishes.

Appellant asserts that the block letters at the top of the document are not in the form the decedent used to sign legal documents and, therefore, it must be found that the document was not properly executed. However, several cases illustrate that the way a testator signs a holographic will does not need to be identical to a signature used to sign other legal documents. In *Estate of Morris* (1969), 268 Cal. App. 2d 638, 640, 74 Cal. Rptr. 32 . . . , the court found that "[t]he use of the initials as a signature was an effective signing of the will. . . ." The words, "Love from 'Muddy'," signed at the end of a holographic will in the form of a letter, were also considered a valid signature. (*Estate of Button* (1930), 209 Cal. 325, 328, 334, 287 P. 964 . . . .) And similarly, in *Estate of Henderson* (1925) 196 Cal. 623, 634, 238 P. 938 . . .), the court found the phrase "Your loving mother" constituted a valid signature. . . .

Other Evidence of Testamentary Intent

. . . Appellant contends that three characteristics of the will undermine the conclusion that the document is testamentary. First, he asserts that the title "Last Will Etc. or What?" creates an ambiguity and implies that the decedent was unaware of what he was writing. Second, he contends the failure of the document to dispose of all of the decedent's property indicates it is not testamentary in nature. Third, appellant asserts that the statement "I would *like* . . ." in the provision regarding the house (italics added) is ambiguous and does not clearly demonstrate an intent on the part of the decedent to dispose of his property. . . .

In determining whether the language of a document is so unclear as to undermine testamentary intent, *Estate of Smilie* (1950), 99 Cal. App. 2d 794, 222 P.2d 692 . . . provides guidance. In that case, . . . [a] letter contained these sentences: "I want you to see that all my bills are paid and that Dot does not get thing. I want you to have all of my after my bill are." . . . The trial court found the document expressed a testamentary intent and construed these sentences to read: "I want you to see that all of my bills are paid and that Dot does not get a thing. I want you to have all." . . . The Court of Appeal upheld the lower court's construction of the will. . . .

"The true test of the character of an instrument is not the testator's realization that it is a *will*, but his intention to create a revocable disposition of his property to accrue and take effect only upon his death and passing no present interest." . . . [Estate of Spitzer, 196 Cal. 301, 307, 237 P. 739 (1925)]. In the instant case, the text of the document indicates that the intent of the decedent was to dispose of his property upon his death. [T]he parts of the text that are confusing or extraneous, such as the words "Etc. or What?" can be ignored as surplusage in order to uphold the intent of the decedent. Intent is demonstrated on the face of the document by the use of the words "Last Will" in the title, the naming of an executor, and the disposal of identified property. The decedent clearly contemplated that the identified property would be disposed of after his death.

Similarly, the inclusion of instructions regarding the decedent's wishes upon a serious illness, and the mention of Deborah Cox as having his power of attorney, which would normally be provisions that would be made effective during the person's lifetime, could also have been properly ignored by the trial court. . . .

Appellant's second contention is that the will is invalid because it does not dispose of all of the decedent's property. However, in *Estate of Rowe*, . . . [(1964) 230 Cal. App. 2d 442, 41 Cal. Rptr. 52], the court found a holographic will to be valid that did not dispose of all of the decedent's property. . . .

Appellant next contends that the words "I would like," with regard to the house, do not show testamentary intent, but are rather a suggestion or recommendation. . . . [T]he language in the holographic will before us does not express a suggestion or wish to a legatee or devisee regarding the future disposition of property being devised. Rather it is an expression of the testator's intent as to the house he and his stepdaughter are living in, in the event of his death. . . . There is no one else named in the will as a devisee of this property. It is reasonable to conclude that the phrase, "I would like," in this context is addressed to the executors of the estate, who had been previously identified in the document. Therefore, . . . this phrase can be construed as an expression of testamentary intent, rather than a suggestion.[4] . . .

In the case before us, Cox's testimony as to the decedent's express wishes upon his death provided evidence, similar to that in *Spies,* that the holographic document, which was consistent with those wishes, was "testamentary in character." . . . [T]estimony regarding the decedent's statements about his will and future intentions were admissible to demonstrate testamentary intent. This testimony, in addition to the title of the document as a "Last Will," the "studied care" with which the decedent set forth the names and addresses of those identified in the will, . . . the indicia of completeness of the document, and the express terms disposing of some of the decedent's property, all support a finding that the document was written with testamentary intent. . . .

The orders are affirmed.

---

[4] We note that in this appeal we are only reviewing the order admitting the holographic will to probate. We express no opinion regarding the eventual interpretation or effect of this provision regarding the house, an issue that is left to be determined by the probate court in further proceedings before that court. We decide only that the language "I would like" in the context of the will is indicative of testamentary intent and not merely precatory.

Incorporation of Material Printed Matter Invalidates Holographic Will

ESTATE of SOUTHWORTH

Court of Appeal, Second District, Division 6
59 Cal. Rptr. 2d 272 (1996), rev. den. (1997)

GILBERT, Associate Justice. A charitable donor card contains printed language showing an intent to make a future gift to the charity. In the blank space following the printed words a testator writes that her entire estate is to be left to the charity. She signs and dates the donor card. Does her handwriting on the donor card constitute a holographic will? No.

The trial court admitted a donor card into probate as a holographic will. Half-siblings, Jeanette Southworth, Jack Southworth, and an heir finder, Francis V. See,[15] appeal from the judgment of the trial court in favor of respondent, North Shore Animal League (NSAL). . . .

FACTS

Decedent never married and had no children. On March 4, 1986, in response to decedent's request for information, NSAL sent a letter to her describing its lifetime pet care program and explaining how to register for it. NSAL asked that she return its enclosed pet care registration card, contact her attorney to include her bequest to NSAL in her estate and send a copy of the bequest to NSAL. NSAL informed her that "[e]ven if you don't currently have a will, we'll accept your Registration on good faith and maintain an Active file on your pet while you're arranging the Bequest." Decedent never returned the registration card to NSAL.

On September 4, 1987, decedent requested registration with The Neptune Society for cremation of her body upon her death. On the registration form, she stated that she never married and that Neptune should contact the Ventura County Coroner to make arrangements. On the same date, decedent sent a letter to NSAL asking whether or not it destroys animals.

Her letter to NSAL states, "I have been terribly upset since I heard [that NSAL destroys animals] because I have always truly believed that you did not destroy animals and this was the determining factor in my selection of you as the beneficiary of my entire estate as I have no relatives and do not want the State of California, courts, or attorneys to benefit from my hard earned labor.

I should appreciate greatly if you would clarify this point about the destruction of animals at your shelter and tell me honestly and truly what your policy is [and] not hedge because I have mentioned leaving my estate to your organization.

On September 9, 1987, NSAL wrote to assure her that it would not destroy any pet. NSAL included a brochure regarding estate planning. The brochure explained that a letter or a verbal

---

[15] Francis V. See, heir finder, was also involved in *Estate of Griswold*, 25 Cal. 4th 904, 24 P.3d 1191, 108 Cal. Rptr. 2d 165 (2001), included in Chapter 2, *supra.*—Ed.

promise will not effectuate a testamentary gift; that a proper written will is required. The mailing urged members to consult an estate planning attorney to avoid the possibility that the estate might end up with "distant relatives whom you didn't even know." Decedent never prepared a formal will.

NSAL sent a donor card to the decedent. It stated: "Your newest gift to the North Shore Animal League will help get more homeless dogs and cats out of cages and into new homes." The donor card thanked her "for your interest in making a bequest to the League." It explained that she could change her life insurance policy or provide for animals in her will by calling her attorney. It sought gifts and legacies and asked her to complete and return the donor card. On April 19, 1989, she returned the donor card to NSAL. . . .

On May 10, 1989, NSAL sent a thank you letter to decedent for "letting us know that you will remember the North Shore Animal League in your will." The letter requested that decedent "have your attorney send us a copy of your will[.]"

The Neptune Society asked for additional information to complete the death certificate, pursuant to amendments to the Probate Code. Decedent returned Neptune's supplemental form and stated that there are "[n]o living relatives" and to "[p]lease notify North Shore Animal League." She included NSAL's address, telephone numbers and the name of the executive director of NSAL. She signed the supplemental form and dated it October 20, 1989.

On September 2, 1992, NSAL sent a letter to decedent acknowledging that in March 1989 she wrote NSAL to state that she intended to take action leading to its becoming one of the beneficiaries of her estate. NSAL requested a meeting with decedent, thanking her for her "kind thoughts and generous support." She never responded to this request.

On January 14, 1994, Dorothy Southworth died. . . .

The trial court concluded that decedent's handwritten statement on the donor card that "[m]y entire estate is to be left to North Shore Animal League" substantially complies with all the Probate Code requirements for a holographic will. The court viewed the preprinted parts of the donor card and the $500,000 sum written in to be immaterial. The court interpreted the preprinted words stating that "I am not taking action now, but my intention is . . ." to mean that she did not want to immediately transfer her funds to NSAL, but intended to bequeath them upon her death. The trial court admitted the donor card to probate as the last will of the decedent. . . .

DISCUSSION

. . . There is no question that the handwriting on the document at issue is that of Dorothy Southworth, and that she signed and dated it. [H]owever, the document is not a commercially-printed will form. It is a donor card for a charity. It was not drafted to serve as a will. The card provides the option of informing NSAL that the donor has or intends to instruct one's attorney to change his or her will.

Furthermore, the printed language Southworth incorporated from the donor card does not evince her present testamentary intent. Instead of striking the material printed words which state "I am not taking action now, but my intention is," she chose to incorporate those words with her handwritten statement, "My entire estate is to be left to North Shore Animal League."

71

The material printed language together with her handwriting evince a future intent; not present testamentary intent.

Although other extrinsic evidence, such as her letter to NSAL of September 4, 1987, and the supplemental Neptune form she signed on October 20, 1989, shows that Southworth desired to leave her estate to NSAL, neither the donor card at issue nor the handwriting on it substantially complies with probate code requirements for holographic wills. Although courts may consider statements made before and after a holographic will is made and the surrounding circumstances, *evidence of present testamentary intent provided by the instrument at issue is paramount*. . . .

Here, Southworth incorporated printed language stating that she was not taking any action when she executed it. It does not establish her testamentary intent at the time she executed it. It only states her intention to make a will in the future.

The judgment is reversed. The parties are to bear their own costs.

FOR ME...HALF FOR YOU   B 1:9E09

                              03/09/.

                                                    153

YOUR HALF

MRS
MISS. D R SOUTHWORTH
6636 TAMARIND
ACOURA HILLS, CA 91301

Dear Mrs. Lewyt:

I know it takes a lot of money to
care for many thousands of homeless
dogs and cats each year, and because
you don't destroy animals, I have
decided:

a. I AM NAMING THE SHELTER AS A
   BENEFICIARY OF A LIFE INSURANCE
   POLICY.

   ( ) My insurance broker has
       already been notified.
   ( ) My broker will be notified
       by . . . . (date)

b. I AM CHANGING MY WILL TO LEAVE
   THE SHELTER . . . .
              (stocks/bonds/cash/etc.)

   ( ) My attorney has already been
       instructed to change my will.
   ( ) My attorney will be instructed
       by . . . . (date)

(c) I AM NOT TAKING ACTION NOW, BUT
    MY INTENTION IS ▓▓▓▓▓▓▓.

    My entire estate
    is to be left to North
    Shore Animal League

The total amount that the animal
shelter will someday receive is
$500,000.00 and I would like the
money used for:

(X) Food and shelter for the animals
( ) Adoption Fund to advertise for
    new owners
(X) Spaying and Neutering Program
    Unrestricted use

                 Sincerely,

          Dorothy Southworth

STREET · PORT WASHINGTON, NY 11050 4/19/89

❧❧

Photocopy of Handwriting Is "In the Handwriting of the Testator"

ESTATE of BRENNER

Court of Appeal, Second District, Division 7
76 Cal. App. 4th 1298, 91 Cal. Rptr. 2d 149 (1999)

NEAL, J. . . . Appellant William James Osborne is a Los Angeles lawyer who formerly represented the decedent Morris Brenner. Respondent Anita Brenner is decedent's daughter, named executrix under Morris Brenner's formal will of November 6, 1990. After Morris died in May 1996, Anita petitioned for probate of Morris' 1990 will. Osborne then filed a petition to probate a handwritten or holographic will prepared by Morris in 1995. . . .

In April 1995 Morris retained Osborne to represent Morris in a personal injury case. In September Morris mentioned his 1990 will to Osborne and asked Osborne to prepare a new will. Morris showed Osborne a copy of the 1990 will, on which Morris had made handwritten changes. Osborne declined to prepare a new will, but made interlineations on the marked-up 1990 will, at Morris' direction, changing some of its dispositions. Morris gave Osborne a copy of this marked-up will.

Soon Morris again asked Osborne to prepare a new will. Osborne again declined, but suggested Morris prepare a holographic will. Morris then sent Osborne a document which Morris said was his holographic will. Morris told Osborne that Morris intended to revoke the 1990 will, and gave Osborne several reasons for desiring to do so.

The purported holographic will which Morris gave Osborne was a three page photocopy of a handwritten list of property dispositions, upon which there appeared handwritten ink additions, including: the note "my will of November 6, 1990 is void"; the signature "Morris Brenner"; the statements "This is my new will"; "my trustee and executor, lawyer James Osborne"; and "Will of Nov. 6, 1990 is void. M.B." The holograph also bore the original ink notation "witness", with the signature of a "Salvador Borja."

Following Osborne's receipt of the 1995 holograph, Morris in several conversations with Osborne referred to "his holographic will." In early 1996 Osborne prepared a draft of a new formal will for Morris, based on the dispositions in the 1995 holograph. Osborne told Morris to take the draft to an estate planning specialist, but Morris did not do so. Morris attempted instead to execute the will without assistance of counsel, did so erroneously, and thus invalidated it.

After Morris died, Borja delivered to Anita the original, yellow paper, handwritten matter which Morris had photocopied and annotated to constitute the holographic will. This was available at trial, and conformed exactly to the photocopied material in the holographic will.

A forensic document expert retained by Osborne testified that all the photocopied and ink handwriting on the holograph was Morris's, except for the notation "witness" and Borja's signature.

The trial court found that Morris had hand-written the text of the 1995 instrument, but the instrument did not qualify as a valid holographic will because the photocopy did not contain Morris's original handwriting. The document also failed to qualify as an attested will, so the court denied it admission to probate. This appeal followed.

DISCUSSION

. . . Looking first only at the formalities, the validity of the holographic will here turns on whether photocopies of the testator's handwritten dispositions satisfy section 6111. The trial court's construction of "handwriting of the testator" as requiring original ink on the page is not implausible. On the other hand, it is also reasonable to refer to a photocopy of someone's handwriting as "in their handwriting." Photocopies of handwritten testamentary dispositions carry pretty much the same assurance of authenticity as original ink. In each instance the genuineness of the testamentary dispositions tends to be shown by the fact that the testator himself wrote them out.

It is true that photocopying could be used to take excerpts from a handwritten document and distort its substance, but this concern usually could be addressed by adequate proof of authenticity—also required for documents in original handwriting.

On balance, we think section 6111 is properly construed to allow photocopies of the testator's handwritten dispositions, properly authenticated, as well as original ink writings. No case has addressed precisely the situation presented here, but several with similar facts support the conclusions reached here. (*Estate of Janes* (1941), 18 Cal. 2d 512, 517, 116 P.2d 438 [handwritten document satisfying holographic will formalities, but with note attached stating "this is a copy of my last will," properly admitted to probate]; *In re Shultz's Estate* (1960), 54 Cal. 2d 513, 516-517, 6 Cal. Rptr. 281, 353 P.2d 921 [series of three letters in decedent's hand, two of them signed, revoking prior will, and containing bequests, properly admitted to probate].)

Moreover . . . [s]ubstantial and uncontroverted extrinsic evidence in this case confirmed that Morris's intent was to replace the 1990 will with the 1995 holographic will. . . .

Section B. Revocation of Wills

Revocation by Writing or by Physical Act

❖ *CPC § 6120. Revocation by Subsequent Will or Physical Act*

A will or any part thereof is revoked by any of the following:

(a) A subsequent will which revokes the prior will or part expressly or by inconsistency.

(b) Being burned, torn, canceled, obliterated, or destroyed, with the intent and for the purpose of revoking it, by either (1) the testator or (2) another person in the testator's presence and by the testator's direction.
(Stats. 1990)

❖ CPC § 6121. Effect of Revoking Duplicate Will

A will executed in duplicate or any part thereof is revoked if one of the duplicates is burned, torn, canceled, obliterated, or destroyed, with the intent and for the purpose of revoking it, by either (1) the testator or (2) another person in the testator's presence and by the testator's direction.
(Stats. 1990)

CPC § 6124. Presumption of Revocation

If the testator's will was last in the testator's possession, the testator was competent until death, and neither the will nor a duplicate original of the will can be found after the testator's death, it is presumed that the testator destroyed the will with intent to revoke it. This presumption is a presumption affecting the burden of producing evidence.
(Stats. 1990)

NOTE: **Estate of Trikha**, 219 Cal. App. 4th 791, 162 Cal. Rptr. 3d 175 (2013), held that wife who contested will leaving all husband's property to children and grandchildren, which could not be found after his death, under § 6124 had burden of proof to establish revocation after son produced substantial evidence tending to overcome the presumption that father had destroyed will with intent to revoke. Wife had several opportunities to take the will and had substantial financial and cultural motives to destroy it.
Photocopy Is Not a "Duplicate Original"

LAUERMANN v. SUPERIOR COURT

Court of Appeal, Fourth District, Division 2
127 Cal. App. 4th 1327, 26 Cal. Rptr. 3d 258 (2005)

KING, Acting P.J. . . . Decedent, Werner . . . Lauermann, was survived by neither spouse nor issue. In 1987 he executed a will leaving certain described real property to real parties in interest Ranu Muongpruan and her children.[3] However, the original of this will could not be

---

[3] The will did not dispose of any residuary estate. Although it expressly indicated decedent's wish not to bequeath anything to any former spouse, it did not specifically mention Gerda Lauermann or her brother. The will does contain a general in terrorem clause.

found following his death. What *was* found, apparently among decedent's possessions, was a photocopy of the will. It bore no indication of intent to revoke; that is, there were no revocatory notations, crossings-out, or other defacement of the copy. . . .

. . . Muongpruan petitioned to have the will admitted to probate . . . . This petition was opposed by decedent's sister, Gerda Lauermann, and Eva Lauermann, . . . personal representative of the estate of decedent's brother, Gerhard.[4] They duly filed a will contest . . . .

Section 6124 provides that, "If the testator's will was last in the testator's possession, the testator was competent until death, and neither the will nor a duplicate original of the will can be found after the testator's death, it is presumed that the testator destroyed the will with intent to revoke it. This presumption is a presumption affecting the burden of producing evidence." . . . In proceedings on the issue, real parties persuaded the trial court that the photocopy of the will qualified as a "duplicate original" so that the presumption would *not* apply. However, the trial court indicated that the issue was one appropriate for immediate resolution by an appellate court. . . . We agreed, and issued an order to show cause on the petition filed by Gerda Lauermann and Eva Lauermann.

DISCUSSION

. . . "Original," in the context before us, is defined as "a primary manuscript from which copies are made." (Webster's 3d New Internat. Dict. (1993) p. 1591.) A duplicate, of course, is simply a copy, so that "duplicate original" may seem to be an oxymoron. However, it need not be so. Section 6121, for example, clearly contemplates that there may be more than one "original" will when it provides that, "A will executed in duplicate . . . is revoked if one of the duplicates is burned, torn, canceled, obliterated, or destroyed, with the intent . . . of revoking it . . . ." It is also clear that "[t]here is no reason why a testator may not execute two valid wills with identical provisions to insure the execution of his wishes should one of them be accidentally lost or destroyed." (Estate of Janes (1941), 18 Cal. 2d 512, 516, 116 P.2d 438, italics added.)

Section 6121 uses the phrase "will executed in duplicate" while section 6124 covers the situation in which "neither the will nor a duplicate original of the will can be found . . . ." The former phrase obviously means that the testator has physically signed two separate *copies* of his will, each of which has also been witnessed and signed by the witnesses. The question is whether "duplicate original" in section 6124 carries the same meaning. . . .

Turning now to the intent and purpose of section 6124, "The stringent requirements for proof of lost or destroyed wills are imposed to avoid fraud." (*Estate of Janes, supra,* . . .) It is plainly in support of this purpose that section 6124 creates a presumption of revocation where a will known or believed to have been executed cannot be found.[8] By contrast, if a testator has

---

[4] Gerhard presumably survived decedent, but has since died.

[8] It is as well to note that the statute clarifies that the presumption is one affecting only the burden of producing evidence rather than the burden of proof. It may therefore be rebutted by evidence showing

personally executed duplicate originals, there is little likelihood of fraud when one copy is available for probate even if the second cannot be found. Although it is true that the intentional destruction by the testator of any copy of a "will executed in duplicate" operates as a revocation (§ 6121), as the Law Revision Commission recognized, a testator who has left an executed copy of his will with, for example, his attorney (or in a safe deposit box) may be less careful to preserve the copy in his personal possession. ... In addition, it is likely that a testator who has executed two or more "duplicate originals" would make an effort to destroy all such copies if he or she wishes to revoke the will.

On the other hand, the existence of mere photocopies, in our view, does *not* suggest that the testator might feel less need to keep track of the original of his or her will. Photocopies are easily made and in common understanding are readily distinguished from an "original." A testator may make several photocopies of his or her will, perhaps to send to relatives or other beneficiaries, or to retain for the purpose of drafting possible changes. It would be unreasonable to expect a testator to track down and destroy all such copies before giving effect to his intended revocation. Thus, the rule urged by real parties in order to carry out a supposed testamentary intent might just as well have the pernicious effect of preserving the validity of a will which the testator had done everything in his power to revoke.

Furthermore, not only are photocopies ubiquitous, but the simplicity of their creation stands in stark contrast to the considerable formalities surrounding the execution of a will. ... Given the importance placed upon the creation and execution of an original will, we do not think that a reasonable testator would believe that a photocopy would be legally effective in place of the original document, and realize that all such copies must be destroyed before a revocation became effective. ...

[T]he trial court erred in ruling that "duplicate original," as used in section 6124, includes a photocopy not personally signed by the testator and the witnesses. ... [T]he presumption of revocation will apply. Let a peremptory writ of mandate issue as prayed. ...

Dependent Relative Revocation and Revival

❖ CPC § 6123. Revival of Revoked Will

(a) If a second will which, had it remained effective at death, would have revoked the first will in whole or in part, is thereafter revoked by acts under Section 6120 or 6121, the first will is revoked in whole or in part unless it is evident from the circumstances of the revocation of the second will or from the testator's contemporary or subsequent declarations that the testator intended the first will to take effect as executed.

---

that it is "equally probable" that the will was destroyed inadvertently or without the intent to revoke it. ...

(b) If a second will which, had it remained effective at death, would have revoked the first will in whole or in part, is thereafter revoked by a third will, the first will is revoked in whole or in part, except to the extent it appears from the terms of the third will that the testator intended the first will to take effect.

(Stats. 1990)

❧❧

Revocation by Operation of Law: Change in Family Circumstances

CPC § 6122. Revocation by Dissolution of Marriage

(a) Unless the will expressly provides otherwise, if after executing a will the testator's marriage is dissolved or annulled, the dissolution or annulment revokes all of the following:

(1) Any disposition or appointment of property made by the will to the former spouse.

(2) Any provision of the will conferring a general or special power of appointment on the former spouse.

(3) Any provision of the will nominating the former spouse as executor, trustee, conservator, or guardian.

(b) If any disposition or other provision of a will is revoked solely by this section, it is revived by the testator's remarriage to the former spouse.

(c) In case of revocation by dissolution or annulment:

(1) Property prevented from passing to a former spouse because of the revocation passes as if the former spouse failed to survive the testator.

(2) Other provisions of the will conferring some power or office on the former spouse shall be interpreted as if the former spouse failed to survive the testator.

(d) For purposes of this section, dissolution or annulment means any dissolution or annulment which would exclude the spouse as a surviving spouse within the meaning of Section 78. A decre of legal separation which does not terminate the status of spouses is not a dissolution for purposes of this section.

(e) Except as provided in Section 6122.1, no change of circumstances other than as described in this section revokes a will.

***

(Stats. 1990, 2001, 2002, 2016)

CPC § 6122.1. Revocation by Termination of Domestic Partnership

(a) Unless the will expressly provides otherwise, if after executing a will the testator's domestic partnership is terminated, the termination revokes all of the following:

(1) Any disposition or appointment of property made by the will to the former domestic partner.

(2) Any provision of the will conferring a general or special power of appointment on the former domestic partner.

(3) Any provision of the will nominating the former domestic partner as executor, trustee, conservator, or guardian.

(b) If any disposition or other provision of a will is revoked solely by this section, it is revived by the testator establishing another domestic partnership with the former domestic partner.

(c) In case of revocation by termination of a domestic partnership:

(1) Property prevented from passing to a former domestic partner because of the revocation passes as if the former domestic partner failed to survive the testator.

(2) Other provisions of the will conferring some power or office on the former domestic partner shall be interpreted as if the former domestic partner failed to survive the testator.

(d) This section shall apply only to wills executed on or after January 1, 2002.
(Stats. 2001)

NOTES:

1. The United States Supreme Court in **Sveen v. Melin**, 138 S. Ct. 1815 (2018), held that Minnesota's automatic revocation-on-divorce statute did not substantially impair pre-existing contractual rights and thus revocation of ex-wife's primary beneficiary designation on life insurance policy made before statute was enacted did not violate the Contracts Clause of the U.S. Constitution.

2. Estate of Coleman, 129 Cal. App. 4th 380, 28 Cal. Rptr. 3d 282 (2005) held that intervivos trust was revoked by marital settlement agreement and order transferring trust property to the spouses individually; residuary devise to trustee of the trust in former spouse's pour-over will created new testamentary trust; provision for ex-spouse was revoked by section 6122.

Gift to Named Stepchildren Contingent on Spouse's Failure to Survive Revoked by Dissolution of Marriage

ESTATE of JONES

Court of Appeal, Third District
122 Cal. App. 4th 326, 18 Cal. Rptr. 3d 637 (2004)

SIMS, J. . . . In 1982, Bruce Alan Jones married appellant's mother Sharon, who had two daughters from a prior marriage-appellant [Kathy Hardie] (then age 21) and Paula Labo (then age 19).

In 1988, while still married, Jones executed the will that is the subject of this appeal. The will stated: "I appoint my wife, Sharon, Executrix hereunder and if she shall fail to qualify, or having qualified shall die, resign, or cease to act as Executrix, then I appoint Kathy Hardie ... to act hereunder." The will also stated: "I give my entire estate to my wife Sharon if she survives me. If she does not survive me, A) I give and bequeath to my sister Susan Peddy all my books, the Jones family pictures, sword, airplane propeller and framed engraved copper plate artwork; B) I give and bequeath to my stepmother Patricia R. Jones the sum of Ten Thousand Dollars ($10,000.00); C) I give and bequeath to my nephew Clayton Peddy the sum of Ten Thousand Dollars ($10,000.00); D) I give and bequeath to my niece Alison Peddy the sum of Ten Thousand Dollars ($10,000.00); E) *all the rest, residue, and remainder of my property, real, personal, and mixed, at whatever time acquired by me and wherever situated, I give, devise, and bequeath (in equal shares) to the following beneficiary or beneficiaries who survive me: my stepdaughters Paula Labo and ... Kathy Hardie.*" (Italics added.)

In 1994, Jones and appellant's mother divorced. In November 2002, Jones died. Appellant's mother died in 2003. ...

DISCUSSION ...

Appellant believes she should inherit under the residuary clause despite her mother's divorce from the testator. We disagree.

Generally, "[t]he intention of the transferor as expressed in the instrument controls the legal effect of the dispositions made in the instrument." (§ 21102.)

The residuary clause in favor of "my stepdaughter[] ... Kathy Hardie ... " was to take effect, as stated in the will, "[i]f she [my wife Sharon] does not survive me." Although Sharon did survive Jones, the divorce revoked the bequest to her pursuant to section 6122. Also pursuant to section 6122, she is treated as having failed to survive him. ... [S]ection 6122 does not address the effect of divorce on bequests to children of the former spouse.

Preliminarily, we note that the will made a bequest to "my *stepdaughters* Paula Labo and ... Kathy Hardie." (Italics added.) However, ... at the time the testator died, appellant was no longer a stepdaughter, because that relationship had ended with appellant's mother's divorce from the testator. Hence, a literal reading of the will excludes appellant from taking. But we do not rest our opinion on this literal, technical reason alone.

Estate of Hermon, ... 39 Cal. App. 4th 1525, 46 Cal. Rptr. 2d 577 [1995], relied upon by the trial court in this case, held, "when a testator provides for his spouse's children, he normally intends to exclude children of an ex-spouse after dissolution, unless a contrary intention is indicated elsewhere in his will." ... We agree.

In *Hermon*, ... a decedent's will, which was executed during a marriage that was dissolved before his death, made bequests—in the event his wife predeceased him—to "my children and my spouse's children" and "my issue and my spouse's issue." ... The children of the former wife argued they were members of a class that continued to exist after the divorce, and they were entitled to share in the estate with the testator's natural children. . . . Since a will speaks as of the date of the testator's death, where there is a testamentary gift to a class, the members of the class are to be determined upon the testator's death. . . .

The Court of Appeal . . . held the bequests to the ex-wife's children failed due to absence of an expression of intent for the bequest to survive the marital dissolution. . . . *Hermon* first observed the case was not controlled by section 6122 (the effect of which is that upon divorce the testator's spouse "dies" for purposes of implementing the provisions of the will), because that statute addressed spouses, not children of spouses. . . . *Hermon* said out-of-state cases, where the operation of "revocation by dissolution" statutes similar to section 6122 triggered gifts in favor of the relatives of the former spouse, were not persuasive because in those cases the testamentary gifts were made to beneficiaries identified by name, whereas in the case before the *Hermon* court, the beneficiaries were described as a class, by their relationship to the testator . . . .

Hermon noted a revised provision of the Uniform Probate Code (a provision that to date has not been adopted in California) revokes not only testamentary bequests to the former spouse but also bequests to the former spouse's relatives. . . . "The general predicate of this provision is that, during the dissolution process or in the aftermath of the dissolution, 'the former spouse's relatives are likely to side with the former spouse, breaking down or weakening any former ties that may previously have developed between the transferor and the former spouse's relatives . . . .' (8 West's U. Laws Ann. (1983) Estate, Probate and Related Laws (1994 pocket supp.) p. 194.)" . . . The *Hermon* court urged the Legislature to adopt a statute similar to the cited provision of the Uniform Probate Code. . . .

The Legislature has not answered the call of the 1995 *Hermon* decision. . . .

[A]ppellant argues this case is different from *Hermon* . . . because here the testator did name her by name . . . not merely by class. Appellant argues that, where a testator leaves property to named individuals, it is reasonable to presume he meant his property to pass to those individuals, even if he supplemented the names with relationship identifiers . . . which he presumably added only to ensure correct identification and not to limit the bequest to a class. She argues such a presumption would be consistent with the general principle expressed in section 21120, that "[p]reference is to be given to an interpretation of an instrument that will prevent intestacy *or failure of a transfer* . . . ." (Italics added.) . . . .

. . . [W]e are not persuaded by appellant's presumption that use of her name in the will displayed an intent to provide for her after divorce. It seems more likely the testator was not contemplating divorce when he prepared his last will and testament six years before the divorce. Appellant was already an adult when her mother married Jones, and so there is no issue of the bond associated with raising a child. . . . The general preference for upholding testamentary transfers does not speak to the circumstances of this case. . . .

[A]ppellant argues California courts have adopted the presumption that a bequest to named individuals is not a bequest to a class. . . . However, none of the cited cases addressed the effect of divorce. . . .

In this case, if appellant enjoyed a continuing relationship with the testator in the eight years between his divorce and his death, we would have expected her to introduce evidence to that effect. She did not. In these circumstances, where we are essentially construing the language of the will without benefit of significant extrinsic evidence, we are constrained to agree with *Estate of Hermon* . . . that "when a testator provides for his spouse's children, he normally intends to exclude children of an ex-spouse after dissolution . . . ." . . .

Devise to Woman Testator Later Married Is Revoked by Subsequent Divorce; Testator's Intent Irrelevant

ESTATE of REEVES

Court of Appeal, Third District
233 Cal. App. 3d 651, 284 Cal. Rptr. 650 (1991)

NICHOLSON, Associate Justice. . . . The decedent, Edward Charles Reeves, married contestant Margaret Lucile Reeves in 1972. The couple divorced in 1982. Two children were born during the ten-year marriage . . . , ages 12 and 10, respectively, at the time of Edward's death. This appeal arises from a will contest filed by Margaret as guardian ad litem for Edward's minor children.

Edward and . . . Marlene A. Reeves, then known as Marlene A. Smith, began living together in March 1983. A month later, while he and Marlene were cohabiting, Edward executed a holographic will which stated: "To Whom it Concerns. In the Event of my death I leave all my properties & money to Marlene A. Smith. Edward C. Reeves. 4/10/83." Marlene kept the will in her possession until Edward's death.

Marlene and Edward married in May 1984, and subsequently divorced. The judgment of dissolution which terminated the marriage on June 18, 1988, included the following notice: "Please review your will, insurance policies, retirement benefit plans, and other matters you may want to change in view of the dissolution or annulment of your marriage. Ending your marriage may automatically change a disposition made by your will to your former spouse."

After the divorce, Edward and Marlene continued to live together, sometimes at his residence, and sometimes at hers. In addition to maintaining separate residences, Edward and Marlene kept separate bank accounts. They also experienced various periods of breakup and reconciliation.

Marlene never showed the holographic will to Edward after she filed it away. She testified Edward had chest pains shortly before his death and made statements concerning the disposition of his property. Marlene also testified she and Edward discussed having formal wills written, but never did so.

Edward died on March 3, 1990, at age 43. On March 8, 1990, Marlene petitioned for probate of Edward's April 10, 1983, holographic will. Margaret filed the will contest shortly thereafter. Following the presentation of oral and documentary evidence, the trial court ordered the holographic will revoked pursuant to section 6122 and denied its admission to probate. . . . This appeal ensued.

DISCUSSION

I. Section 6122 Revokes the Holographic Will

. . . . Marlene maintains section 6122 applies only to a will drawn in favor of a person who was the testator's spouse *at the time the will was drawn* because: (1) in adopting the revocation by divorce statute, California modified the language of Uniform Probate Code section 2-508; (2) California law on statutory wills, which includes a section on revocation by divorce, defines "spouse" as "the testator's husband or wife at the time the testator signs a California statutory will" (§ 6202); . . . and (3) other jurisdictions are split on whether statutes based on Uniform Probate Code section 2-508 apply to wills executed before the testator and former spouse were married. . . . We . . . conclude the trial court was correct in ruling section 6122 revoked Edward's holographic will by operation of law. . . .

Marlene's third argument directs us to other jurisdictions which have considered the question whether revocation by divorce statutes, modeled on Uniform Probate Code section 2-508, apply to wills executed before the testator and former spouse married. . . . California courts ordinarily adopt the construction given a uniform code section by other jurisdictions, unless the construction is manifestly erroneous. . . . While other jurisdictions are divided on the question before us, . . . a majority of the courts which have addressed the question interpret revocation by divorce statutes based on section 2-508 to revoke dispositions to former spouses, regardless of whether the decedent and former spouse were married at the time the will was executed. In reaching this conclusion, the cases rely primarily on statutory language. . . .

We believe this is the proper view. As stated by the Iowa Supreme Court in *Russell v. Johnston* (Iowa 1982) 327 N.W.2d 226, 229, "The clear purpose of [the statute] is to provide an automatic revocation of provisions in a will in favor of a spouse after a marriage is dissolved. The legislature obviously recognized that due to the change in the family structure new moral duties and obligations may have evolved subsequent to the execution of the will, and that due to the turmoil of a dissolution an automatic revocation is in the best interest of the testator." . . .

We conclude the Legislature had a similar purpose here. Section 6122 was a radical departure from prior law which held dissolution had no effect on the wills executed by either spouse. . . . The Legislature changed the law to protect a spouse who neglects to change his or her will following divorce or annulment. This purpose is no less compelling where, as here, the decedent executes his will before he and his former spouse are married. The significant fact is the couple was married and subsequently divorced. . . .

Edward was living with Marlene at the time of his death in March 1990. However, following their divorce, Edward and Marlene suffered various periods of breakups and reconciliation . . . . He may or may not have wanted Marlene to inherit his estate. By notifying Edward the holographic will would be revoked by operation of law on the date the marriage was terminated, and, at the same time, alerting him to the effect of the divorce on his prior will, the California statutory scheme gave Edward the opportunity to execute a new will. . . . Edward did not write a new will in favor of Marlene or anyone else. . . .

II. Evidence of Decedent's Intent Properly Struck

Marlene maintains evidence of Edward's intent she should receive his entire estate was admissible under Evidence Code section 1260. That section states in part: "Evidence of a statement made by a declarant who is unavailable as a witness that he . . . has or has not revoked his will . . . is not made inadmissible by the hearsay rule." . . .

. . . [S]ection 6122 revokes a will automatically if the testator's marriage is dissolved. The will may be revived only by the testator's remarriage to the former spouse. . . . [Edward] never remarried Marlene Reeves. Accordingly, any subsequent statements Edward may have made "right up until the time of his death, that [Marlene] should take his entire estate and evidence of [his] continuing belief that the holographic will was still valid and in full force and effect" were entirely irrelevant. The trial court did not err in striking the testimony which purported to recount such statements. . . .

Section C. Components of a Will

Incorporation by Reference

CPC § 6130. Incorporation by Reference

A writing in existence when a will is executed may be incorporated by reference if the language of the will manifests this intent and describes the writing sufficiently to permit its identification. (Stats. 1990)

CPC § 6132. Writing Directing Disposition of Tangible Personal Property Referred to in Will

(a) Notwithstanding any other provision, a will may refer to a writing that directs disposition of tangible personal property not otherwise specifically disposed of by the will, except for money that is common coin or currency and property used primarily in a trade or business. A writing directing disposition of a testator's tangible personal property is effective if all of the following conditions are satisfied:

(1) An unrevoked will refers to the writing.

(2) The writing is dated and is either in the handwriting of, or signed by, the testator.

(3) The writing describes the items and the recipients of the property with reasonable certainty.

(b) The failure of a writing to conform to the conditions described in paragraph (2) of subdivision (a) does not preclude the introduction of evidence of the existence of the testator's intent regarding the disposition of tangible personal property as authorized by this section.

(c) The writing may be written or signed before or after the execution of the will and need not have significance apart from its effect upon the dispositions of property made by the will. A writing that meets the requirements of this section shall be given effect as if it were actually contained in the will itself, except that if any person designated to receive property in the writing dies before the testator, the property shall pass as further directed in the writing and, in the absence of any further directions, the disposition shall lapse.

(d) The testator may make subsequent handwritten or signed changes to any writing. If there is an inconsistent disposition of tangible personal property as between writings, the most recent writing controls.

(e)(1) If the writing directing disposition of tangible personal property omits a statement as to the date of its execution, and if the omission results in doubt whether its provisions or the provisions of another writing inconsistent with it are controlling, then the writing omitting the statement is invalid to the extent of its inconsistency unless the time of its execution is established to be after the date of execution of the other writing.

(2) If the writing directing disposition of tangible personal property omits a statement as to the date of its execution, and it is established that the testator lacked testamentary capacity at any time during which the writing may have been executed, the writing is invalid unless it is established that it was executed at a time when the testator had testamentary capacity. ***

(g) The total value of tangible personal property identified and disposed of in the writing shall not exceed twenty-five thousand dollars ($25,000). If the value of an item of tangible personal property described in the writing exceeds five thousand dollars ($5,000), that item shall not be subject to this section and that item shall be disposed of pursuant to the remainder clause of the will. The value of an item of tangible personal property that is disposed of pursuant to the remainder clause of the will shall not be counted towards the twenty-five thousand dollar ($25,000) limit described in this subdivision.

(h) As used in this section, the following definitions shall apply:

(1) "Tangible personal property" means articles of personal or household use or ornament, including, but not limited to, furniture, furnishings, automobiles, boats, and jewelry, as well as precious metals in any tangible form, such as bullion or coins and articles held for investment purposes. The term "tangible personal property" does not mean real property, a mobilehome as defined in Section 798.3 of the Civil Code, intangible

property, such as evidences of indebtedness, bank accounts and other monetary deposits, documents of title, or securities.

(2) "Common coin or currency" means the coins and currency of the United States that are legal tender for the payment of public and private debts, but does not include coins or currency kept or acquired for their historical, artistic, collectable, or investment value

apart from their normal use as legal tender for payment.

(Stats. 2006)

Acts of Independent Significance

CPC § 6131. Acts of Independent Significance

A will may dispose of property by reference to acts and events that have significance apart from their effect upon the dispositions made by the will, whether the acts and events occur before or after the execution of the will or before or after the testator's death. The execution or revocation of a will of another person is such an event.

(Stats. 1990)

Section D. Contracts Relating to Wills

Contracts to Make a Will

❖ CPC § 21700. Contract to Make Will, Devise, or Other Instrument

(a) A contract to make a will or devise or other instrument, or not to revoke a will or devise or other instrument, or to die intestate, if made after the effective date of this statute, can be established only by one of the following:

(1) Provisions of a will or other instrument stating the material provisions of the contract.

(2) An expressed reference in a will or other instrument to a contract and extrinsic evidence proving the terms of the contract.

(3) A writing signed by the decedent evidencing the contract.

(4) Clear and convincing evidence of an agreement between the decedent and the claimant or a promise by the decedent to the claimant that is enforceable in equity.

(5) Clear and convincing evidence of an agreement between the decedent and another person for the benefit of the claimant or a promise by the decedent to another person for the benefit of the claimant that is enforceable in equity.

(b) The execution of a joint will or mutual wills does not create a presumption of a contract not to revoke the will or wills.

(c) A contract to make a will or devise or other instrument, or not to revoke a will or devise or other instrument, or to die intestate, if made prior to the effective date of this section, shall be construed under the law applicable to the contract prior to the effective date of this section. (Stats. 2000)

CCP § 366.3. Claims Arising From Promise or Agreement Relating to Distribution from Estate or Trust or Under Other Instrument; Limitation Period

(a) If a person has a claim that arises from a promise or agreement with a decedent to distribution from an estate or trust or under another instrument, whether the promise or agreement was made orally or in writing, an action to enforce the claim to distribution may be commenced within one year after the date of death, and the limitations period that would have been applicable does not apply.

(b) The limitations period provided in this section for commencement of an action shall not be tolled or extended for any reason except as provided in Sections 12, 12a, and 12b of this code, and former Part 3 (commencing with Section 21300)[16] of Division 11 of the Probate Code, as that part read prior to its repeal by Chapter 174 of the Statutes of 2008.

(c) This section applies to actions brought on claims concerning persons dying on or after the effective date of this section. (Stats. 2000, 2006, 2009)

Action for Breach of Contract to Make Will Must Be Brought Within One Year of Death.

STEWART v. SEWARD

Court of Appeal, Second District, Division 3
148 Cal. App. 4th 1513, 56 Cal. Rptr. 3d 651 (2007)

Klein, P.J. . . . The essential issue presented is whether the trial court properly found Stewart's action is barred by the one-year statute of limitations provided in Code of Civil Procedure section 366.3. . . .

. . . Stewart is the daughter of Gowisea Koontz . . . , the predeceased spouse of Wilmer. In early December 1990, Gowisea, who was dying of cancer, entered into an oral agreement with Wilmer regarding the distribution of Gowisea's property upon her death. Gowisea, in the presence of Wilmer and several family witnesses, stated she would not execute a will disposing of her property and would not convert title to their home on 39th Street in Los Angeles from

---

[16] Probate Code section 21300 *et seq.* pertains to no contest clauses.—Ed.

joint tenancy to tenancy in common, in exchange for Wilmer's promise to execute a will leaving 50 percent of the 39th Street property to Stewart and the remaining 50 percent to two grandchildren. Although Stewart urged Gowisea to put the agreement in writing, Gowisea assured Stewart she trusted Wilmer to perform the agreement. Gowisea died intestate on December 12, 1990.

In March 1997, Wilmer executed a will devising 100 percent of the 39th Street property to the two grandchildren, leaving Stewart with no interest in the property. Wilmer died on October 26, 2004. . . .

On July 13, 2005, Stewart filed a "creditor's claim" in Wilmer's probate proceeding, asserting she was entitled to "$150,000.00 or more" from Wilmer's estate, pursuant to an "oral contract for one half the value" of the 39th Street property.

On July 21, 2005, the administrator rejected the creditor's claim, using a mandatory Judicial Council Form . . . captioned "Allowance or Rejection of Creditor's Claim." Pre-printed on the form is the following advisement: "rejected claims: From the date notice of rejection is given, the creditor must act on the rejected claim (*e.g.*, file a lawsuit) as follows: a. Claim due: within three months after notice of rejection. b. Claim not due: within three months after the claim becomes due." The rejection form was mailed to Stewart on July 29, 2005.

After receiving the rejection notice, Stewart filed the instant action against the administrator of Wilmer's estate on October 28, 2005. The complaint alleged causes of action for breach of an oral contract, fraud, negligent misrepresentation, breach of fiduciary duty and equitable estoppel. By way of relief, Stewart sought, inter alia, "[s]pecific performance for a 50% interest in the real property . . . ; . . . [i]n the alternative, . . . damages to equal 50% of the value of the subject property . . . ."

The trial court sustained the administrator's demurrer without leave to amend. . . . Stewart filed a timely notice of appeal . . . .

DISCUSSION . . .

2. Stewart's action arose out of an alleged breach . . . of . . . promise to . . . execute a will . . .
Section 366.2, upon which Stewart relies, provides in relevant part: "(a) If a person against whom an action may be brought on a liability of the person, whether arising in contract, tort, or otherwise, and whether accrued or not accrued, dies before the expiration of the applicable limitations period, and the cause of action survives, an action may be commenced within one year after the date of death, and the limitations period that would have been applicable does not apply. (b) *The limitations period provided in this section for commencement of an* action shall not be tolled or extended for any reason except as provided in any of the following, where applicable: . . . (2) *Part 4 (commencing with Section 9000) of Division 7 of the Probate Code (creditor claims in administration of estates of decedents).*" (Italics added.)

Probate Code section 9000 provides in relevant part: "As used in this division: (a) 'Claim' means a demand for payment for any of the following, whether due, not due, accrued or not accrued, or contingent, and whether liquidated or unliquidated: (1) Liability of the decedent, whether arising in contract, tort, or otherwise . . . ." As to creditors, Probate Code section 9352 provides the *"filing of a claim or a petition . . . tolls the statute of limitations otherwise applicable to the claim until allowance, approval or rejection . . . ."* (Italics added.) If a claim is due at the time notice of rejection is given, the claimant has three months after notice is given to commence an action on the claim. (Prob. Code, § 9353, subd. (a)(1).) . . .

Unlike section 366.2, section 366.3, enacted in 2000, does not provide for tolling for creditor claims. Section 366.3 governs an action arising from a promise or agreement with a decedent to distribution from an estate. It provides: "(a) *If a person has a claim that arises from a promise or agreement with a decedent to distribution from an estate or trust or under another instrument, whether the promise or agreement was made orally or in writing,* an action to enforce the claim to distribution may be commenced within one year after the date of death, and the limitations period that would have been applicable does not apply. (b) *The limitations period provided in this section for commencement of an action shall not be tolled or extended for any reason except* as provided in Sections 12, 12a, and 12b of this code, and Part 3 (commencing with Section 21300) of Division 11 of the Probate Code. . . . " . . .

Stewart contends where a plaintiff "is seeking relief by way of a distribution of specific property from the estate contrary to the express provisions of the will of decedent, the claim is of the type addressed in [section] 366.3. Where, however, the claim at issue is not making a challenge to the distribution called for in the will, but rather is seeking damages from the decedent based on a breach of contract or tort by the decedent, then the claim at issue is of the type covered by the provisions of [section] 366.2." Stewart asserts her complaint "seeks money damages from Wilmer based on his personal liability arising from his acts and omissions that thwarted Gowisea's estate plan, to Stewart's damage as a third party beneficiary of Gowisea's estate plan," and therefore her action is of the type governed by section 366.2 and not section 366.3. . . .

[Stewart's] claim falls squarely within the ambit of section 366.3. . . . [It] arose from an alleged oral promise by Wilmer to Gowisea to "produce a will disposing of 50% of [the 39th Street] property to [Stewart]." Thus, the claim *"arises from a promise or agreement with a decedent to distribution from an estate . . . ."* . . . [T]he pertinent question is not the nature of the relief or remedy being requested but rather, the nature of the claim itself. Because Stewart's claim arose from an alleged oral promise or agreement concerning distribution from Wilmer's estate, the instant action is governed by the limitations period of section 366.3.

3. Stewart's reliance on the doctrines of equitable estoppel and waiver is misplaced. . . .

. . . On July 21, 2005, the administrator signed a form rejecting Stewart's claim; the form was mailed to Stewart on July 29, 2005. Stewart contends if the administrator considered Stewart's creditor's claim to be a claim that was not subject to the creditor claim requirements, and as to which no tolling would apply pursuant to section 366.3, then the eight-day delay in serving the notice of rejection "takes on the appearance of an intentional effort to mislead Stewart with regard to the time limitations for filing an action on her claims, particularly in light of the fact [the administrator] expressly stated in her rejection of the claim that Stewart had three months to file an action on the rejected claim."

The argument is unavailing. Initially, we note "[a] creditor's claim may be deemed rejected at the creditor's option if the personal representatives or court has refused or neglected to act on the claim within *30 days* after the claim was filed." . . . In view of the fact 30 days of inaction may be deemed to be a rejection of the claim, Stewart's contention the administrator's eight-day delay in mailing the rejection notice gives rise to equitable estoppel is unpersuasive.

Moreover, section 366.3 indicates the limitations period provided shall not be tolled or extended *for any reason* except for specific enumerated circumstances. . . . This is confirmed by the legislative history of section 366.3 . . . . Accordingly, the administrator is not equitably estopped to assert the one-year limitations period of section 366.3.[7]

. . . We reject Stewart's theory the administrator's use of the mandatory Judicial Council form to deny Stewart's claim constituted an intentional relinquishment by the administrator of the right to assert the one-year limitations period . . . .

The order of dismissal is affirmed. Respondent shall recover costs on appeal.

NOTE: The judicial council form used in Stewart was subsequently changed to replace "three months" with 90 days and to add: "The 90-day period mentioned above may not apply to your claim because some claims are not treated as creditors' claims or are subject to special statutes of limitations, or for other legal reasons. You should consult with an attorney if you have any questions about or are unsure of your rights and obligations concerning your claim."[17]

1-Year Period of CCP §366.3 Prevails Over 90-Day Period of CPC § 9353 for Filing Suit Based on Breach of Contract to Make Will

ALLEN v. STODDARD

California Court of Appeal, Fourth District, Division 3
212 Cal. App. 4th 807, 152 Cal. Rptr. 3d 71, (2013)

---

[7] We recognize there is nothing on the mandatory Judicial Council form for "Allowance or Rejection of Creditor's Claim," Form DE-174, to indicate why Stewart's claim was rejected, and the form does not apprise a claimant whether the claim was rejected on the ground the claimant does not qualify as a creditor. In the event a claimant is not a creditor for purposes of section 366.2, the advisement on Form DE-174 that the claimant has three months to file a lawsuit can be a trap for the unwary.

[17] Thanks to Pamela Shu, UCLA School of Law, 2010, for bringing this to my attention. She thought the result in Stewart was quite unfair. See http://www.courts.ca.gov/forms.htm for Judicial Council forms.

BEDSWORTH, J. This case of first impression requires us to directly confront the issue of whether Probate Code section 9353 irreconcilably conflicts with Code of Civil Procedure section 366.3.[1] We determine they *do* conflict on the very narrow point of how much time a claimant against an estate has to *file suit* based on a promise to make a distribution from the estate, such as a contract to make a will. Section 9353 gives claimants 90 days from rejection of the claim by the estate to file suit; section 366.3 gives them a year from decedent's death to file suit. Under the longstanding rule of construction that newer and more specific statutes take precedence over older and more general statutes, we conclude it is section 366.3's time limit that controls.

The practical effect of our determination is that plaintiff Richard Allen's suit for breach of contract to make a will, filed 91 days after rejection by the estate of his creditor's claim *but* within a year of the decedent's death, is not time-barred. The judgment of dismissal in favor of the estate, predicated solely on the application of section 9353's 90–day time frame to file suit, must therefore be reversed.

FACTS

This case comes to us on a judgment of dismissal after the defendant's demurrer was sustained without leave to amend . . . .

James Humpert died October 29, 2010. Humpert had been in a stable, long-term committed relationship with plaintiff Richard Allen, and during that relationship Humpert had promised Allen he "would be taken care of" should "anything happen" to Humpert. It is undisputed Humpert died intestate, and there is no evidence Allen and Humpert ever registered as domestic partners, or married during that brief period in 2008 when same-sex couples could marry. . . .

Allen filed a petition with the probate court to be appointed administrator of Humpert's estate, but Humpert's sister, Edith Marlynne Stoddard, filed an opposing petition, and she prevailed. Hence, as administrator of Humpert's estate she is the named defendant in this case.

In April 2011, a little more than five months after Humpert died, Allen filed a creditor's claim against Humpert's estate based on the "would be taken care of" promise made by Humpert. (There is no issue of late notice in making this claim on the estate.) The next month, on May 19, 2011, the estate sent a formal notice of rejection of Allen's claim.

Allen filed this action on August 18, 2011, which, given the 31 days that hath both May and July, ended up being exactly 91 days from May 19, 2011.[3] Stoddard, as estate administrator,

---

[1] Undesignated references to any section 9000 through 9353 in this opinion are to the Probate Code. Any undesignated references to section 366.3 or to section 366.2 are to the Code of Civil Procedure.

[3] This is perhaps an example of the misleading effect of a mandatory Judicial Council rejection form (DE–174), noted by the Rutter Group Probate Treatise to be a "trap for the unwary." . . . The rejection form states that the claimant has "three months"—as distinct from 90 days—to file suit. (Ibid.) [The form has been changed since this case was decided, see Note following *Stewart* case, above.—Ed.]

successfully demurred to the complaint based on it being untimely under section 9353, subdivision (a)(1). A judgment of dismissal ensued, and Allen timely filed this appeal.

DISCUSSION

Preliminarily, we note a small matter not raised by either party. The entire battle at the trial level concerned the operation of section 9353, and specifically whether the time to file a suit might be extended for five days since the notice of rejection was served by mail. (Cf. Code Civ. Proc., § 1013.) Even though the suit was clearly filed within a year of Humpert's death, the possible application of section 366.3 . . . was not raised at the trial level at all. . . .

Since the effect of section 366.3 on this case presents a pristine issue of law, and since the estate makes no attempt to show any prejudice, we exercise our discretion to address the section 366.3 issue. . . .

A. *Applicability of Section 366.3*
Section 366.3 gives persons who have claims against estates based on promises to make a distribution after death (such as contracts to make a will) a full year from the date of the decedent's death to file suit. If section 366.3 governed Allen's claim against Humpert's estate, his suit was timely. . . .

The estate argues section 366.3 doesn't apply at all. That is an argument readily disposed of. The gravamen of Allen's suit is what is often called a "*Marvin* claim" (after *Marvin v. Marvin* (1976) 18 Cal.3d 660, 134 Cal. Rptr. 815, 557 P.2d 106), which is an express or implied enforceable contract between two nonmarital partners, usually arising out of some sort of domestic arrangements between those partners. . . .

The text of section 366.3 (". . . a promise or agreement with a decedent to distribution from an estate . . .") squarely fits claims based on contracts, including *Marvin* contracts, by a decedent to provide for someone after the decedent's death or make some other distribution of an estate. . . . *Stewart v. Seward* . . . .

B. *Applicability of Section 9353*
The estate also argues that section 9353 *does* apply, and therefore its 90-day-from-date-of-rejection time limit bars Allen's suit. This argument is not so readily disposed of. We first review the formidable array of Probate Code statutes bearing on the requirement imposed on persons with claims on estates to file creditor's claims with those estates. . . .

Section 9000, subdivision (a)(1) defines claim to mean "a demand for payment for any of the following, whether due, not due, accrued or not accrued, or contingent, and whether liquidated or unliquidated: (1) *Liability of the decedent,* whether *arising in contract,* tort or otherwise." (Italics added.)

Section 9000, subdivision (c) defines creditor to mean "a person who may have a claim against an estate." Claims that are not filed with estates as provided in Part 4 of the Probate Code are "barred." (§ 9002.) . . .

Section 9351 precludes suit against an estate unless a claim has first been filed with the estate and the claim has been rejected in whole or part. . . .

These requirements then culminate in section 9353. Section 9353 says, plainly, that regardless of any other statute of limitations, any claimant against an estate has 90 days after notice of rejection of the claim by the estate to file suit.

It is not surprising, then, that a claim for breach of an agreement to make a distribution from an *estate* has been squarely held to be a "claim" within the meaning of section 9000, and therefore a creditor's claim was required before the claimant could state a cause of action in a lawsuit on that claim. *Wilkison v. Wiederkehr* (2002) 101 Cal. App. 4th 822, 829, 832, 124 Cal. Rptr. 2d 631.[8]

And there is no basis in the texts of sections 9000, 9002, 9051 and 9053 to say that claims against estates based on promises by decedents to make wills are not within those statutes. Allen suggests that section 9000, subdivision (b) somehow removes such claims (which include *Marvin* claims) from the ambit of the word "claim" as defined in subdivision (a), but that argument is unavailing. The text just doesn't fit. Subdivision (b) provides: "'Claim' does not include a dispute regarding *title* of the decedent to *specific property* alleged to be included in the decedent's estate." (Italics added.) There is nothing in a general promise to "take care" of a domestic partner after one's death which implicates "title" to "specific property."

In short, if section 9353, rather than section 366.3, controls the date of the filing of Allen's suit, affirmance is required.

C. *The Anomaly*

So, does or does not, section 366.3 conflict with section 9353? The answer is: It does, but section 366.3 does not necessarily conflict with the sections of the Probate Code governing claims against estates involving matters *other than the statute of limitations* involving contracts to make a will. But to explain why, we must confront and resolve an anomaly that has arisen in the case law. The anomaly is this: Under *Wilkison,* a claim based on a contract to make a will *is* a claim within the meaning of section 9000 and therefore section 9353 *should* govern the statute of limitations, but *Stewart* says a claim based on a contract to make a will is not a claim against the estate at all, . . . and thus implies section 9353 has nothing to do with the statute of limitations on suits against estates based on contracts to make a will. And here's the real problem: The conflict cannot be solved simply by saying *Wilkison* was decided before section 366.3 was applicable, because section 366.3 ushered in no change in the language of the Probate Code sections—particularly section 9000 which defines claims and creditors—that plainly apply to claims against estates based on contracts to make a will. And furthermore, the actual

---

[8] *Wilkison's* thinking was the claimant had an adequate remedy at law for breach of the contract by filing a claim with the estate, and in the absence of such a filed claim, he could not maintain a legal action based on the contract breach. . . .

text of section 366.3 does not include any language that allows one to say suits based on contracts to make a will are not otherwise governed by the Probate Code sections. The text of section 366.3 doesn't say anything to the effect that claims against estates based on contracts to make a will are not claims within the meaning of section 9000.

The anomaly is only resolved by recognizing that *Stewart's* comment that the claimant there "was not a creditor of the estate" was simply dicta. The central point of the *Stewart* case was that the claim there fell within the meaning of section 366.3, not section 366.2. . . . The court could have reached that determination without adding the thought, contained in the introductory part of the opinion but otherwise never developed, that the plaintiff never was a "creditor" in the first place.

A statutory scheme in which "claims" within the scope of section 366.3 are not held to be "claims" within section 9000 is inconsistent with all applicable statutes and at least one prior Court of Appeal decision.[12] We therefore part company with the redoubtable Rutter Group Probate Treatise when, relying on *Stewart*, it says claims within section 366.3 are not claims "subject to the claim-filing requirements" of the Probate Code. (Cf. Rutter Group Probate Treatise, *supra,* ¶ 8:11:5, p. 8–13 with ¶ 8:98.3, p. 8–49.)

But we must take one more step. No case of which we are aware has applied section 366.3 to countermand the competing 90–day statute of limitations in section 9353. . . . We now take that step.

. . . [T]he two statutes cannot be reconciled. Section 9353 begins with the words, "Regardless of whether the statute of limitations otherwise applicable to a claim will expire before or after the following times . . . ," while section 366.3 affirmatively declares that an action "to enforce the claim to distribution may be commenced within one year after the date of death, and the limitations period that would have been applicable does not apply."

The precise conflict can be resolved for purposes of this case by the well-established rule that where statutes are in irreconcilable conflict, a specific and later enacted statute trumps a general and earlier one. . . . Section 9353 is a general statute. It applies on its face to all claims. Section 366.3 is a specific statute, applying only to a narrow class of claims. Section 9353 was enacted in 1991, about a decade earlier than section 366.3. . . . Thus, if they cannot be reconciled, section 366.3 prevails over section 9353. . . . We hold the two statutes cannot be reconciled on the narrow point of when *suit* must be filed.[14] But we do not go beyond that. . . .

---

[12] But note that sections 366.2 and section 366.3 do nicely dovetail with each other. Section 366.2 is written to apply to claims that clearly arise *before* a decedent's death, while section 366.3 is written so that it can only apply to claims that arise *on or after* a decedent's death.

[14] Stoddard and amici curiae argue the statutes *can* be reconciled simply by reading them to impose the worst of all possible worlds on plaintiffs asserting claims based on contracts to make estate plans. That is, such plaintiffs must meet *both* the section 9351 90-day-from-rejection deadline and the section 366.3 1-year-from-death-of-decedent deadline. We reject this proposed reconciliation because it ignores

We need not take the step in this case of trying to articulate a unified theory of the relationship between the Probate Code claim-filing requirements and section 366.3.[15] We only decide the case before us. . . . [16] And we recognize that by deciding only the case before us we may leave the relationship between sections 9351 and 366.6, to use the argot of science fiction, a bit wibbly wobbly in certain particulars. For example, we do not deal with the case where a *suit* might be timely under section 366.3, but there has been no *claim* to the estate, and thus no compliance with section 9351 at all. . . . Nor do we deal with the obvious problem of an estate that somehow tries to run out the clock on section 366.3. (Cf. *Stewart* . . . [rejecting argument that reliance by estate on mandatory judicial council form constituted some form of waiver of right to assert 366.3's one-year statute of limitations].) It may be there are still unexplored circumstances where section 9351 simply cannot be reconciled with section 366.3.

---

section 366.3's exclusivity clause ("the limitations period that would have been applicable does not apply"), and indeed Stoddard and amici do not deal with that clause in proposing their reconciliation.

[15] One virtue of the *Stewart* dicta is that it does imply a bright line theory of claims against estates based on contracts to make a will—they simply are outside the universe of sections 9000 et seq. of the Probate Code. But saying so is a step we will leave to the Legislature. After all, does the Legislature really want all estates to remain open to possibly *unknown* claims a year after the decedent's death, no matter how diligent an executor or administrator might be in giving notice to creditors? . . .

[16] In a petition for rehearing, Stoddard, joined by amici curiae, invite us to decide another case, namely one involving a plaintiff who came within section 366.2, not section 366.3. Both Stoddard and amici curiae raise the *ad horrendum* argument that applying our reasoning to section 366.2 (which was enacted in 1992, eight years prior to section 366.3, but two years after section 9353, which was enacted in 1990) would nullify section 9353, because, after all, most creditors of and claimants against estates come within section 366.2, not section 366.3.

We reject this *ad horrendum* argument for two reasons. First, Stoddard and amici curiae ignore the big textual difference between sections 366.2 and 366.3. Section 366.2, subdivision (b)(2)—which has no analog in section 366.3—makes explicit reference to Probate Code sections 9000 et seq. So any court construing a scenario in which a "section 366.2 plaintiff" did not meet the section 9353 deadline would have at least some textual basis to say that maybe section 9353 was impliedly intended to survive section 366.2's exclusivity clause. (See *Estate of Yool* (2007) 151 Cal. App. 4th 867, 876, 60 Cal. Rptr. 3d 526 . . . .) We have no such textual basis to say that as regards section 366.3 here.

Second, Stoddard's and amici curiae's argument is essentially one of trying to infer legislative intent about section 366.3, as against what the Legislature plainly said in the statute, based on some section 366.2 hobgoblin. Alas, that's about as easy as pi. We have not been cited to, nor discovered on our own, anything in the legislative history of section 366.3 which clearly states the Legislature intended section 9353 to survive section 366.3's exclusivity clause. What is clear from the legislative history of section 366.3 is that the Legislature intended a "consistent" one-year statute of limitations in the face of several appellate decisions which construed section 366.3's predecessor (former Probate Code section 150) to allow suits against estates based on contracts to make wills for much longer periods than one year. . . . That is, the legislative history of section 366.3 reflects no clear intent to preserve section 9353's statute of limitations as against section 366.3's exclusivity clause. We therefore decline to read such an intent into the statute. . . .

But those are tomorrow's cases. Sufficient unto *this* case are its own complexities. Perhaps the Legislature will make things clearer in the meantime. For now, *this suit* was timely.

Enforcement of Written Contract That Friend and Neighbor Would Receive House in Exchange for Caring for Owner Barred by 1-Year Statute of Limitations, CCP §366.3.

ESTATE of ZIEGLER

California Court of Appeal, Fourth District, Division 2
187 Cal. App. 4th 1357, 114 Cal. Rptr. 3d 863, review denied (2010)

RICHLI, J. The statute of limitations serves noble public policies. . . . Its operation in particular cases, however, can be sadly inequitable.

This is just such a case. The equities in favor of claimant Richard H. LaQue could hardly be more compelling. LaQue and his wife provided food, care, and companionship to their neighbor, Paul Ziegler, when Ziegler was sick and alone. At first, they did so out of the goodness of their hearts. Eventually, however, a grateful Ziegler insisted on entering into a written agreement—the validity of which is unquestioned—that in consideration of continued care, LaQue would receive Ziegler's home upon Ziegler's death.

On the other hand, the equities in favor of appellant W.C. Cox and Company (Cox) are slim to none. Cox is a soulless[1] corporation in the business of locating missing heirs. It is acting as the attorney in fact for nine residents of Germany who claim to be Ziegler's heirs.

After Ziegler died without a will, LaQue simply moved into Ziegler's former home, unopposed. He did not see the need to file any claim in connection with Ziegler's estate until about a year and three weeks after Ziegler's death.

Alas for LaQue, Code of Civil Procedure section 366.3, . . . "[requires that his action] be commenced within *one year after the date of death . . . .*" (Italics added.)

The trial court held that LaQue's claim was not barred by the statute of limitations. Cox appeals.

LaQue argues that Code of Civil Procedure section 366.3 does not apply because the written agreement is not a promise to make a future distribution from Ziegler's estate; rather, it is a present promise to convey Ziegler's house, albeit one that could not have been performed until after Ziegler's death. We will conclude that this is a distinction without a difference. Accordingly, we will reverse.

I. FACTUAL BACKGROUND

---

[1] We use the word "soulless" literally; we do not mean to imply that Cox's employees are not caring people or that they do not provide a valuable service.

. . . On November 10, 2005, Ziegler asked LaQue to come over, along with Irma (who was to bring paper and a pen) and anyone else who was at his house. LaQue brought Victor Oga, his daughter's fiancé. Ziegler told them all that "he wanted Richard to have the house." He then dictated a document to Irma. It provided:

"November 10, 2005,

"2:15 p.m.

"I Paul Daniel Ziegler home owner of 820 E. G St in Colton, California 92324, am signing over my home and property to Richard H. LaQue Sr.

"This written agreement between myself and Richard is for the exchange of my care and daily meals. This written note will be immediately active if and when I no longer can reside in my home due to death." (The Agreement.)

Ziegler read the Agreement and then signed it. He had LaQue sign it. He also had Oga sign it as witness.

After that, the LaQues "started giving [Ziegler] more care . . . ." They checked on him daily and brought him dinner (the only meal he wanted) every day. They were "prepared to take care of [him] for months or years if need be[.]" . . .

LaQue realized that Ziegler had relatives only when he found some unopened year-old Christmas cards from them. He asked Ziegler if he should notify them that he was in the hospital, but Ziegler said no.

On January 15, 2006, Ziegler died in the hospital. He was 60 years old. LaQue took it upon himself to notify Ziegler's relatives. He tried to handle the funeral arrangements but could not, because he was not a family member. He did manage to find where Ziegler's mother was buried; he requested that Ziegler's remains be buried next to her and arranged for a headstone.

In March 2006, in reliance on the Agreement, the LaQues moved into Ziegler's home.

II. PROCEDURAL BACKGROUND

In September 2006, the public administrator filed a petition to probate Ziegler's estate. In October 2006, the trial court appointed him as the administrator of the estate (the Administrator). Nine German nationals who claim to be Ziegler's first cousins (or descendents of his first cousins) through his maternal grandparents appeared through Cox as their attorney in fact. . . .

On February 9, 2007, LaQue filed a creditor's claim for $9,556, representing the value of his services on a quantum meruit theory. On February 13, 2007, LaQue filed an alternative creditor's claim for $318,600, the estimated value of the house, representing the value of his services on a contract theory.

In May 2007, the Administrator filed a petition for instructions (Prob. Code, § 9611), seeking an order that LaQue's creditor's claim for the value of the house be allowed (subject to prior creditor's claims and costs of administration). Cox filed objections to the Administrator's petition, arguing that LaQue's claims were barred by the statute of limitations.[3]

In June 2007, Cox filed a petition to determine persons entitled to distribution of the estate (Prob. Code, § 11700), seeking an order that the estate should be distributed to Ziegler's intestate heirs. . . .

In September 2007, LaQue filed a petition to transfer property of the estate (Prob. Code, § 850 et seq.), seeking an order that the Administrator transfer the house to him. Cox filed objections to LaQue's petition, arguing again that LaQue's claims were barred by the statute of limitations.

The trial court held a combined trial on all three petitions. . . . [I]t ruled that LaQue's claim to the house was not barred . . . .

LAQUE'S CLAIM TO THE HOUSE IS TIME–BARRED UNDER CODE OF CIVIL PROCEDURE SECTION 366.3

. . . The trial court reasoned that the applicable statute of limitations would run from breach of the contract and that the contract had not been breached.[5] It is unclear exactly *which* statute of limitations the trial court had in mind. If it was referring to Code of Civil Procedure section 366.3, clearly it erred; that statute runs from the date of death, not the date on which the cause of action accrues.

LaQue, evidently recognizing this, urges us to treat the trial court's ruling as an implied finding that Code of Civil Procedure section 366.3 did not apply. Even if so, however, the trial court still erred, because, for the reasons we will state, Code of Civil Procedure section 366.3 *did* apply.

According to the legislative history of this section, the Legislature was concerned that existing law did "not provide a uniform statute of limitations for claims arising from a contract to make a will or other promise or agreement with a decedent to a distribution from an estate or trust." (Assem. Com. on Judiciary, Analysis of Assem. Bill No. 1491 (1999–2000 Reg. Sess.), as amended Jan. 3, 2000 . . . .[18]) It was advised that "[c]urrent law has an uncertain statute of limitations in regard to equitable and contractual claims to distribution of estates. In some cases, the statute may run three years from discovery of the action or four years under a contract theory." . . . Accordingly, Code of Civil Procedure section 366.3 would "establish[ ] a one-year statute of limitations for the enforcement of these claims . . . ." . . .

The Legislature was also told that: "The use of the one-year-from-date-of-death statute of limitations is important to the administration of estates and trusts since most are distributed by 18 months after the date of death. Allowing a claim to be commenced against distributees of an estate or trust or other instrument after a year from the date of death would bring

---

[3] In its objections, Cox relied solely on Code of Civil Procedure section 366.2. In its trial brief, however, it additionally relied on Code of Civil Procedure section 366.3.

[5] It is conceivable that a personal representative's indications that he or she intends to perform a decedent's contract could rise to the level of an estoppel to assert the statute of limitations. LaQue has not asserted such an estoppel.

[18] Further references to this Analysis are omitted.—Ed.

hardship to beneficiaries and administrators alike, and would frustrate the policy in favor of the early closing and distribution of estates, proponents state. Using the same statute of limitations for all claims against the estate would also be more convenient for the fiduciaries administering estates." (Sen. Judiciary Com., Analysis of Assem. Bill No. 1491 (1999–2000 Reg. Sess.), as amended Mar. 23, 2000, pp. 11–12 . . . .)

Code of Civil Procedure section 366.3 has been construed to "reach any action predicated upon the decedent's agreement to distribute estate or trust property in a specified manner." (*Ferraro v. Camarlinghi* (2008) 161 Cal. App. 4th 509, 555, 75 Cal. Rptr. 3d 19.) Specifically, it has been held to apply even to fraud and unjust enrichment claims, as long as they are "predicated on a decedent's promise to make specified distributions upon his death." . . . Moreover, it has been held to apply to claims based on a contract to leave certain property by will, even when the claimant is seeking only damages for breach of the contract and is not seeking the property itself. (*Stewart v. Seward* (2007) 148 Cal. App. 4th 1513, 1521–1523, 56 Cal. Rptr. 3d 651.)

It could be argued that LaQue is not claiming a "distribution."[8] "Distribution," when used as a term of art in probate law, means "the process of dividing an estate *after* realizing its movable assets and paying out of them its debts and other claims against the estate." (Black's Law Dict. (8th ed. 2004) p. 508, col. 2, italics added.) . . . One would not normally refer to the payment of a creditor's claim as a "distribution." Likewise, one would not normally refer to the award of specific property to a person who is claiming it as the true owner, adversely to the decedent, as a "distribution."

Once again, however, the Legislature clearly intended Code of Civil Procedure section 366.3 to apply, at a minimum, to a claim based on a contract to make a will. . . . We may assume, without deciding, that a claim based on a contract to make a will is either a creditor's claim or a claim to specific property and hence is not a claim for a "distribution" in the technical sense. . . . Even if so, it is a claim for a "distribution" in the sense that the Legislature intended.

And LaQue's claim here is indistinguishable from a claim on a contract to make a will. The Agreement was a promise to transfer property upon death. It could be performed only after death, by the decedent's personal representative, by conveying property that otherwise belonged to the estate.

LaQue argues that his claim "is not based on a promise or contract to make a distribution from Ziegler's estate; rather, it seeks to enforce a valid and existing written contract." He asserts that the written agreement "is a valid and existing contract that was to be partially performed before Ziegler's death (*i.e.,* the LaQues would provide the services . . .) and partially performed after Ziegler's death (*i.e.,* LaQue would receive title to Ziegler's residence as compensation for those services) . . . . Put a bit differently, the written contract was a present obligation to convey, not a future promise or agreement to make a distribution of Ziegler's estate."

In these respects, however, the Agreement was, once again, indistinguishable from a contract to make a will. . . . At oral argument, LaQue shifted ground slightly. He argued that upon Ziegler's death the house was transferred to him instantly, by operation of law; thus, it was no

---

[8] LaQue himself has never raised this particular argument.

longer an asset of the estate, and he was not claiming a distribution from the estate. He likened the Agreement to a beneficiary designation on a bank or brokerage account.

The difference, however, is that the Agreement was a contract; normally, a beneficiary designation is not. Even though the Agreement was worded in the present tense, it required some further action by the Administrator (representing Ziegler) to make the transfer happen. The notion that the title was instantly transferred, although appealing, is a legal fiction; actually, the estate continued to hold the title.

The appropriate analogy would be that it was as if Ziegler had entered into a contract to make a beneficiary designation naming LaQue but had never actually made such a designation while he lived; it was left up to the Administrator either to perform the contract, by turning over estate assets, or to breach the contract. If he breached, then, as in this case, LaQue would be asserting a "claim that arises from a promise or agreement with a decedent to distribution from an estate" within the meaning of Code of Civil Procedure section 366.3.

Finally, if we had any doubt about the matter, we would be swayed by the Legislature's intent to promote uniformity and to foster "the policy in favor of the early closing and distribution of estates." . . .

We therefore conclude that LaQue's claim to the house is barred by Code of Civil Procedure section 366.3. LaQue also asserted a claim, in the alternative, to the value of his services on a quantum meruit basis. That claim, however, is barred by Code of Civil Procedure section 366.2, which establishes a similar limitations period—i.e., one year from the date of death—for claims that could have been brought against a decedent had he or she lived. . . . Accordingly, we will remand with directions to reject all of LaQue's claims.

V. DISPOSITION

The order appealed from is reversed. The trial court is directed to enter a new order rejecting LaQue's claims. Cox is awarded costs on appeal against LaQue.

NOTES:

1. Yeh v. Tai, 18 Cal. App. 5th 953, 227 Cal. Rptr. 3d 275 (2017), held that § 366.3 did not apply to widow's action to enforce decedent's promise made during his life to put her on the title to a condominium and that it would remain community property because it was not a promise concerning a distribution from an estate or trust.

2. McMackin v. Ehrheart, 194 Cal. App. 4th 128, 122 Cal. Rptr. 3d 902 (2011), held that boyfriend's action against decedent's daughters was governed by one-year statute of limitations because gravamen of the complaint was that decedent had promised boyfriend a life estate in the home upon her death in consideration for 17 years of his "love, affection, care, and companionship."

3. Embree v. Embree, 125 Cal. App. 4th 487, 22 Cal. Rptr. 3d 782 (2004) held that former wife's action against decedent's trust beneficiaries to enforce marital settlement agreement that husband would establish trust or annuity on his death to pay her $1800 per month time was barred under § 366.3 because not filed within one year after his death.

Chapter 4. Wills: Capacity and Contests

Section A. Capacity to Make a Will

❖ CPC § 6100. Who May Make a Will

(a) An individual 18 or more years of age who is of sound mind may make a will.

(b) A conservator may make a will for the conservatee if the conservator has been so authorized by a court order pursuant to Section 2580. Nothing in this section shall impair the right of a conservatee who is mentally competent to make a will from revoking or amending a will made by the conservator or making a new and inconsistent will.

(Stats. 1990, 1995)

CPC § 6100.5. Standard of Competence

(a) An individual is not mentally competent to make a will if at the time of making the will either of the following is true:

> (1) The individual does not have sufficient mental capacity to be able to (A) understand the nature of the testamentary act, (B) understand and recollect the nature and situation of the individual's property, or (C) remember and understand the individual's relations to living descendants, spouse, and parents, and those whose interests are affected by the will.

> (2) The individual suffers from a mental disorder with symptoms including delusions or hallucinations, which delusions or hallucinations result in the individual's devising property in a way which, except for the existence of the delusions or hallucinations, the individual would not have done.

(b) Nothing in this section supersedes existing law relating to the admissibility of evidence to prove the existence of mental incompetence or mental disorders.

(c) Notwithstanding subdivision (a), a conservator may make a will on behalf of a conservatee if the conservator has been so authorized by a court order pursuant to Section 2580.

(Stats. 1990, 1995)

NOTES:

1. California follows the majority rule that the party contesting a will on the ground of lack of capacity has the burden of proof. See, *e.g.*, **Estate of Wright**, 7 Cal. 2d 348, 60 P.2d 434 (1936).

2. Estate of Sobol, 225 Cal. App. 4th 771 (2014), held that the co-executors named in the will lacked standing to challenge the validity of a codicil that revoked their designation as executors and named others to serve as co-executors.

Thorough Discussion of the Statutes and Standards That Govern Mental Capacity Required for Various Transactions, Including Wills

IN RE MARRIAGE OF GREENWAY

Court of Appeal, Fourth District, Division 3
217 Cal. App. 4th 628, 158 Cal. Rptr. 3d 364, review denied (2013)

O'LEARY, P.J. After 48 years of marriage, Lyle B. Greenway (Lyle) sought legal separation from Joann Greenway (Joann). . . . Joann . . . objected to ending the marriage or dividing the estate valued at several million dollars. She asserted Lyle was mentally incompetent and their son, Kurt Greenway (Kurt) was controlling the situation. . . . [T]he sole issue [is] whether Lyle was capable of making a reasoned decision regarding his marital status. . . . The court determined Lyle was mentally capable of making a reasoned decision to end his marriage. . . . [The voluminous facts of the case have been omitted as well as issues other than the standard for determining mental capacity.—Ed.]

The basic starting point for any mental capacity determination is the Due Process in Competence Determinations Act found in Probate Code sections 810 to 813, 1801, 1881, 3201, and 3204 (the Act). In 1995, the Legislature created the Act to clarify the legal capacity of a person who has a mental or physical disorder. The Act expressly states it broadly covers the capacity of such persons to perform all types of actions, "including, but not limited to" contracting, conveying, executing wills and trusts, marrying, and making medical decisions. (§ 810(b).) "The mere diagnosis of a mental or physical disorder shall not be sufficient in and of itself to support a determination that a person is of unsound mind or lacks the capacity to do a certain act." (§ 811.) Moreover, the Act declares there "exist[s] a rebuttable presumption affecting the burden of proof that *all persons have the capacity* to make decisions and to be responsible for their acts or decisions." (§ 810(a), italics added.)

The Act offers a wide range of potential mental deficits that may support a "determination that a person is of unsound mind or lacks the capacity to make a decision or do a certain act[.]" (§ 811(a) [lists 18 mental functions].) The categories of mental functions generally relate to one's ability to understand and recall one's surroundings, and include (but are not limited to) alertness and attention, orientation to time, ability to concentrate, short and long term memory, ability to communicate, recognition of familiar objects and persons, ability to plan and reason logically, delusions, ability to modulate mood, and affect. The Legislature noted a deficit in one of the mental functions listed "may be considered only if the deficit, by itself or in combination with one or more other mental function deficits, significantly impairs the person's ability to understand and appreciate the consequences of his or her actions *with regard to the type of act or decision in question."* (§ 811(b), italics added.) In other words . . . [t]here must be a causal link between the impaired mental function and the issue or action in question. . . . [I]n considering the causal link, courts should also consider "the frequency, severity, and duration of periods of impairment." (§ 811(c).)

. . . [S]ection 812 provides additional criteria to be considered when deciding whether a person lacks "capacity to make decision[s]." It states: "Except where otherwise provided by law, including, but not limited to, [the Probate Code section regarding informed medical consent] and the statutory and decisional law of testamentary capacity, a person lacks the capacity to make a decision unless the person has the ability to communicate verbally, or by any other means, the decision, and to understand and appreciate, to the extent relevant, all of the following: (a) The rights, duties, and responsibilities created by, or affected by the decision; (b) The probable consequences for the decisionmaker and, where appropriate, the persons affected by the decision; (c) The significant risks, benefits, and reasonable alternatives involved in the decision."

. . . [T]he required level of understanding depends entirely on the complexity of the decision being made. There is a large body of case authority reflecting an extremely low level of mental capacity needed before making the decision to marry or execute a will. Marriage arises out of a civil contract, but courts recognize this is a special kind of contract that does not require the same level of mental capacity of the parties as other kinds of contracts. Family Code section 300(a) simply states marriage requires "the consent of the parties capable of making that contract." Generally, "All persons are capable of contracting, except minors, persons of unsound mind, and persons deprived of civil rights." (Civ. Code, § 1556.) However, as described in Probate Code section 811, an "unsound mind" requires more than the diagnosis of a physical or mental disorder. Moreover, a person under a conservatorship, who is generally without contractual power, may be deemed to have marital capacity. (Prob. Code, § 1900 [appointment of conservator does not "affect the capacity of the conservatee to marry"].) Likely in recognition of the fundamental right to marry the Legislature enacted a statute permitting a court to determine a conservatee's capacity to marry based on petition of the conservator, the conservatee or "any relative or friend of the conservatee, or any interested person." (Prob. Code, § 1901(b).) "Whether the conservatee has capacity to marry is determined by the law that would be applicable had no conservatorship been established."[4] (Cal. Law Revision Com. . . .). Thus, the court may rely on subjective information provided by "any interested person" on the conservatee's capacity to marry and must ignore a prior adjudication deeming it necessary to appoint a conservator because the conservatee lacked the legal capacity to enter into all transactions that bind or obligate the conservatorship estate. (Prob. Code, § 1872.) And, as mentioned earlier, there is also a presumption in support of finding the required mental capacity to marry. (Prob. Code, § 810.)

---

[4] Probate Code section 1801 provides: "(a) A conservator of the person may be appointed for a person who is unable to provide properly for his or her personal needs for physical health, food, clothing, or shelter . . . . (b) A conservator of the estate may be appointed for a person who is substantially unable to manage his or her own financial resources or resist fraud or undue influence. . . . Substantial inability may not be proved solely by isolated incidents of negligence or improvidence."

Similarly, the standard for testamentary capacity is exceptionally low. Probate Code section 6100.5, lists criteria stating an individual is not mentally competent to make a will if unable to understand the nature of the testamentary act, understand and recollect the nature of his or her assets, or remember and understand his or her relationship to family members, friends, and those whose interests are affected by the will. In addition, an individual lacks mental competence if he or she suffers from a mental disorder with symptoms such as delusions or hallucinations that cause him or her to devise property in a way the individual "would not have done." Interestingly, this seemingly clearly written statutory authority has been interpreted by the courts to create a very low standard for testamentary capacity. [I]t is well settled, "old age, feebleness, forgetfulness, filthy personal habits, personal eccentricities, failure to recognize old friends or relatives, physical disability, absent-mindedness and mental confusion do not furnish grounds for holding that a testator lacked testamentary capacity." (*Estate of Selb,* (1948) 84 Cal. App. 2d 46, 49, 190 P.2d 277.) Indeed, even hallucinations and delusions do not demonstrate lack of capacity if they are not related to the testamentary act. (*Estate of Perkins* (1925) 195 Cal. 699, 704, 235 P. 45; see *Estate of Fritschi* (1963) 60 Cal.2d 367, 372, 33 Cal. Rptr. 264, 384 P.2d 656 [testator in hospital with fatal cancer, physically weak, disturbed and under heavy dosage of drugs possessed testamentary capacity].) And like marital capacity, the mere fact the testator is under a conservatorship will not support a finding of lack of testamentary capacity without additional evidence of mental incompetence for making a will. (Prob. Code, § 1871(c).)

Turning to the capacity to contract (which includes the capacity to convey, create a trust, make gifts, and grant powers of attorney) the baseline is contained in Probate Code sections 811 and 812. But Civil Code Section 39(b), provides more specific guidelines for determining the capacity to contract. "A rebuttable presumption affecting the burden of proof that a person is of unsound mind shall exist for purposes of this section if the person is substantially unable to *manage his or her own financial resources or resist fraud or undue influence.*" (Italics added.) This is the same showing required for establishment of a conservatorship. (Prob. Code, § 1801(b).) If the Civil Code section 39(b) presumption arises, the burden is placed on the party claiming capacity to contract to prove that while he or she may be unable to manage his or her financial resources or resist fraud or undue influence, he or she is nevertheless still capable of contracting being of sound mind as defined by Probate Code section 811.[5]

It is unclear why testamentary capacity and marital capacity have lower standards than for mental capacity, and a different burden of proof, from what is required before an elderly person diagnosed with mild dementia executes a contract. With respect to marital capacity, we are aware of the many well established statutory safeguards in place to protect spouses and their assets, and therefore, it is understandable why the fundamental right to marry would warrant lowering the mental capacity threshold. As for testamentary capacity, there is also a large body of statutory and case law designed to protect testators and their heirs. And common sense tells us a living person will not be harmed by his or her own testamentary documents. The same

---

[5] Civil Code section 2296 [appointment of agents] and Probate Code section 4120 [appointment of an attorney in fact] contain identical language to state simply that any person with the capacity to contract may appoint an agent or attorney in fact.

cannot be said for the parties to a contract, including the innocent third parties who may have financially relied on the terms of a contract, the elderly person who has made an inappropriate conveyance, or the person who prepared an imprudent grant of a power of attorney. These types of contractual decisions create rights, duties, and responsibilities that require a higher level of understanding and appreciation, and the parties are not afforded the same safety net of laws that protect parties to marriage contracts or testamentary acts.

In light of the above authority, we conclude the mental capacity required to end one's marriage should be similar to the mental capacity required to begin the marriage. As discussed above, the threshold is low. . . . And our Supreme Court, in *Marriage of Higgason,* (1973) 10 Cal.3d 476, 110 Cal. Rptr. 897, 516 P.2d 289, held a conservatee could also initiate a dissolution proceeding as long as he or she has the capacity to express that he or she wants to end the marriage.

The Supreme Court in *Higgason* rejected Husband's argument the petition for dissolution of marriage could not be brought by a guardian ad litem, on behalf of a spouse who is under conservatorship. The court reasoned such a proceeding may be brought "provided it is established that the spouse is capable of exercising a judgment, and expressing a wish, that the marriage be dissolved on account of irreconcilable differences and has done so. [T]his requirement has been met . . . . [T]he trial court found that the wife was not insane and had the ability to think; the record shows that the wife signed and verified the petition for dissolution of marriage and also two declarations in support of . . . injunctive relief against the husband's visiting her premises; and her deposition shows that she desired a dissolution of the marriage." The Supreme Court reasoned appointment of a conservator "does not constitute a determination that the conservatee is in any way 'insane or incompetent' [citations] . . . ."

In *In re Marriage of Straczynski,* (2010) 189 Cal. App. 4th 531, 116 Cal. Rptr. 3d 938, the appellate court extended *Higgason* by holding an incapacitated individual may *maintain* a dissolution proceeding only if he or she remains capable of " 'exercising a judgment, and expressing a wish, that the marriage be dissolved' " throughout the proceedings. . . . [T]he decision to dissolve a marriage is intensely personal. Just as a guardian cannot maintain an action so "'strictly personal'" against the conservatee's wishes, . . . the conservatee must be capable of making the decision to file the petition and expressing his or her desire to end the marriage.

. . . Joann devotes a large portion of her opening brief discussing evidence she claims supports the conclusion Lyle's dementia was so severe he could not exercise a judgment or express a wish his marriage be dissolved, and her theory Lyle filed the petition because of undue influence. But we do not reweigh the evidence. The court had before it substantial evidence of Lyle's mental capacity both in the form of expert opinion and by its first hand observations. And given that courts must presume a person has the capacity to make a decision about ending his or her marriage, and must apply the relevant legal authority requiring a lower level of mental capacity, we find no basis to disturb the trial court's judgment. There was much less information about the conservatee's mental capacity presented in the *Higgason* case, where the court simply relied on the fact Wife personally signed the petition and testified in her deposition she no longer wanted to be married.

The order is affirmed. Respondent shall recover his costs on appeal.

Malpractice Liability

Attorney's Duty to Ascertain Competence of Client with Review of California Cases on Duty to Intended Beneficiaries

MOORE v. ANDERSON ZEIGLER DISHAROON GALLAGHER & GRAY

Court of Appeal, First District
109 Cal. App. 4th 1287, 135 Cal. Rptr. 2d 888 (2003)

KLINE, P.J. In an issue of first impression in this state, we consider whether an attorney has a duty to beneficiaries under a will to evaluate and ascertain the testamentary capacity of a client . . . . Because this appeal is from a pretrial ruling sustaining demurrers without leave to amend, our recitation of the facts assumes the truth of all facts properly pleaded by the plaintiff-appellant . . . and likewise accepts as true all facts that may be implied or inferred from those she expressly alleges. . . .

The first amended complaint alleged as follows: appellants are five of the nine adult children of decedent Clyde P. Smith. Respondents represented Clyde. They prepared and amended estate plan documents for him, including amendments to a trust agreement called the Clyde P. Smith 1985 Trust. Under the terms of the amendment prepared by attorney Disharoon and executed by Clyde in September 1999, upon the death of the trustor (Clyde), certain assets of the trust were to be distributed to two marital trusts and to a trust for Clyde's grandchildren. The residue was to be distributed to eight of Clyde's nine adult children (including appellants). The amendment provided that the ninth child, Michael D. Smith, was not a beneficiary of the trust. . . .

The complaint further alleged that Disharoon had prepared the September 1999 amendments and knew that Clyde intended that Michael not receive anything under the trust amendments and that Clyde intended to benefit his eight other children with equal shares in the remainder of the trust.

Clyde became terminally ill. By June 2000, Clyde was "extremely sick, debilitated, and confused. Clyde had undergone chemotherapy and was under the influence of powerful medications, including pain medication. Clyde had to be hospitalized. By June 2000, Clyde lacked the capacity to know or understand his estate plan. He did not recollect nor understand the nature of his property or trust dispositions, nor recall his relation to his family members and children."

Disharoon was aware that Clyde was terminally ill and extremely weak. Nevertheless, in June 2000, Disharoon prepared new estate planning documents whereby the estate plan was fundamentally changed. . . . The new documents provided that . . . [substantial assets] would be distributed to Michael D. Smith . . . . Clyde executed these documents on June 21, 2000. The complaint alleged that, when Clyde did so, he lacked testamentary capacity, was not competent and did not truly know or understand his appointments and property disposition. Clyde died on June 23, 2000.

A dispute arose among the children as to which trust amendment should govern the disposition of Clyde's property. . . . After extensive discovery, the parties to the trust litigation reached a settlement. No determination was made of Clyde's capacity. The terms of the settlement allocated to appellants a portion of what they would have received under the trust as amended in September 1999, before the June 23, 2000 amendments.

Following settlement of the trust litigation, . . . appellants sued respondents Disharoon and Anderson Zeigler for malpractice. . . . [T]he first amended complaint alleged that a competent estate planning attorney in the circumstances should have recognized that Clyde's testamentary capacity was "questionable because of Clyde's weakened and confused condition and medical treatment. A competent attorney in such circumstances should exercise reasonable care to confirm his client's capacity, competence, and intentions regarding the client's property dispositions, and should document such confirmation. Attorney Disharoon negligently failed to do so in June 2000, and thereby breached the duty of care to effectuate his client's intent to benefit his eight children . . . [and exclude Michael]." The first amended complaint also alleged that "a competent attorney would have recognized that litigation between the children was likely, unless the attorney took reasonable steps to investigate, confirm and document the client's capacity, competence, and testamentary intent."

Respondents demurred . . . . [T]he trial court granted the demurrer without leave to amend . . . . This timely appeal followed.

DISCUSSION

. . . "As a general rule, an attorney has no professional obligation to nonclients and thus cannot be held liable to nonclients for the consequences of the attorney's professional negligence . . . ." . . . As an exception to this general rule, it has been settled in California that an attorney may be liable to nonclients in limited circumstances where the nonclient was the *intended beneficiary* of the attorney's services. (*Lucas v. Hamm* (1961) 56 Cal. 2d 583, 589-591, 15 Cal. Rptr. 821, 364 P.2d 685; accord *Heyer v. Flaig* (1969) 70 Cal. 2d 223, 226, 74 Cal. Rptr. 225, 449 P.2d 161 . . . ; *Bucquet v. Livingston* (1976) 57 Cal. App. 3d 914, 921, 129 Cal. Rptr. 514.) . . . Such liability is not, however, automatic. . . .

"All of the authorities indicate that a determination whether liability exists in a specific case is a matter of policy and involves the balancing of various factors, including: 1) the extent to which the transaction was intended to affect the plaintiff; 2) the foreseeability of harm to him; 3) the degree of certainty that the plaintiff suffered injury; 4) the closeness of the connection between the defendant's conduct and the injury suffered; 5) the moral blame attached to the defendant's conduct; and 6) the policy of preventing future harm . . . ." (*Bucquet v. Livingston* . . . .) These factors were identified by the Supreme Court in *Biakanja v. Irving*, . . . 49 Cal. 2d 647, 320 P.2d 16 . . . in which a notary public was held liable in tort to the intended beneficiary of a will which was ineffective because of the notary's negligent supervision of its attestation.

Later cases have considered two additional factors to be critical to the duty determination. One is the likelihood that imposition of liability might interfere with the attorney's ethical duties to the client. (*Goodman v. Kennedy*, . . . 18 Cal. 3d 335, 344, 134 Cal. Rptr. 375, 556 P.2d 737; *St. Paul Title Co. v. Meier* (1986) 181 Cal. App. 3d 948, 952, 226 Cal. Rptr. 538.) The Supreme Court has also considered the related question of whether the imposition of liability "would impose an undue burden on the profession." (*Lucas v. Hamm* . . . .)

In *Lucas* the court determined that negligence in the drafting of a will that caused a bequest to plaintiff-beneficiaries to be invalid could entitle the beneficiaries named in the will to bring an action against the drafting attorney. [3] The court stated: "We are of the view that the extension of [the attorney's] liability to beneficiaries injured by a negligently drawn will does not place an undue burden on the profession, particularly when we take into consideration that a contrary conclusion would cause the innocent beneficiary to bear the loss." . . .

Heyer v. Flaig . . . similarly involved negligence in the drafting of a document which did not carry out the testator's intent. In that case, the testator had retained the attorney to prepare her will, telling him she wished her estate to pass to her two daughters and that she intended to remarry. The attorney drafted the will providing for the two daughters, but failed to include any mention of the intent of the testator to remarry and to not make any provision for her new spouse. The testator remarried ten days after the will was executed. Upon her death, the new spouse claimed a portion of the estate as a post-testamentary spouse . . . . The attorney was sued by the testator's daughters. . . . "*Heyer* strongly reinforced the theory that an attorney who 'undertakes to fulfill the testamentary instructions of his client . . . assumes a relationship . . . also with the client's intended beneficiaries,' that 'the possibility of injury to an intended beneficiary' is foreseeable should the client's testamentary plan fail after his or her death, and that in such an eventuality 'only the beneficiaries suffer the real loss. We recognized in *Lucas* that unless the beneficiary could recover against the attorney in such a case, no one could do so and the social policy of preventing future harm would be frustrated. . . . [P]ublic policy requires that the attorney exercise his position of trust and superior knowledge responsibly so as not to affect adversely persons whose rights and interests are certain and foreseeable.' . . . ." . . .

These cases were distinguished and no duty to beneficiaries was found in *Radovich v. Locke-Paddon*, [(1995), 35 Cal. App. 4th 946, 954-955, 41 Cal. Rptr. 2d 573.] There, the court held that the defendant attorney and his firm owed no duty of care to the client's husband, as a

---

[3] Although it held that there was no bar to finding a duty to third party beneficiaries in these circumstances, the court ultimately refused to find the attorney liable because the drafting error, a violation of the rule against perpetuities and restraints on alienation, did not show negligence. . . .

potential beneficiary named in an unsigned will. . . . The husband sued the attorney and the firm for malpractice, alleging that they owed a duty to the husband to carry out the decedent's testamentary wishes in a reasonably prompt and diligent fashion and had breached that duty in failing to remind the decedent to execute the will or even to find out whether she had done so . . . . The *Radovich* court distinguished *Biakanja, Lucas* and *Heyer* on the grounds that "the decedent never signed the will Locke-Paddon drafted. While the crux of *Biakanja, Lucas* and *Heyer* was that a will the decedent *had signed* had been rendered wholly or partially ineffective, at least as to the beneficiaries, by the negligence of the person who had prepared the will, the crux of Radovich's claim is that a will potentially beneficial to him had never become effective because, assertedly due to Locke-Paddon's negligence the decedent *had not signed* it." . . . The will was not defective by reason of its draftsmanship. There was no argument that the will would have been ineffective to achieve the disposition of assets the deceased would have preferred. . . . It was not clear that the decedent had not changed her mind. . . . Moreover, the *Radovich* court saw "both practical and policy reasons for requiring more evidence of commitment than is furnished by a direction to prepare a will containing specified provisions . . . . From a policy standpoint, we must be sensitive to the potential for misunderstanding and the difficulties of proof inherent in the fact that disputes such as these will not arise until the decedent—the only person who can say what he or she intended—has died. Thus we must as a policy matter insist on the clearest manifestation of commitment the circumstances will permit." . . .

Most importantly, the *Radovich* court recognized strong "[c]ountervailing policy considerations" that in the circumstances cut against imposition of a duty. "[I]mposition of liability in a case such as this could improperly compromise an attorney's primary duty of undivided loyalty to his or her client, the decedent . . . , '[i]mposition of liability would create an incentive for an attorney to exert pressure on a client to complete and execute estate planning documents summarily,' without the additional consideration the decedent in this case intended to give them, and '[f]ear of liability to potential third party beneficiaries would contravene the attorney's primary responsibility to ensure that the proposed estate plan effectuates the client's wishes and that the client understands the available options and the legal and practical implications of whatever course of action is ultimately chosen.' . . ." On weighing the relevant policy considerations, the court concluded the attorney owed no duty to the beneficiary to inquire whether the decedent had any question or wished further assistance in completing the change in testamentary disposition she had discussed with him. . . .

The considerations identified in *Radovich,* as well as in *Lucas* and the negligent drafting and execution cases, lead to the conclusion that an attorney preparing a will for a testator *owes no duty to the beneficiary of the will or to the beneficiary under a previous will* to ascertain and document the testamentary capacity of the client.

First and foremost, we believe the duty of loyalty of the attorney to the client may be compromised by imposing a duty to beneficiaries in these circumstances. . . .

In the *Biakanja-Lucas-Heyer* line of cases, there is clearly no potential for conflict between the duty the attorney owes to the client and the duty the attorney owes to intended beneficiaries.

. . . Only the negligence of the attorney, resulting in the invalidity of the document or bequest, frustrates the intention of the testator.

In contrast, where the testamentary capacity of the testator is the basis for a will challenge, the true intent of the testator *is* the central question. That intent cannot be ascertained from the will or other challenged estate plan document itself. The attorney who is persuaded of the client's testamentary capacity by his or her own observations and experience, and who drafts the will accordingly, fulfills that duty of loyalty *to the testator*. In so determining, the attorney should not be required to consider the effect of the new will on beneficiaries under a former will or beneficiaries of the new will.

The extension of the duty to intended beneficiaries . . . to this context would place an intolerable burden upon attorneys. Not only would the attorney be subject to potentially conflicting duties to the client and to potential beneficiaries, but counsel also could be subject to conflicting duties to different sets of beneficiaries. The testator's attorney would be placed in the position of potential liability to either the beneficiaries disinherited if the attorney prepares the will or to the potential beneficiaries of the new will if the attorney refuses to prepare it in accordance with the testator's wishes. The instant case, where some children benefited under the previous will and others benefited under the later, challenged will is a perfect illustration of that burden.

Appellants argue that . . . competent counsel has a duty to the testator to ascertain competence before drafting the will and by documenting that exploration, counsel guards against groundless challenges to the testator's competency. We are not persuaded that imposition of such a burden on counsel would result in less litigation. Ascertaining testamentary capacity is often difficult and the potential for liability to beneficiaries who might deem any investigation inadequate would unjustifiably deny many persons the opportunity to make or amend their wills. . . . Any doubts as to capacity might be resolved by counsel by refusing to draft the will as desired by the testator, turning the presumption of testamentary capacity on its head and requiring the testator represented by a cautious attorney to prove his competency.

In the situation presented in *Biakanja, Lucas,* and *Heyer,* intended beneficiaries of the invalid will or trust documents were left with no remedy and no way to secure the undisputed intention of the testator. Their only avenue for redress was via a malpractice action against the negligent attorney. In contrast, beneficiaries disinherited by a will executed by an incompetent testator have a remedy in the probate court. They may contest the probate and challenge the will on the ground that the testator lacked testamentary capacity at the time of executing the will. That is precisely what appellants did in this case. . . .

It may be that prudent counsel should refrain from drafting a will for a client the attorney reasonably believes lacks testamentary capacity or should take steps to preserve evidence regarding the client's capacity in a borderline case. However, that is a far cry from imposing malpractice liability to nonclient potential beneficiaries for the attorney's alleged inadequate investigation or evaluation of capacity or the failure to sufficiently document that investigation. . . .

DISPOSITION

The judgment is affirmed. Respondents are awarded their costs on this appeal.

NOTE:

In **Chang v. Lederman**, 172 Cal. App. 4th 67, 90 Cal. Rptr. 3d 758 2009), Schumert's surviving spouse sued the lawyer who drafted Schumert's trust, claiming that the lawyer refused to carry out Schumert's instructions to amend the trust to leave the entire trust estate to his wife. She claimed that the lawyer refused because Schumert's former wife would sue if the trust, which left the bulk of the estate to his son, was modified and that Schumert, who was seriously ill, should have a psychiatric evaluation before making changes to his estate plan.

The court held that because the surviving spouse had never been the lawyer's client and because her claim that she was an intended beneficiary was not based on an express bequest in an executed will or trust, the lawyer owed her no duty of care. Recognizing a duty of care to a nonclient who alleges she was a potential beneficiary, in the absence of an executed will or trust reflecting the testator/trustor's intent would place an intolerable burden on the legal profession.

Section B. Undue Influence

❖ CPC § 6104. Duress, Menace, Fraud, Undue Influence

The execution or revocation of a will or a part of a will is ineffective to the extent the execution or revocation was procured by duress, menace, fraud, or undue influence.

(Stats. 1990)

What Is Undue Influence?

CPC § 86. Undue Influence

"Undue influence" has the same meaning as defined in Section 15610.70 of the Welfare and Institutions Code. It is the intent of the Legislature that this section supplement the common law meaning of undue influence without superseding or interfering with the operation of that law.

(Stats. 2013)

Welfare & Institutions Code § 15610.70. Undue Influence Defined; Determining When Result Produced by Undue Influence

(a) "Undue influence" means excessive persuasion that causes another person to act or refrain from acting and results in inequity. In determining whether a result was produced by undue influence, all of the following shall be considered:

(1) The vulnerability of the victim, including, but not limited to, incapacity, illness, disability, injury, age, education, impaired cognitive function, emotional distress, isolation, or dependency.

(2) The influencer's apparent authority, including, but not line 36 limited to, status as a fiduciary, family member, care provider, health care professional, legal professional, spiritual adviser, expert, or other qualification, and whether the influencer knew or should have known of the victim's vulnerability.

(3) The actions or tactics used by the influencer, including, but not limited to, all of the following:

(A) Controlling necessaries of life, medication, the victim's interactions with others, access to information, or sleep.

(B) Use of affection, intimidation, or coercion.

(C) Initiation of changes in personal or property rights, use of haste or secrecy in effecting those changes, effecting changes at inappropriate times and places, and claims of expertise in effecting changes.

(4) The equity of the result. Evidence of the equity of the result may include, but is not limited to, the economic consequences to the victim, any divergence from the victim's prior intent or course of conduct or dealing, the relationship of the value conveyed to the value of any services or consideration received, or the appropriateness of the change in light of the length and nature of the relationship.

(b) Evidence of an inequitable result, without more, is not sufficient to prove undue influence. (Stats. 2013)

Amanuensis Rule: Presumption of Undue Influence

ESTATE of STEPHENS

Supreme Court of California
28 Cal. 4th 665, 49 P.3d 1093 (2002)

MORENO, J. . . . Prior to his death, the deceased orally instructed his daughter to sign his name on a grant deed that vested title to his residence in himself and her as joint tenants; she did so outside of his presence and he later orally ratified the conveyance. We granted review to decide whether the transfer was valid. . . .

I.

In 1978, Austin David Stephens (Austin) and his wife, Thelma, executed crossover wills, which provided that when they passed away all their real and personal property would be equally divided between their children, Lawrence Stephens (Lawrence) and Shirley Williams (Shirley).

In 1983, Thelma became seriously ill with cancer. Shirley drove her mother to every chemotherapy treatment and gave her around-the-clock care for five years. Shirley, who lived just two houses from her parents, installed an intercom linking their bedrooms so her mother could reach her at any time. At the same time, Shirley held two jobs. She worked in the daytime as a switchboard operator and in the evening as a cocktail waitress.

Soon after Thelma died in 1988, Austin's health began to suffer. Over the next six years, he had over 170 doctor visits and was hospitalized several times as a result of diabetes, a heart attack, prostate cancer, lip cancer, high blood pressure, glaucoma, and ear and eye surgeries. Shirley, as she did with her mother, took care of her father. She fixed him three meals a day, cleaned his pool and house, washed his clothes, watered his plants, purchased his groceries, gave him daily insulin shots, arranged his medical appointments, purchased his prescriptions, completed his insurance paperwork, medical forms and tax returns, paid his bills and cared for his pets.

Unlike Shirley, Lawrence was not involved in the daily activity of caring for his father. In August of 1989, Lawrence moved from California to Colorado to retire. Thereafter, he visited his father once or twice a year.

Austin began to lose his eyesight from glaucoma. In 1989, he executed a durable power of attorney, naming Shirley his attorney-in-fact. The document specified that she had the power to sell, convey, and transfer his real property. By 1990, Austin was blind and relied on Shirley to read documents for him. In 1991, Austin decided to make a gift of his home to Shirley due in part to her caring for him as well as Lawrence's departure to Colorado at a time when Austin felt he needed help.

A grant deed was typed by Agnes Stephens, who was Lawrence's ex-wife and Shirley's coworker. The deed vested title in Austin and Shirley as joint tenants. Austin's name and address were typed on the deed for return by mailing after recording. Following preparation of the deed, Austin verbally instructed Shirley, in the presence of Austin's best friend and neighbor, Delbert Catron, to sign his name to the deed. Shirley followed her father's instructions. She executed the deed and had it notarized. Austin was not present at the time Shirley signed the deed.

The trial court determined that, after the deed was executed, Austin "orally and expressly" ratified Shirley's signing of his name to the deed. The trial court stated: "a. Shirley immediately told Austin of each step of the execution, notarization, forwarding of the deed to the County Recorder's office for recording, and return of the deed to him after recording. At each of these steps Austin verbally acknowledged to Shirley that that was what he wanted to happen and instructed her to proceed with the next step. b. While the deed was with the County Recorder's office for recording, Austin personally received a telephone call from a person from the County of Orange who inquired as to whether Austin intended the transfer of the real property to be a gift to Shirley. Austin told the caller that that was his intent. c. After the deed was recorded it was mailed to Austin's residence, at which time he verbally acknowledged receiving it and instructed Shirley to place it in safekeeping. d. Subsequent to the recording of the deed, Austin had several conversations with Mr. Catron in which he told Mr. Catron that Shirley had followed his instructions and executed the deed. e. Around Christmas 1991, subsequent to the recording of the deed, Austin traveled to Florida where he stayed for several weeks or months to visit his brother, James Franklin Stephens. During that visit he repeatedly told his brother that he was angry with Larry for leaving California, that he had nothing but praise for Shirley for taking care of him, and that he had 'disinherited Larry.' "

The trial court also determined that Austin was at all times thereafter mentally competent and capable of taking action to disavow the validity of the deed if that was his desire, but that he did not do so despite his knowledge of the execution, notarization, and recording of the deed.

Within a few weeks of Austin's death in 1994, Lawrence filed a petition for probate of the will and a petition to determine title and require transfer of the property to the estate. . . . . Lawrence died before trial, but his daughter, Katherine Stephens Vohs (Katherine), continued with the litigation as his successor in interest. . . .

After a court trial, the trial judge declared Shirley the sole owner of Austin's property under the "amanuensis" rule, which provides that where the signing of a grantor's name is done with the grantor's express authority, the person signing the grantor's name is not deemed an agent but is instead regarded as a mere instrument or amanuensis of the grantor, and that signature is deemed to be that of the grantor.[1] . . .

The trial court stated: "Shirley's signature of Austin's name was a purely ministerial, mechanical act and was not an exercise by Shirley of any authority under the power of attorney. The signature is therefore deemed to be that of Austin made by the hand of Shirley, and not the signature of Shirley as an authorized agent under the power of attorney or otherwise as a fiduciary. . . . By virtue of Austin's antecedent instruction to Shirley and his subsequent ratification, the signature on the deed is deemed to be Austin's as a matter of law, meeting the requirement of [Civil Code §1091] that a deed be executed by the grantor."

Katherine appealed. During the appeal's pendency, Shirley passed away. Her children continued to defend the lawsuit. . . . The Court of Appeal reversed . . . reluctantly . . . . We . . . now reverse.

---

[1] The Oxford English Dictionary (2d ed. 1989) defines "amanuensis" as "one who copies or writes from the dictation of another." Pablo Neruda has penned: "In the center of the earth I will push aside the emeralds so that I can see you—you like an amanuensis, with a pen of water, copying the green sprigs of plants." (Neruda, 100 Love Sonnets (1986) "In the Center of the Earth," p. 211, 1st verse.)

II.

The Court of Appeal correctly determined that Shirley was not authorized to sign the deed as Austin's agent . . . . An agent's authority to execute a deed on behalf of a principal must be conferred in writing. Civil Code section 1091 . . . .

While Shirley had written authority from Austin in the form of a power of attorney, that document specified that she had only the power to sell, convey, and transfer his real property. By law, she lacked authority to convey the property to herself as a gift. . . . (*Shields v. Shields* (1962), 200 Cal. App. 2d 99, 101, 19 Cal. Rptr. 129.)

Nor was the gift authorized by Probate Code section 4264, which provides that a power of attorney may not be construed to grant authority to an attorney-in-fact to "[m]ake or revoke a gift of the principal's property in trust or otherwise" unless such act is "expressly authorized in the power of attorney." . . .

Respondents . . . argue that Austin subsequently ratified her execution of the deed by his oral statements to others. This argument is not persuasive. To be valid, any such ratification must have been made in writing . . . .

Respondents insist that the transaction should be valid as a deed signed by Austin, because Shirley acted as Austin's amanuensis in that she performed a mere mechanical function in signing Austin's name to the deed . . . [and] that the Court of Appeal erred in concluding that Shirley did not qualify as an amanuensis because she did not sign the deed in Austin's presence.

The sole authority cited by the Court of Appeal, *Pitney v. Pitney* (1921), 55 Cal. App. 22, 29, 202 P. 940 (*Pitney*), specifically requires that an amanuensis sign a deed in the presence of the grantor. . . .

Subsequent cases have clarified, however, that application of the amanuensis rule is not confined to the situation in which an agent signs a contract in the principal's immediate presence. It may also apply when an agent, acting with merely mechanical and no discretionary authority, signs the principal's name *outside* the principal's presence. . . . [case discussion omitted.—Ed.]

III.

In the . . . cited cases, however, the amanuensis had no interest in the contract. Here, Shirley claims to be an amanuensis despite the fact that she is also the sole beneficiary of this transfer. No prior California decision has addressed the issue of an "interested amanuensis."[4] Obvious

---

[4] While there is scant authority on the specific issue of the interested amanuensis, other jurisdictions have permitted the practice. . . . [citations omitted]

The dissent correctly notes that several courts and commentators have endorsed the general rule that an agent, acting for one party to a contract of sale required to be in writing, cannot also act as the agent for the other party and validly bind that other party to such contract. . . . Our decision does not conflict

concerns arise; namely, whether the transfer was the product of fraud, duress, or undue influence. Accordingly, if the amanuensis will directly benefit from the transfer of title, the validity of the transfer must be examined under a heightened level of judicial scrutiny.

In an undue influence case, for example, "[w]here the relationship between the parties is that of parent and child and the parent relies on the child for advice in business matters, a gift *inter vivos* . . . which is without consideration and where the parent does not have independent advice, is presumed to be fraudulent and to have been made under undue influence." (*Sparks v. Mendoza* (1948), 83 Cal. App. 2d 511, 514, 189 P.2d 43.) . . . The burden of proof then shifts to the child "to show that the transaction was free from fraud and undue influence, and in all particulars fair." . . . Put differently, this presumption may be rebutted by "evidence that the act in question had its genesis in the mind of the parent and that he was not goaded to a completion by any act of such child." (*Goldman v. Goldman* (1953), 116 Cal. App. 2d 227, 234, 253 P.2d 474.) The child's burden of proof is by a preponderance of the evidence. (*Estate of Gelonese* (1974), 36 Cal. App. 3d 854, . . . 111 Cal. Rptr. 833.)

. . . Because unscrupulous parties could attempt to use the amanuensis rule to sidestep the protections contained in . . . [Civil Code sections 2309 and 2310 and Probate Code section 4264], we hold that the signing of a grantor's name by an interested amanuensis must be presumed invalid. . . . [T]he interested amanuensis bears the burden to show that his or her signing of the grantor's name was a mechanical act in that the grantor intended to sign the document using the instrumentality of the amanuensis.[7]

. . . However, this presumption has been successfully rebutted in this case. The trial court found, based on overwhelming evidence, that Shirley acted as a mere amanuensis, signing the deed at Austin's direct request, albeit not in his immediate presence . . . [; therefore] Austin's oral instruction to Shirley was sufficient. "It is perfectly natural for a parent to be more bountiful to one of his children who has assumed the greatest burden of care and lavished the highest degree of solicitude upon him." (*Camperi v. Chiechi*, . . . 134 Cal. App. 2d at p. 505, 286 P.2d 399.) . . . The judgment of the Court of Appeal is reversed.

WE CONCUR: GEORGE, C.J., BAXTER, WERDEGAR, CHIN and BROWN, JJ.

---

with this line of cases because we recognize that Shirley was not authorized to sign the deed as Austin's agent. Despite its claims to the contrary, however, the dissent cites no case where a court has held that a beneficiary to a will cannot also act as an amanuensis. . . .

[7] The dissent states that the protections outlined above "may look good at first glance, but . . . [a]ny swindler who signs an aging and infirm relative's name to a deed . . . can easily defeat the presumption of invalidity by falsely testifying that the relative asked the swindler to sign as an amanuensis." . . . These fears are unfounded.

. . . [B]ased upon the testimony of several disinterested witnesses, the trial court overwhelmingly found that Shirley acted as Austin's amanuensis. . . . [I]t is unlikely that a "swindler's" testimony, without corroboration, will rebut the presumption of invalidity. Indeed, as seen in undue influence cases . . . upon which our rule is patterned, the presumption of invalidity effectively acts as a safeguard against unscrupulous relatives who would otherwise seek to take advantage of an aging and infirm relative.

Dissenting Opinion by KENNARD, J. . . . A rule permitting an interested party to sign another party's name to a document covered by the statute of frauds creates an exception to the statute that is so broad as to defeat its purpose, which is to prevent perjury by requiring that important transactions be in writing and signed by the parties. Otherwise, a party could write a document implementing such a transaction, sign the other party's name, and then enforce it by falsely testifying that the signature was authorized. . . .

My sympathies lie with Shirley . . . . That, however, is beside the point. The result in this case cannot depend on personal sympathies toward the claimant. In the words of Lowe v. Mohler, . . . 56 Ind. App. 593, 105 N.E. 934, 936: "It is doubtless true that in some instances the application of this doctrine [that an interested party may not sign the name of another party to a document required by the statute of frauds] may work a hardship, and innocent parties may be required to suffer therefrom; but the aggregate good which comes from its strict enforcement so far overshadows the evil that the courts uniformly adhere to the rule as announced. . . .

Bequests to Lawyers and Fiduciary Appointments:

Statutes and Cases on Disqualified Transferees

NOTE:

In 1993, California enacted CPC §§ 21350-21356 which created a presumption that transfers to the drafter of an instrument, to a fiduciary who transcribed or caused an instrument to be transcribed, or to a care custodian of a dependent adult, and to certain persons related to them, are the product of undue influence, with certain exceptions. Exceptions included transfers to relatives and transfers accompanied by a certificate of independent review given to the transferor by an attorney.

Problems with the statutes were revealed by several cases. After a series of cases raising the question whether care custodians covered by the statute were limited to professional caregivers, the Supreme Court in **Bernard v. Foley**, 39 Cal. 4th 794, 139 P.3d 1196, 47 Cal. Rptr. 3d 248 (2006), held they included anyone (other than a relative of the transferor) who provided health services to a dependent adult, including long-time friends who received no compensation. **Osornio v. Weingarten**, 124 Cal. App. 4th 304, 21 Cal. Rptr. 3d 246 (2004), revealed that two attorneys would be required to insure that a gift to a care custodian would not be presumed the product of undue influence: the attorney who drafted the instrument and a separate attorney to give a certificate of independent review. What was required for a valid independent review was also left unclear by the statutes. **Estate of Winans**, 183 Cal. App. 4th 102, 107 Cal. Rptr. 3d 167 (2010), *infra*, filled some of the gaps.

These problems, among others, led to a study by the California Law Revision Commission. Based on its recommendations, the legislature in 2010 enacted CPC §§ 21360-21392, which apply to instruments that become irrevocable after January 1, 2011. Until January 1, 2014, CPC §§ 21350-21356 remained in effect as to instruments that became irrevocable between September 1, 1993 and January 1, 2011. On January 1, 2014, CPC §§ 21350-21356 were repealed, CPC § 21355. Only the statutes that became effective January 1, 2011 are reproduced here. Two cases interpreting the old statutes are also included because they will remain relevant in interpreting the provisions of the new statutes.

NOTE: Jenkins v. Teegarden, 230 Cal. App. 4th 1128, 179 Cal. Rptr. 3d 304 (2014) held that despite repeal of §§ 21350-21356, prior law continues to apply to instruments that became irrevocable before Jan. 1, 2011.

CPC § 21360. Application of Definitions

The definitions in this chapter govern the construction of this part.
(Stats. 2010)

CPC § 21362. Definition of Care Custodian and Health and Social Services

(a) "Care custodian" means a person who provides health or social services to a dependent adult, except that "care custodian" does not include a person who provided services without remuneration if the person had a personal relationship with the dependent adult (1) at least 90 days before providing those services, (2) at least six months before the dependent adult's death, and (3) before the dependent adult was admitted to hospice care, if the dependent adult was admitted to hospice care. As used in this subdivision, "remuneration" does not include the donative transfer at issue under this chapter or the reimbursement of expenses.

(b) For the purposes of this section, "health and social services" means services provided to a dependent adult because of the person's dependent condition, including, but not limited to, the administration of medicine, medical testing, wound care, assistance with hygiene, companionship, housekeeping, shopping, cooking, and assistance with finances.
(Stats. 2010)

CPC § 21366. Definition of Dependent Adult

"Dependent adult" means a person who, at the time of executing the instrument at issue under this part, was a person described in either of the following:

(a) The person was 65 years of age or older and satisfied one or both of the following criteria:

    (1) The person was unable to provide properly for his or her personal needs for physical health, food, clothing, or shelter.

    (2) Due to one or more deficits in the mental functions listed in paragraphs (1) to (4), inclusive, of subdivision (a) of Section 811, the person had difficulty managing his or her own financial resources or resisting fraud or undue influence.

(b) The person was 18 years of age or older and satisfied one or both of the following criteria:

(1) The person was unable to provide properly for his or her personal needs for physical health, food, clothing, or shelter.

(2) Due to one or more deficits in the mental functions listed in paragraphs (1) to (4), inclusive, of subdivision (a) of Section 811, the person had substantial difficulty managing his or her own financial resources or resisting fraud or undue influence.

(Stats. 2010)

CPC § 21370. Definition of Independent Attorney

"Independent attorney" means an attorney who has no legal, business, financial, professional, or personal relationship with the beneficiary of a donative transfer at issue under this part, and who would not be appointed as a fiduciary or receive any pecuniary benefit as a result of the operation of the instrument containing the donative transfer at issue under this part.

(Stats. 2010)

CPC § 21374. Definitions of Related by Blood or Affinity, Spouse or Domestic Partner

(a) A person who is "related by blood or affinity" to a specified person means any of the following persons:

(1) A spouse or domestic partner of the specified person.

(2) A relative within a specified degree of kinship to the specified person or within a specified degree of kinship to the spouse or domestic partner of the specified person.

(3) The spouse or domestic partner of a person described in paragraph (2).

(b) For the purposes of this section, "spouse or domestic partner" includes a predeceased spouse or predeceased domestic partner.

(c) In determining a relationship under this section, Sections 6406 and 6407, and Chapter 2 (commencing with Section 6450) of Part 2 of Division 6, are applicable.

(Stats. 2010)

CPC § 21380. Transfers Presumed Fraudulent or Result of Undue Influence; Burden of Proof; Costs & Attorney Fees

(a) A provision of an instrument making a donative transfer to any of the following persons is presumed to be the product of fraud or undue influence:

(1) The person who drafted the instrument.

(2) A person who transcribed the instrument or caused it to be transcribed and who was in a fiduciary relationship with the transferor when the instrument was transcribed.

(3) A care custodian of a transferor who is a dependent adult, but only if the instrument was executed during the period in which the care custodian provided services to the transferor, or within 90 days before or after that period.

(4) A person who is related by blood or affinity, within the third degree, to any person described in paragraphs (1) to (3), inclusive.

(5) A cohabitant or employee of any person described in paragraphs (1) to (3), inclusive.

(6) A partner, shareholder, or employee of a law firm in which a person described in paragraph (1) or (2) has an ownership interest.

(b) The presumption created by this section is a presumption affecting the burden of proof. The presumption may be rebutted by proving, by clear and convincing evidence, that the donative transfer was not the product of fraud or undue influence.

(c) Notwithstanding subdivision (b), with respect to a donative transfer to the person who drafted the donative instrument, or to a person who is related to, or associated with, the drafter as described in paragraph (4), (5), or (6) of subdivision (a), the presumption created by this section is conclusive.

(d) If a beneficiary is unsuccessful in rebutting the presumption, the beneficiary shall bear all costs of the proceeding, including reasonable attorney's fees.

(Stats. 2010, 2017)

NOTES:

1. Jenkins v. Teegarden, 230 Cal. App. 4th 1128, 179 Cal. Rptr. 3d 304 (2014), held that a donative transfer is not one made for no consideration, but a transfer made for inadequate consideration as determined by the standard applied to a grant of specific performance.

2. AB 328 introduced in the 2019-2020 legislative session, if enacted, would add a subsection (a)(4) to include a care custodian who commenced a marriage, cohabitation, or domestic partnership with a transferor who is a dependent adult while, or within 90 days after, providing services to that dependent adult, if the donative transfer occurred or the instrument was executed less than six months after the marriage, cohabitation, or domestic partnership began.

CPC § 21382. *Exclusion from Presumption for Certain Documents or Transfers*

Section 21380 does not apply to any of the following instruments or transfers:

(a) A donative transfer to a person who is related by blood or affinity, within the fourth degree, to the transferor or is the cohabitant of the transferor.

(b) An instrument that is drafted or transcribed by a person who is related by blood or affinity, within the fourth degree, to the transferor or is the cohabitant of the transferor.

(c) An instrument that is approved pursuant to an order under Article 10 (commencing with Section 2580) of Chapter 6 of Part 4 of Division 4,[19] after full disclosure of the relationships of the persons involved.

---

[19] Action of conservator approved by court.—Ed.

(d) A donative transfer to a federal, state, or local public entity, an entity that qualifies for an exemption from taxation under Section 501(c)(3) or 501(c)(19) of the Internal Revenue Code, or a trust holding the transferred property for the entity.

(e) A donative transfer of property valued at five thousand dollars ($5,000) or less, if the total value of the transferor's estate equals or exceeds the amount stated in Section 13100.[20]

(f) An instrument executed outside of California by a transferor who was not a resident of California when the instrument was executed.

(Stats. 2010)

NOTE: AB 328 introduced in the 2019-2020 legislative session, if enacted, would change subsection (a) to read "Except as provided in paragraph (4) of subdivision (a) of Section 21380, a donative transfer to a person who is related by blood or affinity, within the fourth degree, to the transferor or is the cohabitant of the transferor."

CPC § 21384. Donative Transfers Excluded From Presumption; Certificate of Independent Review

(a) A donative transfer is not subject to Section 21380 if the instrument is reviewed by an independent attorney who counsels the transferor, out of the presence of any heir or proposed beneficiary, about the nature and consequences of the intended transfer, including the effect of the intended transfer on the transferor's heirs and on any beneficiary of a prior donative instrument, attempts to determine if the intended transfer is the result of fraud or undue influence, and signs and delivers to the transferor an original certificate in substantially the following form:

"CERTIFICATE OF INDEPENDENT REVIEW

I, _____ , have reviewed
                    (attorney's name)

_____ and have counseled the transferor,
            (name of instrument)

_____ , on the nature and consequences of
            (name of transferor)

any transfers of property to _____
(name of person described in Section 21380 of the Probate Code)

---

[20] $150,000.—Ed.

that would be made by the instrument.

I am an "independent attorney" as defined in Section 21370 of the Probate Code and am in a position to advise the transferor independently, impartially, and confidentially as to the consequences of the transfer.

On the basis of this counsel, I conclude that the transfers to

_____ that would

    (name of person described in Section 21380 of the Probate Code)

be made by the instrument are not the product of fraud or undue influence.

"

_____   _____

(Name of Attorney)   (Date)

(b) An attorney whose written engagement, signed by the transferor, is expressly limited solely to compliance with the requirements of this section, shall not be considered to otherwise represent the transferor as a client.

(c) An attorney who drafts an instrument can review and certify the same instrument pursuant to this section, but only as to a donative transfer to a care custodian. In all other circumstances, an attorney who drafts an instrument may not review and certify the instrument.

(d) If the certificate is prepared by an attorney other than the attorney who drafted the instrument that is under review, a copy of the signed certification shall be provided to the drafting attorney.

(Stats. 2010, 2017)

NOTE: AB 327 introduced in the 2019-2020 legislature, if enacted, would add a new § 21385 that would read:

(a) An at-death transfer, as defined in Section 21104, between spouses by will, revocable trust, beneficiary form, or other instrument is not subject to Section 721 of the Family Code or any presumptions of undue influence created by that section.

(b) This section does not limit the application of any other statutory or common law presumptions of undue influence that may apply to an at-death transfer between spouses.

CPC § 21386. Failed Donative Transfer Passes as if Beneficiary Predeceased Without Spouse, Domestic Partner, or Issue

If a donative transfer fails under this part, the instrument making the donative transfer shall operate as if the beneficiary had predeceased the transferor without spouse, domestic partner, or issue.

(Stats. 2010. 2017)

CPC § 21388. Personal Liability for Certain Property Transfers

(a) A person is not liable for transferring property pursuant to an instrument that is subject to the presumption created under this part, unless the person is served with notice, prior to transferring the property, that the instrument has been contested under this part.

(b) A person who is served with notice that an instrument has been contested under this part is not liable for failing to transfer property pursuant to the instrument, unless the person is served with notice that the validity of the transfer has been conclusively determined by a court.

(Stats. 2010)

CPC § 21390. Contrary Provision in Instrument Not Effective

This part applies notwithstanding a contrary provision in an instrument.

(Stats. 2010)

CPC § 21392. Applicability Date; Statutes Supplement Common Law on Undue Influence

(a) This part shall apply to instruments that become irrevocable on or after January 1, 2011. For the purposes of this section, an instrument that is otherwise revocable or amendable shall be deemed to be irrevocable if, on or after January 1, 2011, the transferor by reason of incapacity was unable to change the disposition of the transferor's property and did not regain capacity before the date of the transferor's death.

(b) It is the intent of the Legislature that this part supplement the common law on fraud and undue influence, without superseding or interfering in the operation of that law. Nothing in this part precludes an action to contest a donative transfer under the common law or under any other applicable law. This subdivision is declarative of existing law.

(Stats. 2010, 2017)

Meaning of "A Person in a Fiduciary Relationship with the Transferor Who Transcribed the Instrument or Caused It To Be Transcribed"

RICE v. CLARK

Supreme Court of California

28 Cal. 4th 89, 47 P.3d 300, 120 Cal. Rptr. 2d 522 (2002)

WERDEGAR, J. . . . The issue presented in this case is whether the class of persons disqualified because they *cause* an instrument to be transcribed is broad enough to include a person who provides information needed in the instrument's preparation and who encourages the donor to execute it, but who does not direct or otherwise participate in the instrument's transcription to final written form. Like the trial and appellate courts below, we conclude the category of persons disqualified . . . is not so broad.

FACTUAL AND PROCEDURAL BACKGROUND

Petitioner Owen S. Rice seeks to invalidate gifts decedent Cecilia M. Clare made by will, trust and other instruments that left Clare's entire estate to respondent Richard L. Clark (Clark) and his wife, respondent Janet A. Clark. Because the trust instrument names Rice as the contingent beneficiary if the Clarks predecease Clare, and because a person disqualified under section 21350 is treated as having predeceased the transferor (§21353), Rice would take under the trust if the Clarks were disqualified.

Clare, 76 years old when her husband died in 1988, owned several pieces of income-producing real property, as well as her Santa Maria home. She had no children or other close relatives. Clark, 42 years old in 1988, was working as a building inspector for the City of Santa Maria and as a handyman, and was managing his own investment properties.

Clark first met Clare in 1988, after her husband's death, when he repaired the garage door at her home. Over the next few months, he performed numerous repairs on her properties, receiving $200 per day in pay. In the summer of 1988, Clark quit his job with the City of Santa Maria, began attending a local college, and continued doing maintenance and small repair work for Clare. In 1989, having finished his course work, he worked increased hours on the Clare properties, taking on more extensive projects. From 1989 through 1993, Clare paid Clark $1,200 per week to take care of her properties.

Toward the end of 1994, Clark's weekly compensation was raised to $1,400 and he took on additional duties. He began helping Clare with her bill paying, bookkeeping, and tax information, and sometimes spoke with tenants on Clare's behalf. He began accompanying Clare to the grocery store and to the bank, which she visited several times each week. Clare also gave Clark a key to her safety deposit box. Beginning in December 1994, Clare wrote checks to cash and gave Clark cash gifts of about $250 to $350 per day.

In 1992, Clare executed a will prepared by Maurice Twitchell, an attorney who had previously done real estate work for her. That instrument bequeathed a farm property and personal property from Clare's home to Richard and Janet Clark, but gave the residue of the estate to Allan Hancock College in Santa Maria, to establish and endow a school of music.

In January 1995, at a meeting between Clark, Clare and Twitchell, Clark said, and Clare appeared to agree, that Clare wished to change her will so as to leave everything to the Clarks with the exception of one ranch, which she wanted to give to Rice, the longtime tenant. However, Clare, acting through Clark, fired Twitchell in March 1995 without executing a new will; Clark told Twitchell that Clare found him too "pushy."

Clare and Clark met with a new attorney, Michael Hardy, on May 4, 1995. Clark had made the appointment at the request of Clare, who had known Hardy's former partner. Hardy had heard of Clare's late husband, but did not know Clare or Clark before the meeting. Clark told Hardy that Clare wanted him to prepare a new will or a trust. During or after the meeting, Clark also gave Hardy lists of Clare's assets, including real property holdings, stocks and bank accounts.

Hardy asked Clare how she wished to leave her estate. She said she wanted to leave her entire estate to Richard and Janet Clark, or to the survivor of them if one of them died before her. If both Clarks predeceased Clare, she wanted the next contingent beneficiary to be Owen Rice. Clare, having decided she wanted a living trust, stated in answer to Hardy's question that she wanted Richard Clark to succeed her as trustee, with Janet Clark as her second choice if Richard were unable to serve. Hardy did not ask Clare about her prior estate plan or why she wanted to change it. Clark was present throughout the meeting. According to Hardy, Clare appeared mentally competent and expressed her testamentary wishes clearly.

Sometime after the May 4 meeting, Clark telephoned Hardy's office and asked the secretary to ask Hardy to prepare the necessary documents promptly. Hardy and his secretary prepared the necessary documents for a will and trust and, through Clark, scheduled a signing appointment for Clare for June 14, 1995. That morning, Clare told Clark she did not like Hardy and did not want to see him. Clark phoned Hardy about an hour before the appointment and said, "I don't think that I can get her in," but Clark and Clare arrived at the appointed time. Hardy went through the documents he had prepared one by one. Clare did not ask any questions and seemed impatient, but appeared to understand Hardy's presentation. But when Hardy asked if she was ready to sign, she said she was not ready and left abruptly. Clark followed Clare, telling Hardy he would talk to her.

Clark and Clare picked up breakfast at a fast-food restaurant and ate it in the park, as was their custom. Clare seemed unhappy. Clark told her that any other attorney she hired would prepare the same type of documents and she would simply end up paying additional legal fees. Clare then agreed to return to Hardy's office and sign the documents. About an hour after they had left, Clark and Clare returned to Hardy's office, where Hardy briefly reviewed the documents again and Clare signed them.

The documents signed June 14, 1995, were an individual living trust instrument, a pour-over will, grant deeds transferring two of Clare's real properties into the trust, and durable powers of attorney for Clark to handle Clare's health care and financial affairs if she became incapacitated. Other deeds remained to be prepared in order to fully fund the trust. The trust instrument named Richard Clark as successor trustee. On Clare's death, the trust estate was to be distributed to Richard and Janet Clark in equal shares, to the survivor if either predeceased Clare, or to Owen Rice if both Clarks predeceased Clare.

Clare did not return to Hardy for further work in funding the trust, instead retaining attorneys Mark Henbury and, after Henbury's sudden death, Karen Mehl to prepare the necessary documents. Mehl prepared several grant deeds conveying property into the trust, which Clare signed in October 1995. Mehl believed Clare was fully competent when she executed the deeds.

Through Henbury, Clare and Clark had been referred to a stockbroker. Clark told the broker that Clare wanted to give all her stocks to him and his wife, and that the documentation should be done in such a way that Clare, who suffered from a muscular palsy in her hand, would not have to sign numerous documents. In August 1995, with the broker's assistance, Clark used his power of attorney to transfer the 68 stock certificates into the Clare trust, after which Clare signed a transfer moving them into a separate trust established by and for the benefit of the Clarks.

In late December 1995 and early 1996, Clare's physical and mental health deteriorated sharply. Clark contacted adult protective services for help, and, in March 1996, Clare entered a nursing home. On February 28, 1996, a physician examined Clare and found her unable to manage her personal, medical or financial affairs, a conclusion with which Clark agreed. Earlier that day, however, Clark had taken Clare to the stockbroker's office, where she signed a transfer into her trust of stock that had been missed in the earlier transactions. Also in February 1996, Clare cashed several large checks Clark had prepared and gave Clark much of the cash.

On March 28, 1996, Clark, represented by Michael Hardy, filed a petition to act as conservator of Clare's person and estate. Clare died on May 10, 1996, before the court acted on the conservatorship petition. The real property in her estate was valued at more than $4.5 million.

In an earlier proceeding, Allan Hancock College, the residuary beneficiary under Clare's 1992 will, sought to invalidate the 1995 will and trust, claiming that these instruments had been procured by Clark's undue influence. . . . In August 1997, the superior court gave judgment for the Clarks, finding that Richard Clark had not unduly benefited from the 1995 will and trust. In light of Clare's lack of close family or other friends, the court found, Richard Clark, as Clare's "longtime employee and friend," was a natural recipient of her bounty. Rice, who was not a beneficiary of the 1992 will, was not a party to this earlier action.

In December 1997, Rice brought the present action, petitioning for a declaration that the donative transfers to the Clarks were invalid under section 21350 . . . .

After . . . trial, the superior court found that Rice had not proven the Clarks were disqualified persons . . . . The court found that Richard Clark was in a fiduciary relationship with Clare at all material times and, "because he was helpful to her and he was the closest human being in her life," had exercised considerable influence over Clare. But Clark did not meet the other criteria of section 21350. To cause an instrument to be transcribed within the meaning of section 21350(a)(4), the trial court concluded, is to take an action "that leads directly, substantially, and uninterruptedly to the writing down or causing to be printed the words of another." While Clark had taken part in "arranging for preparation" of the challenged instruments, he did not draft the instruments, transcribe them, or cause them to be transcribed because "he did none of the thinking or writing himself nor did he order or request any other person to do so." The court therefore entered judgment for the Clarks without making any finding on undue influence.

The Court of Appeal affirmed . . . .

DISCUSSION

I. Legal Background

The principle that a will is invalid if procured by the undue influence of another predates the 1931 adoption of the Probate Code . . . but is now codified in section 6104. . . . Undue influence is pressure brought to bear directly on the testamentary act, sufficient to overcome the testator's free will, amounting in effect to coercion destroying the testator's free agency. (*Estate of Fritschi* (1963), 60 Cal. 2d 367, 373-374, 33 Cal. Rptr. 264, 384 P.2d 656; *Estate of Sarabia* (1990), 221 Cal. App. 3d 599, 604-605, 270 Cal. Rptr. 560; see also *Hagen v. Hickenbottom* (1995), 41 Cal. App. 4th 168, 182, 48 Cal. Rptr. 2d 197 [principles of undue influence applicable to estate plan formalized by simultaneously executed inter vivos trust and will].)

Although a person challenging the testamentary instrument ordinarily bears the burden of proving undue influence (§8252), this court and the Courts of Appeal have held that a presumption of undue influence, shifting the burden of proof, arises upon the challenger's showing that (1) the person alleged to have exerted undue influence had a confidential relationship with the testator; (2) the person actively participated in procuring the instrument's preparation or execution; and (3) the person would benefit unduly by the testamentary instrument. . . .

Supplementing the foregoing, the Legislature in 1993 added the statutory scheme at issue in this case, part 3.5 of division 11 of the Probate Code (hereafter part 3.5), comprising sections 21350 to 21356, and substantially amended it in 1995. . . . The 1993 legislation was introduced in response to reports that an Orange County attorney who represented a large number of Leisure World residents had drafted numerous wills and trusts under which he was a major or exclusive beneficiary, and had abused his position as trustee or conservator in many cases to benefit himself or his law partners. . . .

The scheme set out in part 3.5 differs from the preexisting decisional law relating to undue influence (and section 6104) in several respects. Section 21350 applies to all donative transfers by instrument, not only to wills and other testamentary transfers, but it invalidates only gifts to drafters and to fiduciaries (and to persons close to them) who transcribe the instrument or cause it to be transcribed. Unlike the common law, section 21350 does not require, as the predicate for a presumption of invalidity, that the transferee would receive an "undue" benefit. The transferee, under part 3.5, bears an elevated proof burden in rebutting the presumption: he or she must show the absence of undue influence, fraud or duress *by clear and convincing evidence,* and without reliance on the testimony of any presumptively disqualified person.[21] . . . Section 21351, moreover, makes the presumption of disqualification conclusive as to a drafter-transferee. . . . Thus, for example, if an attorney drafted a client's will so as to benefit himself, he would (assuming no other exception in section 21351 applied) be conclusively disqualified; if he drafted the will so as to benefit his relative or law partner, the presumption would be rebuttable, but only by clear and convincing evidence other than the drafter's testimony that the client freely chose that disposition. . . .

II. Applicability of the 1995 Amendments

As enacted in 1993, subdivision (a)(1) of section 21350 disqualified any person, including attorneys and other fiduciaries, who "drafted, transcribed, or caused to be drafted or transcribed, the instrument." . . . The 1995 amendments, while retaining the disqualification of all drafters, expressly limited disqualification of transcribers, and those who cause the instrument to be transcribed, to fiduciaries. . . . Most important for present purposes, the 1995 amendments eliminated any reference to a person who "caused [the instrument] to be drafted."

Most of the instruments at issue in this case (including the will and trust, the deeds, and most of the stock transfers) were executed in 1995, before the January 1, 1996, effective date of the 1995 amendments. . . . T]he question arises whether the 1995 amendments apply to instruments executed before those amendments became effective.

[Probate Code] Section 3 provides rules for applicability of changes to the Probate Code. Subdivision (c) . . . states: "Subject to the limitations provided in this section, a new law [defined . . . to include an amendment to a Probate Code section] applies on the operative date to all matters governed by the new law, regardless of whether an event occurred or circumstance existed before, on, or after the operative date, including, but not limited to, creation of a fiduciary relationship, death of a person, commencement of a proceeding, making of an order, or taking of an action."

The Clarks contend that section 3, subdivision (c) mandates application of the law as amended in 1995, even though the trust and will were executed prior to that amendment's effectiveness. We agree. . . . [discussion omitted].

III. Scope of Section 21350(a)(4)

. . . There being no contention that Clark falls within any other provision of section 21350, subdivision (a), we must decide whether the lower courts were correct in interpreting subdivision (a)(4) as too narrow to include Clark.

"Transcribe" is, in the present context at least, clear enough in meaning: "To make a copy of (something) in writing; to copy out from an original." (18 Oxford English Dict. (2d ed. 1989)

---

[21] The language that proof be made "without reliance on the testimony of any presumptively disqualified person" is omitted in new § 21380(b).—Ed.

p. 392 . . . . Neither party proposes a meaning different from this, or suggests the Legislature used the term in any way other than its ordinary meaning.

There is no evidence that Clark actually transcribed any donative instrument. . . . The question, then, is whether Clark can be said to have "caused" the instruments' transcription. "Cause" does not have as clear a meaning as "transcribe." As was observed in *Estate of Swetmann* (2000), 85 Cal. App. 4th 807, 102 Cal. Rptr. 2d 457 . . . , the only published decision addressing the precise question before us, "[t]he concept of causation has been given various meanings in the law, ranging from an indirect, peripheral contribution to an immediate and necessary precedent of an event." . . .

Here, the lower courts construed "cause to be transcribed" as limited to direct involvement in the instrument's transcription, as by ordering another person to transcribe a document. This was in accord with the *Swetmann* court, which concluded that "a person who causes the document to be transcribed is one who directs the drafted document to be written out in its final form and, like the transcriber, is in a position to subvert the true intent of the testator." . . . Rice, on the other hand, argues that a person causes an instrument's transcription if he "makes use of other persons to draft and transcribe the instruments, and . . . then persuades the testator to execute them." . . . Rice argues [that] the presumption of disqualification should apply to any fiduciary "whose conduct is a substantial factor in the creation or execution of the donative instruments."

In *Swetmann*, the elderly testator's next door neighbor and conservator, who had for many years helped the testator and his wife with errands and who exercised the testator's power of attorney, arranged for the testator to meet with an estate planning firm, provided information to the estate planner regarding the testator's financial affairs, and paid the planning firm from the conservatorship account. The conservator did not, however, directly participate in preparing the resulting will and trust. . . .

The appellate court concluded the conservator had not caused the will or trust to be transcribed . . . because "none of [his] activities pertained to the physical preparation of the documents." . . . Unlike a drafter, transcriber, or person who directs the instrument's transcription, the conservator was not peculiarly positioned "to subvert the true intent of the testator." . . . His involvement in the will and trust's preparation thus came within neither the spirit nor the letter of section 21350. . . .

Because of the ambiguity inherent in the term "causes," neither party's construction of the statute can be absolutely excluded by the plain language. Our interpretation must in addition be guided by an understanding of the legislative purposes and history. . . .

. . . The "overriding intent" of the new law, according to a committee report, was "to clearly and unambiguously prohibit the most patently offensive actions of [the attorney] while not unreasonably encumbering the practice of probate law." (Sen. Com. on Judiciary, Analysis of Assem. Bill No. 21 (1993-1994 Reg. Sess.), as amended June 17, 1993, p. 5.) The bill would do so, its author stated, by " 'strictly forbid[ding] attorneys from drafting (or causing to be drafted) wills that leave themselves, or relatives or business partners, any gifts.' "

Part 3.5 was thus structured to be more absolute in certain respects, but narrower in the persons targeted, than the preexisting law under section 6104. It is more absolute in that all gifts, not only those involving an undue benefit to the transferee, are presumptively invalidated; in that the presumption of disqualification is conclusive as to drafters; and in that others subject to the presumption must prove absence of undue influence or fraud by clear and convincing evidence and without relying on their own testimony. It is narrower in applying only to drafters and to fiduciaries (and persons close to them) involved in the instrument's transcription, and in excluding relatives of the transferor, whereas the preexisting law (§ 6104) invalidates testamentary gifts procured by *any* recipient's undue influence or fraud. Part 3.5, in short, supplemented existing law by adding an especially strict prohibition focused relatively narrowly on a particular class of transferees.

. . . While virtually anyone acquainted with a testator might in some circumstance use fraud, duress or undue influence to obtain a testamentary gift—a gift that would be ineffective under section 6104 and the decisional law—those who directly participate in the instrument's physical preparation, whether by drafting or transcribing it, are particularly well situated to insert gifts to themselves, their families or business associates, and to secure the instrument's execution. Transcription—the process of reducing an instrument to final written form—obviously carries with it the opportunity to fraudulently alter the terms of the document to the transcriber's advantage." (*Swetmann*.) In the same manner, one who *directs* an instrument's transcription can easily cause the inclusion of provisions benefiting him- or herself, as can a person who drafts an instrument. Only as to this restricted class of persons directly involved in the donative instrument's physical preparation did the Legislature, in enacting part 3.5, prohibit the receipt of gifts by a stricter standard than the preexisting law provided.

Our conclusion is reinforced by the amendment history of section 21350. . . . The 1995 amendments, among many other changes, removed the reference to a person who "caused [the instrument] to be drafted." . . . The definition of "cause to be transcribed" Rice urges us to adopt, which includes any person "whose conduct is a substantial factor in the creation . . . of the donative instruments," would include as well any person who "caused [the instrument] to be drafted," at least as Rice urges causation be understood. As the Legislature has deliberately removed one category from its description of the persons to be disqualified, we should not interpret a remaining category to effectively reinsert it. . . .

Clark materially assisted Clare to dictate the contents of her will and trust to an attorney and to execute the instruments drafted by the attorney, but did not himself directly participate in transcribing the instruments. For this reason, as the lower courts concluded, he did not "cause[ ] [the instruments] to be transcribed" . . . .

WE CONCUR: GEORGE, C.J., KENNARD, BAXTER, CHIN, BROWN and MORENO, JJ.

Whether Transferee Is Related to Testator Determined at Time Instrument Is Drafted

ESTATE of LIRA

California Court of Appeal, 2d Dist. Div. 6
212 Cal. App. 4th 1368, 152 Cal. Rptr. 3d 1 (2012)

PERREN, J. The will and trust of Oligario Lira named his three natural children and three of his six stepchildren as beneficiaries. . . . Oligario executed his will and trust while he was married to Mary Terrones, the mother of his stepchildren, but after she had commenced dissolution proceedings. The judgment dissolving their marriage was entered four months before Oligario's death.

Oligario's natural daughter, appellant Mary Lira Ratcliff (Mary Ratcliff) challenged his will and trust. She contended that Oligario's donative transfers to his stepson beneficiaries were disqualified under Probate section 21350, subdivision (a)(2), . . . because they were related to the lawyer who drafted the will and trust (Oligario's step-grandson).[3] In opposition, respondent Robert Terrones, successor trustee of the trust (Robert) claimed that the disqualification did not apply because Oligario (the transferor) was related by marriage to his stepson beneficiaries. . . . The trial court concluded that the transfers were valid because section 21351, subdivision (a) exempted them from disqualification. Mary Ratcliff contends that the section 21351, subdivision (a) exemption did not apply because the transfers did not occur until after Oligario's death, and after the end of his relationship with his stepsons.

We hold that the section 21351, subdivision (a) exemption from disqualification applies where the transferor and transferee are related at the time that the transferor executes the donative instruments. Section 21351, subdivision (a) does not require that the transferor and transferee be related upon the death of the transferor. In this case, Oligario was related to his stepson beneficiaries upon his execution of the donative instruments. Accordingly, we conclude that his transfers to them were valid and affirm the findings and orders of the trial court. . . .

DISPOSITION
The judgment is affirmed. Costs on appeal to respondent.

---

[3] Oligario's step-grandson, attorney Glenn Terrones (Glenn) drafted his will and trust. Glenn was related to three beneficiaries, Oligario's stepsons Robert C. Terrones, John C. Terrones and Narcizo C. Terrones.

Certificate of Independent Review Ineffective for Lack of Proper Counseling

ESTATE of WINANS

California Court of Appeal, 1st Dist. Div. 1
183 Cal. App. 4th 102, 107 Cal. Rptr. 3d 167 (2010)

MARGULIES, J. In 2005 and 2006, Eugene Winans (Winans) executed wills excluding his half brother and leaving most or all of his property to appellants, Winans's nieces and nephews by a different brother. Barely one month before his death in 2007, using a different attorney, Winans executed a new will that differed considerably by including his half brother, excluding appellants, and leaving substantial property to his care custodian, respondent Elizabeth Timar and other nonrelatives who were not beneficiaries in the prior wills. Appellants challenged the validity of the new will on the grounds of undue influence by Timar and lack of testamentary capacity. They also challenged with respect to the bequest to Timar the validity of the certificate of independent review obtained by Winans under Probate Code section 21351. After substantial discovery by the parties, the trial court granted summary judgment in favor of Timar, dismissing appellants' will contest.

Appellants contend triable issues of fact exist precluding summary judgment. Regarding the certificate of independent review, appellants contend the certifying attorney (1) failed properly to counsel Winans with respect to the "nature and consequences" of the bequest to Timar because he did not explain the statutory scheme under section 21350 and spent only a brief time in counseling, (2) did not conduct the counseling in a confidential manner because others were in the room at the time the counseling occurred, and (3) could not be considered an "independent" attorney because he was designated as executor in the will and stood to earn a substantial fee if appointed. We agree with appellants . . . . Accordingly, we reverse the trial court's grant of summary judgment.

I. BACKGROUND

. . . [Attorney Patrick Coyle was contacted to help Winans make a new will. Winans lived in lived in Canterbury, a six-bed residential care facility in Santa Rosa, owned and operated by Timar.—Ed.] After meeting with Winans, Coyle arranged for Ira Lowenthal, an attorney who shared office space with Coyle, to draft one. Coyle and Lowenthal met with Winans on June 8, 2007. Winans told the attorneys he wanted to leave the house in Forestville to Timar because she had taken care of him over the last few years. Winans also wanted to give bequests to a few longtime tenants in his other properties. . . . Winans selected Coyle as his executor.

Following these discussions, Lowenthal drafted a will . . . for Winans devising the Forestville property to Timar. The remaining beneficiaries, who divided the residue, were . . . tenants of Winans's properties, and Joan Schefer, a piano player at Canterbury with a "30 year plus history" with Winans. Expressly omitted from the 2007 will were [brother] Byron and appellants [Byron's children], thereby reversing the family bequests in the 2006 will executed less than a year earlier. . . . Because Coyle and Lowenthal were unaware of the earlier wills, they did not inquire about this change.

On June 11, Coyle and Lowenthal met with Winans at Canterbury for execution of the 2007 will. Also present was a notary public Lowenthal had brought to witness the signing. After Lowenthal read the terms of the will to Winans, Coyle counseled Winans pursuant to section 21351, informing Winans he was giving property to Timar, asking whether he had been pressured to give the bequest or whether any threats or promises had been made to obtain the bequest, and telling Winans if he had any "problems" with Timar he and Lowenthal could take care of them. Winans said his bequest was voluntary. This interaction took no more than one to five minutes. Coyle later prepared a certificate of independent review . . . and sent it to Winans.

II. DISCUSSION . . .

A. *Certificate of Independent Review*

. . . The statutory bar of section 21350 supplements the preexisting common law doctrine that a presumption of undue influence arises when a person in a confidential relationship with the testator actively participates in procuring a will and benefits unduly under it. . . . The ban of section 21350 is . . . avoided if a "certificate of independent review" is prepared with respect to the transfer. (§ 21351, subd. (b).) . . .

1. *Adequacy of the Substance of Coyle's Counseling*

. . . [S]ection 21351 "does not discuss a minimum, adequate level of counseling" regarding a donative transfer to a disqualified person. . . . [S]ubdivision (b) of section 21351 contains only the barest description of the necessary counseling. The text of the statute requires the attorney to "counsel[ ] the client (transferor) about the nature and consequences of the intended transfer." . . .

Coyle testified that, immediately prior to execution of the will, "I went through some questions about was [Winans] under any pressure. You are giving this to [Timar]. You don't have to do this. I told him if he had any problems that [Lowenthal] and I would take care of them; that he didn't have to do this. Had she, you know—or had there been any pressure? Was there any promises, any requests? All of which he said 'no.' And I did that before he signed the will."

. . . [T]he independent attorney's duty under the statute is to counsel the transferor about the "nature and consequences" of the gift—in essence, to make sure the transferor knows exactly what he or she is doing in executing the instrument. The transferor does not need to know about the existence of the statute or understand its workings in order to understand the nature of his or her bequest. . . .

. . . [W]e conclude a triable issue of fact existed as to the adequacy of the substance of Coyle's counseling. . . . [T]the purpose of the statute [is] to ensure that testators who make bequests to disqualified persons do so voluntarily and in full awareness of the scope of their acts. . . .

Proper counseling about the nature and consequences of a bequest to a disqualified person . . . requires the attorney to ensure the testator understands (1) the nature of the property bequeathed; (2) that a disqualified person will receive the property; and (3) that the "natural objects" of the testator's bounty, if any, will not receive the property. The certifying attorney must also ensure the testator voluntary intends this result and does not believe himself or herself to be under any compulsion, whether legal, financial or otherwise, to make the bequest. This may require the certifying attorney to confirm, for example, the testator is aware the disqualified person has already been fully compensated for the services provided to the testator or otherwise has no legal claim on the testator's bounty. While Coyle appears to have confirmed Winans's awareness of the nature of the Forestville property and his intent to give it to Timar, the remainder of his counseling was, at best, weak. There is no evidence, for example, Coyle discussed with Winans his decision to exclude appellants, or even that Coyle was fully aware of the identity of the natural objects of Winans's bounty.

Appellants also argue the counseling session, which lasted between one and five minutes, was too brief and occurred too late in the process to be effective, since the will had already been prepared and read when the counseling occurred. Timar responds that, while the counseling session at the time of execution of the will lasted only a short time, Coyle had extended discussions with Winans prior to the preparation of the will that should be included when considering the extent of Coyle's counseling under the statute.

In every situation to which section 21350 applies, the attorneys involved in preparing the will, if they are acting competently and in good faith, will have discussed the required subjects with the testator as part of the drafting process. Because the statute expressly requires the independent attorney to review the "instrument," section 21351, subdivision (b) necessarily anticipates a counseling session subsequent to and separate from that process. To include Coyle's earlier discussions with Winans as counseling under the statute would undercut this intent and weaken the nature and significance of the separate counseling session.

2. *Confidentiality*

Section 21351, subdivision (b) does not specifically require the counseling to be "confidential," but . . . [b]ecause the certificate must be executed "on the basis" of independent, impartial, and confidential counsel, we agree with appellants the statute requires the counseling to occur confidentially. Timar does not contend otherwise.

Appellants correctly point out that most of Coyle's conversations with Winans were conducted under less than confidential conditions. Timar was described as "in and out" of Winans's room during the various consultations that occurred prior to execution of the will, and the door to his room was sometimes open. Because Winans was hard of hearing, the conversations could likely be overheard by Canterbury staff or other residents and visitors. Both attorneys testified, however, that the session during which the will was executed occurred with the door closed and in the presence only of Coyle, Lowenthal, and a notary public who was present to witness the signing.

The statute does not define "confidential," and the dictionary definition of "private, secret" is of little help in this context. . . . Plainly, the best practice is to hold the counseling session in complete privacy, with only the testator and the certifying attorney present. The task of the certifying attorney is to ensure the testator understands the implications of his or her bequest and to attempt to determine whether the bequest has been improperly secured. This is best accomplished if the testator is able to speak frankly with the certifying attorney, and such frankness is most likely to be achieved by counseling in complete privacy.

Nonetheless, we are unwilling to adopt such a bright line rule, recognizing there might be circumstances under which a third party's presence would be necessary to effect the counseling. . . .

Viewing the meaning of the words in context and in light of the statutory purpose, we conclude the Legislature intended the counseling to occur under circumstances that would insulate the transferor from any improper influences giving rise to the donative transfer and encourage the transferor to speak frankly with the certifying attorney about those influences, if any. At a minimum, therefore, the disqualified person and any person associated with the disqualified person must be absent. Further, the counseling session must occur in the absence of any person whose presence might discourage the testator from speaking frankly with the attorney about the subject bequest. Accordingly, if any person other than the certifying attorney is present . . . , the burden is on the disqualified person to demonstrate the session was nonetheless "confidential" by showing the presence of the additional persons either (1) was necessary to accomplish the counseling session, or (2) did not interfere with the transferor's full and honest disclosure to the independent attorney regarding the transfer to the disqualified person.

Although Timar was absent during the counseling session before the will was executed, the presence of Lowenthal and the notary public raises a triable issue regarding the confidentiality of this session. [N]either person was necessary to accomplish the counseling. There is no evidence they assisted Coyle in any manner. Nor, on the evidence provided, can we conclude as a matter of law that neither person's presence interfered with Winans's full and honest communication with Coyle. As drafter, Lowenthal was acquainted with Timar and had been responsible for implementing the bequest. If undue pressure was involved, Winans would have been required to disavow his prior statements to Lowenthal in order to acknowledge the pressure, something he might have been reluctant to do in Lowenthal's presence. The notary public was a complete stranger to Winans. There is no testimony her presence was explained to Winans to his satisfaction, nor any other reason to believe he would have been at ease discussing an intimate and difficult subject in her presence. . . .

3. *"Independent" Attorney*
. . . The statutory text of section 21351, subdivision (b) does not define "independent." . . . [Discussion of legislative history omitted—Ed.] . . . [11] [We conclude] an attorney is

---

[11] Timar also argues we should adopt the definition of "independent attorney" found in a recent report of the California Law Revision Commission, which was directed by the Legislature in 2006 to study various aspects of donative transfer restrictions. (Stats. 2006, ch. 215, § 1.) The report recommends defining "independent attorney" to require an attorney with no "legal, business, financial, professional, or personal relationship" with the disqualified person. (Recommendation: Donative Transfer Restrictions (Oct. 2008) 38 Cal. Law Revision Com. Rep. 107 (2008) pp. 133–134, 145.) The report

"independent" . . . if the attorney's personal circumstances do not prevent him or her from forming a disinterested judgment about the validity of the bequest.

There is clearly a triable issue of fact as to Coyle's ability to form a disinterested judgment about the validity of the bequest. . . . Because of the large size of the estate, his statutory fee as executor would be quite large. Had he refused to certify the bequest to Timar, he could have placed his participation as executor in jeopardy, thereby risking loss of the fee. In addition, Coyle shared an office with the drafter, Lowenthal, and had been involved in Winans's formulation of his bequests. Together, these factors raise a triable issue of fact as to Coyle's ability to evaluate the validity of the bequest to Timar with disinterest. . . .

III. DISPOSITION

Because we find a triable issue of fact with respect to the validity of the certificate of independent review and the issues of undue influence and testamentary capacity, summary judgment on appellants' will contest is reversed. The matter is remanded to the probate court for further proceedings consistent with this decision.

NOTES:

1. The definition of "independent attorney" adopted in § 21370 includes the language mentioned by the court in footnote 11 and also includes a provision disqualifying an attorney who would be appointed as a fiduciary or receive any pecuniary benefit as a result of the operation of the instrument reviewed.

2. Attorney found to have drafted or transcribed will and trust naming himself trustee and beneficiary properly held liable for $1,256,971 attorney fees, denied compensation for services as trustee, and denied reimbursement for expenses; fees and expenses benefited only attorney, not the trust. **Butler v. LeBoeuf**, 248 Cal. App. 4th 198, 203 Cal. Rptr. 3d 572 (2016).

Planning for and Avoiding a Will Contest: California's No-Contest Clause Statutes

California adopted a set of no contest clause statutes in 1990 as a result of a Law Revision Commission recommendation. Section 21320, the so-called safe harbor provision, allowed a declaratory judgment action to determine whether a particular action would trigger application of a no contest clause. So much litigation followed that the Law Revision Commission was directed in 2005 to revisit the no contest clause statutes.

---

provides no explanation for the source of the proposed definition, and we find it unpersuasive as evidence of legislative intent.

As a result of the Commission's 2007 recommendation, a new set of no contest clause statutes was adopted in 2008 to become effective January 1, 2010. The statutes that follow are the new ones, which apply to instruments that become irrevocable on or after January 1, 2001. For the statutes that apply prior to January, 2010, and to instruments that became irrevocable before 2001, see CPC §§ 21300-21307 and § 21320.

NOTE: In **Donkin v. Donkin**, 58 Cal. 4th 412, 314 P.3d 780 (2013), the California Supreme Court thoroughly reviewed the history of the no contest clause statutes and concluded that the old law allowing a safe harbor petition applied to petitions pending on the effective date of the new law with respect to instruments that became irrevocable after January 1, 2001, but that the new law applies to determine enforceability of the no-contest clauses in the instrument.

CPC § 21310. Contest Clause Definitions

As used in this part:

(a) "Contest" means a pleading filed with the court by a beneficiary that would result in a penalty under a no contest clause, if the no contest clause is enforced.

(b) "Direct contest" means a contest that alleges the invalidity of a protected instrument or one or more of its terms, based on one or more of the following grounds:

(1) Forgery.

(2) Lack of due execution.

(3) Lack of capacity.

(4) Menace, duress, fraud, or undue influence.

(5) Revocation of a will pursuant to Section 6120, revocation of a trust pursuant to Section 15401, or revocation of an instrument other than a will or trust pursuant to the procedure for revocation that is provided by statute or by the instrument.

(6) Disqualification of a beneficiary under Section 6112 21350, or 21380.

(c) "No contest clause" means a provision in an otherwise valid instrument that, if enforced, would penalize a beneficiary for filing a pleading in any court.

(d) "Pleading" means a petition, complaint, cross-complaint, objection, answer, response, or claim.

(e) "Protected instrument" means all of the following instruments:

(1) The instrument that contains the no contest clause.

(2) An instrument that is in existence on the date that the instrument containing the no contest clause is executed and is expressly identified in the no contest clause, either individually or as part of an identifiable class of instruments, as being governed by the no contest clause.

(Stats. 2008, 2010)

CPC § 21311. Enforcement of No Contest Clause

(a) A no contest clause shall only be enforced against the following types of contests:

(1) A direct contest that is brought without probable cause.

(2) A pleading to challenge a transfer of property on the grounds that it was not the transferor's property at the time of the transfer. A no contest clause shall only be enforced under this paragraph if the no contest clause expressly provides for that application.

(3) The filing of a creditor's claim or prosecution of an action based on it. A no contest clause shall only be enforced under this paragraph if the no contest clause expressly provides for that application.

(b) For the purposes of this section, probable cause exists if, at the time of filing a contest, the facts known to the contestant would cause a reasonable person to believe that there is a reasonable likelihood that the requested relief will be granted after an opportunity for further investigation or discovery.

(Stats. 2008)

NOTE: Urick v. Urick, 15 Cal. App. 5th 1182, 224 Cal. Rptr. 3d 125 (2017) held that the anti-SLAPP statute (CCP § 425.16) applies to a petition to enforce a no-contest clause. The contest, a petition to reform the trust to change beneficiaries, is a pleading filed with the probate court, which is a protected activity. But the order granting contestant's motion to strike was reversed because the beneficiary who filed the petition to enforce the no-contest clause established a reasonable probability of prevailing on the merits.

CPC § 21312. Construction of No Contest Clause

In determining the intent of the transferor, a no contest clause shall be strictly construed.

(Stats. 2008)

CPC § 21313. Not Complete Codification; Common Law Continues to Apply

This part is not intended as a complete codification of the law governing enforcement of a no contest clause. The common law governs enforcement of a no contest clause to the extent this part does not apply.

(Stats. 2008)

CPC § 21314. Application Despite Contrary Provision in Instrument

This part applies notwithstanding a contrary provision in the instrument.

(Stats. 2008)

CPC § 21315. Effective Date

(a) This part applies to any instrument, whenever executed, that became irrevocable on or after January 1, 2001.

(b) This part does not apply to an instrument that became irrevocable before January 1, 2001. (Stats. 2008)

Third amendment to trust not a "protected instrument": general incorporation by reference of terms of second amendment which included a no-contest clause not sufficient

AVILES v. SWEARINGEN

Court of Appeal, Second District, Division 6
16 Cal. App. 5th 485, 224 Cal. Rptr. 3d 686 (2017)

YEGAN, J. In this case of first impression, we apply newly enacted Probate Code section 21310. If, in theory, this could lead to a debatable result, so be it. There is no "play in the joints" in probate law, as Chief Justice Rehnquist would say. We "strictly" follow probate law as given to us by the Legislature.

Tracy J. Swearingen appeals from an order denying her petition to enforce a no contest clause and disinherit Jose Francisco Aviles as a trust beneficiary of the Margaret B. Chappell Living Trust. The trial court found that the trust Third Amendment and Restatement (hereafter Third Amendment), which contains general language of incorporation of a prior trust amendment, did not specifically refer to a no contest clause. It also found that the Third Amendment was not a "protected instrument" within the meaning of Probate Code section 21310.[1] Finally, it ordered appellant's removal as trustee, pendente lite, without prejudice to her reinstatement should she prevail at trial on Aviles' petition to invalidate the Third Amendment.

We affirm the order denying the petition to disinherit respondent. The purported appeal from the order removing appellant as trustee pending trial is dismissed because it is not a final appealable order.[2]

Facts and Procedural History

Margaret B. Chappell (Peggy) created the . . . Trust in 2010 and amended the trust three times before succumbing to cancer on January 12, 2016. The original trust instrument was a comprehensive 34-page document drafted by counsel. It provided that Peggy's boyfriend, respondent Jose Francisco Aviles, would receive all the trust assets on Peggy's death. The First Amendment provided that Aviles would receive Peggy's real property and directed that the

---

[1] All statutory references are to the Probate Code.

[2] At the eleventh hour, the parties declare that they have settled the underlying case. They ask for dismissal of the appeal. The request is denied. It is untimely. In addition, we elect to reach the merits of the first impression issue which has statewide importance to the probate bar.

remaining trust assets be distributed as follows: 50 percent to Peggy's brother and 50 percent to be divided equally between the children of Peggy's nieces and nephews. The Second Amendment provided that Aviles would receive Peggy's real property and 50 percent of the remaining trust assets would be distributed to her brother and 50 percent to Peggy's godchildren.

In 2015, Peggy suffered a relapse of cancer and entrusted appellant with her estate planning documents. Peggy complained to others that appellant had read the trust documents. Appellant confronted Peggy about the disposition of trust assets. In the months that followed, Peggy executed the Third Amendment without the advice of counsel.[3] The Third Amendment changed the trust remainder beneficiary provision to make appellant the sole remainder beneficiary and successor trustee. It incorporated by reference the unchanged provisions of the Second Amendment and provided: "These Articles once included, and along with any Articles not amended, shall result in the Third Amendment and Restatement of the Trust Agreement for the Living Trust of Margaret B. Chappell."

After Peggy died, Aviles filed a petition to invalidate the Third Amendment on the ground that it was the product of undue influence and financial abuse. The petition alleged that appellant and her husband owned and operated a marijuana dispensary, that they supplied Peggy marijuana without a medical approval, that Peggy became addicted to marijuana, and was a dependent adult within the meaning of section 21366. It also alleged that appellant was Peggy's "care custodian" (§ 21362), and coerced Peggy to disinherit her brother and godchildren and name appellant remainder beneficiary of the trust. While Peggy was on her deathbed, appellant and her agents allegedly took 1. a valuable collection of vintage wine from Peggy's home; 2. her Mercedes; 3. an expensive collection of purses; 4. Peggy's jewelry box; and 5. control of Peggy's bank accounts including a safe deposit box that held a $100,000 jewelry collection.

Appellant opposed the petition and filed a counter petition to disinherit Aviles alleging that he violated the no contest clause in the Second Amendment by challenging the Third Amendment.

Thereafter, respondent filed a motion to enjoin appellant from using trust assets to fund her defense of the trust contest. (See *Doolittle v. Exchange Bank* (2015) 241 Cal.App.4th 529, 546, 193 Cal.Rptr.3d 818 [trial court may enjoin trustee's use of trust funds to defend a challenge to a trust where there is a likelihood of prevailing on the contest].) The motion and appellant's petition to disinherit respondent were heard at the same time. Denying the petition, the trial court ruled that the Third Amendment was not a "protected instrument" as defined by section 21310 because the instrument did not contain a no contest clause or expressly reference the no contest clause in the Second Amendment. With respect to the motion to enjoin appellant's use of the trust funds to defend against the petition to invalidate the Third Amendment, the

---

[3] Where, as here, the settler has substantial assets, he or she should not attempt to dispose of them without the guiding hand of counsel. As Rankeillor, the lawyer, said, "I often think the happiest consequences seem to flow when a gentleman consults his lawyer, and takes all the law allows him." (Stevenson, Kidnapped (1913) p. 268.)

trial court removed appellant as trustee, pendente lite, and appointed a professional fiduciary to act as trustee.

No Contest Clause

. . . No contest clauses are valid in California and are favored by the public policies of discouraging litigation and giving effect to the settlor's expressed purposes. Competing public policies, however, also exist. The court must strictly construe a no contest clause because it works a forfeiture and may not be extended beyond its plainly intended function. Our courts have narrowly construed no contest clauses even where the trust amendment expressly confirms and ratifies the provisions of the trust. (*Perrin v. Lee* (2008) 164 Cal.App.4th 1239, 1242, 79 Cal.Rptr.3d 885; *Townsend v. Townsend* (2009) 171 Cal.App.4th 389, 392, 89 Cal.Rptr.3d 760.)

. . . Appellant concedes the Third Amendment does not have a no contest clause. At issue is whether the Third Amendment is a "protected instrument" because it incorporates by reference the no contest clause in the Second Amendment without specifically mentioning it. Appellant claims that Peggy intended to include the no contest clause in the Third Amendment because the Third Amendment incorporates all of the terms of the Second Amendment not amended by the Third Amendment. Article 16 of the Second Amendment, which contains the no contest clause, states that a "protected instrument" shall include "any and all amendments" to the Trust Agreement.

The no contest clause and its application to future trust amendments is strictly construed. (§ 21312.) Under . . . § 21310, subd. (e)(2), the no contest clause is not enforceable unless it is set forth verbatim in the Third Amendment or the Third Amendment expressly refers to the no contest clause in the Second Amendment. Section 21310, subdivision (e), which became operative January 1, 2010, requires that the "protected instrument" either contain the no contest clause (subd. (e)(1)), or that the instrument be *"in existence on the date that the instrument containing the no contest is executed and is expressly identified in the no contest clause . . . ."* . . .

Simply stated, the no contest clause in the Second Amendment, does not apply to future trust amendments, such as the Third Amendment, unless the amendment specifically refers to the no contest clause.

In 2008, the Legislature enacted Section 21310 based on the recommendation of the Law Revision Commission to simplify the law, to balance conflicting public policies, and to limit the enforcement of no contest clauses to direct contests brought without probable cause, to creditor claims, and to challenges to the transferor's (i.e., settlor's) ownership of property at time of transfer. (*Donkin v. Donkin* (2013) 58 Cal.4th 412, 426, 165 Cal.Rptr.3d 476, 314 P.3d 780.) The Law Revision Commission warned "that other public policy concerns 'can trump a transferor's intention to create a no contest clause.' . . . It noted that " '[e]xperienced practitioners are well aware that the no contest clause is a favorite device of undue influencers and those who use duress to become the (unnatural) object of a decedent's bounty.' " (Recommendation on Revision of No Contest Clause Statute (Jan. 2008) 37 Cal. Law Revision

Com. Rep. (2007) p. 388 (Revision Rep.).)

Appellant claims that the no contest clause in the Second Amendment trumps section 21310, subdivision (e)(2), but that would violate section 21314 which provides that "[t]his part applies notwithstanding a contrary provision in the instrument." (See *Giammarrusco v. Simon* (2009) 171 Cal.App.4th 1586, 1615, 91 Cal.Rptr.3d 50 [if instrument contains a no contest clause that is inconsistent with the revised law, the clause will be disregarded].) Although no contest clauses are favored by the public policies of discouraging litigation and giving effect to the trustor's intent, they are also disfavored by the policy against forfeitures and may not extend beyond what plainly was the settlor's intent. (*Meyer v. Meyer* (2008) 162 Cal.App.4th 983, 991, 76 Cal.Rptr.3d 546.) "In determining the intent of the [settlor], a no contest clause shall be strictly construed." (§ 21312.)

We cannot say that Peggy unequivocally expressed her intent to apply the no contest clause to petitions contesting trust amendments that are the product of fraud or undue influence. Application of the clause here would defy common sense. "An instrument that is the product of menace, duress, fraud, or undue influence is not an expression of the transferor's free will and should not be enforced." (Revision Rep., *supra*, at p. 370.) We are guided by the fundamental truism that—put bluntly—the law is not an ass. (See Charles Dickens, *Oliver Twist* 333 (Dover Thrift ed., Dover Publications 2002) (1983) [" 'If the law supposes that,' said Mr. Bumble, squeezing his hat emphatically in both hands, 'the law is a ass—a idiot' "].)

Pendente Lite Order Removing Appellant as Trustee

Appellant contends that the trial court abused its discretion in removing her as trustee. This was a pendente lite order and "without prejudice." It is not appealable. Section 1304, subdivision (a) makes appealable any *"final order"* under section 17200 including an order removing a trustee (§ 17200, subd. (b)(1)).

Disposition

The judgment (order denying petition to disinherit respondent) is affirmed. The purported appeal from the (order removing appellant as trustee) is dismissed. In light of the settlement of the underlying litigation, we do not award costs.

We concur: GILBERT, P. J., PERREN, J.

No Contest Clause Forcing Election Between Filing Creditors' Claims for Child & Spousal Support and Gifts Under Trust Not Against Public Policy

COLBURN v. THE NORTHERN TRUST COMPANY

Court of Appeal, Second District, Division 1
151 Cal. App. 4th 439, 59 Cal. Rptr. 3d 828 (as modified June 4, 2007)

VOGEL, J. . . . Richard D. Colburn married Jacqueline Colburn in May 1998. They had two children, Daisy (born in 1998) and Franklin (born in 2000), then divorced in January 2002.

The Dissolution Judgment

A final judgment based on a stipulated marital settlement agreement obligated Richard (and, in the event of his death, his estate) to pay child support (tax free to Jacqueline) of $4,000 per month per child until majority, marriage, emancipation, or death . . . , to provide medical and dental care for the children. . . , and to pay monthly spousal support of $8,333 to Jacqueline until her death, non-modifiable and not terminable on her remarriage or his death . . . . In addition, the marital judgment obligated Richard to deposit into a separate irrevocable trust the amount of $950,000 for the children . . . , and to include in his estate plan an irrevocable trust or annuity sufficient to make annual tax-free payments of $100,000 to Jacqueline until her death, with any remainder passing to the Colburn Foundation, a charitable trust.

The Richard D. Colburn Trust

Richard created the Richard D. Colburn Trust in 1969, and amended and restated it in November 2002 (after the dissolution of his marriage to Jacqueline). The trust includes various provisions designed to comply "with and . . . carry out the obligations imposed upon [Richard] and [his] estate by the [marital] judgment." . . .

In addition to and independent of Richard's obligations under the marital judgment, the trust creates separate $3 million trusts for Daisy and Franklin. . . .

The trust includes this no contest clause:

"1. I have intentionally and with full knowledge omitted to provide for my heirs, except for such provisions, if any, as are made specifically in this trust and my Will. If any person, who is or claims under or through a beneficiary of this trust, in any manner whatsoever, directly or indirectly, contests or attacks this trust or my Will, takes any action that would frustrate the dispositive plan contemplated in this trust or my Will, conspires or cooperates with anyone attempting to contest, attack, or frustrate this trust or my Will, or takes any of the actions set forth in items (a) through (d) below of this paragraph . . . , then in that event I specifically disinherit each such Objector. In that event, any portion of the trust estate not disposed of under the foregoing provisions of this trust shall be distributed to the Colburn Foundation. For purposes of this Part, the following actions shall constitute a contest: (a) filing a creditor's claim or prosecution of an action based thereon, (b) commencing any legal action or proceeding to determine the character of property, (c) challenging the validity of any instrument, contract, agreement, beneficiary designation, or other document executed by me and pertaining to the disposition of my assets (including the beneficiary designation of any annuity, insurance policy, retirement plan, or buy-sell agreement), and (d) petitioning for settlement or for compromise affecting the terms of this trust or my Will, or for interpretation of this trust or my Will. Notwithstanding the foregoing but subject to paragraph 2 below, this paragraph 1 shall not apply to any person solely by reason of such person taking an action described in items (a) through (d) above, if such action is unopposed by the Trustee . . . .

"2. On January 30, 2002, a judgment of dissolution of marriage was entered . . . dissolving my marriage to [Jacqueline] . . . . I have set forth provisions above in this instrument to fulfill all obligations I may have to [Jacqueline], Daisy, and Franklin pursuant to the terms of the [dissolution judgment]. I specifically intend that if [Jacqueline] (or any personal representative or agent of [Jacqueline]) (a) raises any claim that she has a community property interest in any asset of this trust or my estate, (b) files a creditor's claim in my estate or against this trust or prosecutes any action based thereon, or (c) in any other manner makes any claim against this trust, my estate, the Colburn Music Fund, the Colburn Foundation, then, in that event, [Jacqueline] and all of her descendants (including Daisy and Franklin) shall be deemed to be Objectors as provided in paragraph 1 above, and for all purposes hereof, they each shall be deemed to have predeceased me . . . .

"3. If [Jacqueline], either on her own behalf or in any other manner [or through any other person] commences . . . any legal proceeding of any form and/or nature against me and/or [the individual trustees], my estate, this Trust or any other trust established by me during my lifetime, my personal representatives [or any of his charitable entities or family members], then I hereby provide that such action shall constitute a contest of this trust and my Will, and I hereby disinherit [Jacqueline] and all [of her] descendants . . . (including Daisy and Franklin). . . ."

The Northern Trust Company and three of Richard's six adult children (Richard W. Colburn, Keith W. Colburn, and Carol C. Hogel) were named as the Trustees of Richard's trust.

Richard died on June 3, 2004, and the Trustees thereafter initiated procedures to require anyone asserting a claim against the trust's assets (including claims based on money judgments) to first present a creditor's claim to the Trustees. . . .

In October, Jacqueline filed two safe harbor applications (one for herself, and one on behalf of the children which was subsequently prosecuted by Barbara D. Bergstein as the children's guardian ad litem) in which she asked the probate court to determine whether creditor's claims for spousal and child support and other funds she claimed pursuant to the marital judgment (a total of $8,551,890 for her and $4,687,000 for the children) or, in the children's case, an order to show cause for modification of child support as an alternative to a creditor's claim ($4,687,000), would violate the trust's no contest clause. . . . In a nutshell, Jacqueline and the children claimed the provisions of Richard's trust did not fully satisfy the obligations imposed on his estate by the marital judgment, and that their proposed creditor's claims would carry out, not frustrate, his stated intention to have the trust fulfill his obligations under the marital judgment.

The Trustees, joined by the Colburn Foundation, opposed both applications . . . .

In July 2005, the probate court signed and filed an order finding (1) that Jacqueline's proposed creditor's claim, if filed, *would* violate the trust's no contest clause, (2) that the children's proposed creditor's claim, if filed, *would* violate the trust's no contest clause, but (3) that an application for an order to show cause for modification of child support, if filed, would *not* violate the no contest clause because the clause is "unenforceable as against public policy with respect to modification of child support."

Jacqueline and the guardian ad litem appeal from the order insofar as it finds that their proposed creditor's claims would violate the no contest clause, and the Trustees appeal from the order to the extent it holds that an application for an order to show cause for modification of child support would not violate the no contest clause.

DISCUSSION

I. Jacqueline's and the Children's Appeals

Jacqueline and the children contend their proposed creditor's claims would not violate the no contest clause. We disagree. . . .

A no contest clause may result in a "forced election" where a beneficiary is obligated to choose between two inconsistent or alternative rights or claims because the testator or trustor clearly intended that the beneficiary not enjoy both. . . . Put another way, a claimant cannot at the same time take the benefits under a testamentary instrument and repudiate the losses; she must accept the terms in toto, or reject them in toto. . . . Where a beneficiary has rights independent of the testamentary document, a no contest clause necessarily creates a forced election. . . .

Richard's no contest clause is a paradigm of clarity and unequivocally states his intent. . . .

By its plain terms, the no contest clause bars the creditor's claims proposed by Jacqueline and the children. . . . By its substantive provisions, the trust itself confirms Richard's intent to have the trust perform all of his obligations under the marital judgment-while at the same time giving $3 million gifts to each of his children. Quite plainly, he did everything within his power to ensure that Jacqueline and the children would accept his gifts without challenging his overall testamentary plan, while at the same time forcing their election so that their challenge to the trust, if made, would leave them to their remedies under the marital dissolution judgment.

To avoid this result, Jacqueline and the children offer a variety of arguments, none of which have merit. . . .

Jacqueline and the children contend that, assuming their proposed creditor's claims trigger the no contest clause, public policy considerations (the enforcement of spousal and child support

147

orders) bar enforcement of the no contest clause in this case. We disagree.

Enforcement of the no contest clause extinguishes Richard's testamentary gifts to Jacqueline and the children but it in no way prevents them from enforcing Richard's support obligations under the marital judgment. As our Supreme Court explained in *Burch v. George* . . . [7 Cal. 4th 246, 866 P.2d 92 (1994)], where the decedent's widow advanced essentially the same argument, claiming that enforcement of a no contest clause impaired and effectively prohibited enforcement of her community property rights, "while the enforcement of a no contest clause might work a forfeiture of a surviving spouse's conditional right to take under the trust instrument, it does not . . . work any forfeiture or conversion of the spouse's community property." . . . The same is true about spousal and child support because here, as in *Burch,* the no contest clause does not deprive the former spouse or children of their right to support under the marital judgment, nor does it hinder their ability to assert those interests. To the extent Jacqueline and the children believe their claims under the marital judgment are payable by Richard's estate, they are free to pursue those claims at their option. . . .

That Jacqueline and the children would thereby relinquish their conditional right to take under Richard's trust is a given—because equity supports enforcement of the no contest clause against beneficiaries asserting support claims against the trust's assets when those claims would plainly frustrate the trustor's intent and expectations. "There is considerable unfairness in allowing a [former] spouse [and her children] to accept a will or trust instrument to the extent it confers a benefit, and at the same time attack the instrument to the extent it does not. Under such circumstances, the [former] spouse [and her children] would receive a windfall to the detriment of other beneficiaries." (*Burch v. George,* . . . [9])

We reject the children's challenge to the specific provision in the trust that a creditor's claim by Jacqueline would disinherit not only her but also the children (as Jacqueline's "descendants"). First, the issue was not raised in either of the safe harbor petitions and thus is not before us on this appeal. Second, the issue is premature—and will ripen only if Jacqueline ultimately relinquishes her rights under the trust and pursues a creditor's claim but the children do the opposite by choosing the trust and relinquishing their rights under the marital judgment. . . . For this reason, and because the public policy issue could not be determined without factual findings about the benefits and burdens of the compelled election, the point is outside the scope of the safe harbor petitions. (Compare *Estate of Ferber* (1998), 66 Cal. App. 4th 244, 251, 77 Cal. Rptr. 2d 774 [when a public policy issue is raised in a safe harbor petition, it may be considered only when it can be disposed of as a matter of law, without

---

[9] Conversely, there is nothing patently unfair about this compelled election. As we noted in *Tunstall v. Wells* (2006) 144 Cal. App. 4th 554, 565, 50 Cal. Rptr. 3d 468, a testator has the right to grant bequests subject to any lawful conditions he may select, and it is not for us or any court to question the testator's selected approach. Unlike us, Richard knew Jacqueline and did everything required to compel her to choose between keeping the rights she had negotiated and obtained under the marital judgment or relinquishing those rights in order to gain some other benefit under his trust. It is also worth noting that, in addition to Jacqueline and her children, Richard had five adult children and one adult stepson from a prior marriage—and was contemplating a new marriage at the time of his 2002 amendment to his trust.

reference to factual matters].) . . .

II. *The Trustees' Appeal*

The Trustees contend the trial court erred in finding that an application for an order to show cause to modify child support would not violate the no contest clause. We agree.

As the children concede, a creditor's claim is a prerequisite to an application for an order to show cause to modify child support. (§§ 19004, 19300.) As explained above, a creditor's claim would violate the no contest clause. As necessarily follows, the children must choose between their rights under the marital judgment and those given by the trust. Any other result would be a windfall for the children, a disservice to the trust's other beneficiaries, and a blatant violation of Richard's testamentary plan. . . .

Section E. Tortious Interference with an Expectancy

California Recognizes Tort of Intentional Interference with Expected Inheritance

BECKWITH v. DAHL

Court of Appeal, Fourth District, Division 3
205 Cal. App. 4th 1039, 141 Cal. Rptr. 3d 142 (2012)

O'LEARY, P.J. Brent Beckwith appeals from a judgment of dismissal entered after the trial court sustained without leave to amend Susan Dahl's demurrer to his complaint alleging intentional interference with an expected inheritance (IIEI) and deceit by false promise. Beckwith argues we should join the majority of other states in recognizing the tort of IIEI as a valid cause of action.[1] We agree it is time to officially recognize this tort claim. In addition, in this opinion we have clarified why IIEI and the cause of action, deceit by false promise, address different wrongs. We conclude Beckwith's complaint alleged sufficient facts to support a claim for deceit, but there are currently insufficient facts stated to allege IIEI. Given the unique circumstances of this case, Beckwith must be afforded an opportunity to amend the complaint if he believes he can allege the facts necessary to support an IIEI claim as delineated in this opinion. We reverse the judgment of dismissal and the order sustaining the demurrer. The matter is remanded for further proceedings.

FACTS & PROCEDURE

1. Marc Christian MacGinnis

Beckwith and his partner, Marc Christian MacGinnis (MacGinnis), were in a long-term, committed relationship for almost 10 years. They leased an apartment together and were occasional business partners. MacGinnis had no children and his parents were deceased. His

---

[1] This court invited amicus curiae briefing from the Consumer Attorneys of California, the Civil Justice Association of California, the Family Research Council, and the National Center for Lesbian Rights.

sister, Susan Dahl, with whom he had an estranged relationship, was his only other living family. At some point during their relationship, MacGinnis showed Beckwith a will he had saved on his computer. The will stated that upon MacGinnis's death, his estate was to be divided equally between Beckwith and Dahl. MacGinnis never printed or signed the will.

In May 2009, MacGinnis's health began to decline. On May 25, 2009, MacGinnis was in the hospital awaiting surgery to repair holes in his lungs. He asked Beckwith to locate and print the will so he could sign it. Beckwith went to their home and looked for the will, but he could not find it. When Beckwith told MacGinnis that he could not locate the will, MacGinnis asked Beckwith to create a new will so he could sign it the next day. That night, Beckwith created a new will for MacGinnis using forms downloaded from the Internet. The will stated: " 'I [MacGinnis] give all the rest, residue and remainder of my property and estate, both real and personal, of whatever kind and wherever located, that I own or to which I shall be in any manner entitled at the time of my death (collectively referred to as my "residuary estate"), as follows: (a) If Brent Beckwith and Susan Dahl survive me, to those named in clause (a) who survive me in equal shares.' "

Before Beckwith presented the will to MacGinnis, he called Dahl to tell her about the will and e-mailed her a copy. Later that night, Dahl responded to Beckwith's e-mail stating: " 'I really think we should look into a Trust for [MacGinnis]. There are far less regulations and it does not go through probate. The house and all property would be in *our names* and if something should happen to [MacGinnis] *we* could make decisions without it going to probate and the taxes are less on a trust rather than the normal inheritance tax. I have [two] very good friends [who] are attorneys and I will call them tonight.' [Emphasis added.]" After receiving the e-mail, Beckwith called Dahl to discuss the details of the living trust. Dahl told Beckwith not to present the will to MacGinnis for signature because one of her friends would prepare the trust documents for MacGinnis to sign "in the next couple [of] days." Beckwith did not present the will to MacGinnis.

Two days later, on May 27, MacGinnis had surgery on his lungs. Although the doctors informed Dahl there was a chance MacGinnis would not survive the surgery, the doctors could not discuss the matter with Beckwith since he was not a family member under the law. Nor did Dahl tell Beckwith about the risks associated with the surgery. Dahl never gave MacGinnis any trust documents to sign. After the surgery, MacGinnis was placed on a ventilator and his prognosis worsened. Six days later, Dahl, following the doctors' recommendations, removed MacGinnis from the ventilator. On June 2, 2009, MacGinnis died intestate. He left an estate worth over $1 million.

2. The Probate Proceedings
Following MacGinnis's death, Beckwith and Dahl met to discuss the disposition of MacGinnis's personal property. After Beckwith suggested they find the will that MacGinnis prepared, Dahl told Beckwith "we don't need a will." Two weeks after MacGinnis' death, on June 17, 2009, Dahl opened probate in Los Angeles Superior Court. Dahl verbally informed Beckwith that she had opened probate, but she did not send him any copies of the probate filings. In the filing, she did not identify Beckwith as an interested party. Dahl also applied to

become the administrator of the estate.

In September 2009, Beckwith began to ask Dahl for details of the probate case. Dahl informed Beckwith that she had not had any contact with the probate attorney so she did not know anything. On October 2, 2009, Beckwith looked up the probate case online. He then sent Dahl an e-mail stating: "'In case you hadn't had a chance to talk to speak [*sic*] with the probate attorney, I looked up [MacGinnis's] probate case on-line *http://www.lasuperiorcourt.org/ Probate/* and the next hearing date is not until 8/27/10, so unfortunately as expected it is going to take over a year from [MacGinnis's] passing until we get *our proceeds* from the estate.' [Emphasis added.]" When Dahl did not respond, Beckwith sent her another e-mail on December 2, 2009, asking if she needed any information from him regarding the distribution of MacGinnis's assets. Again, Dahl did not respond. Beckwith e-mailed Dahl again on December 18, 2009, asking about the probate proceedings. This time Dahl responded by e-mail, stating: "'Because [MacGinnis] died without a will, and the estate went into probate, I was made executor of his estate. The court then declared that his assets would go to his only surviving family member which is me.'" A few weeks later, in January 2010, Dahl filed a petition with the probate court for final distribution of the estate. Beckwith filed an opposition to Dahl's petition in March 2010. After a hearing, at which Beckwith was present in *pro se*, the probate judge found that Beckwith had no standing because he was "not a creditor of the estate" and he had "no intestate rights" with regard to MacGinnis's estate.

3. The Civil Action and Demurrer
On July 30, 2010, while the probate case was still pending, Beckwith filed the instant civil action against Dahl alleging IIEI, deceit by false promise, and negligence. In the complaint, Beckwith asserted Dahl interfered with his expected inheritance of one half of MacGinnis's estate by lying to him about her intention to prepare a living trust for MacGinnis to sign. Beckwith further alleged Dahl made these false promises in order to "caus[e] a sufficient delay to prevent [MacGinnis] from signing his will before his surgery" because she knew that if MacGinnis died without a will, she would inherit the entire estate. Finally, Beckwith claimed that as a result of his reliance on Dahl's promises, "he was deprived of his . . . share of [MacGinnis's] estate," and because he had no standing in probate court, a civil action against Dahl was his only remedy.

Dahl demurred to all three causes of action. . . .

DISCUSSION
. . . [T]he threshold question before this court is whether California should recognize a tort remedy for IIEI.

a. Background of the Tort
. . . "Twenty-five of the forty-two states that have considered . . . [the tort of IIEI] have validated it." (Klein, "*Go West, Disappointed Heir*": *Tortious Interference with Expectations of Inheritance—A Survey with Analysis of State Approaches, in the Pacific States* (2009) 13 Lewis & Clark L.Rev. 209, 226 (hereafter *Go West*).) The United States Supreme Court called the tort "widely recognized." (*Marshall v. Marshall* (2006) 547 U.S. 293, 312 . . . .) In addition, IIEI is outlined

in section 774B of the Restatement Second of Torts. . . .

In general, most states recognizing the tort adopt it with the following elements: (1) an expectation of receiving an inheritance; (2) intentional interference with that expectancy by a third party; (3) the interference was independently wrongful or tortious; (4) there was a reasonable certainty that, but for the interference, the plaintiff would have received the inheritance; and (5) damages. . . . Most states prohibit an interference action when the plaintiff already has an adequate probate remedy. . . .

b. Policy Considerations

. . . The tort of IIEI developed under the "general principle of law that whenever the law prohibits an injury it will also afford a remedy." . . . Similarly, it is a maxim of California jurisprudence that, "[f]or every wrong there is a remedy." (Civ. Code, § 3523.) . . .

One policy concern that stands out is the effect that recognition of the tort could have on the probate system. . . . Recognition of the IIEI tort could enable plaintiffs to usurp a testator's true intent by bypassing the. . . stringent probate requirements. . . . "'If we were to permit, much less encourage, dual litigation tracks for disgruntled heirs, we would risk destabilizing the law of probate and creating uncertainty and inconsistency in its place. We would risk undermining the legislative intent inherent in creating the Probate Code as the preferable, if not exclusive, remedy for disputes over testamentary documents.'" . . . *Wilson v. Fritschy* (N.M.Ct.App.2002) . . . 55 P.3d 997, 1002.) These are very valid concerns that warrant this court's attention.

. . . A "majority of the states which have adopted the tort of interference with an inheritance have achieved such a balance by prohibiting a tort action to be brought where the remedy of a will contest is available and would provide the injured party with adequate relief." . . . [citation omitted] By applying a similar last recourse requirement to the tort in California, the integrity of the probate system is protected because where a probate remedy is available, it must be pursued. In addition, the only plaintiffs who will be able to utilize the tort are those who lack an adequate probate remedy *because of the interference of another*. In a sense, the interfering tortfeasor has "obtained the benefit of the testamentary intent rule by committing a tort against a third party . . . ." (*Allen v. Hall* (1999) 328 Or. 276, 974 P.2d 199, 203 . . . .) Allowing those so harmed to bring a tort action "still would give defendants all the benefits that the testamentary intent rule calls for them to receive. Once possessed of those benefits, however, defendants would be liable to respond in damages for torts that they may have committed—a separate legal inquiry with its own societal justifications." . . .

Another common reason cited against recognition is that the IIEI tort is contrary to the principle that gratuitous promises are generally not enforceable. . . . Therefore, the argument goes, it would be inconsistent to allow a prospective beneficiary to recover against a third party for interfering with an expectancy when the prospective beneficiary could not legally enforce the same promise against the testator. However, California already recognizes other interference torts that protect only *expectancies* of future economic benefits that could not be enforced directly. (See *Reeves v. Hanlon* (2004) 33 Cal. 4th 1140, 1144, 17 Cal. Rptr. 3d 289, 95

P.3d 513 [interference with at-will employment relations]; *Korea Supply Co. v. Lockheed Martin Corp.* (2003) 29 Cal. 4th 1134, 1153, 131 Cal. Rptr. 2d 29, 63 P.3d 937 [interference with prospective economic advantage]; *Speegle v. Board of Fire Underwriters* (1946) 29 Cal.2d 34, 39, 172 P.2d 867 [interference with at-will contract] . . . .)

Closely related is the concern that an expectancy in an inheritance is too speculative to warrant a tort remedy because the testator may have changed his mind notwithstanding any interference from a third party. . . . However, where there is a strong probability that an expected inheritance would have been received absent the alleged interference, whether or not the decedent changed his mind is a question of fact necessary to prove an element of the tort and is not a reason to refuse to recognize the existence of the tort altogether. . . . Courts have dealt with this issue with respect to other interference torts by developing "a threshold causation requirement . . . for maintaining a cause of action . . . namely, proof that it is reasonably *probable* that the lost economic advantage would have been realized but for the defendant's interference." . . . [A] similar threshold requirement is built into the IIEI tort because one of the tort's required elements is that there exists a reasonable certainty that, but for the interference, the plaintiff would have received the inheritance. . . .

[W]e conclude that a court should recognize the tort of IIEI if it is necessary to afford an injured plaintiff a remedy. . . .

c. Application to Beckwith's Complaint
. . . [A]n IIEI defendant must direct the independently tortious conduct at someone other than the plaintiff. The cases firmly indicate a requirement that "[t]he fraud, duress, undue influence, or other independent tortious conduct required for this tort is directed at the testator. *The beneficiary is not directly defrauded* or unduly influenced; the testator is." (*Whalen v. Prosser* (Fla.Dist.Ct.App 1998) 719 So.2d 2, 6, . . . italics added.) In other words, the defendant's tortious conduct must have induced or caused the testator to take some action that deprives the plaintiff of his expected inheritance. . . . ; see also *Schilling v. Herrera* (Fla.Dist.Ct.App.2007) 952 So.2d 1231 [defendant unduly influenced testator to execute a new will in her favor]; *Cardenas v. Schober* (Pa.Super.Ct.2001) 783 A.2d 317, 326 [defendant's intentional failure to adhere to an agreement he made with testator to draft a will in favor of the plaintiffs constituted fraud and supported a claim for intentional interference with expected inheritance].) Even in the relatively few IIEI cases we found where the defendant's wrongful conduct was directed at someone other than the testator, the defendant's interference was never directed only at the plaintiff. (See *Allen, supra,* 974 P.2d at p. 205 [defendant interfered with testator's attempts to change his will by falsely telling testator's attorney testator was not lucid].)

We must also emphasize the tort of IIEI is one for wrongful interference with an expected inheritance and not an independent action for the underlying tortious conduct such as fraud or undue influence. The underlying tort is only the means by which the interference occurs. This distinction explains the development of the tort as one designed to provide a remedy for disappointed legatees. In the absence of an IIEI cause of action, when tortious conduct causing injury to an expected legatee is directed at the testator, the injured party has no independent action in tort. Thus, probate remedies developed to provide a remedy and method of challenging a tortiously induced bequest even when no independent tort action was available. (See Prob. Code, § 6104 ["The execution or revocation of a will or a part of a will is ineffective to the extent the execution or revocation was procured by duress, menace, fraud, or undue influence"].) Similarly, the tort of IIEI developed to provide a remedy when both of these avenues failed, *i.e.*, when the plaintiff had no independent tort action because the underlying tort was directed at the testator and when the plaintiff had no adequate remedy in probate. . . . [W]hen the defendant's tortious conduct is directed at the plaintiff, rather than at the testator, the plaintiff has an independent tort claim against the defendant and asserting the IIEI tort is unnecessary and superfluous. . . .

Here, Beckwith alleged he had an expectancy in MacGinnis's estate that would have been realized but for Dahl's intentional interference. However, Beckwith did not allege Dahl directed any independently tortious conduct at MacGinnis. The only wrongful conduct alleged in Beckwith's complaint was Dahl's false promise to him. Accordingly, Beckwith's complaint failed to sufficiently allege the IIEI tort. . . .

3. Promissory Fraud

The trial court also sustained without leave to amend Beckwith's second cause of action for deceit by false promise. Under Civil Code section 1709, one is liable for fraudulent deceit if he "deceives another with intent to induce him to alter his position to his injury or risk . . . ." (Civ. Code, § 1709.) Section 1710 of the Civil Code defines deceit for the purposes of Civil Code section 1709 as, inter alia, "[a] promise, made without any intention of performing it." (Civ. Code, § 1710.) " 'The elements of fraud, which give rise to the tort action for deceit, are (a) misrepresentation (false representation, concealment, or nondisclosure); (b) knowledge of falsity (or 'scienter'); (c) intent to defraud, *i.e.*, to induce reliance; (d) justifiable reliance; and (e) resulting damage.' [Citation.]" (*Lazar v. Superior Court* (1996) 12 Cal. 4th 631, 638, 49 Cal. Rptr. 2d 377, 909 P.2d 981.) . . . As explained in more detail below, we conclude Beckwith's complaint sufficiently alleged each of the elements of fraud with the requisite specificity and particularity. . . .

. . . Beckwith alleged in his complaint he "was harmed in that he was deprived of his one half (1/2) share of [MacGinnis's] estate, and [his] reliance on [Dahl's] false promise was a substantial factor in causing that harm." Dahl contends Beckwith's damages were not causally related to the alleged fraud because the actual cause of Beckwith's injuries was MacGinnis's failure to make a will. On demurrer, however, the appropriate inquiry is whether Beckwith would have suffered the alleged damages even if he had presented MacGinnis with the will. Beckwith has alleged a causal relationship between his actions induced by Dahl's promises and his resulting damage. . . . [T]here are no facts showing Beckwith would have been damaged even if he had presented MacGinnis with the will. . . .

3. Justifiable Reliance

. . . Here, the complaint alleged that "[g]iven the circumstances, [MacGinnis's] condition, [Beckwith's] emotionally vulnerable state, and [Beckwith's] trust in [Dahl] to help effectuate [MacGinnis's] wishes, [Beckwith] reasonably relied on [Dahl's] representations that she would have trust documents prepared and that no will was necessary." Thus, the complaint contained specific allegations of facts showing why Beckwith's reliance on Dahl's promises was reasonable under the circumstances.

Dahl argues Beckwith's reliance on her promise was not justifiable because he "relied on a vague suggestion from a virtual stranger (who was purportedly estranged from the decedent at that time and had everything to gain by not having that will signed) that he should not have the decedent sign his already prepared will." However, the law is clear that "'[n]o rogue should enjoy his ill-gotten plunder for the simple reason that his victim is by chance a fool.'" (*Boeken v. Philip Morris, Inc.* (2005) 127 Cal. App. 4th 1640, 1667, 26 Cal. Rptr. 3d 638 . . . .)

Conversely, a plaintiff's reliance is not reasonable when he "put[s] faith in representations which are preposterous, or which are shown by facts within his observation to be so patently and obviously false that he must have closed his eyes to avoid discovery of the truth. . . . " (*Boeken, supra* . . . .) . . .

In this case, Dahl's alleged misrepresentations are not so preposterous or obviously false as to preclude tort liability. Beckwith has adequately pled that his reliance on Dahl's promises was reasonable under the circumstances. Therefore, Beckwith has alleged all the necessary elements of causation to sustain a claim for fraudulent deceit. . . . Beckwith has sufficiently alleged all of the elements of promissory fraud with the required specificity to state a claim. Accordingly, we conclude the trial court erred in sustaining Dahl's demurrer.

DISPOSITION
The judgment of dismissal is reversed and the matter remanded. The trial court is directed to overrule the demurrer to the promissory fraud cause of action and grant leave to amend the IIEI cause of action. Appellant shall recover his costs on appeal.

Chapter 5. Wills: Construction

General Rules for Construction of Wills, Trusts & Other Instruments

CPC § 21101. Application of Division 11, Part I (Rules for Interpreting Instruments)

Unless the provision or context otherwise requires, this part applies to a will, trust, deed, and any other instrument.

(Stats. 1994, 2002)

CPC § 21102. Intent, Construction, Extrinsic Evidence

(a) The intention of the transferor as expressed in the instrument controls the legal effect of the dispositions made in the instrument.

(b) The rules of construction in this part apply where the intention of the transferor is not indicated by the instrument.

(c) Nothing in this section limits the use of extrinsic evidence, to the extent otherwise authorized by law, to determine the intention of the transferor.

(Stats. 1994, 2002)

CPC § 21103. Transferor Can Select Law Governing Instrument

The meaning and legal effect of a disposition in an instrument is determined by the local law of a particular state selected by the transferor in the instrument unless the application of that law is contrary to the rights of the surviving spouse to community and quasi-community property, to any other public policy of this state applicable to the disposition, or, in the case of a will, to Part 3 (commencing with Section 6500) of Division 6.

(Stats. 1994, 2002)

❖ CPC § 21105. Will Passes All Property Owned at Death

Except as otherwise provided in Sections 641 and 642,[22] a will passes all property the testator owns at death, including property acquired after execution of the will.

(Stats. 1994, 2002)

---

[22] Sections 641 and 642 concern the exercise of powers of appointment. Section 641 is set forth in Chapter 12.—Ed.

Section A. Mistaken or Ambiguous Language in Wills

Issue Defined as Lineal Descendants Excluding Children Adopted in and out of Trustor's Bloodline Not Ambiguous; Review of California Cases on Finding Ambiguity

CITIZENS BUSINESS BANK v. CARRANO

Court of Appeal, Second District, Division 8
189 Cal. App. 4th 1200, 117 Cal. Rptr. 3d 119 (2010)

O'CONNELL, J. This matter stems from a dispute over whether a child born out of wedlock is a beneficiary to his biological grandparents' trust. The trial court found the trust instrument ambiguous and that his grandparents did not intend for him to be a beneficiary under their trust. We reverse because we find the terms of the trust are unambiguous and remand with instructions.

FACTS

. . . Charles and Serena Papaz created the Papaz Family Trust on August 2, 1966. Charles and Serena have one child, Christopher. Christopher fathered three children out of wedlock: . . . Only [one,] Jonathan's status is the subject of this appeal.

1. Christopher Fathers a Child Out of Wedlock

Christopher met Jonathan's mother, Kathy Carrano, when he was shot in the leg in 1984. She was Christopher's physical therapist while he was in the hospital and she continued to care for him during his recovery at his parents' home. One night, Christopher gave Kathy a drug and had sex with her without her knowledge. Jonathan was conceived that night. Kathy was married to another man at the time. Jonathan was born in August 1985. Kathy and her husband raised Jonathan as their child. A few years after he was born, Kathy learned that Jonathan was Christopher's son and not her husband's. Jonathan was never formally adopted by Kathy's husband.

Christopher, however, appeared to be aware that Jonathan was his son from the beginning. He bragged to his friend, Vahe Tatoian, when Kathy was pregnant that, "I know this is my kid." He again acknowledged Jonathan as his son to Vahe in 2004, but refused to tell his father, Charles. Serena also appeared to know that Christopher had fathered a child. At or around the time of Jonathan's birth, she mentioned to her sister that Christopher may have had a child with a nurse. Serena's sister understood that the nurse she referred to was the one who cared for Christopher while he was recovering from his gunshot wound. In any event, it is undisputed that Jonathan is Christopher's biological son.

Charles and Serena did not approve of Christopher's behavior, particularly his relationships with women and fathering children out of wedlock. They also did not trust Christopher with money and did not want to leave their entire fortune to him outright, believing he would squander it.

2. The Trust Instrument is Amended to Redefine "Issue"

As a result, they amended their trust in 1988 (the Eighth Amendment) to, among other things, enable him to receive income from the trust but not the assets themselves. . . . Under the . . . Amendment to the trust, Christopher's "issue" would receive the trust assets in the event Christopher did not survive his parents. "Issue" was defined . . . as follows:

"As used in this trust, the term 'issue' shall refer to lineal descendants of all degrees and the terms 'child,' 'children' and 'issue' shall include persons adopted into the Trustors' bloodline and shall exclude persons adopted out of the Trustors' bloodline. . . ." In 1991, Charles and Serena amended the trust a ninth time to redefine the term "issue" to expressly exclude "persons adopted into the Trustors' bloodline" and "persons adopted out of the Trustors' bloodline." If Christopher had no issue, then one half of the trust assets would go to Charles's heirs—his sister's children—and one half to Serena's heirs—her sister. . . .

In December 2006, Christopher became paralyzed from his neck down and could no longer speak. In January 2007, Kathy told both Jonathan and Charles that Christopher was Jonathan's biological father. Jonathan introduced himself to Charles, saying, "I am Jonathan, your grandson, Christopher's son." Charles "reached over and grabbed [Jonathan's] hand and said, 'I know.' " Though Jonathan visited both Christopher and Charles regularly thereafter, Charles never acknowledged him as his grandson, and in fact referred to him as "Leroy." However, there was evidence Charles acknowledged to his attorney and banker that Jonathan was his grandson during financial discussions where Jonathan was present. . . . Christopher died on June 22, 2007. His father died shortly afterwards on July 8, 2007. Serena pre-deceased Charles and Christopher . . . .

3. The Trial Over the Trust Beneficiaries

. . . In an order dated March 9, 2009, the trial court found that "Jonathan is not considered a child of Christopher." To reach this decision, the trial court held that "[t]he trust is not specific concerning the rights of someone in Jonathan's circumstances. The trust does not in its language suggest whether Christopher's child born out of wedlock and into an extant family that does not include Christopher should be included as a lineal descendant under the trust." As a result of the ambiguity, the court considered extrinsic evidence to determine the Trustors' intent. . . .

DISCUSSION

. . . Our Supreme Court's opinion in *Estate of Russell* (1968) 69 Cal.2d 200, 205–206, 70 Cal. Rptr. 561, 444 P.2d 353 lays the foundation for our interpretation of a trust instrument: "'The paramount rule in the construction of wills, to which all other rules must yield, is that a will is to be construed according to the intention of the testator as expressed therein, and this intention must be given effect as far as possible.' [Citation.]" . . . However, the court acknowledged that extrinsic evidence is "admissible 'to explain any ambiguity arising on the face of a will, or to resolve a latent ambiguity which does not so appear.' [Citation.]" . . .

Likewise, *Estate of Dye* (2001) 92 Cal. App. 4th 966, 112 Cal. Rptr. 2d 362, is instructive. The will provided that the estate be given to his wife as her "sole and separate property." An adopted-in son claimed the phrase "sole and separate property" was ambiguous thereby requiring the introduction of extrinsic evidence. The son attempted to introduce evidence to show that his adopted-out brothers should not receive anything under the will. The Court of Appeal held that the phrase was not a latent ambiguity. . . .

In contrast, the Supreme Court found ambiguity in *Estate of Dominici* (1907) 151 Cal. 181, 90 P. 448. There, the trial court found a latent ambiguity where the decedent's will identified a beneficiary by name but described a completely different person. . . . The Supreme Court upheld the admission of extrinsic evidence to explain the discrepancy. We find that this is not a case where extrinsic evidence reveals an ambiguity that must be resolved . . . .

According to respondents, the term "issue" is fairly susceptible of two or more constructions because Charles and Serena intended to restrict the meaning of "issue." They argue that it is reasonable to interpret "that a person born out of wedlock, and legally a member of another family should be treated as outside the class of 'issue.' " We disagree.

[W]e are not at liberty to rewrite the Papaz Family Trust to attach restrictions to the term "issue" that Serena and Charles did not expressly include. . . . Serena and Charles, through their lawyers, chose to define the term "issue" as a class of people who were lineal descendants of Christopher and . . . who had not been adopted into or out of the bloodline. The definition of "issue" was drafted by lawyers and amended. Neither of those restrictions apply to Jonathan, plainly Christopher's lineal descendant.[4] That Charles and Serena failed to expressly describe Jonathan's "special case" does not create a latent ambiguity. The extrinsic evidence further supports this conclusion. Christopher boasted that Jonathan was his son. Serena stated to others that she suspected Jonathan was her grandson. Charles spoke to his banker and lawyer describing Jonathan as his grandson.

While Charles and Serena were religious, conservative and disapproving of Christopher's affairs, that does not reasonably imply they intended to disinherit their biological grandchildren born out of wedlock. If Charles and Serena intended Christopher's issue only to include children who are biologically related to him and the issue of a legal marriage, they could have said so. (Estate of Casey (1982) 128 Cal. App. 3d 867, 874, 198 Cal. Rptr. 170 ["Extrinsic evidence of any type cannot be used to reach an interpretation which substitutes affirmative dispository language for silence. That would amount to rewriting the will"].)

Neither is this a case where the critical terms are undefined and we are left to interpret the trust by statutory means, as urged by respondents. In *Newman v. Wells Fargo Bank*, supra, 14 Cal. 4th 126, 59 Cal. Rptr. 2d 2, 926 P.2d 969, a case relied upon by respondents, the term "issue" was not defined. As a result, the question facing the court was, given an ambiguous provision in

---

[4] Though they indicate that the term "lineal descendent" may be ambiguous, respondents fail to provide any alternate definition for the term or even clearly state why they consider the term ambiguous. Importantly, respondents do not seriously argue that Jonathan is not Christopher's lineal descendent.

the will, which law should apply to determine whether a child adopted out of the family was among the "issue" of the testator—the law in effect at the time the will was executed or at the time of the testator's death. . . .

. . . [T]he term "issue" was clearly, simply and specifically defined by Serena and Charles. . . . Because the term "issue" is not ambiguous, we need not resort to the Probate Code or Family Code to interpret the term.

DISPOSITION

. . . The matter is remanded for entry of a new order instructing the trustee to distribute the trust assets to Jonathan Carrano as the issue of Christopher Papaz within the meaning of the trust. Each party to bear his or her own costs on appeal.

We concur: RUBIN, Acting P.J., and FLIER, J.

Unambiguous Will May Be Reformed If Clear and Convincing Evidence Establishes Mistake in Expression and Testator's Actual Specific Intent When Will Was Drafted

ESTATE of DUKE

Supreme Court of California
61 Cal. 4th 871, 352 P.3d 863 (2015)

CANTIL–SAKAUYE, C.J. Irving Duke prepared a holographic will providing that, upon his death, his wife would inherit his estate and that if he and his wife died at the same time, specific charities would inherit his estate. The handwritten will, however, contained no provision addressing the disposition of his estate if, as occurred here, he lived longer than his wife. The specified charities contend that at the time the testator wrote his will, he specifically intended to provide in his will that the charities would inherit his estate in the event his wife was not alive when he died. The courts below excluded extrinsic evidence of the testator's intent, finding that the will was unambiguous and failed to provide for the circumstance in which his wife predeceased him. Therefore, finding that Duke died intestate, the court entered judgment in favor of the heirs at law, Seymour and Robert Radin [the Radins].

We granted review to reconsider the historical rule that extrinsic evidence is inadmissible to reform an unambiguous will. We conclude that the categorical bar on reformation of wills is not justified, and we hold that an unambiguous will may be reformed if clear and convincing evidence establishes that the will contains a mistake in the expression of the testator's intent at the time the will was drafted and also establishes the testator's actual specific intent at the time the will was drafted. We further conclude that the charities' theory that the testator actually intended at the time he drafted his will to provide that his estate would pass to the charities in the event his wife was not alive to inherit the estate is sufficiently particularized, with respect to the existence of such a mistake and the testator's intent, that the remedy of reformation is available so long as clear and convincing evidence on both points is demonstrated. Therefore, we will direct this matter to be remanded to the probate court for consideration of whether clear and convincing evidence establishes that such a mistake occurred at the time the will was written and that the testator at that time intended his estate to pass to the charities in the event his wife was not alive to inherit the estate when he died.

I. FACTS

In 1984, when Irving Duke was 72 years of age, he prepared a holographic will in which he left all of his property to "my beloved wife, Mrs. Beatrice Schecter Duke," who was then 58 years of age. He left to his brother, Harry Duke, "the sum of One dollar." He provided that "[s]hould my wife . . . and I die at the same moment, my estate is to be equally divided—One-half is to be donated to the City of Hope in the name and loving memory of my sister, Mrs. Rose Duke Radin. One-half is to be donated to the Jewish National Fund to plant trees in Israel in the names and loving memory of my mother and father—Bessie and Isaac Duke."

Irving further provided in his will that "I have intentionally omitted all other persons, whether heirs or otherwise, who are not specifically mentioned herein, and I hereby specifically disinherit all persons whomsoever claiming to be, or who may lawfully be determined to be my heirs at law, except as otherwise mentioned in this will. If any heir, devisee or legatee, or any other person or persons, shall either directly or indirectly, seek to invalidate this will, or any part thereof, then I hereby give and bequeath to such person or persons the sum of one dollar ($1.00) and no more, in lieu of any other share or interest in my estate."

. . . Beatrice died in July 2002, but the will was not changed . . . .

Irving died in November 2007, leaving no spouse or children. In February 2008, a deputy public administrator for the County of Los Angeles obtained the will from Irving's safe deposit box. In March 2008, two charities, the City of Hope (COH) and the Jewish National Fund (JNF), petitioned for probate and for letters of administration. In October 2008, the Radins [sons of Irving's sister, Rose, who predeceased Irving] filed a petition for determination of entitlement to estate distribution. . . . Their petition alleged that they are entitled to the distribution of Irving's estate as Irving's sole intestate heirs.

The Radins moved for summary judgment. They did not challenge the validity of the will. Instead, they asserted that the estate must pass to Irving's closest surviving intestate heirs . . . because . . . there is no provision in the will for disposition of the estate in the event Irving survived Beatrice. In opposition to the motion, COH and JNF offered extrinsic evidence to prove that Irving intended the will to provide that in the event Beatrice was not alive . . . when Irving died, the estate would be distributed to COH and JNF. The probate court concluded that the will was not ambiguous, and on that ground, it declined to consider extrinsic evidence of Irving's intent, and granted summary judgment for the Radins.

The Court of Appeal affirmed, based on our opinion in *Estate of Barnes* (1965) 63 Cal.2d 580, 47 Cal.Rptr. 480, 407 P.2d 656 (*Barnes*). In *Barnes*, the testatrix's will provided that all of her property was to go to her husband, and if she and her husband died simultaneously or within two weeks of each other, her entire estate was to go to her nephew, Robert Henderson. Her will included a disinheritance clause, stating that " 'I hereby declare that I have thought of and considered each and every person who would inherit from me had I died intestate and who is

162

not mentioned in this Will, and I hereby declare that I do not desire to devise or bequeath to such person or persons any sum whatsoever and I hereby disinherit such person or persons.' " The testatrix's husband predeceased her, but she did not alter her will after his death.

When the testatrix died, 13 years after executing the will, she had various heirs at law, but Robert Henderson was not an heir at law because his mother was still alive. In the heirship proceeding, Henderson's mother testified that at the time the will was executed, Henderson frequently visited the testatrix at her home and spent many holidays with her, the two had a close relationship, and the testatrix was fond of him and often introduced him as her son. She also testified that the other relatives did not visit. The trial court found the will ambiguous, admitted the extrinsic evidence, and construed it in favor of Henderson.

We reversed the judgment. We stated that the extrinsic evidence concerning Henderson's relationship with the testatrix did not assist in interpreting the will. Although that evidence might have explained why the testatrix named Henderson as an alternate beneficiary in the event she died within two weeks of her husband, it shed no light on her intention in the event her husband died years before she did. We further observed that the will made no disposition of her property in the event she outlived her husband by several years, and noted that although a disinheritance clause could prevent a claimant from inheriting under the will, it could not prevent heirs from inheriting pursuant to the statutory rules of intestacy.

Turning to the will, we acknowledged that "a will is to be construed according to the intention of the testator, and so as to avoid intestacy." We added, "However, a court may not write a will which the testator did not write." The terms of the testatrix's will reflected that she wanted all of her property to go to her husband, and "also demonstrate[d] an awareness that [if she died within two weeks of her husband] she might well have no further opportunity to designate an alternate, and therefore she named [Henderson]. However, . . . the will is devoid of a provision or suggestion as to testatrix' intent if, as occurred, she was afforded sufficient time to review the will following the death of her husband." We noted that if the absence of a disposition of her property had come to her attention after her husband died, she might have provided that her estate would go to Henderson, or she might have made other provisions. "Under such circumstances any selection by the courts now would be to indulge in forbidden conjecture." Finally, we found no " 'dominant dispositive plan' " that might warrant the finding of a gift by implication. Therefore, finding the extrinsic evidence offered no assistance, we reversed the order distributing the estate to Henderson.

The Court of Appeal noted that the will in this case is similar to the will in *Barnes*. " . . . Irving's will is not ambiguous . . . . It simply made no disposition whatsoever of the property in the event Irving outlived his wife by several years, as eventually occurred." The Court of Appeal also found the will sufficiently similar to the will in *Barnes* to compel the conclusion that it does not reflect a dominant dispositive plan to leave the estate to JNF and COH. Finally, it rejected the admission of extrinsic evidence because the evidence did not address any ambiguity in the will.

The Court of Appeal added that it was "mindful of the fact that the ultimate disposition of Irving's property . . . does not appear to comport with his testamentary intent. It is clear that [Irving] meant to dispose of his estate through his bequests, first to his wife and, should she predecease him, then to the charities. It is difficult to imagine that after leaving specific gifts to the charities in the names and memories of beloved family members, Irving intended them to take effect only in the event that he and his wife died " 'at the same moment.' " It concluded, however, that because the will is unambiguous, *Barnes* precluded consideration of the extrinsic evidence.

We granted review to consider whether the rule applied in *Barnes* should be reconsidered. For the reasons set forth below, we hold that the categorical bar on reformation of unambiguous wills is not justified and that reformation is permissible if clear and convincing evidence establishes an error in the expression of the testator's intent and establishes the testator's actual specific intent at the time the will was drafted.

II. DISCUSSION

California law allows the admission of extrinsic evidence to establish that a will is ambiguous and to clarify ambiguities in a will. (Prob.Code, § 6111.5; *Estate of Russell* (1968) 69 Cal.2d 200, 206–213, 70 Cal.Rptr. 561, 444 P.2d 353.) As COH and JNF acknowledge, however, California law does not currently authorize the admission of extrinsic evidence to correct a mistake in a will when the will is unambiguous. To evaluate whether there are circumstances in which this court should authorize the admission of extrinsic evidence to correct a mistake in an unambiguous will, we first consider whether the Legislature's actions in this field preclude this court from altering the rule. As explained below, a review of the development of the law in California reflects that the Legislature has codified judicial expansions of the admissibility of evidence with respect to a testator's intent, but has not acted in a manner that restricts the authority of courts to develop the common law in this area. Second, we consider whether the common law rule categorically barring the reformation of wills is warranted, in light of the evolution of the law of probate and modern theories of interpretation of writings, and we conclude that the categorical bar on reformation is not justified. Third, we consider principles of stare decisis, and conclude that a change in the law is warranted to allow the reformation of an unambiguous will when clear and convincing evidence establishes that the will contains a mistake in the expression of the testator's intent at the time the will was executed and also establishes the testator's actual and specific intent at the time the will was executed. Finally, we conclude that the remedy of reformation is potentially available with respect to the theory of mistake articulated by COH and JNF in this case. Therefore, we will direct the case to be remanded for the probate court's consideration of whether clear and convincing evidence establishes that the testator intended, at the time he drafted his will, to provide in his will that his estate was to pass to COH and JNF in the event his wife was not alive at the time the testator died.

A. Statutory and judicial development of the law concerning the admission of extrinsic evidence regarding wills

Beginning with the original Statute of Wills in 1540, statutory law has required that wills be in writing. (32 Hen. VIII, ch. 1, July 20, 1540; see Prob.Code, §§ 6110, 6111; . . . . The principles governing the interpretation and enforcement of wills, however, have been developed by the courts. In California, common law principles governing the interpretation of wills were generally reflected in the Civil Code as enacted in 1872, which was based on the draft Field Code's summary of New York common law. . . . Discussion of California cases governing interpretation of wills and statutory developments after 1872 omitted.—Ed.]

This history of statutory provisions concerning the admissibility of evidence of a testator's intent reflects that the Legislature has codified legal principles developed by the courts, and has taken steps to ensure that its enactments do not restrict the admissibility of extrinsic evidence beyond the principles established by the courts. Nothing in this history suggests that the Legislature intended to foreclose further judicial developments of the law concerning the admissibility of evidence to discern the testator's intent . . . .

B. No sound basis exists to forbid the reformation of unambiguous wills in appropriate circumstances

As discussed below, extrinsic evidence is admissible to correct errors in other types of donative documents, even when the donor is deceased. Extrinsic evidence is also admissible to aid in the construction of a will, and in some cases, the resulting "construction" has essentially reformed the will. Extrinsic evidence is also admissible to determine whether a document was intended to be a will, and to prove the contents of a will that has been lost or destroyed. Because extrinsic evidence is not inherently more reliable when admitted for these various purposes than when admitted to correct an error in a will, concerns about the reliability of evidence do not justify a categorical bar on reformation of wills. To the extent categorical resistance to reformation is based instead on a concern that reformed language would not comply with the formalities required by the statute of wills, . . . principles developed in the context of the statute of frauds, which similarly requires a signed writing to evidence specified documents, illustrate that the purposes of the statute of wills are satisfied by the testator's execution of a writing that complies with the statutory requirements. With the statutory purposes satisfied, only the concerns regarding the reliability of evidence might justify a categorical bar on reformation of wills, and those concerns are addressed by imposing a burden of clear and convincing evidence. . . . [Discussion of use of extrinsic evidence in California omitted.—Ed.]

Thus, extrinsic evidence is admitted to correct donative documents other than wills after the donor's death. Moreover, myriad circumstances exist in which California courts appropriately admit evidence to establish a testator's intentions. Because extrinsic evidence is not inherently more reliable when admitted for these various purposes than when admitted to correct an error in a will, Professors John Langbein and Lawrence Waggoner, leading advocates of an extension of the doctrine of reformation to unambiguous wills, conclude that evidentiary concerns do not explain or justify the bar on reformation of wills. In their view, a greater obstacle to reformation has been concern with the formalities required in the execution of a will by the statute of wills. (Langbein & Waggoner, *Reformation of Wills on the Ground of Mistake: Change of Direction in American Law?* (1982) 130 U. Pa. L. Rev. 521, 524–529 (hereafter Langbein and Waggoner).) To overcome the objection that reformed language is unattested, they look to principles related to the statute of frauds.

Like the statute of wills, the statute of frauds requires certain documents to be evidenced by a writing subscribed by the party. If not evidenced by such a writing, a contract subject to the statute of frauds is invalid. " 'The primary purpose of the Statute [of Frauds] is evidentiary, to require reliable evidence of the existence and terms of the contract and to prevent enforcement through fraud or perjury of contracts never in fact made.' " Once sufficient written evidence of an agreement is presented, the evidentiary purpose is served, and extrinsic evidence is admissible to clarify ambiguous terms and to reform the writing to correct a mistake, even when the writing is intended to be a complete and exclusive statement of the parties' agreement. . . .

In correcting a contract subject to the statute of frauds, a court is not enforcing an oral contract, but is instead enforcing a written contract in accordance with the parties' actual agreement. To overcome the presumption that the writing is accurate, we have required clear and convincing evidence of a mistake before allowing reformation of a contract. . . .

In contrast to cases involving the statute of frauds, which may or may not involve a party who is deceased, cases arising under the statute of wills always involve a testator who is deceased and therefore cannot explain his or her intentions. We have already recognized, however, in the context of inheritance rights, that imposing a burden of proof by clear and convincing evidence is a means to address evidentiary concerns related to the circumstances that the principal witness is deceased and statutory formalities were not followed. (*Estate of Ford* (2004) 32 Cal.4th 160, 172, 8 Cal.Rptr.3d 541, 82 P.3d 747 [one seeking to inherit based on the doctrine of equitable adoption must meet the clear and convincing evidence standard, in part because the adoptive parent is deceased and can no longer testify, and the relief sought is outside the ordinary course of intestate succession and without the formalities required by the adoption statutes].) In addition, discerning intent in the context of a will is eased by the fact that the court must ascertain only the subjective intent of a single individual. (Langbein & Waggoner, *supra,* 130 U. Pa. L. Rev. at p. 569.) Therefore, the fact that the testator will always be unavailable to testify does not warrant a categorical bar on the admission of extrinsic evidence to reform a will.

Applying the analysis developed with respect to the statute of frauds, Langbein and Waggoner observe, "Whereas an oral will instances total noncompliance with the Wills Act formalities, a duly executed will with a mistakenly rendered term involves high levels of compliance with both the letter and the purpose of the Wills Act formalities. To the extent that a mistake case risks impairing any policy of the Wills Act, it is the *evidentiary* policy that is in question." (130 U. Pa. L. Rev. at p. 569, italics added.) With respect to evidentiary concerns, the authors advocate that reformation be allowed only in cases of clear and convincing evidence of the alleged mistake and the testator's intent. . . .

In cases in which clear and convincing evidence establishes both a mistake in the drafting of the will and the testator's actual and specific intent at the time the will was drafted, it is plain that denying reformation would defeat the testator's intent and result in unjust enrichment of unintended beneficiaries. Given that the paramount concern in construing a will is to determine the subjective intent of the testator (*Estate of Russell*) only significant countervailing considerations can justify a rule categorically denying reformation.

The Radins cite various factors in support of their contention that reformation of wills should never be allowed, some of which we have addressed above. First, they distinguish wills from other written instruments, noting that probate of a will always occurs after the testator's death, whereas contract litigation typically occurs when the parties to the contract are alive, and trust administration "frequently" begins before the testator's death. In addition, anyone may claim to be an intended beneficiary of a will, but the parties to a contract typically are few. We are not persuaded by these arguments in favor of a categorical bar on reformation. As we have noted, the death of a principal witness has not been viewed as a reason to deny reformation in other contexts. Also, although anyone may claim to be an intended beneficiary of a will, an appropriately tailored reformation remedy will alleviate concerns regarding unintended beneficiaries; it is unlikely that there will be many persons who have a connection to a testator and can produce clear and convincing evidence both of a mistake in the drafting of the will at the time the will was written and of the testator's specific intentions concerning the disposition of property. . . .

Second, the Radins express concern that reformation overrides the formalities required to execute a will. The fact that reformation is an available remedy does not relieve a testator of the requirements imposed by the Statute of Wills. (See Prob.Code, § 6111.) . . . To the extent reformation is inconsistent with the formalities' evidentiary purpose of establishing the testator's intent in a writing, the inconsistency is no different from the tension between reformation and the statute of frauds. As explained above, the evidentiary concern is addressed by requiring clear and convincing evidence of a mistake in expression and the testator's actual and specific intent. We should not allow stringent adherence to formalities to obscure the ultimate purpose of the statute of wills, which is to transfer an estate in accordance with the testator's intent.

Third, the Radins assert that allowing reformation in circumstances in which the estate would otherwise pass pursuant to the laws of intestacy constitutes an attack on the laws of intestacy. We disagree. The purpose of reformation is to carry out the wishes of the testator, and the remedy reflects no judgment other than a preference for disposition pursuant to the wishes of the testator. This preference is consistent with the statutory scheme. (See Prob.Code, §§ 6110 [a will that is not properly executed is enforceable if clear and convincing evidence establishes it was intended to constitute the testator's will], 21120 ["Preference is to be given to an interpretation of an instrument that will prevent intestacy or failure of a transfer, rather than one that will result in an intestacy or failure of a transfer"].)

Fourth, the Radins assert that allowing reformation will result in a significant increase in probate litigation and expenses. Claimants have long been entitled, however, to present extrinsic evidence to establish that a will is ambiguous despite the fact that it appears to be unambiguous. (*Estate of Russell*) Therefore, probate courts already receive extrinsic evidence of testator intent from claimants attempting to reform a will through the doctrine of ambiguity. . . . The task of deciding whether the evidence establishes by clear and convincing evidence that a mistake was made in the drafting of the will is a relatively small additional burden . . . . To the extent additional claims are made that are based on a theory of mistake rather than a theory of ambiguity, the heightened evidentiary standard will help the probate court to filter out weak claims. Finally, fear of additional judicial burdens is not an adequate reason to deny relief that would serve the paramount purpose of distributing property in accordance with the testator's intent. . . .

Fifth, the Radins discount justifications for allowing reformation in appropriate circumstances. They assert that section 6110(c)(2), which allows the probate of a will that was not executed in compliance with statutory attestation requirements if clear and convincing evidence establishes that the testator intended the writing to be a will, was not intended to lessen required formalities. Although section 6110 does not reduce the formalities of attestation, it reflects a judgment that the formalities should not be allowed to defeat the testator's intent when clear and convincing evidence satisfies the evidentiary concerns underlying the formalities of the statute of wills. The Radins also reject as a factor in support of a reformation remedy the avoidance of unjust enrichment. They state that no one has a right to inherit, and they recite various facts that they believe reflect that it is more just for Irving's relatives to inherit his estate than for the charities to receive it. If, however, a testator did not intend to devise property to a particular party, that party's receipt of the property as a result of a mistake constitutes unjust enrichment.

In sum, the Radins identify no countervailing considerations that would justify denying reformation if clear and convincing evidence establishes a mistake in the testator's expression of intent and the testator's actual and specific intent at the time the will was drafted.

C. Principles of stare decisis do not compel adherence to precedent in this context

. . . Rather than introducing uncertainty into estate planning, allowing reformation of a will upon a clear and convincing showing of a mistake in expression and the testator's actual and specific intent helps ensure that the testator's affairs are settled as intended. And because the doctrine is relevant only in the context of litigation, and it affects the distribution of an estate only upon a determination by clear and convincing evidence of a mistake in the will and of the testator's actual intent at the time the will was drafted, adoption of the doctrine will not diminish the principles of law that encourage the preparation of well-drafted, properly executed wills. "Precisely because the reformation doctrine is a rule of litigation, no draftsman would plan to rely on it when proper drafting can spare the expense and hazard of litigation." (Langbein & Waggoner, *supra*, 130 U. Pa. L. Rev. at p. 587.)

In addition, the principles we are reconsidering are entirely court created, and the Legislature's inaction does not weigh against allowing reformation. As explained above, the Legislature has followed the courts' lead in adopting more flexible rules concerning the interpretation of wills, and has been attentive to codifying principles established by our cases without barring the continued evolution of the law. Furthermore, the technical requirements applicable to wills have become more flexible, the evidence admissible to interpret wills has been expanded, and existing doctrines concerning the resolution of ambiguities in wills have been stretched to allow the correction of mistakes.

Finally, allowing reformation in these circumstances is consistent with the Legislature's efforts to apply the same rules of construction to all donative documents (see Prob.Code, § 21101 et seq.), and will promote fairness in the treatment of estates, regardless of the tools used for estate planning. . . . Moreover, allowing reformation of trusts and other instruments, but never of wills, appears to favor those with the means to establish estate plans that avoid probate proceedings, and to deny a remedy with respect to the estates of individuals who effect their plans through traditional testamentary documents. Denying reformation in these circumstances seems particularly harsh with respect to individuals who write wills without the assistance of counsel, and are more likely to overlook flaws in the expression of their intent.

As the Radins note, to date only a few states allow reformation of wills. However, both the Restatement Third of Property and the Uniform Probate Code now support the remedy. . . .

[W]e are persuaded that authorizing the reformation of wills under the circumstances and with the protections discussed above serves the paramount purpose of the law governing wills without compromising the policies underlying the statutory scheme and the common law rules. If a mistake in expression and the testator's actual and specific intent at the time the will was drafted are established by clear and convincing evidence, no policy underlying the statute of wills supports a rule that would ignore the testator's intent and unjustly enrich those who would inherit as a result of a mistake.

D. The charities have articulated a valid theory that will support reformation if established by clear and convincing evidence

COH and JNF contend that Irving actually intended at the time he wrote his will to provide that his estate would pass to COH and JNF in the event Beatrice was not alive to inherit his estate when he died, but that his intent was inartfully expressed in his will and thus there is a mistake in the will that should be reformed to reflect his intent when the will was drafted. Their contention, if proved by clear and convincing evidence, would support reformation of the will to reflect Irving's actual intent.

First, the alleged mistake concerns Irving's actual intent at the time he wrote the will. . . . If Irving's only intent at the time he wrote his will was to address the disposition of his estate in the circumstances in which he died before Beatrice or they died simultaneously, his will accurately reflects his intent. In that circumstance, his mistake, if any, would be in failing subsequently to modify the will after Beatrice died, and that mistake would not be related to the will he wrote and that COH and JNF seek to have reformed.

Second, the alleged mistake and intent are sufficiently specific. The allegations are precise with respect to the error and the remedy: the charities assert Irving specifically intended when he wrote his will to provide that his estate would pass to COH and JNF not only upon the simultaneous death of Irving and Beatrice, as the will expressly states, but also in the event Beatrice was not alive to inherit the estate at the time of his death. Although COH and JNF do not allege that the error was merely clerical, but instead assert that Irving's intent was inartfully expressed, their theory alleges "a mistake in the rendering of terms that the testator has authored or approved. The remedy in such a case has exactly the dimensions of the mistake. The term that the testator intended is restored." (Langbein & Waggoner, *supra*, 130 U. Pa. L. Rev. at pp. 583–584.)

The charities' theory, which sets forth a specific disposition of assets Irving allegedly intended when he wrote his will, distinguishes this case from circumstances in which it is alleged that the testator had a more general intent regarding the disposition of the estate which was not accomplished by the will as written. An example of an error involving general intent would be a case in which a testator intended in his or her will to provide adequate resources to one of the will's beneficiaries to support that beneficiary for a lifetime, but the specific gift set forth in the will proves to be inadequate for that purpose. Thus, that will accurately sets forth the testator's specific intent with respect to the distribution of assets, but due to a mistake with respect to the value of those assets or the needs of the beneficiary, the will fails to effect the testator's intent to provide adequate assets to support the beneficiary. In contrast to cases in which the alleged error is in the rendering of the specific terms intended by the testator, cases in which the alleged error is in failing to accomplish a general intent of the testator would require a court to determine the testator's putative intent: if the testator had known of the mistake, how would the testator have changed the will? The case before us presents only the issue of whether a will may be reformed when extrinsic evidence establishes that the will fails to set forth the actual specific intent of the testator at the time the will was executed, and we express no opinion on the availability of reformation in cases involving claims of general and putative intent.

Finally, for the reasons discussed above, evidence of the testator's intent must be clear and convincing. Among the evidence to be considered is the will itself, but when reformation rather than construction of a will is at issue, the rules of construction, which set forth principles for determining disposition of estate assets where the testator's intention is not reflected in the will, do not apply where extrinsic evidence supplies the missing terms. (Langbein and Waggoner, 130 U. Pa. L. Rev. at pp. 579–580.) Other doctrines of interpretation are also supplanted by the remedy of reformation. For example, although the terms of a will may be inadequate alone to establish a dominant dispositive plan that would warrant a gift by implication, those aspects of the will that tend to reflect an intent to make a particular gift should be considered together with the extrinsic evidence of intent to determine whether there is clear and convincing evidence of an intent to make a gift. Similarly, although a disinheritance clause cannot prevent heirs from inheriting pursuant to the statutory rules of intestacy, any intent reflected in such a clause may be relevant when reformation is sought.

III. CONCLUSION

We hold that an unambiguous will may be reformed to conform to the testator's intent if clear and convincing evidence establishes that the will contains a mistake in the testator's expression of intent at the time the will was drafted, and also establishes the testator's actual specific intent at the time the will was drafted. We reverse the judgment of the Court of Appeal and remand the matter to the Court of Appeal with directions to remand the case to the trial court for its consideration of extrinsic evidence as authorized by our opinion.

WE CONCUR: WERDEGAR, CHIN, CORRIGAN, LIU, CUÉLLAR, and KRUGER, JJ.

NOTE: Schwan v. Permann, 28 Cal. App. 5th 678, 239 Cal. Rptr. 427 (2018), held that trust's requirement that named beneficiaries be employed at the time of life tenants' deaths was not ambiguous even though settlor did not anticipate selling the company when the trust was executed. But beneficiaries who were employed at time of the sale were excused from complying with the condition because it had become impossible to perform. Trial court properly considered evidence of settlor's motive for the employment condition in declining to infer from his failure to modify the trust after sale of the company that settlor intended the gifts to lapse.

Section B. Death of Beneficiary Before Transferor

Lapsed and Void Devises

CPC § 21104. Meaning of "At-Death Transfer"

As used in this part, "at-death transfer" means a transfer that is revocable during the lifetime of the transferor, but does not include a joint tenancy or joint account with right of survivorship.

(Stats. 1994, 2002)

❖ *CPC § 21109. Survival Requirements*

(a) A transferee who fails to survive the transferor of an at-death transfer or until any future time required by the instrument does not take under the instrument.

(b) If it cannot be determined by clear and convincing evidence that the transferee survived until a future time required by the instrument, it is deemed that the transferee did not survive until the required future time.

(Stats. 1994, 2002)

Antilapse Statutes

❖ *CPC § 21110. Anti-Lapse Statute*

(a) Subject to subdivision (b), if a transferee is dead when the instrument is executed, or fails or is treated as failing to survive the transferor or until a future time required by the instrument, the issue of the deceased transferee take in the transferee's place in the manner provided in Section 240. A transferee under a class gift shall be a transferee for the purpose of this subdivision unless the transferee's death occurred before the execution of the instrument and that fact was known to the transferor when the instrument was executed.

(b) The issue of a deceased transferee do not take in the transferee's place if the instrument expresses a contrary intention or a substitute disposition. A requirement that the initial transferee survive the transferor or survive for a specified period of time after the death of the transferor constitutes a contrary intention. A requirement that the initial transferee survive until a future time that is related to the probate of the transferor's will or administration of the estate of the transferor constitutes a contrary intention.

(c) As used in this section, "transferee" means a person who is kindred of the transferor or kindred of a surviving, deceased, or former spouse of the transferor, but does not mean a spouse of the transferor.

(Stats. 1994, 2002, 2018)

CPC § 21111. *Disposition of Failed Transfer*

(a) Except as provided in subdivision (b) and subject to Section 21110, if a transfer fails for any reason, the property is transferred as follows:

(1) If the transferring instrument provides for an alternative disposition in the event the transfer fails, the property is transferred according to the terms of the instrument.

(2) If the transferring instrument does not provide for an alternative disposition but does provide for the transfer of a residue, the property becomes a part of the residue transferred under the instrument.

(3) If the transferring instrument does not provide for an alternative disposition and does not provide for the transfer of a residue, or if the transfer is itself a residuary gift, the property is transferred to the decedent's estate.

(b) Subject to Section 21110, if a residuary gift or a future interest is transferred to two or more persons and the share of a transferee fails for any reason, and no alternative disposition is provided, the share passes to the other transferees in proportion to their other interest in the residuary gift or the future interest.

(c) A transfer of "all my estate" or words of similar import is a residuary gift for purposes of this section.

(d) If failure of a future interest results in an intestacy, the property passes to the heirs of the transferor determined pursuant to Section 21114.

(Stats. 1994, 1996, 2001, 2002)

Person Claiming That Beneficiary Survived Bears Burden of Proof by Clear and Convincing Evidence

ESTATE of LENSCH

California Court of Appeal, First District, Division 2
177 Cal. App. 4th 667, 99 Cal. Rptr. 3d 246 (2009)

HAERLE, Acting P.J. . . . . On March 12, 2008, at 2:30 a.m. Gladys Lensch died . . . . She was 98 years old. She left the following three-sentence holographic will:

> "I Gladys Lensch do hereby declare, being of sound mind, that my estate be equally divided between my daughter Claudia and my son Jay. Claudia being married has 2 daughters, and my son by a previous marriage has 2 sons. They will provide for the well being of my grandchildren in the event of my death or serious incapacity due to lengthy illness. God Bless the Family.
>
> Gladys Clausen Lensch May 10, 1993."

Eleven hours after Gladys died, Jay, Gladys's son, was found dead . . . . He had shot himself with a 12–gauge shotgun. The time of death on Jay's death certificate was recorded as the time his body was found: 1:15 p.m. on March 12, 2008. Jay's body was cremated without an autopsy and his remains were buried five days later.

. . . [Jay's will left the] residue of his estate . . . in equal shares to the Unitarian Universalist Service Committee and Direct Relief International. He left nothing . . . to his two sons, appellants Jason and Ean Lensch.

On June 25, 2008, Jason and Ean Lensch filed a "Petition to Determine Survival and to Determine Persons Entitled to Distribution." This petition was verified by petitioner's attorney because petitioners reside "out of this county and state." . . .

The petition stated that "Shortly after noon [on the same day Gladys Lensch died] the body of her son, Jay Lensch was found. Jay Lensch died in his Trinity County home of a self-inflicted gunshot wound. Petitioners and their attorney spoke to the Trinity County Deputy Coroner who investigated Jay Lensch's death and the Deputy Coroner said that he could not determine the precise time of Jay Lensch's death. To Ean Lensch, the Deputy Coroner said that Jay Lensch had been dead at least 24 hours before his body was found and that death might have occurred two or more days earlier. To Petitioner's attorney, the Deputy Coroner said that Jay Lensch had last spoken to another person two days before his body was discovered and that death could have occurred any time between that conversation and the time of discovery. On the death certificate, the Deputy Coroner used the time of discovery as the time of death, as is customary in cases like this. The Deputy Coroner is certain that Jay died earlier than the time stated on the death certificate, 1:15 p.m., but explained to Petitioner's counsel that there is no way to tell what was the actual time of death." Petitioners asked the court to find that "it cannot be determined by clear and convincing evidence who died first, Gladys Clausen Lensch or Jay Alfred Lensch," and that the court deem Gladys to have survived Jay for the purpose of the transfers created by Gladys's will and that the court rule that the transfer made to Jay in Gladys's will fails.

On July 25, 2008, Jay's executor . . . filed an opposition to . . . [the] petition . . . . He argued that Jason and Ean had the burden of proving that Jay did not survive Gladys. He also argued that survival was not required by the terms of Gladys's will. Relying on the death certificate of both decedents, respondent argued that because death certificates are proof of time of death, and claimant's petition was based on "inadmissible opinions, speculation, and hearsay," the only evidence of time of death was the death certificate.

At a brief hearing on July 30, 2008, the court noted that its tentative ruling was that "there is no requirement for survival in the testamentary document." Petitioners immediately requested an evidentiary hearing. Counsel argued that Jay was required to survive Gladys in order to take under her will. The court rejected this argument and also ruled, in the alternative, that even if there was a survival requirement "the only evidence before the court being the death certificates demonstrate that . . . Mr. Lensch did survive his mother." . . .

The court denied the petition to determine survival. The court held that "the evidence offered shows that decedent's will did not require survival, but nevertheless, that Jay Lensch survived decedent . . . and that no further evidentiary hearing is required." . . .

III. DISCUSSION

A. *Survivorship*

. . . We . . . conclude that, although the trial court was correct in finding that Gladys's will contains no survivorship requirement, it erred in denying appellants' petition on this basis, apparently because it did not understand the legal consequences of the lack of a survivorship requirement in Gladys's will. . . . Gladys's bequest was not conditioned on Jay's survival. Nor did she make an alternate disposition. Therefore, under sections 21109 and 21110, if Jay died before Gladys, then Gladys's bequest to Jay fails under section 21109 and passes to Jay's children . . . .

Respondent, who seems to understand at this point in the proceedings the significance of the fact that Gladys's will contained neither a survival requirement nor an alternate disposition, argues that Jay's will, in which Jay complains about his sons' conduct toward him, constitutes extrinsic evidence from which the probate court "could reasonably infer . . . that Gladys knew and disapproved of [Jason and Ean]'s conduct, and for that reason intended in her will to give Jay complete discretion over his bequest whether he survived her or not. In other words, respondent contends that the trial court should have construed Gladys's will as containing a provision that Jay was not required to survive her based on language contained in Jay's will, which was written well after Gladys's. We disagree. . . .

Jay's will demonstrates only that Jay appears to have disapproved of his sons when he wrote *his* will. There is no evidence that Gladys was even aware of her son's difficult relationship with his children or that she agreed with her son's assessment of his children's behavior. . . .

B. *Evidentiary Hearing*

Appellants argue that the trial court erred in finding, based on the time of death reported in Jay's death certificate, that Gladys predeceased Jay. This conclusion led to the denial of appellants' claim that, under the antilapse statute, they were entitled to a share of Gladys's estate. The probate court should have held an evidentiary hearing on this issue and erred in denying appellants' request for one. . . .

C. *Standard and Burden of Proof* . . .

1. *Standard* . . .

. . . When it was first enacted in 1994, section 21109 contained a subdivision (b) that provided "[i]f it cannot be established by clear and convincing evidence that the transferee has survived the transferor, it is deemed that the beneficiary did not survive the transferor." . . . In 2002, section 21109, subdivision (b) was deleted. . . . The Law Revision Commission comment to this change . . . is as follows: "Former subdivision (b) is deleted as unnecessary. The general 'clear and convincing evidence' standard of Section 220 applies." (31 Cal. L. Rev. Comm. Reports 195.) Section 220 provides that "if the title to property or the devolution of property depends upon priority of death and it cannot be established by clear and convincing evidence that one of the persons survived the other, the property of each person shall be administered or distributed, or otherwise dealt with, as if that person had survived the other." . . .

Respondent, however, argues that, because section 21109 does not specify what standard of proof applies in determining whether the transferee fails to survive the transferor (as opposed to a failure to survive until "the required future time" covered by section 21109, subdivision (b)), then the clear and convincing standard of proof does not apply to the issue of whether a beneficiary survived the transferor of an at-death transfer. Respondent's argument fails for the very basic reason that it ignores the relevant legislative history of section 21109, which makes quite clear that section 220 applies to this issue.

2. *Burden of Proof*

It is well-established that the party whose claim is "dependent on survivorship" bears the burden of proof in an action to determine order of death. (Estate of Rowley (1967) 257 Cal. App. 2d 324, 333, 65 Cal. Rptr. 139 (Rowley).) . . . Respondent's claim, like the claim of the beneficiary in Rowley depends on his survival of Gladys. Respondent, therefore, bears the burden of proof. . . .

Finally, respondent argues that the burden of proof in this case is established . . . by Health and Safety Code section 103550 . . . .[3] Respondent argues that appellants must controvert the prima facie evidence contained in the death certificates of Gladys and Jay and, therefore, appellants bear the overall burden of proof on the question of survivorship.

We cannot agree. Health and Safety Code section 103550 creates a presumption that the evidence contained in certain public records is correct, a presumption designed to permit the introduction of such records over hearsay objections and to obviate the need for live testimony in instances in which a fact contained in these records is not in dispute. . . . Existing case law makes clear that respondent bears the burden of proof on this issue.

IV. DISPOSITION

The order is reversed and the cause is remanded for an evidentiary hearing consistent with the views expressed in this opinion. Appellants shall recover costs on appeal.

---

[3] Health and Safety Code section 103550 provides: "Any birth, fetal death, death, or marriage record that was registered within a period of one year from the date of the event under the provisions of this part, or any copy of the record or part thereof, properly certified by the State Registrar, local registrar, or county recorder, is prima facie evidence in all courts and places of the facts stated therein." Of course, a death certificate is "'subject to rebuttal and to explanation.'" (*Morris v. Noguchi* (1983) 141 Cal. App. 3d 520, 523, fn. 1, 190 Cal. Rptr. 347; see also *People v. Holder* (1964) 230 Cal. App. 2d 50, 56, 40 Cal. Rptr. 655.) And a party may correct a statement in a death certificate by calling as a witness the person who made the death certificate. (See *Estate of Scott* (1942) 55 Cal. App. 2d 780, 782–783, 131 P.2d 613.) [Location of footnote changed.—Ed.]

NOTE & PROBLEMS:

1. Testator's will gave $10,000 to each of two granddaughters, children of her deceased son, and the residue to her daughter, Miller. The gifts to the granddaughters provided they should lapse if they predeceased testator. The residuary gift did not provide for lapse or make an alternate disposition if Miller predeceased. The will contained a disinheritance clause stating that testator intentionally omitted to provide for any of her heirs. Miller predeceased testator and her son claimed the residue of the estate. **Estate of Tolman**, 181 Cal. App. 4th 1433, 104 Cal. Rptr. 3d 924 (2010) held that grandson was entitled to entire residue under antilapse statute. Disinheritance clause did not indicate contrary intent; grandson's right to take was based on being a lineal descendant of the residuary beneficiary, not on being an heir.

2. Jean Mooney's will, executed in 1961, left the residue of her estate to her father, or if he predeceased her, to her two sisters, Doris and Lucile in equal shares. When Jean Mooney died in 2007, her father and two sisters had predeceased her. Jean was survived by the four children of sister Doris and the three children of sister Lucile. How should Jean's property be distributed under the will? See **Estate of Mooney**, 169 Cal. App. 4th 654, 87 Cal. Rptr. 3d 115 (2008) (½ to children of Doris and ½ to children of Lucile).

3. Ethel Begley's holographic will, executed in 1960, provided: "All of my real estate and personal property is to sold and be divided share and share alike between my two Sisters Lulu L Bolton, Lena S Ford, and one Brother John H. Dickey, all of Willits, California, and the Heirs of my late Sister Viola Davis." When Ethel died in 1985, none of the named beneficiaries was living. Lulu and John had died without issue. Nine of Lena's eleven children were alive as were four issue of one deceased child and two issue of the other deceased child. All three of Viola's children had predeceased, but one had four surviving issue and each of the other two one surviving issue.

How should Ethel's property be distributed under the will? See **Estate of Begley**, 201 Cal. App. 3d 791, 247 Cal. Rptr. 632 (1988) (Lena's issue take under antilapse statute; Viola's issue take directly as her heirs, determined as if Viola had died just before Ethel's death; Lulu's and John's shares lapsed and passed to the other takers of the estate under the predecessor to § 21111(b) "in proportion to their other interest in the residuary gift." Result: Half the estate passes to Viola's four grandchildren in equal shares. The other half of the estate passes to Lena's living and deceased children in eleven equal shares, with the share of one deceased child being divided among four living issue and the share of the other deceased child being divided among two living issue.

Section C. Changes in Property After Execution of Will

Classification of At-Death Transfers

CPC § 21117. Classification of Gifts

At-death transfers are classified as follows:

(a) A specific gift is a transfer of specifically identifiable property.

(b) A general gift is a transfer from the general assets of the transferor that does not give specific property.

(c) A demonstrative gift is a general gift that specifies the fund or property from which the transfer is primarily to be made.

(d) A general pecuniary gift is a pecuniary gift within the meaning of Section 21118.

(e) An annuity is a general pecuniary gift that is payable periodically.

(f) A residuary gift is a transfer of property that remains after all specific and general gifts have been satisfied.

(Stats. 1994, 2002)

NOTE: Blech v. Blech, 25 Cal. App. 5th 989, 236 Cal. Rptr. 3d 430 (2018) held that trust paragraph headed "Division of Remaining Trust Estate," which directed division into separate shares for his four children with specified percentages for each, was a residuary gift even though shares for two of the children were to include particular parcels of real property. The directions as to real property were methods of funding those two shares, not specific gifts of the described real property.

Ademption by Extinction

CPC § 21133. Ademption

A recipient of an at-death transfer of a specific gift has a right to the property specifically given, to the extent the property is owned by the transferor at the time the gift takes effect in possession or enjoyment, and all of the following:

(a) Any balance of the purchase price (together with any security agreement) owing from a purchaser to the transferor at the time the gift takes effect in possession or enjoyment by reason of sale of the property.

(b) Any amount of an eminent domain award for the taking of the property unpaid at the time the gift takes effect in possession or enjoyment.

(c) Any proceeds unpaid at the time the gift takes effect in possession or enjoyment on fire or casualty insurance on or other recovery for injury to the property.

(d) Property owned by the transferor at the time the gift takes effect in possession or enjoyment and acquired as a result of foreclosure, or obtained in lieu of foreclosure, of the security interest for a specifically given obligation.

(Stats. 1994, 2002)

CPC § 21134. No Ademption in Certain Circumstances

(a) Except as otherwise provided in this section, if, after the execution of the instrument of gift, specifically given property is sold, or encumbered by a deed of trust, mortgage, or other instrument, by a conservator, by an agent acting within the authority of a durable power of attorney for an incapacitated principal, or by a trustee acting for an incapacitated settlor of a trust established by the settlor as a revocable trust, the transferee of the specific gift has the right to a general pecuniary gift equal to the net sale price of the property unreduced by the payoff of any such encumbrance, or the amount of the unpaid encumbrance on the property as well as the property itself.

(b) Except as otherwise provided in this section, if an eminent domain award for the taking of specifically given property is paid to a conservator, to an agent acting within the authority of a durable power of attorney for an incapacitated principal, or to a trustee acting for an incapacitated settlor of a trust established by the settlor as a revocable trust, or if the proceeds on fire or casualty insurance on, or recovery for injury to, specifically gifted property are paid to a conservator, to an agent acting within the authority of a durable power of attorney for an incapacitated principal, or to a trustee acting for an incapacitated settlor of a trust established by the settlor as a revocable trust, the recipient of the specific gift has the right to a general pecuniary gift equal to the eminent domain award or the insurance proceeds or recovery unreduced by the payoff of any encumbrance placed on the property by the conservator, agent, or trustee, after the execution of the instrument of gift.

(c) For the purpose of the references in this section to a conservator, this section does not apply if, after the sale, mortgage, condemnation, fire, or casualty, or recovery, the conservatorship is terminated and the transferor survives the termination by one year.

(d) For the purpose of the references in this section to an agent acting with the authority of a durable power of attorney for an incapacitated principal, or to a trustee acting for an incapacitated settlor of a trust established by the settlor as a revocable trust, (1) "incapacitated principal" or "incapacitated settlor" means a principal or settlor who is an incapacitated person, (2) no adjudication of incapacity before death is necessary, and (3) the acts of an agent within the authority of a durable power of attorney are presumed to be for an incapacitated principal. However, there shall be no presumption of a settlor's incapacity concerning the acts of a trustee.

(e) The right of the transferee of the specific gift under this section shall be reduced by any right the transferee has under Section 21133.

(Stats. 1994, 2002, 2012)

CPC § 21139. Rules Not Intended to Increase Incidence of Ademption

The rules stated in Sections 21133 to 21135, inclusive, are not exhaustive, and nothing in those sections is intended to increase the incidence of ademption under the law of this state.
(Stats. 1994, 2002)

NOTE:

Brown v. LaBow, 157 Cal. App. 4th 795, 69 Cal. Rptr. 3d 417 (2007), held that no ademption of a specific gift of corporate shares on the trustor's death occurred when, during the trustor's incapacity, the trustee of a revocable inter vivos trust, which held the controlling interest in the corporation, agreed to a sale of the corporate assets. Although CPC § 21134 did not apply, the same result followed under California case law. The trustee in that case, who was also the trustor's conservator, was Frumeh Labow, a professional conservator, described as "Los Angeles' busiest" who only takes estates worth at least $300,000, in Robin Fields, Evelyn Larrubia and Jack Leonard, *When a Family Matter Turns Into a Business*, L.A. Times, Nov. 13, 2005,
https://www.latimes.com/archives/la-xpm-2005-nov-13-me-conserve13-story.html.

Stock Splits and the Problem of Increase

CPC § 21132. Entitlement to Stock Splits, Dividends, Etc.

(a) If a transferor executes an instrument that makes an at-death transfer of securities and the transferor then owned securities that meet the description in the instrument, the transfer includes additional securities owned by the transferor at death to the extent the additional securities were acquired by the transferor after the instrument was executed as a result of the transferor's ownership of the described securities and are securities of any of the following types:

(1) Securities of the same organization acquired by reason of action initiated by the organization or any successor, related, or acquiring organization, excluding any acquired by exercise of purchase options.

(2) Securities of another organization acquired as a result of a merger, consolidation, reorganization, or other distribution by the organization or any successor, related, or acquiring organization.

(3) Securities of the same organization acquired as a result of a plan of reinvestment.

(b) Distributions in cash before death with respect to a described security are not part of the transfer.

(Stats. 2002)

Satisfaction of General Pecuniary Bequests

CPC § 21135. Satisfaction

(a) Property given by a transferor during his or her lifetime to a person is treated as a satisfaction of an at-death transfer to that person in whole or in part only if one of the following conditions is satisfied:

(1) The instrument provides for deduction of the lifetime gift from the at-death transfer.

(2) The transferor declares in a contemporaneous writing that the gift is in satisfaction of the at-death transfer or that its value is to be deducted from the value of the at-death transfer.

(3) The transferee acknowledges in writing that the gift is in satisfaction of the at-death transfer or that its value is to be deducted from the value of the at-death transfer.

(4) The property given is the same property that is the subject of a specific gift to that person.

(b) Subject to subdivision (c), for the purpose of partial satisfaction, property given during lifetime is valued as of the time the transferee came into possession or enjoyment of the property or as of the time of death of the transferor, whichever occurs first.

(c) If the value of the gift is expressed in the contemporaneous writing of the transferor, or in an acknowledgment of the transferee made contemporaneously with the gift, that value is conclusive in the division and distribution of the estate.

(d) If the transferee fails to survive the transferor, the gift is treated as a full or partial satisfaction of the gift, as the case may be, in applying Sections 21110 and 21111 unless the transferor's contemporaneous writing provides otherwise.

(Stats. 1994, 2002)

Exoneration of Liens

CPC § 21131. No Right of Exoneration

A specific gift passes the property transferred subject to any mortgage, deed of trust, or other lien existing at the date of death, without right of exoneration, regardless of a general directive to pay debts contained in the instrument.

(Stats. 1994, 2002)

Abatement

CPC § 21400. Transferor's Plan Trumps Statutory Abatement

Notwithstanding any other provision of this part, if the instrument provides for abatement, or if the transferor's plan or if the purpose of the transfer would be defeated by abatement as provided in this part, the shares of beneficiaries abate as is necessary to effectuate the instrument, plan, or purpose.

(Stats. 1990)

CPC § 21401. Application of Statutory Abatement

Except as provided in Sections 21612 (omitted spouse) and 21623 (omitted children) and in Division 10 (commencing with Section 20100) (proration of taxes), shares of beneficiaries abate as provided in this part for all purposes, including payment of the debts, expenses, and charges specified in Section 11420,[23] satisfaction of gifts, and payment of expenses on specifically devised property pursuant to Section 12002, and without any priority as between real and personal property.

(Stats. 1990, 2003)

CPC § 21402. Statutory Abatement Order

(a) Shares of beneficiaries abate in the following order:

    (1) Property not disposed of by the instrument.

    (2) Residuary gifts.

    (3) General gifts to persons other than the transferor's relatives.

    (4) General gifts to the transferor's relatives.

    (5) Specific gifts to persons other than the transferor's relatives.

    (6) Specific gifts to the transferor's relatives.

(b) For purposes of this section, a "relative" of the transferor is a person to whom property would pass from the transferor under Section 6401 or 6402 (intestate succession) if the transferor died intestate and there were no other person having priority.

(Stats. 1990)

CPC § 21403. Abatement Within Class; Treatment of Annuities & Demonstrative Gifts

(a) Subject to subdivision (b), shares of beneficiaries abate pro rata within each class specified in Section 21402.

---

[23] Expenses of administration, obligations secured by a lien, funeral expenses, expenses of last illness, family allowance, wage claims, and general debts in that order.—Ed.

(b) Gifts of annuities and demonstrative gifts are treated as specific gifts to the extent they are satisfied out of the fund or property specified in the gift and as general gifts to the extent they are satisfied out of property other than the fund or property specified in the gift.
(Stats. 1990)

NOTE: Siegel v. Fife, 234 Cal. App. 4th 988, 184 Cal. Rptr. 3d 531 (2015), held that trustee could sell real estate designated as a specific gift before selling residuary assets because trust provides broad authority to sell trust assets for life beneficiary's care and that "rights of any remaindermen shall be considered of secondary importance." Trustee listed all of trust's real estate for sale, but specifically given property was first to sell. Life beneficiary's needs far exceeded cash available in the trust. If any funds remain when the life beneficiary dies, the probate court will fix the amount that the various remaindermen will receive.

Chapter 6. Trusts: Characteristics and Creation

Section A. The Trust in American Law

California's Trust Law, found in Division 9 of the Probate Code, has 9 parts:

1. General Provisions, §§ 15000 *et seq.*
2. Creation, Validity, Modification, and Termination of Trusts, §§ 15200 *et seq.*
3. Trustees and Beneficiaries, §§ 15600 *et seq.*
4. Trust Administration, §§ 16000 *et seq.*
5. Judicial Proceedings Concerning Trusts, §§ 17000 *et seq.*
6. Rights of Third Persons, §§ 18000 *et seq.*
7. Uniform Prudent Management of Institutional Funds Act, §§ 18500 *et seq.*
8. Payment of Claims, Debts, and Expenses from Revocable Trust of Deceased Settlor, §§ 19000 *et seq.*
9. Uniform Trust Decanting Act, §§ 19501 *et seq.*

CPC § 82. Definition of Trust

(a) "Trust" includes the following:

(1) An express trust, private or charitable, with additions thereto, wherever and however created.

(2) A trust created or determined by a judgment or decree under which the trust is to be administered in the manner of an express trust.

(b) "Trust" excludes the following:

(1) Constructive trusts, other than those described in paragraph (2) of subdivision (a), and resulting trusts.

(2) Guardianships and conservatorships.

(3) Personal representatives.

(4) Totten trust accounts.

(5) Custodial arrangements pursuant to the Uniform Gifts to Minors Act or the Uniform Transfers to Minors Act of any state.

(6) Business trusts that are taxed as partnerships or corporations.

(7) Investment trusts subject to regulation under the laws of this state or any other jurisdiction.

(8) Common trust funds.

(9) Voting trusts.

(10) Security arrangements.

(11) Transfers in trust for purpose of suit or enforcement of a claim or right.

(12) Liquidation trusts.

(13) Trusts for the primary purpose of paying debts, dividends, interest, salaries, wages, profits, pensions, or employee benefits of any kind.

(14) Any arrangement under which a person is nominee or escrowee for another.

(Stats. 1990)

CPC § 15002. Common Law as Law of State

Except to the extent that the common law rules governing trusts are modified by statute, the common law as to trusts is the law of this state.

(Stats. 1990)

Section B. Creation of a Trust

CPC § 15200. Methods of Creating Trusts

Subject to other provisions of this chapter, a trust may be created by any of the following methods:

(a) A declaration by the owner of property that the owner holds the property as trustee.

(b) A transfer of property by the owner during the owner's lifetime to another person as trustee.

(c) A transfer of property by the owner, by will or by other instrument taking effect upon the death of the owner, to another person as trustee.

(d) An exercise of a power of appointment to another person as trustee.

(e) An enforceable promise to create a trust.

(Stats. 1990)

CPC § 15201. Intention to Create Trust

A trust is created only if the settlor properly manifests an intention to create a trust.

(Stats. 1990)

Declaration of Trust That Specifically Describes Real Property Is Effective To Include Real Property in Trust; No Deed Is Necessary

ESTATE of HEGGSTAD

California Court of Appeal, First District, Division 2
16 Cal. App. 4th 943, 20 Cal. Rptr. 2d 433 (1993)

PHELAN, Associate Justice. . . . On May 10, 1989, decedent Halvard L. Heggstad executed a will naming his son, respondent Glen P. Heggstad, as executor. Concurrently, the decedent executed a valid revocable living trust, naming himself as the trustee and his son Glen, the successor trustee (hereafter the Heggstad Family Trust). All the trust property was identified in a document titled schedule A, which was attached to the trust document. The property at issue was listed as item No. 5 on schedule A, and was mislabeled as "Partnership interest in 100 Independence Drive, Menlo Park, California."

In truth, decedent had an undivided 34.78 percent interest in that property as a tenant in common. . . . This property remained in decedent's name, as an unmarried man, and there was no grant deed reconveying this property to himself as trustee of the revocable living trust. Both sides agree that decedent had formally transferred by separate deeds, all the other real property listed in Schedule A to himself as trustee of the Heggstad Family Trust.

About one month after executing these documents, the decedent married appellant Nancy Rhodes Heggstad. She was not provided for in either the will or the trust documents, and all parties agree that she is entitled to one-third of the decedent's estate (her intestate share)[1] as an omitted spouse pursuant to Probate Code section 6560. She takes nothing under the terms of the trust and makes no claim thereto.

Decedent died on October 20, 1990, and his son was duly appointed executor of his estate and became successor trustee under the terms of the Heggstad Family Trust. The trust documents were recorded following decedent's death on January 10, 1991.

During the probate of the will, Glen, the successor trustee, petitioned the court for instructions regarding the disposition of the 100 Independence Drive property. The trustee claimed that the trust language was sufficient to create a trust in the subject property and that the property was not part of his father's estate.

. . . [A]rticle 1 of the trust provided: "HALVARD L. HEGGSTAD, called the settlor or the trustee, . . . declares that he has set aside and transfers to HALVARD L. HEGGSTAD in trust, as trustee, the property described in schedule A attached to this instrument."

Appellant objected, arguing: the trustee is asking for a change of title, which is not available as a remedy in a petition for instructions; the property was not transferred to the trust by a properly executed document or by operation of law; and the trustee is also a beneficiary of the trust and should be removed because of this conflict of interest.

The probate court concluded that the trust document, specifically article 1, was sufficient to create a trust in the subject property.

DISCUSSION

Appellant contends that a written declaration of trust is insufficient, by itself, to create a revocable living trust in real property, and the decedent was required to have executed a grant

---

[1] Decedent was survived by his son Glen and daughter Susan and a granddaughter.

deed transferring the property to himself as trustee . . . . None of the authorities cited by appellant require a settlor, who also names himself as trustee of a revocable living trust, to convey his property to the trust by a separate deed.[3] Our independent research has uncovered no decisional law to support this position. To the contrary, all the authorities we have consulted support the conclusion that a declaration by the settlor that he holds the property in trust for another, alone, is sufficient. . . .

. . . [The] two methods for creating a trust are codified in Probate Code section 15200: "(a) A declaration by the owner of property that the owner holds the property as trustee," and "(b) A transfer of property by the owner during the owner's lifetime to another person as trustee." (. . . ; see also Rest. 2nd Trusts, § 17.)

Where the trust property is real estate, the statute of frauds requires that the declaration of trust must be in writing signed by the trustee. (§ 15206; accord Rest.2d, Trusts, § 40, com. *b*, at p. 105.) Here, the written document declaring a trust in the property described in Schedule A was signed by the decedent at the time he made the declaration and constitutes a proper manifestation of his intent to create a trust. Contrary to appellant's assertion, there is no requirement that the settlor/trustee execute a separate writing conveying the property to the trust. . . .

II

Appellant next contends the probate court lacked jurisdiction to determine the testamentary nature of 100 Independence Drive, *i.e.*, whether it was part of the estate or trust property. She claims that a petition for instruction to the trustee, under section 17200, cannot resolve the legal status of disputed trust property. This contention defies common sense and finds no support in the law. . . .

The probate court has general subject matter jurisdiction over the decedent's property and as such, it is empowered to resolve competing claims over the title to and distribution of the decedent's property. . . . It is of no legal significance that respondent/trustee chose to seek relief through a petition for instruction (§ 17200), rather than the equivalent petition for conveyance or transfer (§ 9860). . . . [I]t is a fruitless exercise in semantics for appellant to argue that the probate court may only decide this issue as part of its administration of the decedent's estate. Appellant's contention fails.

The probate court's order declaring that the property identified as "100 Independence Way, Menlo Park, San Mateo County," is included in the living trust is affirmed.

KLINE, P.J., and BENSON, J., concur.

---

[3] The case of Nichols v. Emery (1895) 109 Cal. 323, 41 P. 1089 cited by respondent is inapposite. That decision involves a revocable living trust, created by conveyance of the trust property, by deed, to a third party trustee. It has no application to the situation before us-the creation of a revocable living trust by declaration of the settlor.

NOTES:

1. Osswald v. Anderson, 49 Cal. App. 4th 812, 57 Cal. Rptr. 2d 23 (4th Dist. Div. 3, 1996) held that even though settlors intended their home to be the corpus of the trust, signed trust document naming themselves as trustees was not effective as declaration of trust of the home because home was not described in the trust document. Nor was a second trust document that did describe the home as trust property effective to create a trust of the home because third parties, not the settlors, were named as trustees.

2. Luna v. Brownell, 185 Cal. App. 4th 668, 110 Cal. Rptr. 3d 573 (2d Dist. Div. 3, 2010) held that a deed from an individual to himself as trustee of a trust that had not yet been created was valid and effective to transfer the property to the trust when it was later created.

3. Ukkestad v. RBS Asset Finance, Inc., 235 Cal. App. 4th 156, 185 Cal. Rptr. 3d 145 (2015), held that statement in trust instrument that trustor, who was also the trustee, "hereby assigns, grants and conveys to the Trustees . . . all of the Grantor's right, title and interest in and to all of his real and personal property, including . . . real property . . . and all other property owned by the Grantor . . . " was a declaration of trust that satisfied the Statute of Frauds.

4. Carne v. Worthington, 246 Cal. App. 4th 548, 200 Cal. Rptr. 920 (2016) held statement in 2009 trust that "I transfer to my Trustee the property listed in Schedule A" was sufficient to transfer property listed in Schedule A, which was then held in 1985 revocable trust, to 2009 trust. Liebler was trustor and trustee of 1985 trust and signed 2009 trust as grantor/trustor. No separate deed was required.

CPC § 15202. Trust Property

A trust is created only if there is trust property.

(Stats. 1990)

CPC § 15203. Trust Purpose

A trust may be created for any purpose that is not illegal or against public policy.

(Stats. 1990)

NOTE: Trust created to defraud creditors is illegal and may be disregarded. Trustee holds title on resulting trust for the trustor. Designating a minor child as beneficiary does not validate a trust created with an improper purpose. **In re Schwarzkopf**, 626 F.3d 1032 (9th Cir. 2010). Seven-year statute for action to set aside fraudulent transfer does not begin to run until resulting trustee repudiates the trust.

Ascertainable Beneficiaries

CPC § 15204. Trust for Indefinite or General Purpose

A trust created for an indefinite or general purpose is not invalid for that reason if it can be determined with reasonable certainty that a particular use of the trust property comes within that purpose.

(Stats. 1990)

CPC § 15205. Beneficiary Is Ascertainable or to Be Selected by Another

(a) A trust, other than a charitable trust, is created only if there is a beneficiary.

(b) The requirement of subdivision (a) is satisfied if the trust instrument provides for either of the following:

> (1) A beneficiary or class of beneficiaries that is ascertainable with reasonable certainty or that is sufficiently described so it can be determined that some person meets the description or is within the class.

> (2) A grant of a power to the trustee or some other person to select the beneficiaries based on a standard or in the discretion of the trustee or other person.

(Stats. 1990)

CPC § 15211. Duration of Trust for Noncharitable Purpose

A trust for a noncharitable corporation or unincorporated society or for a lawful noncharitable purpose may be performed by the trustee for only 21 years, whether or not there is a beneficiary who can seek enforcement or termination of the trust and whether or not the terms of the trust contemplate a longer duration.

(Stats. 1991)

CPC § 15212. Trust for Care of Domestic or Pet Animal

(a) Subject to the requirements of this section, a trust for the care of an animal is a trust for a lawful noncharitable purpose. Unless expressly provided in the trust, the trust terminates when no animal living on the date of the settlor's death remains alive. The governing instrument of the animal trust shall be liberally construed to bring the trust within this section, to presume against the merely precatory or honorary nature of the disposition, and to carry out the general intent of the settlor. Extrinsic evidence is admissible in determining the settlor's intent.

(b) A trust for the care of an animal is subject to the following requirements:

> (1) Except as expressly provided otherwise in the trust instrument, the principal or income shall not be converted to the use of the trustee or to any use other than for the benefit of the animal.

> (2) Upon termination of the trust, the trustee shall distribute the unexpended trust property in the following order:

>> (A) As directed in the trust instrument.

(B) If the trust was created in a nonresiduary clause in the settlor's will or in a codicil to the settlor's will, under the residuary clause in the settlor's will.

(C) If the application of subparagraph (A) or (B) does not result in distribution of unexpended trust property, to the settlor's heirs under Section 21114.[24]

(3) For the purposes of Section 21110,[25] the residuary clause described in subparagraph (B) of paragraph (2) shall be treated as creating a future interest under the terms of a trust.

(c) The intended use of the principal or income may be enforced by a person designated for that purpose in the trust instrument or, if none is designated, by a person appointed by a court. In addition to a person identified in subdivision (a) of Section 17200,[26] any person interested in the welfare of the animal or any nonprofit charitable organization that has as its principal activity the care of animals may petition the court regarding the trust as provided in Chapter 3 (commencing with Section 17200) of Part 5.

(d) If a trustee is not designated or no designated or successor trustee is willing or able to serve, a court shall name a trustee. . . .

(e) The accountings required by Section 16062[27] shall be provided to the beneficiaries who would be entitled to distribution if the animal were then deceased and to any nonprofit charitable corporation that has as its principal activity the care of animals and that has requested these accountings in writing. However, if the value of the assets in the trust does not exceed forty thousand dollars ($40,000), no filing, report, registration, periodic accounting, separate maintenance of funds, appointment, or fee is required by reason of the existence of the fiduciary relationship of the trustee, unless ordered by the court or required by the trust instrument.

(f) Any beneficiary, any person designated by the trust instrument or the court to enforce the trust, or any nonprofit charitable corporation that has as its principal activity the care of animals may, upon reasonable request, inspect the animal, the premises where the animal is maintained, or the books and records of the trust.

(g) A trust governed by this section is not subject to termination pursuant to subdivision (b) of Section 15408.[28]

(h) Section 15211 does not apply to a trust governed by this section.

(i) For purposes of this section, "animal" means a domestic or pet animal for the benefit of which a trust has been established.

(Stats. 2008)

---

[24] Section 21114 is included in Chapter 13.—Ed.

[25] Section 21110, included in Chapter 5, is the antilapse statute.—Ed.

[26] Section 17200 is included in Chapter 9.—Ed.

[27] Section 16062 is included in Chapter 9.—Ed.

[28] Section 15408, which allows termination of a trust with uneconomically low principal, is included in Chapter 10.—Ed.

A Written Instrument?

CPC § 15206. Statute of Frauds

A trust in relation to real property is not valid unless evidenced by one of the following methods:

(a) By a written instrument signed by the trustee, or by the trustee's agent if authorized in writing to do so.

(b) By a written instrument conveying the trust property signed by the settlor, or by the settlor's agent if authorized in writing to do so.

(c) By operation of law.

(Stats. 1990)

CPC § 15207. Oral Trust of Personal Property

(a) The existence and terms of an oral trust of personal property may be established only by clear and convincing evidence.

(b) The oral declaration of the settlor, standing alone, is not sufficient evidence of the creation of a trust of personal property.

(c) In the case of an oral trust, a reference in this division or elsewhere to a trust instrument or declaration means the terms of the trust as established pursuant to subdivision (a).

(Stats. 1990)

Secret Trusts and the Wills Act

Oliffe v. Wells Rejected: Semisecret Trust Enforced by Constructive Trust in Favor of Intended Beneficiary.

CURDY v. BERTON

Supreme Court of California
21 Pac. 858 (1889)

McFARLAND, J. Madeline Curdy died February 9, 1877, in Alameda county, Cal. She left a will duly executed, in which, after bequests to several persons, including the plaintiff herein, there occurs the following: "I give in trust to Francis Berton, now Swiss consul in San Francisco, all the moneys I possess in France . . . to be distributed according to the private instructions I give him."

Berton was present when the will was made, and wrote it for the testatrix at her request; and at the time of the making of the will she verbally instructed him to distribute said property or its proceeds to certain relations and others in France, other than the plaintiff herein, and gave him an order for said property. The facts in proof show that he at least impliedly agreed to accept the trust. After her death, and before the commencement of this action, said Berton faithfully distributed said property in accordance with the said instructions of said testatrix.

This action is brought by plaintiff . . . one of . . . [the] heirs-at-law, to have it decreed that Berton held the legal title to said property in trust for the heirs . . . , for an accounting, and for the payment to him of his proportionate share of said property . . . . The court gave judgment for defendant, and plaintiff appeals . . . .

[T]he position of appellant is, in brief, that, as the statute law of this state requires a will to be in writing, therefore, "where a testator devises property in trust to be applied to such uses as the testator has verbally specified to the devisee, the trust attempted to be created by parol fails, and the devisee takes the property in trust for the heirs of the testator."

The contention of respondent is, in brief, that, independent of the statute of wills, where a testator bequeaths property in trust to a legatee without specifying in the will the purposes of the trust, and at the same time communicates those purposes to the legatee orally, or by unattested writings, and the legatee, either expressly or by silent acquiescence, promises to perform the trust, and the trust itself is not unlawful, there a court of equity will raise a constructive trust in favor of the beneficiaries intended by the testator, and will charge the legatee as a constructive trustee for them, upon the ground that the legatee will not be countenanced in perpetrating a fraud by encouraging the testator to make a bequest which would not otherwise have been made, and then refusing to execute his promise.

We think that respondent's view of the law, as above stated, is correct. There are some cases which support the proposition of appellant, notably, the case of *Olliffe v. Wells*, 130 Mass. 221; but the weight of authority and the better reason are the other way. . . .

We concur: THORNTON, J.; SHARPSTEIN, J.

Secret Trust: Creditor of Beneficiary May Be Able to Reach Assets via Constructive Trust

CABRAL v. SOARES

Court of Appeal, First District
157 Cal. App. 4th 1234, 69 Cal. Rptr. 3d 242 (2007)

POLLAK, Acting P.J. . . . Plaintiff . . . [Tammy Cabral's] complaint alleges that as of November 2005 . . . [her former husband James E. Cabral] was delinquent in paying court-ordered spousal and child support in the approximate amount of $134,000, and that since 1998 he has "on several occasions been found in contempt" for the failure to pay his support obligations. The complaint alleges that James has taken various steps to avoid enforcement of the support obligations, including "not having a regular job with wages . . . and working in a way that he would be paid in a manner that prevented plaintiff from enforcing the support obligations." The complaint continues, "Until shortly before her death, the will of Edwina Cabral provided that her three children would each receive a one-third interest in her estate," which included the family home in Newark, California with a free and clear market value in excess of $500,000, so that James "would have received enough money to pay the past due support obligations in full." "Defendants Mary Soares and James E. Cabral realized that the one-third interest of James E. Cabral would end up getting used to pay the past due support owed to plaintiff. In order to prevent that from happening, those defendants conspired and agreed to have the will modified shortly before Edwina Cabral died. The modification was to have the one-third interest of James E. Cabral instead get paid to Mary Soares so that she would end up with a two thirds interest . . . . [¶] The intent of this arrangement . . . was that Mary Soares would take the one-third interest of James E. Cabral, that Mary Soares would then hold that money, and that Mary Soares would then later get that money to James E. Cabral in a manner to prevent plaintiff from receiving it for the past due support obligations."

The complaint further alleges that Edwina's will was so modified on May 10, 2005 (with a bequest to James of "the paltry sum of $1,000"), that Edwina died less than two months later, that the will was filed with the probate court in July 2005, and that Mary is the executor under the will . . . . Paragraph 22, the final introductory paragraph of the complaint, reads in full as follows: "The last minute change in the will of Edwina Cabral very shortly before her death was probably done at a time when Edwina Cabral was not aware of what she was doing, was not mentally competent, was subject to undue influence by Mary Soares and James E. Cabral . . . . Alternatively, if Edwina Cabral was aware of what was being done, then she also was doing it for the purpose of defrauding plaintiff and of manufacturing a charade to have the money go to James E. Cabral through Mary Soares in a way that was designed to keep plaintiff from being paid what the court ordered James E. Cabral to pay for support." . . .

The trial court sustained defendants' demurrer to this complaint without leave to amend, with the following explanation: "This court lacks jurisdiction of plaintiff's claims. Plaintiff's claim for declaratory relief seeks to contest the validity of the second will and must be brought in the probate court as a will contest. Code of Civil Procedure § 1060. Plaintiff's other claims are dependent upon her claim that the second will should be set aside. . . . [In denying her motion for reconsideration, the judge said:] "The court remains convinced that plaintiff cannot proceed directly against Mary Soares based on decedent's decision to exclude James Cabral from her will. And, the court is not persuaded that a viable claim can be made against Mary Soares and James Cabral based on an alleged agreement between them unless and until James receives some distribution of assets, in which case the family court assignment order appears to provide an adequate remedy."

The assignment order to which the court referred is an order entered in the family law department in the proceedings giving rise to the support orders against James. The court assigned to plaintiff "until such time as the judgment herein is fully satisfied or this order is amended [a]ll rights to payment that [James] has from any third party" including "any right to payment that [James] may have now or in the future from Mary Soares or from Joseph Cabral or from any other source that relates to the will of Edwina Cabral, the estate of Edwina Cabral, and/or any assets or funds from the will and/or estate of Edwina Cabral." . . .

Discussion

The trial court correctly sustained the demurrer insofar as plaintiff challenges the validity of Edwina's will or the administration of her estate.

. . . A dispute concerning the meaning or validity of the provisions of a will cannot be resolved by declaratory judgment. (Code Civ. Proc., § 1060 [declaratory relief action may be brought by "[a]ny person interested under a written instrument, excluding a will or a trust"] . . . . Despite plaintiff's protestations, her complaint is essentially directed to the validity of the will. . . . The claim that the amended will should be disregarded because executed as the result of undue influence can be maintained only in the probate proceedings. . . .

To the extent that the complaint relies on the alternative allegation that Edwina knowingly participated in a scheme to defraud James' creditors by changing her will as she did, the complaint is equally defective. . . . [T]here was no fraudulent conveyance . . . . While his mother still lived, James had no right to any of her property. His mother was under no obligation to leave any of it to him, and she was under no obligation to plaintiff. . . .

The trial court erred in denying leave to amend to properly allege a constructive trust

. . . [P]laintiff may well be able to allege a right to impose a constructive trust on one-half of what Mary receives under Edwina's will, that is, upon the one-third of Edwina's estate received by Mary that allegedly was intended for James.

Plaintiff's potential right to recover under such a theory involves a two-step analysis. The first question is whether James is entitled to assert a constructive trust upon the one-third interest in the estate that Edwina allegedly intended for him that, under the terms of the amended will, goes to Mary. Although inartfully pleaded, the complaint appears to allege that Mary agreed that if Edwina changed her will to leave Mary the one-third beneficial interest then designated for James, Mary would hold the property for James and "later get that money" to him. What is significant in this allegation is . . . that Mary and Edwina so agreed and that Edwina allegedly changed her will in reliance on that agreement.

"[W]here A is induced to make a will in favor of B . . . by the oral promise of B to hold for C, the courts are nearly unanimous in England in decreeing that B must hold in trust for C, and the same is true as to the courts of the United States." (Bogert, Trusts and Trustees (2007) Constructive Trusts, § 499, fns. & italics omitted.) That unquestionably is the rule in California. . . . (*Sears v. Rule* (1945), 27 Cal. 2d 131, 139, 163 P.2d 443.)

. . . Thus, the allegations in plaintiff's complaint suggest that Mary will receive one-third of Edwina's estate subject to a constructive trust for the benefit of James.

The second step in the analysis is to determine whether plaintiff is entitled to enforce James's right to impose such a constructive trust. Several procedures exist by which a judgment creditor such as plaintiff may enforce a judgment against intangible or contingent rights that a debtor such as James may have. . . . Section 708.510, subdivision (a) of the Code of Civil Procedure provides that except as otherwise provided by law, "upon application of the judgment creditor on noticed motion, the court may order the judgment debtor to assign to the judgment creditor . . . all or part of a right to payment due or to become due, whether or not the right is conditioned on future developments." . . . [I]n the family court proceedings the court has in fact entered an order assigning to plaintiff any right James may have to payment from Mary that "relates to" Edwina's will or estate.

In refusing to reconsider its order denying plaintiff leave to amend her complaint, the trial court suggested that no claim could be made against Mary and James "based on an alleged agreement between them unless and until James receives some distribution of assets," in which case the trial court believed the assignment order would provide an adequate remedy. However, imposition of a constructive trust on a portion of the devise to Mary would not be based on an agreement between James and Mary but on an agreement between Mary and Edwina. More importantly, James may never—or at least, never within the foreseeable future—receive a distribution of assets from the estate (other than the "paltry" $1,000 bequest). If James declines to enforce a claim for imposition of a constructive trust, or if Mary disputes the validity of such a claim, plaintiff's rights will not be enforced . . . .

A so-called creditor's suit, authorized by Code of Civil Procedure section 708.210, is designed to address exactly such a situation. . . . Section 708.210 provides, "If a third person has possession or control of property in which the judgment debtor has an interest or is indebted to the judgment debtor, the judgment creditor may bring an action against the third person to have the interest or debt applied to the satisfaction of the money judgment." . . . In many situations the assignment entered in family court would be sufficient to enforce a creditor's rights. However, a creditor's suit may be necessary if there is a dispute concerning ownership of the property held by the third party—in this instance a dispute concerning the right to impose a constructive trust on one half the amounts distributed to Mary from Edwina's estate . . . . Given the allegations of the complaint in this case, it is entirely reasonable for plaintiff to anticipate that Mary may dispute the right to impose a constructive trust on any portion of the legacy from her mother, or may otherwise fail to cooperate in honoring the family court assignment. In all events, plaintiff's right to maintain a creditor's suit is not dependent on establishing that other less onerous procedures provide an inadequate remedy. . . .

The record does not disclose whether there have as yet been any distributions in the probate proceedings. If Mary has already received a distribution from the estate but has not delivered any portion to James, plaintiff unquestionably is entitled to maintain a creditor's suit to enforce whatever right James has to one-half of those funds. Mary may deny that she agreed to hold any portion of the legacy for James, and the action will provide the means for resolving that critical issue. If funds have not yet been distributed from the estate, Mary will not yet have received any property potentially subject to a constructive trust. In that event there may be an appropriate basis for declaratory relief, not with respect to plaintiff's right to an interest in Edwina's estate, . . . but with respect to plaintiff's right to enforce a constructive trust against a portion of the funds that Mary is entitled to receive from the estate. If plaintiff were to show a basis for anticipating action by Mary that might frustrate plaintiff's ability to enforce a constructive trust, injunctive relief might be appropriate. We do not anticipate what new or revised allegations plaintiff may make to her complaint . . . . We are satisfied, however, that plaintiff is entitled to amend her complaint to attempt to state a claim on which relief may be granted.

Disposition

The judgment is reversed, and the matter is remanded to the trial court with directions to grant plaintiff leave to file an amended complaint. The parties are to bear their respective costs on appeal . . . .

Chapter 7. Nonprobate Transfers and Planning for Incapacity

Section B. Revocable Trusts

Revoking or Amending a Revocable Trust

Mental Capacity

Test for Testamentary Capacity Appropriate for Simple Amendments to Revocable Trust

ANDERSEN v. HUNT

California Court of Appeal, Second District, Division 4
196 Cal. App. 4th 722, 126 Cal. Rptr. 3d 736, Review Denied (2011)

SUZUKAWA, J. . . . Plaintiffs and respondents Stephen Andersen . . . and Kathleen Brandt . . . are the children of decedent Wayne Andersen . . . , who died April 28, 2006. . . . Plaintiff John Andersen . . . , not a party to this appeal, is Stephen's son and Wayne's grandson. Appellant Pauline Hunt . . . was Wayne's long-term romantic partner. Taylor Profita . . . is Pauline's grandson.

In 1992, Wayne and his wife established a family trust that named Stephen and Kathleen the sole beneficiaries after their parents' deaths. Wayne's wife died in 1993. In 2003, after suffering a stroke, Wayne amended his trust to leave a 60 percent portion of his estate to Pauline, with the remainder going to Stephen, Kathleen, and John. He made subsequent amendments later in 2003 and in 2004, but retained the provision leaving 60 percent of his estate to Pauline.

After Wayne's death in 2006, Stephen and Kathleen brought the present action to, among other things, invalidate the 2003 and 2004 trust amendments and recover funds placed in accounts held jointly by Wayne and Pauline. The probate court found that Wayne lacked capacity to execute the trust amendments, transfer funds from the trust to joint tenancy accounts, and change the beneficiary of his life insurance policy, and that Pauline exerted undue influence with respect to the amendments and transfers.

In the published part of the opinion, we conclude the probate court erred when it evaluated Wayne's capacity to execute the trust amendments by the general standard of capacity set out in Probate Code sections 810 to 812, instead of the standard of testamentary capacity set out in Probate Code section 6100.5.[29] . . . In the unpublished part, we find there is no substantial evidence that Wayne lacked testamentary capacity to execute the 2003 and 2004 trust

---

[29] Section 6100.5 is set forth in Chapter 4.

amendments or that the amendments were the product of Pauline's undue influence. We also determine there is substantial evidence that Wayne lacked capacity to open joint tenancy accounts and to change the beneficiary of his life insurance policy. Thus, we reverse the part of the judgment invalidating the trust amendments and affirm in all other respects.

DISCUSSION

III. The Trial Court Erred in Evaluating Wayne's Capacity to Execute the Trust Amendments by Standards of Contractual Capacity, Not Testamentary Capacity

. . . Pauline contends that the trial court erred in evaluating Wayne's capacity to execute the trust amendments by the standard of contractual capacity, rather than testamentary capacity. . . . [W]e agree.

A. Testamentary Capacity

. . . " 'It is thoroughly established by a series of decisions that: "Ability to transact important business, or even ordinary business, is not the legal standard of testamentary capacity . . . ." . . . Rather, testamentary capacity involves the question whether, at the time the will is made, the testator ' "has sufficient mental capacity to understand the nature of the act he is doing, to understand and recollect the nature and situation of his property and to remember, and understand his relations to, the persons who have claims upon his bounty and whose interests are affected by the provisions of the instrument." ' . . . It is a question . . . of the testator's mental state in relation to a specific event, the making of a will." (*Conservatorship of Bookasta* (1989) 216 Cal. App. 3d 445, 450, 265 Cal. Rptr. 1.)

. . . 'It has been held over and over in this state that old age, feebleness, forgetfulness, filthy personal habits, personal eccentricities, failure to recognize old friends or relatives, physical disability, absent-mindedness and mental confusion do not furnish grounds for holding that a testator lacked testamentary capacity.' (*Estate of Selb* (1948) 84 Cal. App. 2d 46, 49 [190 P.2d 277].) Nor does the mere fact that the testator is under a guardianship support a finding of lack of testamentary capacity without evidence that the incompetence continues at the time of the will's execution. (. . . *Estate of Wochos* (1972) 23 Cal. App. 3d 47 [99 Cal. Rptr. 782].) . . .

B. Capacity Generally

Sections 810 to 813 set out the standard for capacity to make various kinds of decisions, transact business, and enter contracts. Section 810 provides:

"(a) For purposes of this part, there shall exist a rebuttable presumption affecting the burden of proof that all persons have the capacity to make decisions and to be responsible for their acts or decisions.

"(b) A person who has a mental or physical disorder may still be capable of contracting, conveying, marrying, making medical decisions, executing wills or trusts, and performing other actions.

"(c) A judicial determination that a person is totally without understanding, or is of unsound mind, or suffers from one or more mental deficits so substantial that, under the circumstances, the person should be deemed to lack the legal capacity to perform a specific act, should be based on evidence of a deficit in one or more of the person's mental functions rather than on a diagnosis of a person's mental or physical disorder."

Section 811 sets out the findings necessary to support a conclusion of lack of capacity, as follows:

"(a) A determination that a person is of unsound mind or lacks the capacity to make a decision or do a certain act, including, but not limited to, the incapacity to contract, to make a conveyance, to marry, to make medical decisions, to execute wills, or to execute trusts, shall be supported by evidence of a deficit in at least one of the following mental functions, subject to subdivision (b), and evidence of a correlation between the deficit or deficits and the decision or acts in question:

"(1) Alertness and attention, including, but not limited to, the following: (A) Level of arousal or consciousness. (B) Orientation to time, place, person, and situation. (C) Ability to attend and concentrate.

"(2) Information processing, including, but not limited to, the following: (A) Short- and long-term memory, including immediate recall. (B) Ability to understand or communicate with others, either verbally or otherwise. (C) Recognition of familiar objects and familiar persons. (D) Ability to understand and appreciate quantities. (E) Ability to reason using abstract concepts. (F) Ability to plan, organize, and carry out actions in one's own rational self-interest. (G) Ability to reason logically.

"(3) Thought processes. Deficits in these functions may be demonstrated by the presence of the following: (A) Severely disorganized thinking. (B) Hallucinations. (C) Delusions. (D) Uncontrollable, repetitive, or intrusive thoughts.

"(4) Ability to modulate mood and affect. Deficits in this ability may be demonstrated by the presence of a pervasive and persistent or recurrent state of euphoria, anger, anxiety, fear, panic, depression, hopelessness or despair, helplessness, apathy or indifference, that is inappropriate in degree to the individual's circumstances.

"(b) A deficit in the mental functions listed above may be considered only if the deficit, by itself or in combination with one or more other mental function deficits, significantly impairs the person's ability to understand and appreciate the consequences of his or her actions *with regard to the type of act or decision in question.*

"(c) In determining whether a person suffers from a deficit in mental function so substantial that the person lacks the capacity to do a certain act, the court may take into consideration the frequency, severity, and duration of periods of impairment . . . ." (Italics added.)

Section 812 provides: "Except where otherwise provided by law, including, but not limited to, Section 813 and the statutory and decisional law of testamentary capacity, a person lacks the capacity to make a decision unless the person has the ability to communicate verbally, or by any other means, the decision, and to understand and appreciate, to the extent relevant, all of the following: (a) The rights, duties, and responsibilities created by, or affected by the decision. (b) The probable consequences for the decisionmaker and, where appropriate, the persons affected by the decision. (c) The significant risks, benefits, and reasonable alternatives involved in the decision."

C. Wayne's Capacity to Execute the Disputed Trust Amendments Should Have Been Evaluated by the Standard of Testamentary Capacity (Section 6100.5)

. . . California courts have not applied consistent standards in evaluating capacity to make or amend a trust. . . . [Case discussion omitted.—Ed.] The cases . . . offer little assistance in resolving the question we now address—the measure by which a court should evaluate a decedent's capacity to make an after-death transfer by trust. . . .

As Stephen and Kathleen correctly note, section 6100.5 defines mental competency to make a "will," not a testamentary transfer more generally. Thus, they appear to be correct that Wayne's capacity must be evaluated under sections 810 to 812, not section 6100.5.

Stephen and Kathleen err, however, in suggesting that sections 810 to 812 set out a single standard of "contractual capacity." They do not. To the contrary, section 811, subdivision (a) provides that a determination that a person lacks capacity to make a decision or do a certain act, including without limitation "to contract, . . . to execute wills, or to execute trusts," must be supported by evidence of a deficit in one of the statutorily identified mental functions *and evidence of a correlation between the deficit and the decision or act in question.* Section 811, subdivision (b) contains similar language, stating that a deficit in one of the statutorily defined mental functions may be considered *only* if it significantly impairs the person's ability to appreciate the consequences of his or her actions *with regard to the type or act or decision in question.* And section 812 provides that a person lacks capacity to make a decision only if he or she cannot appreciate the rights, duties, consequences, risks and benefits *"involved in the decision."* (Italics added.) Accordingly, sections 810 to 812 do not set out a single standard for contractual capacity, but rather provide that capacity to do a variety of acts, including to contract, make a will, or execute a trust, must be evaluated by a person's ability to appreciate the consequences *of the particular act he or she wishes to take.* More complicated decisions and transactions thus would appear to require greater mental function; less complicated decisions and transactions would appear to require less mental function.

When determining whether a trustor had capacity to execute a trust amendment that, in its content and complexity, closely resembles a will or codicil, we believe it is appropriate to look to section 6100.5 to determine when a person's mental deficits are sufficient to allow a court to conclude that the person lacks the ability "to understand and appreciate the consequences of his or her actions with regard to the type of act or decision in question." . . . In other words, while section 6100.5 is not directly applicable to determine competency to make or amend a trust, it is made applicable through section 811 to trusts or trust amendments that are analogous to wills or codicils.

In the present case, while the original trust document is complex, the amendments are not. . . . Indeed, none of the contested amendments does more than provide the percentages of the trust estate Wayne wished each beneficiary to receive. The May 28, 2003 amendment provided that Pauline was to receive 60 percent of the trust residue, and Stephen, Kathleen, and John were to receive the remaining 40 percent in equal shares; the November 18, 2003 amendment specified the same 60 percent/40 percent allocation if Wayne predeceased Pauline, but provided that if Pauline died first, Taylor should receive a portion of the trust assets; and the July 6, 2004 amendment eliminated John as a beneficiary, providing that "Steve will have the portion that had been set aside for his son."

In view of the amendments' simplicity and testamentary nature, we conclude that they are indistinguishable from a will or codicil and, thus, Wayne's capacity to execute the amendments should have been evaluated pursuant to the standard of testamentary capacity articulated in section 6100.5. The trial court erred in evaluating Wayne's capacity under a different, higher standard of mental functioning. . . .

DISPOSITION

The part[s] of the judgment invalidating the trust amendments are reversed, and the probate court is directed to enter a new and different judgment affirming the validity of the trust amendments. In all other respects, the judgment is affirmed. The parties are to bear their own costs on appeal.

Estate Plan Changes Including Creation of New Trusts, Transmutation of Community Property, and Disinheritance of Children Required Greater Capacity than CPC § 6100.5

LINTZ v. LINTZ

Court of Appeal, Sixth District, California.
222 Cal. App. 4th 1346, 167 Cal. Rptr. 3d 50 (2014)

Grover, J. Defendant Lois . . . Lintz appeals from a judgment of financial elder abuse, undue influence, breach of fiduciary duty, conversion of separate property, and constructive trust. Defendant challenges only the remedial aspect of the judgment. She argues that the probate court erred by voiding her deceased husband's testamentary trusts and trust amendments executed after May 2005 without proof of undue influence in connection with the execution of those documents. She argues further that the probate court's invalidation of the trust documents unconstitutionally interferes with her marital relationship.

Although the probate court applied the incorrect standard for legal capacity and failed to apply a presumption of undue influence to the interspousal transactions at issue here, we will affirm the judgment because it is amply supported by the evidence, especially in light of the higher burdens incorrectly placed on plaintiffs below, and we find no error in the remedy.

I. FACTUAL AND PROCEDURAL BACKGROUND

Defendant was the third wife of decedent Robert Lintz. The couple married in 1999, divorced approximately six months later, and remarried in February 2005. Their second marriage ended when decedent died in October 2009 at age 81. Defendant has two children from a previous marriage. Decedent had three children from two previous marriages, and two grandchildren. When decedent remarried defendant in 2005, he was a retired real estate developer worth millions of dollars. Decedent had a complicated estate plan, with holdings in both northern and southern California. Decedent's northern California estate plan was contained in the Robert Lintz Trust (the trust) and a series of amendments to the trust, prepared over the years by decedent's estate lawyers. The ninth amendment to the trust, in effect when decedent and defendant remarried, provided for decedent's children, grandchildren, and former son-in-law upon decedent's death.

In May 2005 decedent executed a tenth amendment to the trust. The tenth amendment provided defendant with fifty percent of decedent's assets upon his death, with the remaining fifty percent to be distributed among decedent's children and grandchildren. Between May 2005 and 2008 decedent executed several additional trust amendments, increasingly providing defendant with more of decedent's assets upon his death and disinheriting his two eldest children. Ultimately, in June 2008 defendant and decedent, as joint settlors and trustees, executed the Lintz Family Revocable Trust. The trust, prepared by defendant's attorney at defendant's direction, purportedly designated all of decedent's property as community property, gave defendant an exclusive life interest in decedent's estate, and gave defendant the right to disinherit decedent's youngest child and leave any unspent residue to defendant's two children.

Upon decedent's death, decedent's older children, plaintiffs Susan Lintz and James Lintz, as decedent's successors in interest, filed a second amended complaint against defendant alleging several causes of action including fiduciary abuse of an elder, breach of fiduciary duty, conversion, constructive trust, and undue influence.[1] Following a 15–day bench trial, the probate court issued a 25–page statement of decision finding defendant liable for financial elder abuse under Welfare and Institutions Code section 15610.30, breach of fiduciary duty, conversion of separate property funds, and finding defendant in constructive trust of decedent's converted funds and trust property. The court ruled that decedent had testamentary capacity to execute the trust instruments, but it found defendant liable for undue influence in the procurement of decedent's estate plans.

Among several remedies, the probate court voided all trusts and trust amendments following the tenth amendment to the trust, invalidated real property deeds, and took

---

[1] Plaintiffs commenced the lawsuit before decedent's death in conjunction with a conservatorship petition as proposed guardians ad litem.

steps to implement the terms of the tenth amendment. The court concluded that much of defendant's spending during her marriage to decedent constituted acts of financial abuse and conversion, and awarded plaintiffs attorney's fees and costs for proving financial elder abuse under Welfare and Institutions Code section 15610.30.

II. DISCUSSION

A. LEGAL CAPACITY STANDARD

. . . In *Andersen v. Hunt* (2011) 196 Cal. App. 4th 722, 730, 126 Cal. Rptr. 3d 736 (*Andersen*) the court addressed "the measure by which a court should evaluate a decedent's capacity to make an after-death transfer by trust." *Andersen* ruled that Probate Code section 6100.5 applied to the mental competency to make a will, not to a testamentary transfer in general. . . . The court explained that Probate Code sections 810 through 812 do not impose a single standard of contractual capacity. Because each section provides that capacity be evaluated in light of the complexity of the decision or act in question capacity to execute a trust "must be evaluated by a person's ability to appreciate the consequences *of the particular act he or she wishes to take.*" Indeed, "[m]ore complicated decisions and transactions thus would appear to require greater mental function; less complicated decisions and transactions would appear to require less mental function."

Andersen further concluded that, when a trust amendment closely resembles a will or codicil "in its content and complexity," a court should look to Probate Code section 6100.5 to determine whether, under Probate Code section 811, subdivision (b), a person lacks the mental function " 'to understand and appreciate the consequences of his or her actions with regard to the type of act or decision in question.' " . . . Because the trust amendments in *Anderson* merely reallocated the percentage of the trust estate among beneficiaries, the court considered them indistinguishable from a will or codicil and concluded that the decedent's capacity should have been evaluated under the lower capacity standard of Probate Code section 6100.5.

Adopting the reasoning of *Andersen,* we conclude that the probate court erred by applying the Probate Code section 6100.5 testamentary capacity standard to the trusts and trust amendments at issue in this case instead of the sliding-scale contractual standard in Probate Code sections 810 through 812. The trust instruments here were unquestionably more complex than a will or codicil. They addressed community property concerns, provided for income distribution during the life of the surviving spouse, and provided for the creation of multiple trusts, one contemplating estate tax consequences, upon the death of the surviving spouse.

B. UNDUE INFLUENCE PRESUMPTION

In property-related transactions between spouses, Family Code section 721,[30] subdivision (b) "imposes a duty of the highest good faith and fair dealing on each spouse . . . ." This duty stems from the "general rules governing fiduciary relationships which control the actions of persons occupying confidential relations with each other," prohibiting each spouse from taking "any unfair advantage of the other." . . . The presumption is rebuttable; the spouse advantaged by the transaction must establish that the disadvantaged spouse acted freely and voluntarily, with " 'full knowledge of all the facts, and with a complete understanding of the effect of' the transaction.' "

Family Code section 721 applies here. Although we were not provided with transcripts of the two-day closing arguments, there is no indication in the record before us that the probate court applied the presumption of undue influence arising from that section. The presumption should have been applied to the transmutation of decedent's separate property to community property and to the huge sums of money decedent transferred to defendant. It also should have been applied to the Lintz Family Revocable Trust, which was a contract between decedent and defendant both as settlors and as trustees. . . . The trust advantaged defendant by granting her an exclusive and virtually unfettered life estate in decedent's property, disinheriting two of decedent's three children, and giving defendant the right to disinherit decedent's third child and pass decedent's property either to her own children or to her individual estate.

The probate court should have applied the presumption of undue influence, thereby shifting the burden to defendant to rebut the presumption. Even without that burden, defendant did not prevail on the issue of undue influence below. Our conclusion that the presumption applies only weakens her position on appeal.

C. CHALLENGES TO UNDUE INFLUENCE FINDING

. . . Defendant argues that the probate court erred by voiding all trust instruments executed after the May 2005 tenth amendment based on a finding that defendant exerted undue influence, without evidence of such influence being exercised at the time the documents were actually signed. Defendant concedes the court's factual findings are sufficient to support liability for financial elder abuse under Welfare and Institutions Code section 15610.30, but she argues that they are insufficient to void a testamentary document. . . .

1. Undue Influence May Be Proven By Circumstantial Evidence

In *In re Welch* (1954) 43 Cal.2d 173, 272 P.2d 512, . . . the Supreme Court recognized

---

[30] Family Code § 721 is set out in Chapter 8.

the settled law that undue influence requires a showing that the testator's free will was overpowered "at the very time the will was made." Defendant relies on the quoted language . . . to argue that no evidence established that decedent's free will was overborne at the time the testamentary documents were executed. Given the extensive circumstantial evidence supporting the probate court's undue influence finding, we can only understand defendant to be arguing that plaintiffs failed to produce any direct evidence of undue influence at the time decedent signed the testamentary documents. But plaintiffs are not required to prove their case by direct evidence.

"Direct evidence as to undue influence is rarely obtainable and hence a court or jury must determine the issue of undue influence by inferences drawn from all the facts and circumstances." (*Griffith v. Hannam* (1951) 106 Cal. App. 2d 782, 786, 236 P.2d 208; . . . .) [citations omitted.—Ed.] Thus, while pressure must be brought to bear directly on the testamentary act, the pressure, or undue influence, may be established by circumstantial evidence. As a matter of law, the probate court's undue influence finding need not be supported by direct evidence of undue influence at the moment decedent signed the trust instruments.

2. The Undue Influence Finding was Separate from the Welfare and Institutions Code Financial Elder Abuse Finding

We reject defendant's assertion that the probate court's undue influence finding was made under Welfare and Institutions Code section 15610.30 . . . .[3]

The probate court cited Welfare and Institutions Code section 15610.30 to impose financial elder abuse liability as to plaintiffs' first cause of action for fiduciary abuse of an elder. This liability is supported by the court's findings that "[decedent] did not know the extent of [defendant's] spending," and that "[w]hile it is not uncommon for a spouse to spend money or purchase items of which the other is unaware, and the line between such conduct and financial abuse is not always clear, what [defendant] did in this case went well beyond the line of reasonable conduct and constituted financial abuse," and the court's further conclusion that much of defendant's credit card spending and writing herself checks from decedent's bank account during the marriage amounted to financial abuse.

---

[3] During the pendency of this appeal, the Legislature amended Welfare and Institutions Code section 15610.30, subdivision (a)(3) replacing "by undue influence, as defined in Civil Code section 1575" with "by undue influence, as defined by section 15610.70." . . . The Legislature added a new section 15610.70 . . . defining undue influence as "excessive persuasion that causes another person to act or refrain from acting by overcoming that person's free will and results in inequity," and listing factors to be considered in making an undue influence determination under section 15610.30. . . . The Legislature also added section 86 to the Probate Code, providing that undue influence under the Probate Code has the same meaning as it does under Welfare and Institutions Code section 15610.70. . . .

In addition to finding defendant liable for Welfare and Institutions Code section 15610.30 financial elder abuse, the probate court found defendant liable under plaintiffs' separately pleaded fifth cause of action for undue influence. On that cause of action, the court concluded defendant exerted undue influence specifically "to procure estate plans and control over assets, according to [defendant's] wishes and contrary to the wishes of [decedent]." . . . It is clear from the statement of decision that the court made the undue influence finding as to the fifth cause of action under the Probate Code, not the Welfare and Institutions Code.

3. The Probate Court Applied the Proper Undue Influence Standard to Void the Trust Documents

We are also unpersuaded by defendant's argument that the probate court conflated the former Welfare and Institutions Code section 15610.30 undue influence standard with the standard for undue influence under Probate Code section 6104. We note that defendant does not challenge the findings of fact or conclusions of law contained in the statement of decision, and we therefore presume them to be correct on appeal. . . . We presume the evidence supports the conclusion that defendant used undue influence over decedent "to procure estate plans . . . , according to her wishes and contrary to the wishes of decedent." But even without that presumption, the statement of decision establishes the undue influence required to void a testamentary document; defendant's influence overcame decedent's free will and operated directly on the testamentary acts voided by the trial court. . . .

The probate court described decedent as "helpless[ ] and susceptible[ ] to [defendant's] wishes and influence beyond the susceptibility which is normal incident of [*sic*] a marital relationship." According to the statement of decision, decedent was fearful of defendant and unable to exercise his free will over her when it came to his money. Defendant took an increasingly active role in procuring decedent's estate plans following the tenth amendment, increasingly benefiting from the later amendments. Defendant misinformed decedent's lawyers of decedent's testamentary wishes and ultimately discontinued the services of decedent's long-standing estate planning lawyers under the pretext of a fee dispute. The probate court also noted that decedent signed the Lintz Family Revocable Trust—the most recent estate plan prepared by defendant's lawyer—outside the presence of his new counsel and against new counsel's advice. That document provided for unspent residue to be left to defendant's children, and it gave defendant the power to disinherit decedent's youngest child whom he adored. Decedent's execution of that estate plan was inconsistent with the statement he made to his lawyer ("Why shouldn't we leave the property to [decedent's youngest child]?") on the same day defendant insisted to the lawyer that decedent wanted everything left to her. It was also inconsistent with decedent's great dislike for one of defendant's children. . . . We conclude the probate court applied the proper undue influence standard to void the trust documents.

* * *

E. DEFENDANT'S SANCTITY OF MARRIAGE ARGUMENT

Defendant argues that voiding the trust documents because she "spent 'too much' of her husband's money during his lifetime" violates the sanctity of her marriage to decedent under the California Constitution. This argument fails because, as we explained above, the probate court did not void the trust documents on that basis. Apart from the probate court's findings establishing that defendant spent decedent's money without his knowledge and against his wishes, the trial court made additional findings to support its undue influence determination. Further, while the right to marry is protected by the California Constitution (*In re Marriage Cases* (2008) 43 Cal. 4th 757, 809, 76 Cal. Rptr. 3d 683, 183 P.3d 384), the Constitution does not diminish defendant's fiduciary obligations to her husband, nor shield her from liability for unlawful conduct.

III. DISPOSITION

The judgment of the probate court is affirmed.

Time Limit on Action to Contest Trust

CPC § 16061.8. Limitations of Actions to Contest Trust

No person upon whom the notification by the trustee is served pursuant to this chapter, whether the notice is served on him or her within or after the time period set forth in subdivision (f) of Section 16061.7, may bring an action to contest the trust more than 120 days from the date the notification by the trustee is served upon him or her, or 60 days from the date on which a copy of the terms of the trust is delivered pursuant to Section 1215 to him or her during that 120-day period, whichever is later.

(Stats. 1997, 2000, 2010, 2017)

Filing Petition, But Not Service, Within 120 Days Is Required by CPC § 16061.8

STRALEY v. GAMBLE

Court of Appeal, Second District, Division 2
217 Cal. App. 4th 533, 158 Cal. Rptr. 484 (2013)

ASHMANN-GERST, J. Steven M. Straley appeals from a trial court order denying his petition for an order to determine the validity of a trust amendment. He contends that the trial court erred in finding that the petition was untimely pursuant to Probate Code sections 16061.7 and

16061.8 and that it was barred by the principle of laches. We agree with appellant that he timely brought an action to contest the trust. Accordingly, we reverse.

FACTUAL AND PROCEDURAL BACKGROUND

Factual Background

Rebecca S. Straley, appellant's mother, was the trustor and settlor of the Rebecca S. Straley Living Trust Dated May 27, 2009 (the trust). Appellant was deliberately not named as a beneficiary of the trust. But, under the provisions of the trust, Mrs. Straley had the right, as settlor, to amend the trust in writing as she elected.

On April 3, 2011, Mrs. Straley executed (or attempted to sign) some sort of amendment to the trust (the amendment), purportedly distributing her entire estate to appellant. According to appellant's opening brief, Mrs. Straley had reconciled with appellant and wanted to amend the trust to include him as a beneficiary. Respondent William O. Gamble III (trustee), the successor trustee, challenges the validity of the amendment, pointing out that the amendment does not mention the trust, does not state that it was amending the trust, was likely "typed" by someone when Mrs. Straley was on her deathbed, and a shaky "R" is supposed to be Mrs. Straley's signature. Mrs. Straley passed away on April 6, 2011.

Procedural Background

On April 21, 2011, the successor trustee served appellant with notice of the administration of the trust, pursuant to section 16061.7. Five days later, appellant was served with a copy of the trust.

On August 18, 2011, appellant filed the petition. In the petition, appellant asked the trial court to determine whether the entire trust distribution had been changed pursuant to the amendment. Appellant did not, however, serve notice of his petition until he served notice of hearing on October 28, 2011.

On November 28, 2011, the trustee filed and served his response to the petition, asserting, inter alia, that the petition was time-barred, pursuant to section 16061.7 and the doctrine of laches, and that the amendment was invalid. Specifically, the trustee claimed that the delay in serving notice of hearing on the petition for 187 days exceeded the 120–day statutory period to "bring an action" to contest the trust under sections 16061.7 and 16061.8. Appellant filed a brief memorandum of points and authorities in rebuttal.

At the hearing on November 30, 2012, the trial court denied appellant's petition for the reasons set forth in the trustee's response. In particular, the trial court found that the petition was time-barred by section 16061.7 and by the equitable doctrine of laches. Appellant's timely appeal ensued.

DISCUSSION

I. *Standard of review*

As the parties agree, we review the trial court's order to the extent it is based upon the interpretation of sections 16061.7 and 16061.8 de novo. ... We review the trial court's finding that the doctrine of laches applies for abuse of discretion. ...

II. *The trial court erred in finding that appellant's petition was time-barred by the statute of limitations and the doctrine of laches*

A trustee or beneficiary of a trust may petition the court to determine the validity of a trust provision. (§ 17200(b)(3).) "A proceeding under this chapter is commenced by filing a petition stating facts showing that the petition is authorized under this chapter. The petition shall also state the grounds of the petition and the names and addresses of each person entitled to notice of the petition." (§ 17201.) At the time the petition is filed, the clerk's office sets a hearing date on the petition. (See, e.g., Super. Ct. L.A. County, Local Rules, rule 4.9.) Then, "[a]t least 30 days before the time set for the hearing on the petition, the petitioner shall cause notice of hearing to be mailed." (§ 17203(a.).)

The timeframe in which to bring an action to contest a trust is delineated by statute. Section 16061.8 provides, in relevant part: "No person upon whom the notification by the trustee is served pursuant to this chapter ... may bring an action to contest the trust more than 120 days from the date the notification by the trustee is served upon him."

Here, the trustee served the notification on appellant on April 21, 2011. Thus, appellant had until August 24, 2011, to "bring an action" to contest the trust. Because appellant filed his petition on August 18, 2011, the petition was timely filed. ...

In defending the trial court's order, the trustee argues that to "bring an action," appellant was required to file *and serve* his petition within the 120-day statutory period. In light of the procedure set forth above, we cannot agree. Appellant was not required to serve his petition at the time it was filed. Rather, he was required to serve his petition after the clerk set the hearing date, and at least 30 days before that hearing date.

Our conclusion is bolstered by the definition of the phrase "bring suit." To "bring suit" is to initiate legal proceedings in a legal action; "a suit is 'brought' at the time it is commenced." (Black's Law Dict. (6th ed. 1990) p. 192, col. 2.) If something more than just filing the petition was required, either the Judicial Council or the Legislature could have said so. ...

While the statute does not use the word "filed," we believe that the statutory phrase "bring an action" is clear: Appellant brought the action when he filed his petition. Service of the petition was not required to timely bring an action.

Having determined that appellant's petition was timely under the terms of the statute, we next consider whether the petition was nonetheless barred by the doctrine of laches. "Laches is an equitable defense to the enforcement of stale claims. It may be applied where the complaining party has unreasonably delayed in the enforcement of a right, and where that party has either acquiesced in the adverse party's conduct or where the adverse party has suffered prejudice. . . . [Citations.]" . . .

Despite the deferential standard of review, we conclude that the trial court erred in finding that appellant's petition was barred by the doctrine of laches. In particular, there is no indication that the trustee was prejudiced by any sort of delay in the timely filing and subsequent service of the petition. Certainly trusts are supposed to be administered expeditiously. . . . But, there is no evidence here that the trust's assets were in fact administered before appellant's petition was heard. . . .

DISPOSITION

The order is reversed. Appellant is entitled to costs on appeal.

NOTES:

1. Drake v. Pinkham, 217 Cal. App. 4th 400, 158 Cal. Rptr. 3d 115 (2013), held that sister who waited until after mother's death to contest validity of amendments to revocable trust that eliminated her interest was barred by laches. Sister was aware of the amendments and filed a petition alleging that her mother was incompetent in 2005, but entered a settlement agreement in 2006, and did not file petition to invalidate trust amendments until 2010. Sister had standing during her mother's lifetime to challenge validity of amendments on ground of mother's lack of capacity and her failure to bring the action until mother had died was necessarily prejudicial because all causes of action centered on mother's mental capacity, defendant's influence over her, and mother's understanding of the amendments.

2. Filing petition to probate will that expressly revoked trust was action to contest trust; no separate action was necessary. Petition was filed within 120 days after trustee gave notice pursuant to §§ 16061.7 and 16061.8. **Estate of Stoker**, 193 Cal. App. 4th 236, 122 Cal. Rptr. 3d 529 (2011).

3. Yeh v. Tai, 18 Cal. App. 5th 953, 227 Cal. Rptr. 3d 275 (2017) held that widow's action under Family Code § 1101 to recover property husband wrongfully transferred to trust for his children was not an action to contest the trust subject to 120 day requirement.

Presumption of Revocability; Methods of Revocation and Amendment

CPC § 15400. Presumption of Revocability

Unless a trust is expressly made irrevocable by the trust instrument, the trust is revocable by the settlor. This section applies only where the settlor is domiciled in this state when the trust

is created, where the trust instrument is executed in this state, or where the trust instrument provides that the law of this state governs the trust.
(Stats. 1990)

CPC § 15401. Methods of Revoking Revocable Trust

(a) A trust that is revocable by the settlor or any other person may be revoked in whole or in part by any of the following methods:

(1) By compliance with any method of revocation provided in the trust instrument.

(2) By a writing, other than a will, signed by the settlor or any other person holding the power of revocation and delivered to the trustee during the lifetime of the settlor or the person holding the power of revocation. If the trust instrument explicitly makes the method of revocation provided in the trust instrument the exclusive method of revocation, the trust may not be revoked pursuant to this paragraph.

(b)(1) Unless otherwise provided in the instrument, if a trust is created by more than one settlor, each settlor may revoke the trust as to the portion of the trust contributed by that settlor, except as provided in Section 761 of the Family Code.

(2) Notwithstanding paragraph (1), a settlor may grant to another person, including, but not limited to, his or her spouse, a power to revoke all or part of that portion of the trust contributed by that settlor, regardless of whether that portion was separate property or community property of that settlor, and regardless of whether that power to revoke is exercisable during the lifetime of that settlor or continues after the death of that settlor, or both.

(c) A trust may not be modified or revoked by an attorney in fact under a power of attorney unless it is expressly permitted by the trust instrument.

(d) This section shall not limit the authority to modify or terminate a trust pursuant to Section 15403 or 15404 in an appropriate case.

(e) The manner of revocation of a trust revocable by the settlor or any other person that was created by an instrument executed before July 1, 1987, is governed by prior law and not by this section.
(Stats. 1990, 1994, 2012)

CPC § 15402. Modification by Revocation Procedure

Unless the trust instrument provides otherwise, if a trust is revocable by the settlor, the settlor may modify the trust by the procedure for revocation.
(Stats. 1990)

Family Code § 761. Revocation as to Community Property Share

(a) Unless the trust instrument or the instrument of transfer expressly provides otherwise, community property that is transferred in trust remains community property during the marriage, regardless of the identity of the trustee, if the trust, originally or as amended before or after the transfer, provides that the trust is revocable as to that property during the marriage and the power, if any, to modify the trust as to the rights and interests in that property during the marriage may be exercised only with the joinder or consent of both spouses.

(b) Unless the trust instrument expressly provides otherwise, a power to revoke as to community property may be exercised by either spouse acting alone. Community property, including any income or appreciation, that is distributed or withdrawn from a trust by revocation, power of withdrawal, or otherwise, remains community property unless there is a valid transmutation of the property at the time of distribution or withdrawal.

***

(Stats. 1992, 2014)

NOTE: Community property held in revocable trust for spouses for life with remainder to wife's son became separate property on wife's death under CPC § 100. Even though husband could have revoked the entire trust during her lifetime under Family Code § 761, his revocation after her death was effective only as to his half of the property. **Estate of Powell**, 83 Cal. App. 4th 1434, 100 Cal. Rptr. 2d 501 (2000).

CPC § 15800. *Rights of Beneficiaries of Revocable Trusts*

Except to the extent that the trust instrument otherwise provides or where the joint action of the settlor and all beneficiaries is required, during the time that a trust is revocable and the person holding the power to revoke the trust is competent:

(a) The person holding the power to revoke, and not the beneficiary, has the rights afforded beneficiaries under this division.

(b) The duties of the trustee are owed to the person holding the power to revoke.

(Stats. 1990)

Husband's Revocation of Trust Effective Despite Lack of Notice to Co-Trustor Wife

MASRY v. MASRY

California Court of Appeal, Second District
166 Cal. App. 4th 738, 82 Cal. Rptr. 3d 915, as modified (2008)

GILBERT, P.J. How may a settlor revoke a revocable trust? Probate Code section 15401, subdivision (a)(2) provides the answer: (1) by compliance with the method stated in the trust, (2) by a writing (other than a will) signed by the settlor and delivered to the trustee during the lifetime of the settlor. Subdivision (a)(2) also tells us that its provisions do not apply if the trust instrument *explicitly* makes its language the exclusive method of revocation. . . .

In 2004, Edward Masry and appellant Joette Masry, husband and wife, created the Edward and Joette Masry Family Trust (Family Trust), which consisted of the property acquired during their marriage. Each was a trustor and trustee. . . . [T]he Family Trust . . . states in pertinent part: "Each of the Trustors hereby reserves the right and power to revoke this Trust, in whole or in part, from time to time during their joint lifetimes, by written direction delivered to the other Trustor and to the Trustee."

A little over a year after the Family Trust was created, and shortly before his death, Edward executed a "Notice of Revocation of Interest in Trust and Resignation as Trustee." His purpose was to transfer his assets from the Family Trust to a new trust, the Edward L. Masry Trust (Edward Trust). He designated two of his children from a previous marriage . . . as successor cotrustees. Joette was not given notice of the revocation until two weeks after Edward's death. . . .

Joette filed a revocation petition and a petition to ascertain beneficiaries. She argued, among other things, that Edward's revocation was invalid because she was not given notice during his lifetime. The trial court found that the Family Trust did not explicitly make delivery of the revocation to Joette, the other Trustor, during Edward's lifetime the exclusive method of revocation. The court ruled that Edward's delivery of the revocation to himself as trustee satisfied Probate Code section 15401, subdivision (b), and Family Code section 761. . . .

DISCUSSION . . .

We agree with respondents that . . . the Family Trust does not state that the method of revocation it provides is explicitly exclusive. It is simply one method of revocation in addition to that provided in Probate Code section 15401 . . . . Edward complied with section 15401, subdivision (a)(2), by giving notice to himself as trustee. If the language in the trust were sufficient to qualify as the explicitly exclusive method, then the language in section 15401, subdivision (a)(2) would be unnecessary. . . .

. . . [We conclude that] absent language in the trust that its method of revocation is exclusive, the trustor has the option of revoking according to the method provided in Probate Code section 15401, subdivision (a)(2), delivering notice to himself as trustee. That there are two trustees here does not change our view. Under subdivision (a)(2), Edward's notice to himself is sufficient as notice to "the trustee." . . .

Joette argues that such an interpretation of Probate Code section 15401 and its subdivisions is not good public policy, because it allows a "secret" revocation and represents one spouse taking advantage of the other. It is true that had Joette been given notice of the revocation as provided in the Family Trust, she could have tried to persuade Edward to change his mind or could have made changes in the disposition of her community share of the trust property.

But married parties are permitted to dispose of their share of the community without the consent of the other spouse. And if the Legislature sees an overriding public policy argument that the method of revocation used here violates public policy, it can certainly once again amend the statute. . . . The judgment is affirmed. Costs are awarded to respondents.

We concur: YEGAN and PERREN, JJ.

NOTES:

1. Estate of Stoker, 193 Cal. App. 4th 236, 122 Cal. Rptr. 3d 529 (2011) held that trust providing decedent could revoke it "at any time during his lifetime" was revoked when he executed will that specifically revoked the trust.

2. Gardenhire v. Superior Court, 127 Cal. App. 4th 882, 26 Cal. Rptr. 3d 143 (2005) held that a trust provision for revocation by "a written notice signed by the Trustor and delivered to the Trustee" allowed revocation by a later will.

3. Estate of Coleman, 129 Cal. App. 4th 380, 28 Cal. Rptr. 3d 282 (2005) held that intervivos trust was revoked by marital settlement agreement and order transferring trust property to the spouses individually; residuary devise to trustee of the trust in former spouse's pour-over will created new testamentary trust; provision in new trust for ex-spouse was § revoked by section 6122.

Trust Can Be Amended Only by Method Specified in Trust Instrument

KING v. LYNCH

California Court of Appeal, Fifth District
204 Cal. App. 4th 1186, 139 Cal. Rptr. 3d 553 review denied (2012)

LEVY, Acting P.J. . . . In July 2004, Zoel Night Lynch and Edna Mae Lynch, a married couple, created a revocable trust. . . . The trust designated the settlors, Zoel and Edna, as initial trustees of the trust. The trust provided that during the lifetime of the settlors, the income and principal of the trust would be used for the support of the settlors.

Article "FOURTH" of the trust concerned modification and revocation. That article provided, with omissions not pertinent to this appeal, the following:

> "During the joint lifetimes of the Settlors, this Trust may be amended, in whole or in part, with respect to jointly owned property by an instrument in writing signed by both Settlors and delivered to the Trustee, and with respect to separately owned property by an instrument in writing signed by the Settlor who contributed that property to the Trust, delivered to the Trustee.
>
> "During the joint lifetimes of the Settlors, this Trust may be revoked, in whole or in part, with respect to jointly owned property by an instrument in writing signed by either Settlor and delivered to the Trustee and the other Settlor, and with respect to

> separately owned property by an instrument in writing signed by the Settlor who contributed that property to the Trust, delivered to the Trustee . . . .
>
> "The first Settlor to die shall be called the 'Deceased Spouse' and the living Settlor shall be called the 'Surviving Spouse.' The Surviving Spouse shall have the powers to amend or revoke this Trust in whole or in part . . . .
>
> "The powers of the Settlors to revoke or amend this instrument are personal to Settlors and shall not be exercisable in Settlors' behalf by any conservator, guardian or other fiduciary, except that revocation or amendment may be authorized, after notice to the Trustee, by the court that appointed the conservator, guardian or other fiduciary."

Zoel and Edna had five children, David Eric Lynch, Nancy Street, Mary Jo Tirman, Judith E. King, and Thomas Francis Lynch. Thomas predeceased his parents leaving two daughters surviving, Sandra Lynch and Susan Lynch.

The original trust provided that after the death of Zoel and Edna, Nancy, Mary, Judith, and David were each to receive a distribution of $100,000 from the trust, and Sandra and Susan were each to receive $50,000. The remainder of the trust was to be given to David. The trust established David as successor trustee upon the death of the last settlor.

In 2005 and 2006, Zoel and Edna executed three amendments to the trust. The net result of these amendments was to bequeath four parcels of real estate to David. Both of the settlors signed these amendments and their validity is not questioned in the present proceeding.

Later in 2006, Edna suffered a severe brain injury that left her incompetent to handle her own affairs, although it does not appear that she was adjudicated incompetent.

After Edna's injury, Zoel executed three further amendments to the trust, which are designated fourth, fifth, and sixth amendments. The fourth amendment modified the trustee designation, noting that Edna was no longer able to serve and appointed Zoel as sole trustee. The fifth amendment reduced all monetary bequests by half, so that the four children were allocated $50,000 each and Sandra and Susan were allocated $25,000 each. The sixth amendment further reduced the monetary bequests, allocating $10,000 each for the children and $5,000 each for Sandra and Susan. Each of the amendments left intact the bequest of real estate to David and the designation of David as the remainder beneficiary.

Zoel died on January 18, 2010, and Edna died on August 10, 2010. By letter from David's attorney dated October 27, 2010, the trustee gave notice concerning the administration of the trust, pursuant to Probate Code section 16061.7. . . . On February 15, 2011, Nancy, Mary, Judith, Sandra, and Susan filed the present proceeding . . . .

Following a hearing, the trial court entered an order finding that the fourth, fifth, and sixth amendments to the trust were invalid . . . on the ground that these amendments were signed by only one of the settlors in contravention of the express terms of the trust. . . . David appealed. The remaining beneficiaries have appeared jointly as respondents. . . .

DISCUSSION

In general, a revocable trust can be revoked, in whole or in part, in any manner provided in the trust instrument. (§ 15401, subd. (a)(1).) In addition, the trust may be revoked by a writing, other than a will, signed by the trustor and delivered to the trustee, unless the method of revocation provided in the trust instrument is explicitly exclusive. (§ 15401, subd. (a)(2).)

Under section 15402, unless the trust instrument provides otherwise, a revocable trust may be modified by the procedure for revocation. This appeal involves the construction of this section.

The trust provides that, during the joint lifetimes of the settlors, the trust may be amended by a writing signed by both settlers and delivered to the trustee. Appellant contends that this provision, is not expressly or impliedly exclusive and therefore, Zoel alone could amend the trust by the revocation procedures set forth in section 15401. This analysis requires concluding that, under sections 15401 and 15402, no distinction exists between trust amendment provisions and trust revocation provisions. However, the genesis and language of section 15402 belie this result. . . .

Section 15402 states: "Unless the trust instrument provides otherwise, if a trust is revocable by the settlor, the settlor may modify the trust by the procedure for revocation." Thus, if the trust instrument is silent on modification, the trust may be modified in the same manner in which it could be revoked, either statutorily or as provided in the trust instrument. . . . Here, however, the trust instrument specifies how the trust is to be modified. . . .

The qualification "unless the trust instrument provides otherwise," indicates that if any modification method is specified in the trust, that method must be used to amend the trust. . . .

If we were to adopt appellant's position and hold that a trust may be modified by the revocation procedures set forth in section 15401 unless the trust explicitly provides that the stated modification method is exclusive, section 15402 would become surplusage. Rather than enacting section 15402, the Legislature could have combined revocation and modification into one statute. . . .

Therefore, in this case, to be effective, the amendments needed to be signed by both Zoel and Edna. . . . The trust specified a modification method and thus, under section 15402 the trust could only be amended in that manner. The settlors bound themselves to a specific method of modification. If we were to hold otherwise, especially where, as here, the amendment provision is more restrictive than the revocation provision, we would cause the amendment provision to become superfluous and would thereby thwart the settlors' intent.[5]

---

[5] We recognize that, due to Edna's incompetence, Edna could not execute a trust amendment. However, as recited above, the trust instrument provided a remedy for this situation. If a conservator or guardian

DISPOSITION

The motion to dismiss the appeal is denied. The order is affirmed. Costs on appeal are awarded to respondents.

I CONCUR: DAWSON, J.
DETJEN, J. (Dissenting) . . .

Surviving Spouse Cannot Remove Her Half of Community Property from Trust After It Has Become Irrevocable

AGUILAR v. AGUILAR

California Court of Appeal, Fourth District, Division 3
168 Cal. App. 4th 35, 85 Cal. Rptr. 3d 193 (2008) review denied (2009)

MOORE, J. In a case of buyer's remorse, a wife entered into a joint estate plan with her husband—more particularly, an inter vivos trust that became irrevocable in its entirety on the death of the first spouse to die. More than nine years after the husband died, the wife purported to withdraw her share of the community property from the trust. . . .

I. FACTS

Joe Aguilar (Joe) and Manuela S. Aguilar (Manuela), husband and wife, executed several estate planning documents on November 10, 1992—an inter vivos trust, a property agreement, and pour-over wills. They, as trustors, created the Aguilar Living Trust dated November 10, 1992 (the joint trust). In the joint trust, they declared that their principal residence, located in the City of Lompoc, California (the Lompoc property), which they were transferring into the joint trust, was their community property. Joe and Manuela further declared that the Lompoc property, as an asset of the joint trust, was to retain its community property character. . . . In their wills, Joe and Manuela left all of their property to the trustee of the joint trust.

Joe died in February 1994. In June 1995, Manuela made a new will. In that will, she left all of her property to her one child—Oscar Sosa.

In August 2003, Manuela, as trustee of the joint trust, executed a deed (the deed) purporting to convey one-half of the Lompoc property to herself as trustee of the Manuela Sosa Aguilar Living Trust (the individual trust). The deed was recorded in September 2003.

. . . In November 2006, [James Aguilar, Joe's son] filed a petition to declare the joint trust irrevocable, to cancel the deed, to quiet title to the Lompoc property in the joint trust, and to

---

had been appointed for Edna, the court that appointed the guardian or conservator could have authorized a trust amendment.

obtain damages from Manuela individually and as trustee of the individual trust. . . .

The court found that the provisions of the joint trust confirmed that the property in question was community property. . . and that Manuela did not violate either the law or the terms of the joint trust by withdrawing her one-half interest in that community property and transferring it to the individual trust. . . . James appeals.

II. DISCUSSION

A. Introduction:

The arguments are simple. James contends that the joint trust was irrevocable following Joe's death and precluded Manuela from withdrawing any property therefrom, even her community property share of the joint trust assets. Manuela argues that she was at liberty to withdraw her share of the community property from the joint trust, irrespective of whether the joint trust was irrevocable. . . .

B. Joint Trust Provisions:

. . . Paragraph 3.03 of the joint trust provided that when the first of the trustors died, the trust became "irrevocable and not subject to amendment, revocation, or termination . . . ." Paragraph 4.02, subparagraph B.2 made clear that, after that first death, the trustee had no power to "pay to or apply for the benefit of the surviving trustor any sums out of the principal of the trust estate." . . .

The purpose of this arrangement was clear. . . . [U]pon the surviving trustor's death, the trust estate [was to] be divided in equal shares . . . and distributed . . . to the trustors' eight children and stepchildren, or their issue, by right of representation. . . . [S]even of the . . . remainder beneficiaries are Joe's children and one is Manuela's. . . .

The attorney who prepared the joint trust had some concern over the fact that it became irrevocable on the first death. He wrote a clear and cogent letter to Joe and Manuela emphasizing the irrevocability.

The attorney stated: "[A]s I have explained to you the trust becomes totally IRREVOCABLE once one of you dies. This means that the survivor *may not* amend, modify or terminate the trust. The assets held by the trust must pass to the beneficiaries of the trust, who are your children and stepchildren. Also, the survivor has no power to invade or spend the principal held in the trust. If the only asset held [in] the trust is your home then the survivor may [live] in the home but may not remove the home or any proceeds from the sale of the home for any reason. It must remain in the trust for the children and stepchildren upon the survivor's death." The attorney continued: "I explained to you that it is unusual to draft a living trust that becomes totally irrevocable upon the first [spouse's] death, however, after having discussed this you still desire to proceed in this manner." He asked Joe and Manuela to review the letter and make sure it correctly stated their understanding of the joint trust he had prepared.

Joe and Manuela then signed the letter . . . . They placed their signatures immediately below the following language: "We have read this letter and it correctly sets forth our understanding as to the reasons we are signing the trust discussed in the letter. We understand that the trust is IRREVOCABLE as soon as one of us dies. This means the survivor may not amend[,] modify or terminate the trust. *We also understand that the survivor may not withdraw principal from the trust.*" (Italics added.)

Manuela makes no contention that she did not understand the letter she signed, or that she did not understand the provisions of the joint trust. It would simply appear that, some years after Joe's death, she had a change of heart in terms of her desired estate plan with respect to the principal of the joint trust. Unfortunately, it was too late for her to effectuate a change. She had already entered into an irrevocable estate plan with Joe. . . .

Rights of Creditors in Revocable Trusts

CPC § 18200. Revocable Trusts: Creditors' Rights During Settlor's Lifetime

If the settlor retains the power to revoke the trust in whole or in part, the trust property is subject to the claims of creditors of the settlor to the extent of the power of revocation during the lifetime of the settlor.

(Stats. 1990)

CPC § 19000. Definitions for Part 8 (Payment of Claims, Debts, and Expenses from Revocable Trust of Deceased Settlor)

As used in this part . . .

(g) "Probate estate" means a decedent's estate subject to administration pursuant to Division 7 (commencing with Section 7000).

(h) "Trust estate" means a decedent's property, real and personal, that is titled in the name of the trustee of the deceased settlor's trust or confirmed by order of the court to the trustee of the deceased settlor's trust.

(Stats. 1991, 1996, 2007, 2015)

CPC § 19001. Revocable Trusts: Creditors' Rights at Settlor's Death

(a) Upon the death of a settlor, the property of the deceased settlor that was subject to the power of revocation at the time of the settlor's death is subject to the claims of creditors of the deceased settlor's estate and to the expenses of administration of the probate estate to the extent that the deceased settlor's probate estate is inadequate to satisfy those claims and expenses.

(b) The deceased settlor, by appropriate direction in the trust instrument, may direct the priority of sources of payment of debts among subtrusts or other gifts established by the trust at the deceased settlor's death. Notwithstanding this subdivision, no direction by the settlor shall alter

the priority of payment, from whatever source, of the matters set forth in Section 11420[31] which shall be applied to the trust as it applies to a probate estate.
(Stats. 1992, 2015)

NOTE: Division 9. Trust Law, Part 8. Payment of Claims, Debts, and Expenses from Revocable Trust of Deceased Settlor, commencing with CPC § 19000 provides an optional procedure for publishing notice to creditors, which results in a time limit of 4 months or 60 days after the date notice is mailed or delivered to the creditor. If the trustee does not publish notice to creditors, CCP § 366.2 provides a one-year from the date of death statute of limitations. See **Wagner v. Wagner**, 162 Cal. App. 4th 249, 75 Cal. Rptr. 3d 511 (2008) (trustee's claim for compensation for caring for trustor during last 4 years of her life not timely filed).

1. Rumbaugh v. Harley, 2018 WL 4002854 (E.D. Calif. 2018) held that an action by successor trustee seeking return of $776,647.71 converted by previous trustee was time-barred under CCP § 366.2 because not brought within one year after death of previous trustee.

2. County Line Holdings, LLC v. McClanahan, 22 Cal. App. 5th 1067, 232 Cal. Rptr. 3d 272 (2018) held that one-year period of CCP § 366.2 does not apply to execution of judgment lien obtained before debtor's death.

3. Yeh v. Tai, 18 Cal. App. 5th 953, 227 Cal. Rptr. 3d 275 (2017) held that widow's action to recover property from decedent's trust under Family Code § 1101 was not subject to CCP § 366.2.

4. Wagner v. Wagner, 162 Cal. App. 4th 249, 75 Cal. Rptr. 3d 511 (2008) (trustee's claim for compensation for caring for trustor during last 4 years of her life not timely filed).

Revocable Trusts in Contemporary Practice

The Pour-Over Will

CPC § 6300. Testamentary Additions to Trusts (Pour-Over Wills)

(a) A devise, the validity of which is determinable by the law of this state, may be made by a will to the trustee of a trust established or to be established by the testator or by the testator and some other person or by some other person (including a funded or unfunded life insurance trust, although the settlor has reserved any or all rights of ownership of the insurance contracts) if the trust is identified in the testator's will and its terms are set forth in a written instrument (other than a will) executed before or concurrently with, or within 60 days after the execution

---

[31] Expenses of administration, obligations secured by a lien, funeral expenses, expenses of last illness, family allowance, wage claims, and general debts in that order.—Ed.

of the testator's will or in the valid last will of a person who has predeceased the testator (regardless of the existence, size, or character of the trust property). The devise is not invalid because the trust is amendable or revocable, or both, or because the trust was amended after the execution of the will or after the death of the testator.

(b) Unless the testator's will provides otherwise, the property so devised (1) is not deemed to beheld under a testamentary trust of the testator but becomes a part of the trust to which it is given and (2) shall be administered and disposed of in accordance with the provisions of the instrument or will setting forth the terms of the trust, including any amendments thereto made before or after the death of the testator (regardless of whether made before or after the execution of the testator's will).

(c) Unless otherwise provided in the will, a revocation or termination of the trust before the death of the testator causes the devise to lapse.

(Stats. 1990, 2017)

Section C. The Other Will Substitutes

Pay-on-Death and Transfer-on-Death Contracts

CPC § 5000. Pay on Death Provisions Not Invalid

(a) A provision for a nonprobate transfer on death in an insurance policy, contract of employment, bond, mortgage, promissory note, certificated or uncertificated security, account agreement, custodial agreement, deposit agreement, compensation plan, pension plan, individual retirement plan, employee benefit plan, trust, conveyance, deed of gift, revocable transfer on death deed, marital property agreement, or other written instrument of a similar nature is not invalid because the instrument does not comply with the requirements for execution of a will, and this code does not invalidate the instrument.

(b) Included within subdivision (a) are the following:

(1) A written provision that moneys or other benefits due to, controlled by, or owned by a decedent before death shall be paid after the decedent's death to a person whom the decedent designates either in the instrument or in a separate writing, including a will, executed either before or at the same time as the instrument, or later.

(2) A written provision that moneys due or to become due under the instrument shall cease to be payable in the event of the death of the promisee or the promisor before payment or demand.

(3) A written provision that any property controlled by or owned by the decedent before death that is the subject of the instrument shall pass to a person whom the decedent designates either in the instrument or in a separate writing, including a will, executed either before or at the same time as the instrument, or later.

(c) Nothing in this section limits the rights of creditors under any other law.

(Stats. 1990, 2015)

CPC § 5020. *Spouse's Written Consent Needed for Community Property*

A provision for a nonprobate transfer of community property on death executed by a married person without the written consent of the person's spouse (1) is not effective as to the nonconsenting spouse's interest in the property and (2) does not affect the nonconsenting spouse's disposition on death of the nonconsenting spouse's interest in the community property by will, intestate succession, or nonprobate transfer.

(Stats. 1992)

 familia

Effect of Dissolution of Marriage on Nonprobate Transfers to Former Spouse

CPC § 5040. *When Nonprobate Transfer to Former Spouse or Domestic Partner Fails*

(a) Except as provided in subdivision (b), a nonprobate transfer to the transferor's former spouse, in an instrument executed by the transferor before or during the marriage or registered domestic partnership, fails if, at the time of the transferor's death, the former spouse is not the transferor's surviving spouse as defined in Section 78, as a result of the dissolution or annulment of the marriage or termination of registered domestic partnership. A judgment of legal separation that does not terminate the status of spouses is not a dissolution for purposes of this section.

(b) Subdivision (a) does not cause a nonprobate transfer to fail in any of the following cases:

(1) The nonprobate transfer is not subject to revocation by the transferor at the time of the transferor's death.

(2) There is clear and convincing evidence that the transferor intended to preserve the nonprobate transfer to the former spouse.

(3) A court order that the nonprobate transfer be maintained on behalf of the former spouse is in effect at the time of the transferor's death.

(c) Where a nonprobate transfer fails by operation of this section, the instrument making the nonprobate transfer shall be treated as it would if the former spouse failed to survive the transferor.

(d) Nothing in this section affects the rights of a subsequent purchaser or encumbrancer for value in good faith who relies on the apparent failure of a nonprobate transfer under this section or who lacks knowledge of the failure of a nonprobate transfer under this section.

(e) As used in this section, "nonprobate transfer" means a provision, other than a provision of a life insurance policy, of either of the following types:

(1) A provision of a type described in Section 5000.

(2) A provision in an instrument that operates on death, other than a will, conferring a power of appointment or naming a trustee.

(Stats. 2001, 2015, 2016)

CPC § 5042. Severance of Joint Tenancy with Former Spouse or Domestic Partner

(a) Except as provided in subdivision (b), a joint tenancy between the decedent and the decedent's former spouse, created before or during the marriage or registered domestic partnership, is severed as to the decedent's interest if, at the time of the decedent's death, the former spouse is not the decedent's surviving spouse as defined in Section 78, as a result of the dissolution or annulment of the marriage or registered domestic partnership. A judgment of legal separation that does not terminate the status of spouses is not a dissolution for purposes of this section.

(b) Subdivision (a) does not sever a joint tenancy in either of the following cases:

(1) The joint tenancy is not subject to severance by the decedent at the time of the decedent's death.

(2) There is clear and convincing evidence that the decedent intended to preserve the joint tenancy in favor of the former spouse.

(c) Nothing in this section affects the rights of a subsequent purchaser or encumbrancer for value in good faith who relies on an apparent severance under this section or who lacks knowledge of a severance under this section.

(d) For purposes of this section, property held in "joint tenancy" includes property held as community property with right of survivorship, as described in Section 682.1 of the Civil Code.

(Stats. 2001, 2015, 2016)

CPC § 5046. Court Order to Maintain Former Spouse as Beneficiary

Nothing in this chapter is intended to limit the court's authority to order a party to a dissolution or annulment of marriage to maintain the former spouse as a beneficiary on any nonprobate transfer described in this chapter, or to preserve a joint tenancy in favor of the former spouse.

(Stats. 2001, 2015)

CPC § 5048. Operative Date and Application

(a) This chapter, formerly Part 4 (commencing with Section 5600), is operative on January 1, 2002.

(b) Except as provided in subdivision (c), this chapter applies to an instrument making a nonprobate transfer or creating a joint tenancy whether executed before, on, or after the operative date of this chapter.

(c) Sections 5040 and 5042 do not apply, and the applicable law in effect before the operative date of this chapter applies, to an instrument making a nonprobate transfer or creating a joint tenancy in either of the following circumstances:

(1) The person making the nonprobate transfer or creating the joint tenancy dies before the operative date of this chapter.

(2) The dissolution of marriage or other event that terminates the status of nonprobate transfer beneficiary or joint tenant as a surviving spouse occurs before the operative date of this chapter.

(Stats. 2001, 2015)

Multiple-Party Bank and Brokerage Accounts

CPC § 5301. Ownership of Account

(a) An account belongs, during the lifetime of all parties, to the parties in proportion to the net contributions by each, unless there is clear and convincing evidence of a different intent.

(b) In the case of a P.O.D. account, the P.O.D. payee has no rights to the sums on deposit during the lifetime of any party, unless there is clear and convincing evidence of a different intent.

(c) In the case of a Totten trust account, the beneficiary has no rights to the sums on deposit during the lifetime of any party, unless there is clear and convincing evidence of a different intent. If there is an irrevocable trust, the account belongs beneficially to the beneficiary.

(Stats. 1990, 2012)

NOTE: Subdivision (a) of Section 5301 was amended in 2012 to reverse the holding of **Lee v. Yang**, 111 Cal. App. 4th 481, 3 Cal. Rptr. 3d 819 (2003) that a party withdrawing funds from a joint account owns the funds withdrawn without regard to the source of the funds.

CPC § 5302. Rights on Death of Party to Joint Account

Subject to Section 5040:

(a) Sums remaining on deposit at the death of a party to a joint account belong to the surviving party or parties as against the estate of the decedent unless there is clear and convincing evidence of a different intent. If there are two or more surviving parties, their respective ownerships during lifetime are in proportion to their previous ownership interests under Section 5301 augmented by an equal share for each survivor of any interest the decedent may have owned in the account immediately before the decedent's death; and the right of survivorship continues between the surviving parties.

(b) If the account is a P.O.D. account:

(1) On death of one of two or more parties, the rights to any sums remaining on deposit are governed by subdivision (a).

(2) On death of the sole party or of the survivor of two or more parties, (A) any sums remaining on deposit belong to the P.O.D. payee or payees if surviving, or to the survivor of them if one or more die before the party, (B) if two or more P.O.D. payees survive, any sums remaining on deposit belong to them in equal and undivided shares unless the terms of the account or deposit agreement expressly provide for different shares, and (C) if two or more P.O.D. payees survive, there is no right of survivorship in the event of death of a P.O.D. payee thereafter unless the terms of the account or deposit agreement expressly provide for survivorship between them.

(c) If the account is a Totten trust account:

(1) On death of one of two or more trustees, the rights to any sums remaining on deposit are governed by subdivision (a).

(2) On death of the sole trustee or the survivor of two or more trustees, (A) any sums remaining on deposit belong to the person or persons named as beneficiaries, if surviving, or to the survivor of them if one or more die before the trustee, unless there is clear and convincing evidence of a different intent, (B) if two or more beneficiaries survive, any sums remaining on deposit belong to them in equal and undivided shares unless the terms of the account or deposit agreement expressly provide for different shares, and (C) if two or more beneficiaries survive, there is no right of survivorship in event of death of any beneficiary thereafter unless the terms of the account or deposit agreement expressly provide for survivorship between them.

(d) In other cases, the death of any party to a multiparty account has no effect on beneficial ownership of the account other than to transfer the rights of the decedent as part of the decedent's estate.

(e) A right of survivorship arising from the express terms of the account or under this section, a beneficiary designation in a Totten trust account, or a P.O.D. payee designation, cannot be changed by will.

(Stats. 1990, 2001, 2015)

NOTE: Estate of Betty Lou O'Connor, 16 Cal. App. 5th 159, 224 Cal. Rptr. 3d 243 (2017) held that accounts mother opened with daughter who saw her five to six times a week and helped her with various business affairs during last years of mother's life were joint accounts that belonged to daughter on mother's death. Signed signature card creating right of survivorship is not necessary to create a joint account that passes to surviving account holder in absence of clear and convincing evidence of contrary intent.

PROBLEM:

In 2001, Lucia Howery opened a Totten Trust account at Bank of America, naming Lori Younkin, her stepdaughter, as beneficiary. Lucia was the only person authorized to withdraw funds from the account during her lifetime.

In 2005, Lucia created a revocable inter vivos trust by a Declaration that all assets listed on Schedule A were held in the trust. Schedule A listed the Bank of America Totten Trust account. Under the terms of the trust, on Lucia's death, her automobile was to be distributed to Lori and the Bank of America Totten Trust Account was to be distributed to Gabriella Reeves.

Who is entitled to the Bank of America Totten Trust account on Lucia's death? See **Ariaza v. Younkin**, 188 Cal. App. 4th 1120, 116 Cal. Rptr. 3d 315 (2010) (Gabriella. Trust provision is clear and convincing evidence of different intent under § 5302(c)(2) and trust is not a will under § 5302(e).

❧❧

CPC § 5303. Terms of Account Determine Rights of Survivorship

(a) The provisions of Section 5302 as to rights of survivorship are determined by the form of the account at the death of a party.

(b) Once established, the terms of a multiple-party account can be changed only by any of the following methods:

(1) Closing the account and reopening it under different terms.

(2) Presenting to the financial institution a modification agreement that is signed by all parties with a present right of withdrawal. If the financial institution has a form for this purpose, it may require use of the form.

(3) If the provisions of the terms of the account or deposit agreement provide a method of modification of the terms of the account, complying with those provisions.

(4) As provided in subdivision (c) of Section 5405.

(c) During the lifetime of a party, the terms of the account may be changed as provided in subdivision (b) to eliminate or to add rights of survivorship. Withdrawal of funds from the account by a party also eliminates rights of survivorship upon the death of that party with respect to the funds withdrawn to the extent of the withdrawing party's net contribution to the account.

(Stats. 1990, 2012)

NOTE: Section 5303 was amended in 2012 to make clear that a party's ownership interest in an account, and the power to terminate a right of survivorship by withdrawing funds from the account, is determined by the party's net contribution to the account. This codified the rule in **Estate of Propst**, 50 Cal. 3d 448, 461-62, 268 Cal. Rptr. 114, 788 P.2d 628 (1990), 34 Cal. L. Rev. Comm. Reports 199 (2004).

CPC § 5304. Transfers Not Testamentary

Any transfers resulting from the application of Section 5302 are effective by reason of the account contracts involved and this part and are not to be considered as testamentary. The right under this part of a surviving party to a joint account, or of a beneficiary, or of a P.O.D. payee, to the sums on deposit on the death of a party to a multiple-party account shall not be denied, abridged, or affected because such right has not been created by a writing executed in accordance with the laws of this state prescribing the requirements to effect a valid testamentary disposition of property.

(Stats. 1990)

CPC § 5305. Community Property Presumption; No Change of Beneficiary by Will

(a) Notwithstanding Sections 5301 to 5303, inclusive, if parties to an account are married to each other, whether or not they are so described in the deposit agreement, their net contribution to the account is presumed to be and remain their community property. . . .

(c) Except as provided in Section 5307, a right of survivorship arising from the express terms of the account or under Section 5302, a beneficiary designation in a Totten trust account, or a P.O.D. payee designation, may not be changed by will. . . .

(Stats. 1990, 1992, 1993)

CPC § 5306. No Right of Survivorship in Tenancy in Common Account

For the purposes of this chapter, if an account is expressly described in the deposit agreement as a "tenancy in common" account, no right of survivorship arises from the terms of the account or under Section 5302 unless the terms of the account or deposit agreement expressly provide for survivorship.

(Stats. 1990)

CPC § 5307. Ownership of Community Property Account

For the purposes of this chapter, except to the extent the terms of the account or deposit agreement expressly provide otherwise, if the parties to an account are married to each other and the account is expressly described in the account agreement as a "community property" account, the ownership of the account during lifetime and after the death of a spouse is governed by the law governing community property generally.

(Stats. 1990)

NOTE: California's Uniform TOD (transfer on death) Security Registration Act is located in Probate Code Division 5, Part 3, § 5500 *et seq.*

Nonprobate Transfer of Real Property

Joint Tenancy

Civil Code § 683. Creation of Joint Tenancy in Real or Personal Property

(a) A joint interest is one owned by two or more persons in equal shares, by a title created by a single will or transfer, when expressly declared in the will or transfer to be a joint tenancy, or by transfer from a sole owner to himself or herself and others, or from tenants in common or joint tenants to themselves or some of them, or to themselves or any of them and others, or from spouses, when holding title as community property or otherwise to themselves or to themselves and others or to one of them and to another or others, when expressly declared in the transfer to be a joint tenancy, or when granted or devised to executors or trustees as joint tenants. A joint tenancy in personal property may be created by a written transfer, instrument, or agreement.

(b) Provisions of this section do not apply to a joint account in a financial institution if Part 2 (commencing with Section 5100) of Division 5 of the Probate Code applies to such account.
(Stats. 1872, 1929, 1935, 1955, 1983, 1989, 1990, 2016)

Civil Code § 683.1. Safe-Deposit Box Contract Does Not Create Joint Tenancy

No contract or other arrangement made after the effective date of this section between any person, firm, or corporation engaged in the business of renting safe-deposit boxes and the renter or renters of a safe-deposit box, shall create a joint tenancy in or otherwise establish ownership in any of the contents of such safe-deposit box. Any such contract or other arrangement purporting so to do shall be to such extent void and of no effect.
(Stats. 1949)

Civil Code § 683.2. Unilateral Severance of Joint Tenancy

(a) Subject to the limitations and requirements of this section, in addition to any other means by which a joint tenancy may be severed, a joint tenant may sever a joint tenancy in real property as to the joint tenant's interest without the joinder or consent of the other joint tenants by any of the following means:

(1) Execution and delivery of a deed that conveys legal title to the joint tenant's interest to a third person, whether or not pursuant to an agreement that requires the third person to reconvey legal title to the joint tenant.

(2) Execution of a written instrument that evidences the intent to sever the joint tenancy, including a deed that names the joint tenant as transferee, or of a written declaration that, as to the interest of the joint tenant, the joint tenancy is severed.

(b) Nothing in this section authorizes severance of a joint tenancy contrary to a written agreement of the joint tenants, but a severance contrary to a written agreement does not defeat the rights of a purchaser or encumbrancer for value in good faith and without knowledge of the written agreement.

(c) Severance of a joint tenancy of record by deed, written declaration, or other written instrument pursuant to subdivision (a) is not effective to terminate the right of survivorship of the other joint tenants as to the severing joint tenant's interest unless one of the following requirements is satisfied:

(1) Before the death of the severing joint tenant, the deed, written declaration, or other written instrument effecting the severance is recorded in the county where the real property is located.

(2) The deed, written declaration, or other written instrument effecting the severance is executed and acknowledged before a notary public by the severing joint tenant not earlier than three days before the death of that joint tenant and is recorded in the county where the real property is located not later than seven days after the death of the severing joint tenant.

(d) Nothing in subdivision (c) limits the manner or effect of:

(1) A written instrument executed by all the joint tenants that severs the joint tenancy.

(2) A severance made by or pursuant to a written agreement of all the joint tenants.

(3) A deed from a joint tenant to another joint tenant.

(e) Subdivisions (a) and (b) apply to all joint tenancies in real property, whether the joint tenancy was created before, on, or after January 1, 1985, except that in the case of the death of a joint tenant before January 1, 1985, the validity of a severance under subdivisions (a) and (b) is determined by the law in effect at the time of death. Subdivisions (c) and (d) do not apply to or affect a severance made before January 1, 1986, of a joint tenancy.
(Stats. 1984, 1985)

NOTE: Inclusion of joint tenancy property in revocable trust for settlors for life with remainder to wife's son severed joint tenancy; recordation not necessary because both settlors signed the trust agreement. **Estate of Powell**, 83 Cal. App. 4th 1434, 100 Cal. Rptr. 501 (2000).

Civil Code § 682.1. Community Property with Right of Survivorship

(a) Community property of spouses, when expressly declared in the transfer document to be community property with right of survivorship, and which may be accepted in writing on the face of the document by a statement signed or initialed by the grantees, shall, upon the death of one of the spouses, pass to the survivor, without administration, pursuant to the terms of the instrument, subject to the same procedures, as property held in joint tenancy. Prior to the death of either spouse, the right of survivorship may be terminated pursuant to the same procedures by which a joint tenancy may be severed. Part 1 (commencing with Section 5000) of Division 5 of the Probate Code and Chapter 2 (commencing with Section 13540),[32] Chapter 3 (commencing with Section 13550),[33] and Chapter 3.5 (commencing with Section 13560)[34] of Part 2 of Division 8 of the Probate Code apply to this property.

(b) This section does not apply to a joint account in a financial institution to which Part 2 (commencing with Section 5100) of Division 5 of the Probate Code applies.

---

[32] Right of surviving spouse to dispose of community and quasi-community real property after death of spouse.—Ed.

[33] Liability for debts of deceased spouse chargeable against property passing to surviving spouse without administration.—Ed.

[34] Liability for decedent's property in possession or control of surviving spouse.—Ed.

(c) This section shall become operative on July 1, 2001, and shall apply to instruments created on or after that date.

(Stats. 2000, 2016)

❧❧

No Severance of Joint Tenancy: Deed Not Recorded Within 7 Days of Joint Tenant's Death

DORN v. SOLOMON

California Court of Appeal, Fourth District, Division 3
57 Cal. App. 4th 650, 67 Cal. Rptr. 2d 311 (1997)

SILLS, Presiding Justice. Donald and Dixie Dorn were married in 1975. In 1981, they purchased a home in Fullerton taking title as "husband and wife, as joint tenants." In 1992, the marriage fell apart and Dixie moved out. However, a few months later she discovered she was dying from cancer.

On September 20, 1993, and while she was in the hospital, Dixie executed a quitclaim deed purporting to transfer the family home to "Dixie D. Dorn, Irrevocable Trust dated September 20, 1993." The purpose of the deed, so we are told, was to enable Dixie to transfer her interest in the family home to her daughter by a former marriage, Tammy Gutermuth. Dixie unexpectedly died the following day.

On September 30, 1993, Donald recorded an "Affidavit-Death of Joint Tenant" with the county recorder. On October 25, 1993, Juanita Solomon, as trustee of the irrevocable trust, recorded the quitclaim deed. Donald, complaining that the property was uninsurable with the quitclaim deed of record, filed this action for declaratory relief, quiet title, and to cancel it. Following completion of discovery Donald filed a motion for summary judgment, which was granted. The trustee appeals. ...

[T]he thrust of the appeal is that Dixie had a right to transfer her community property interest in the family home without Donald's consent. Relying on Family Code section 2581, which provides that for "the purpose of division of property on dissolution of marriage" there is a rebuttable presumption that property acquired during marriage in joint tenancy is community property, the trustee asserts there was a triable issue of fact as to whether the property was held in joint tenancy or as community property, and the burden was on Donald to prove that he and Dixie did not hold the property as community property.

[T]he flaw in this argument is that the presumption found in Family Code section 2581 only applies "for purposes of a property division upon marriage dissolution or legal separation." (Hogoboom & King, Cal. Practice Guide: Family Law . . . .) It does not apply when a joint tenant dies. In that case, the property passes by right of survivorship. ... Accordingly, because title to the family home was acquired in joint tenancy, the presumption was that title to the property passed to Donald when Dixie died, and the burden was on the trustee to demonstrate

230

there was a triable issue of material fact as to whether the property was held as community property. This the trustee failed to do. . . .

Of course, Dixie still could have legally severed the joint tenancy by following the provisions of Civil Code section 683.2, which sets forth the requirements for severing a joint tenancy. It appears from the record before us that this is what she was trying to do. However, subdivision (c)(2) of section 683.2 explicitly provides that the deed must be recorded "not later than seven days after the death of the severing joint tenant." Here, the trustee did not record the deed until a month after Dixie died, and thus it was invalid under this section. Accordingly, the judgment is affirmed. Donald shall recover his costs on appeal.

Transfer on Death Deed for Real Property

In October, 2006, the California Law Revision Commission recommended that legislation be enacted to authorize a Revocable Transfer on Death (TOD) Deed, also called a beneficiary deed (http://www.clrc.ca.gov/L3032.html). After unsuccessful attempts in the 2007-2008, 2009-2010, and 2011-2012 legislative sessions, the Revocable Transfer on Death Deed was finally enacted in 2015 and codified as Probate Code Division 5, Part 4, Sections 5600-5696, effective for transfers made by a person who dies on or after January 1, 2016. Section 5600 (c) provides that these statutes are effective only until January 1, 2021, unless a later statute enacted before that date deletes or extends the date. The California Law Revision Commission is directed to study the effects of use of the deed and whether it should be extended to include a broader range of property. It is to report its findings to the Legislature by January 1, 2020. For progress on the study, see California Law Revision Commission Study L-3032.1, http://www.clrc.ca.gov/L3032.1.html.

The deed can only be used to make a donative transfer of real property that is improved with not less than one nor more than four residential dwelling units, a condominium unit, or a single tract of agricultural real estate consisting of 40 acres or less that is improved with a single-family residence. The deed must be signed, dated, and acknowledged by the transferor before a notary public and recorded on or before 60 days after it was executed. The deed must be substantially in the form prescribed in Sections 5642 and 5626 and the transferee must be a named beneficiary (class gift terms and trusts are not allowed). The deed is revocable until death of the transferor, the property remains subject to the payment of decedent-transferor's debts, and the property is part of the estate for the purpose of Medi-Cal eligibility and reimbursement. The deed is not effective as to property the transferor holds as community property or in joint tenancy at the time of the transferor's death.

Section D. Planning for Incapacity

Durable Power of Attorney

Powers of attorney, including durable powers, are covered in Probate Code Division 4.5 §§ 4000-4545.

CPC § 4231.5. Breach of Duty, Remedy

(a) If the attorney-in-fact breaches a duty pursuant to this division, the attorney-in-fact is chargeable with any of the following, as appropriate under the circumstances:

(1) Any loss or depreciation in value of the principal's property resulting from the breach of duty, with interest.

(2) Any profit made by the attorney-in-fact through the breach of duty, with interest.

(3) Any profit that would have accrued to the principal if the loss of profit is the result of the breach of duty.

(b) If the attorney-in-fact has acted reasonably and in good faith under the circumstances as known to the attorney-in-fact, the court, in its discretion, may excuse the attorney-in-fact in whole or in part from liability under subdivision (a) if it would be equitable to do so.

(c) If a court finds that a person has in bad faith wrongfully taken, concealed, or disposed of property that belongs to a principal under a power of attorney, or has taken, concealed, or disposed of property that belongs to a principal under a power of attorney by the use of undue influence in bad faith or through the commission of elder or dependent adult financial abuse, as defined in Section 15610.30 of the Welfare and Institutions Code, the person shall be liable for twice the value of the property recovered by an action to recover the property or for surcharge. In addition, except as otherwise required by law, including Section 15657.5 of the Welfare and Institutions Code, the person may, in the court's discretion, be liable for reasonable attorney's fees and costs to the prevailing party. The remedies provided in this section shall be in addition to any other remedies available in law to the principal or any successor in interest of the principal.

(Stats. 2010, 2013)

NOTE:

In **Estate of Kraus**, 184 Cal. App. 4th 103, 108 Cal. Rptr. 3d 760 (2010) the court upheld a probate court order that the attorney in fact (decedent's brother who had her execute a durable power two days before she died) restore misappropriated funds to the principal's estate and pay statutory double damages under CPC § 859.

The facts stated by the court include the following:

> After counsel for one of the beneficiaries demanded the funds be repaid, David [decedent's brother] threatened to expose their greed to the media. David further also wrote: "I am prepared to expose this entire ugly matter in open court. If you think you can bully me into anything, you are truly mistaken. I know the law very well, and you have no standing in the eyes of the court. [¶] Once you bring this ridiculous matter in front of the judge, you will forever be prejudiced in front of her before you begin any new trial. It's a small circle of players in Probate in Los Angeles, and judges have a long memory for anyone that engages in this fraudulent activity. You will long be remembered in her court." (184 Cal. App. 4th at 109, 108 Cal. Rptr. 3d at 764-65).

Directives Regarding Health Care and Disposition of the Body

Health care directives are covered in Probate Code Division 4.7, §§ 4600-4806.

Chapter 8. Limits on Freedom of Disposition: Protection of the Spouse and Children

Section A. Protection of the Surviving Spouse

See Chapter 2, Section B, *supra*, for surviving spouse's rights in the decedent's intestate property.

Waiver by Premarital or Postnuptial Agreement

❖ CPC § 140. Meaning of "Waiver"

As used in this chapter, "waiver" means a waiver by the surviving spouse of any of the rights listed in subdivision (a) of Section 141, whether signed before or during marriage.

(Stats. 1990)

❖ CPC § 141. What May Be Waived

(a) The right of a surviving spouse to any of the following may be waived in whole or in part by a waiver under this chapter:

(1) Property that would pass from the decedent by intestate succession.

(2) Property that would pass from the decedent by testamentary disposition in a will executed before the waiver.

(3) A probate homestead.

(4) The right to have exempt property set aside.

(5) Family allowance.

(6) The right to have an estate set aside under Chapter 6 (commencing with Section 6600) of Part 3 of Division 6.

(7) The right to elect to take community or quasi-community property against the decedent's will.

(8) The right to take the statutory share of an omitted spouse.

(9) The right to be appointed as the personal representative of the decedent's estate.

(10) An interest in property that is the subject of a nonprobate transfer on death under Part 1 (commencing with Section 5000) of Division 5.

(b) Nothing in this chapter affects or limits the waiver or manner of waiver of rights other than those referred to in subdivision (a), including, but not limited to, the right to property that would pass from the decedent to the surviving spouse by nonprobate transfer upon the death of the decedent, such as the survivorship interest under a joint tenancy, a Totten trust account, or a pay-on-death account.

(Stats. 1990, 1992)

❖ CPC § 142. Requirements for Making Waiver

(a) A waiver under this chapter shall be in writing and shall be signed by the surviving spouse.

(b) Subject to subdivision (c), a waiver under this chapter is enforceable only if it satisfies the requirements of subdivision (a) and is enforceable under either Section 143 or Section 144.

(c) Enforcement of the waiver against the surviving spouse is subject to the same defenses as enforcement of a contract, except that:

(1) Lack of consideration is not a defense to enforcement of the waiver.

(2) A minor intending to marry may make a waiver under this chapter as if married, but the waiver becomes effective only upon the marriage.

(Stats. 1990)

❖ CPC § 143. Waiver Enforceable Unless Surviving Spouse Proves . . .

(a) Subject to Section 142, a waiver is enforceable under this section unless the surviving spouse proves either of the following:

(1) A fair and reasonable disclosure of the property or financial obligations of the decedent was not provided to the surviving spouse prior to the signing of the waiver unless the surviving spouse waived such a fair and reasonable disclosure after advice by independent legal counsel.

(2) The surviving spouse was not represented by independent legal counsel at the time of signing of the waiver.

(b) Subdivision (b) of Section 721 of the Family Code does not apply if the waiver is enforceable under this section.

(Stats. 1990, 1992)

❖ CPC § 144. Waiver Enforceable if the Court Determines . . .

(a) Except as provided in subdivision (b), subject to Section 142, a waiver is enforceable under this section if the court determines either of the following:

(1) The waiver at the time of signing made a fair and reasonable disposition of the rights of the surviving spouse.

(2) The surviving spouse had, or reasonably should have had, an adequate knowledge of the property and financial obligations of the decedent and the decedent did not violate the duty imposed by subdivision (b) of Section 721 of the Family Code.

(b) If, after considering all relevant facts and circumstances, the court finds that enforcement of the waiver pursuant to subdivision (a) would be unconscionable under the circumstances existing at the time enforcement is sought, the court may refuse to enforce the waiver, enforce the remainder of the waiver without the unconscionable provisions, or limit the application of the unconscionable provisions to avoid an unconscionable result.

(c) Except as provided in paragraph (2) of subdivision (a), subdivision (b) of Section 721 of the Family Code does not apply if the waiver is enforceable under this section.

(Stats. 1990, 1992)

❖ CPC § 145. Effect of Waiver of "All Rights"

Unless the waiver or property settlement provides to the contrary, a waiver under this chapter of "all rights" (or equivalent language) in the property or estate of a present or prospective spouse, or a complete property settlement entered into after or in anticipation of separation or dissolution or annulment of marriage, is a waiver by the spouse of the rights described in subdivision (a) of Section 141.

(Stats. 1990)

❖ CPC § 146. Altering, Amending, Revoking a Waiver

(a) As used in this section, "agreement" means a written agreement signed by each spouse or prospective spouse altering, amending, or revoking a waiver under this chapter.

(b) Except as provided in subdivisions (c) and (d) of Section 147, unless the waiver specifically otherwise provides, a waiver under this chapter may not be altered, amended, or revoked except by a subsequent written agreement signed by each spouse or prospective spouse.

(c) Subject to subdivision (d), the agreement is enforceable only if it satisfies the requirements of subdivision (b) and is enforceable under either subdivision (e) or subdivision (f).

(d) Enforcement of the agreement against a party to the agreement is subject to the same defenses as enforcement of any other contract, except that:

(1) Lack of consideration is not a defense to enforcement of the agreement.

(2) A minor intending to marry may enter into the agreement as if married, but the agreement becomes effective only upon the marriage.

(e) Subject to subdivision (d), an agreement is enforceable under this subdivision unless the party to the agreement against whom enforcement is sought proves either of the following:

(1) A fair and reasonable disclosure of the property or financial obligations of the other spouse was not provided to the spouse against whom enforcement is sought prior to the signing of the agreement unless the spouse against whom enforcement is sought waived such a fair and reasonable disclosure after advice by independent legal counsel.

(2) The spouse against whom enforcement is sought was not represented by independent legal counsel at the time of signing of the agreement.

(f) Subject to subdivisions (d) and (g), an agreement is enforceable under this subdivision if the court determines that the agreement at the time of signing made a fair and reasonable disposition of the rights of the spouses.

(g) If, after considering all relevant facts and circumstances, the court finds that enforcement of the agreement pursuant to subdivision (f) would be unconscionable under the circumstances existing at the time enforcement is sought, the court may refuse to enforce the agreement, enforce the remainder of the agreement without the unconscionable provisions, or limit the application of the unconscionable provisions to avoid an unconscionable result.

(h) Subdivision (b) of Section 721 of the Family Code does not apply if the agreement is enforceable under this section.

(Stats. 1990, 1992)

❖ CPC § 147. Effective Dates; Relation to Premarital Agreement & Community Property

(a) Subject to subdivisions (c) and (d), a waiver, agreement, or property settlement made after December 31, 1984, is invalid insofar as it affects the rights listed in subdivision (a) of Section 141 unless it satisfies the requirements of this chapter.

(b) Nothing in this chapter affects the validity or effect of any waiver, agreement, or property settlement made prior to January 1, 1985, and the validity and effect of such waiver, agreement, or property settlement shall continue to be determined by the law applicable to the waiver, agreement, or settlement prior to January 1, 1985.

(c) Nothing in this chapter affects the validity or effect of any premarital property agreement, whether made prior to, on, or after January 1, 1985, insofar as the premarital property agreement affects the rights listed in subdivision (a) of Section 141, and the validity and effect of such premarital property agreement shall be determined by the law otherwise applicable to the premarital property agreement. Nothing in this subdivision limits the enforceability under this chapter of a waiver made under this chapter by a person intending to marry that is otherwise enforceable under this chapter.

(d) Nothing in this chapter limits any right one spouse otherwise has to revoke a consent or election to disposition of his or her half of the community or quasi-community property under the will of the other spouse.

(Stats. 1990)

Family Code § 721. Contracts and Fiduciary Relationship Between Spouses

(a) Subject to subdivision (b), either spouse may enter into any transaction with the other, or with any other person, respecting property, which either might if unmarried.

(b) Except as provided in Sections 143, 144, 146, 16040, and 16047 of the Probate Code, in transactions between themselves, spouses are subject to the general rules governing fiduciary relationships that control the actions of persons occupying confidential relations with each other. This confidential relationship imposes a duty of the highest good faith and fair dealing on each spouse, and neither shall take any unfair advantage of the other. This confidential relationship is a fiduciary relationship subject to the same rights and duties of nonmarital business partners, as provided in Sections 16403, 16404, and 16503 of the Corporations Code, including, but not limited to, the following:

> (1) Providing each spouse access at all times to any books kept regarding a transaction for the purposes of inspection and copying.

(2) Rendering upon request, true and full information of all things affecting any transaction that concerns the community property. Nothing in this section is intended to impose a duty for either spouse to keep detailed books and records of community property transactions.

(3) Accounting to the spouse, and holding as a trustee, any benefit or profit derived from any transaction by one spouse without the consent of the other spouse that concerns the community property.

(Stats. 1992, 2002, 2014)

NOTE: AB 327 introduced in the 2019-2020 legislature would, if enacted, add to subsection (b) an exception for a new CPC § 21385 which would cover at-death transfers between spouses by will, revocable trust, beneficiary form, or other instrument. The text of proposed § 21385 is set forth in Chapter 4.

NOTE: Premarital Agreements Under Family Code

Family Code § 1615 provides a different and more stringent set of requirements for enforcement of a premarital agreement than the Probate Code. It was determined in **Estate of Will**, 170 Cal. App. 4th 902, 88 Cal. Rptr. 3d 502 (2d Dist. 2009), that a waiver meeting the requirements of the Probate Code, but not the requirements of the Family Code, is enforceable against a spouse after the death of the other spouse.

Domestic Partnership Agreement Waiving Rights to Estate Remained Valid After Marriage

ESTATE of WILSON

Court of Appeal, First District, Division 2
211 Cal. App. 4th 1284, 150 Cal. Rptr. 3d 699 (2012)

LAMBDEN, J. In 2006, Dr. Philip Timothy Wilson and Antipas Johnlang Konou executed a "Pre Registration Domestic Partnership Agreement" (the domestic partnership agreement or the agreement) and then registered as domestic partners. The agreement included waivers of any rights, claims or interest in the future property, income, or estate of the other, and required a signed writing to amend or terminate this agreement. A couple of years later, in 2008, Wilson and Konou married during the brief period that same-sex marriages were legal in California. Shortly thereafter, Wilson died.

Konou filed a petition claiming an omitted spouse's interest in Wilson's estate. The probate court rejected Konou's claim and found that Konou was an omitted spouse but that the domestic partnership agreement remained valid after the marriage and Konou waived his rights to any interest in Wilson's estate in this agreement.

Konou appeals and argues that the probate court erred because a marriage is not the same as a domestic partnership and there was no prenuptial agreement. He claims that the marriage license constituted a signed writing that terminated the domestic partnership agreement.

We hold that domestic partnership agreements that are enforceable under the Uniform Premarital Agreement Act (Fam. Code, §§ 1600-1617) . . . and made after statutes were enacted providing domestic partners with essentially the same California State property rights as spouses, are not automatically invalidated by a marriage license. Since Konou expressly waived his rights to any interest in Wilson's estate in the domestic partnership agreement and the validity of this agreement under the Uniform Premarital Agreement Act is not an issue, he cannot claim any interest as a pretermitted spouse in Wilson's estate. Accordingly, we affirm the trial court's order. . . .

We concur: KLINE, P.J., HAERLE, J.

Migrating Couples and Multistate Property Holdings

Moving from a Separate Property State to a Community Property State

CPC § 66. Quasi-Community Property Defined

"Quasi-community property" means the following property, other than community property as defined in Section 28:

(a) All personal property wherever situated, and all real property situated in this state, heretofore or hereafter acquired by a decedent while domiciled elsewhere that would have been the community property of the decedent and the surviving spouse if the decedent had been domiciled in this state at the time of its acquisition.

(b) All personal property wherever situated, and all real property situated in this state, heretofore or hereafter acquired in exchange for real or personal property, wherever situated, that would have been the community property of the decedent and the surviving spouse if the decedent had been domiciled in this state at the time the property so exchanged was acquired.

(Stats. 1990)

❖ CPC § 101. Rights to Quasi-Community Property

(a) Upon the death of a married person domiciled in this state, one-half of the decedent's quasi-community property belongs to the surviving spouse and the other half belongs to the decedent.

(b) Notwithstanding subdivision (a), spouses may agree in writing to divide their quasi-community property on the basis of a non pro rata division of the aggregate value of the quasi-community property, or on the basis of a division of each individual item or asset of quasi-community property, or partly on each basis. Nothing in this subdivision shall be construed to require this written agreement in order to permit or recognize a non pro rata division of quasi-community property.

(Stats. 1990, 1998, 2016)

❖ *CPC § 102. Spouse's Right to Recover Quasi-Community Property*

(a) The decedent's surviving spouse may require the transferee of property in which the surviving spouse had an expectancy under Section 101 at the time of the transfer to restore to the decedent's estate one-half of the property if the transferee retains the property or, if not, one-half of its proceeds or, if none, one-half of its value at the time of transfer, if all of the following requirements are satisfied:

(1) The decedent died domiciled in this state.

(2) The decedent made a transfer of the property to a person other than the surviving spouse without receiving in exchange a consideration of substantial value and without the written consent or joinder of the surviving spouse.

(3) The transfer is any of the following types:

(A) A transfer under which the decedent retained at the time of death the possession or enjoyment of, or the right to income from, the property.

(B) A transfer to the extent that the decedent retained at the time of death a power, either alone or in conjunction with any other person, to revoke or to consume, invade, or dispose of the principal for the decedent's own benefit.

(C) A transfer whereby property is held at the time of the decedent's death by the decedent and another with right of survivorship.

(b) Nothing in this section requires a transferee to restore to the decedent's estate any life insurance, accident insurance, joint annuity, or pension payable to a person other than the surviving spouse.

(c) All property restored to the decedent's estate under this section belongs to the surviving spouse pursuant to Section 101 as though the transfer had not been made.

(Stats. 1990)

❧❧

Right of Nondomiciliary Decedent's Surviving Spouse in California Real Estate

CPC § 120. Surviving Spouse's Right to Elect Against Will of Nondomiciliary Decedent for Interest in California Real Estate

If a married person dies not domiciled in this state and leaves a valid will disposing of real property in this state which is not the community property of the decedent and the surviving spouse, the surviving spouse has the same right to elect to take a portion of or interest in such property against the will of the decedent as though the property were located in the decedent's domicile at death.

(Stats. 1990)

Miscellaneous Additional Rights

Homestead, Personal Property Set Aside & Family Allowance

Provisions for probate homestead and family allowance are located in Probate Code Division 6, Part 3, §§ 6520-6614. The court may set apart a probate homestead under § 6524 and order payment of family allowance for the surviving spouse, minor children of the decedent, and under certain circumstances, for the adult children and parents who were actually dependent on the decedent, under CPC § 6540. Under § 6602, the decedent's estate may be set aside to the surviving spouse and minor children, or one or more of them if the net value of the estate over and above all liens and encumbrances and the value of any probate homestead set apart does not exceed $20,000. In calculating the value of the estate, property held in joint tenancy and multiple-party accounts are excluded.

Probate Code Division 8, Part 1, §§ 13000-13210 allows the successors to a decedent to collect estates of $150,000 or less without probate.

NOTE: AB 473 introduced in the 2019-2020 legislative session, if adopted, would increase the amount that could be set aside under § 6602 from $20,000 to $85,900 and increase the estate that can be collected without probate from $150,000 to $166,250 and add a requirement that the amounts be adjusted every three years.

Section B. Intentional Omission of a Child

Family Code § 3952. Estate of Deceased Parent; Action for Support of Child

If a parent chargeable with the support of a child dies leaving the child chargeable to the county or leaving the child confined in a state institution to be cared for in whole or in part at the expense of the state, and the parent leaves an estate sufficient for the child's support, the supervisors of the county or the director of the state department having jurisdiction over the institution may claim provision for the child's support from the parent's estate, and for this purpose has the same remedies as a creditor against the estate of the parent and may obtain reimbursement from the successor of the deceased parent to the extent provided in Division 8 (commencing with Section 13000) of the Probate Code.

(Stats. 1992)

❦❧

Section C. Protection Against Unintentional Omission

Spouse Omitted from Premarital Will

CPC § 21601. "Testamentary Instruments" Include Revocable Trust; "Estate" Includes Property Held in Revocable Trust

(a) For purposes of this part, "decedent's testamentary instruments" means the decedent's will or revocable trust.

(b) "Estate" as used in this part shall include a decedent's probate estate and all property held in any revocable trust that becomes irrevocable on the death of the decedent.

(Stats. 1997)

CPC § 21630. Statutes Applicable Before & After Jan. 1, 1998

This part [§§ 21600-21630] is not applicable if decedent died before Jan. 1, 1998. The law applicable prior to January 1, 1998 [§§ 6560-6580] applies if the decedent died before January 1, 1998.

(Stats. 1997)

❖ CPC § 21610. Share of Omitted Spouse

Except as provided in Section 21611, if a decedent fails to provide in a testamentary instrument for the decedent's surviving spouse who married the decedent after the execution of all of the decedent's testamentary instruments, the omitted spouse shall receive a share in the decedent's estate, consisting of the following property in said estate:

(a) The one-half of the community property that belongs to the decedent under Section 100.

(b) The one-half of the quasi-community property that belongs to the decedent under Section 101.

(c) A share of the separate property of the decedent equal in value to that which the spouse would have received if the decedent had died without having executed a testamentary instrument, but in no event is the share to be more than one-half the value of the separate property in the estate.

(Stats. 1997)

NOTE: Omitted spouse found liable for elder abuse is not treated as predeceased for purposes of determining entitlement to a share of decedent's estate under § 21610. CPC § 259 only restricts the value of the estate to which his or her share is applied. **Estate of Dito**, 198 Cal. App. 4th 791, 130 Cal. Rptr. 279 (2011).[35]

---

[35] See Chapter 2, Bars to Succession, for the opinion in *Estate of Dito*.

❖ CPC § 21611. When Omitted Spouse Does Not Receive Share

The spouse shall not receive a share of the estate under Section 21610 if any of the following is established:

(a) The decedent's failure to provide for the spouse in the decedent's testamentary instruments was intentional and that intention appears from the testamentary instruments.

(b) The decedent provided for the spouse by transfer outside of the estate passing by the decedent's testamentary instruments and the intention that the transfer be in lieu of a provision in said instruments is shown by statements of the decedent or from the amount of the transfer or by other evidence.

(c) The spouse made a valid agreement waiving the right to share in the decedent's estate.
(Stats. 1997)

NOTE: AB 328 introduced in the 2019-2020 legislative session, if enacted, would add a subsection (d) designed to exclude from protection a spouse who was a care custodian, if the decedent was a dependent adult and the marriage began while the care custodian provided services to the decedent, or within 90 days after the services were last provided, and the decedent died less than six months after the marriage began, unless the spouse proves by clear and convincing evidence that the marriage was not the product of fraud or undue influence.

❖ CPC § 21612. Property to Satisfy Omitted Spouse's Share

(a) Except as provided in subdivision (b), in satisfying a share provided by this chapter:

(1) The share will first be taken from the decedent's estate not disposed of by will or trust, if any.

(2) If that is not sufficient, so much as may be necessary to satisfy the share shall be taken from all beneficiaries of decedent's testamentary instruments in proportion to the value they may respectively receive. The proportion of each beneficiary's share that may be taken pursuant to this subdivision shall be determined based on values as of the date of the decedent's death.

(b) If the obvious intention of the decedent in relation to some specific gift or devise or other provision of a testamentary instrument would be defeated by the application of subdivision (a), the specific devise or gift or provision may be exempted from the apportionment under subdivision (a), and a different apportionment, consistent with the intention of the decedent, may be adopted.
(Stats. 1997, 2003)

Unintentional Disinheritance of a Child

❖ CPC § 21620. Share of Omitted Child

Except as provided in Section 21621, if a decedent fails to provide in a testamentary instrument for a child of decedent born or adopted after the execution of all of the decedent's testamentary instruments, the omitted child shall receive a share in the decedent's estate equal in value to that which the child would have received if the decedent had died without having executed any testamentary instrument.

(Stats. 1997)

❖ CPC § 21621. When Omitted Child Does Not Receive Share

A child shall not receive a share of the estate under Section 21620 if any of the following is established:

(a) The decedent's failure to provide for the child in the decedent's testamentary instruments was intentional and that intention appears from the testamentary instruments.

(b) The decedent had one or more children and devised or otherwise directed the disposition of substantially all the estate to the other parent of the omitted child.

(c) The decedent provided for the child by transfer outside of the estate passing by the decedent's testamentary instruments and the intention that the transfer be in lieu of a provision in said instruments is shown by statements of the decedent or from the amount of the transfer or by other evidence.

(Stats. 1997)

❖ CPC § 21622. Unknown Child or Child Believed Dead

If, at the time of the execution of all of decedent's testamentary instruments effective at the time of decedent's death, the decedent failed to provide for a living child solely because the decedent believed the child to be dead or was unaware of the birth of the child, the child shall receive a share in the estate equal in value to that which the child would have received if the decedent had died without having executed any testamentary instruments.

(Stats. 1997)

❖ CPC § 21623. Property to Satisfy Omitted Child's Share

(a) Except as provided in subdivision (b), in satisfying a share provided by this chapter:

   (1) The share will first be taken from the decedent's estate not disposed of by will or trust, if any.

   (2) If that is not sufficient, so much as may be necessary to satisfy the share shall be taken from all beneficiaries of decedent's testamentary instruments in proportion to the value they may respectively receive. The proportion of each beneficiary's share that may be taken pursuant to this subdivision shall be determined based on values as of the date of the decedent's death.

(b) If the obvious intention of the decedent in relation to some specific gift or devise or other provision of a testamentary instrument would be defeated by the application of subdivision (a), the specific devise or gift or provision of a testamentary instrument may be exempted from the apportionment under subdivision (a), and a different apportionment, consistent with the intention of the decedent, may be adopted.

(Stats. 1997, 2003)

Chapter 9. Trusts: Fiduciary Administration

Section A. From Limited Powers to Fiduciary Administration

Trustees' Powers & Duty to Administer Trust

California's trustee powers statutes are largely drawn from the Uniform Trustees Powers Act (1964). Specific powers are set forth in CPC §§ 16220-16249.

CPC § 16200. General Powers

A trustee has the following powers without the need to obtain court authorization:

(a) The powers conferred by the trust instrument.

(b) Except as limited in the trust instrument, the powers conferred by statute.

(c) Except as limited in the trust instrument, the power to perform any act that a trustee would perform for the purposes of the trust under the standard of care provided in Section 16040 or 16047.

(Stats. 1990, 1995)

CPC § 16201. Power of Court to Grant Relief from Restrictions on Powers

This chapter does not affect the power of a court to relieve a trustee from restrictions on the exercise of powers under the trust instrument.

(Stats. 1990)

CPC § 16202. Exercise of Powers Subject to Fiduciary Duties

The grant of a power to a trustee, whether by the trust instrument, by statute, or by the court, does not in itself require or permit the exercise of the power. The exercise of a power by a trustee is subject to the trustee's fiduciary duties.

(Stats. 1990)

CPC § 16000. Duty to Administer Trust

On acceptance of the trust, the trustee has a duty to administer the trust according to the trust instrument and, except to the extent the trust instrument provides otherwise, according to this division.

(Stats. 1990)

CPC § 16440. Liability for Breach of Trust; Discretion to Excuse Liability for Good Faith Actions

(a) If the trustee commits a breach of trust, the trustee is chargeable with any of the following that is appropriate under the circumstances:

(1) Any loss or depreciation in value of the trust estate resulting from the breach of trust, with interest.

(2) Any profit made by the trustee through the breach of trust, with interest.

(3) Any profit that would have accrued to the trust estate if the loss of profit is the result of the breach of trust.

(b) If the trustee has acted reasonably and in good faith under the circumstances as known to the trustee, the court, in its discretion, may excuse the trustee in whole or in part from liability under subdivision (a) if it would be equitable to do so.

(Stats. 1990)

No abuse of discretion in excusing trustee from liability for failure to evict destitute life beneficiary for failure to pay maintenance expenses and for two-year delay in sale of residence

ORANGE CATHOLIC FOUNDATION v. ARVIZU

Court of Appeal, Fourth District Division 3
28 Cal. App. 5th 283, 239 Cal. Rptr. 3d 60 (2018)

MOORE, J. Probate Code section 16440, subdivision (b) provides that if a "trustee has acted *reasonably and in good faith* under the circumstances as known to the trustee," a court has discretion to excuse him or her from liability for a breach of trust if it would be equitable to do so.[1] (Italics added.) Acting under this express authority, the trial court denied a petition brought by Orange Catholic Foundation[2] and Kevin W. Vann, the Roman Catholic Bishop of Orange (collectively, the Church) to remove Rosie Mary Arvizu from her position as trustee of the Josephine Kennedy Trust (Trust) and for damages. Finding no abuse of discretion, we affirm the judgment.

The Trust gave a life estate in Kennedy's house (the Residence) to Paul Senez, her very dear family friend of over 60 years, provided that he pay for certain expenses related to the Residence. The Trust further provided that upon Senez's death, the Residence was to be sold and the proceeds were to be given to the Church for the benefit of the needy elderly and abused children. The Church alleged that Arvizu (Kennedy's niece and the successor trustee) breached

---

[1] All further undesignated statutory references are to the Probate Code.

[2] Orange Catholic Foundation is a not-for-profit corporation that administers all gifts for the Roman Catholic Diocese of Orange. The Roman Catholic Bishop of Orange appointed and authorized Orange Catholic Foundation to litigate this petition on the Church's behalf.

her duties as trustee by: (1) improperly using Trust funds to pay expenses that should have been borne by Senez (who was elderly, destitute, suffering from dementia, and unable to cover the expenses himself); (2) failing to evict Senez when he could not pay those expenses; and (3) not promptly renting out or selling the Residence after Senez's death (a delay which occurred in part due to Arvizu's cancer treatment and other health issues, and which fortuitously benefited the Church because the Residence *appreciated* by $136,000 during the period of Arvizu's inaction).

The trial court denied the Church's petition, invoking its equitable power under section 16440(b) to excuse Arvizu from liability. The court observed that the Church's argument that Senez should have been evicted, while perhaps technically correct, is "both unrealistic and not particularly charitable." The court went on: "How could Arvizu in good conscience boot out a man who essentially was a member of her family, had lived in the house for 40 years, was suffering from dementia and had minimal financial assets? . . . Under the circumstances, it is hard to imagine that anyone would take that step." As detailed below, we conclude that substantial evidence supported the trial court's finding that Arvizu acted reasonably and in good faith, and we find no abuse of discretion in the trial court's exercise of its equitable powers under section 16440(b).

I. FACTS AND PROCEDURAL HISTORY

A. The Parties and the Trust

Senez was a longtime friend of the Kennedy family. Although not related to the Kennedys by blood, he was considered a member of the family, spent holidays with them, and was affectionately known as "Uncle." He lived with the Kennedy family for 60 years, including 40 years spent at the Residence. When Kennedy's husband was alive, Senez worked as a driver for his extermination business. After Kennedy's husband passed away, Senez continued to live with Kennedy at the Residence and took care of her in her old age. Kennedy treated Senez like a son.

Kennedy established the Trust in 1997, naming herself as Trustee. . . . [T]he Trust provided that upon her death, "The Trustee shall retain, IN TRUST, all of the Trustor's interest in the [Residence] . . . , for the use and benefit of PAUL A. SENEZ for the remainder of his life; provided, however, that during the period that PAUL A. SENEZ is residing in said residence, he shall be responsible for payment of all expenses incurred in the upkeep of said residence, including but not limited to mortgage payments, taxes, utilities, insurance, and any other expenses which may be incurred. Upon the death of PAUL A. SENEZ, or in the event he shall choose not to reside in said residence, the property shall be sold and . . . [T]he Trustee shall distribute the rest, residue and remainder of the Trust Estate to the ORANGE COUNTY CATHOLIC DIOCESE, to be used for the benefit of abused and needy children and the needy elderly, as said Diocese shall determine."

In 2003, Kennedy executed a Second Amended Declaration of Trust. That Amendment . . . removed any obligation to pay mortgage payments and required Senez to pay only for "ordinary maintenance expenses" (as opposed to "any other expenses which may be incurred").

The Trust named Kennedy's niece, Arvizu, as the successor trustee. Kennedy and Arvizu were very close, and Arvizu regarded Kennedy as a mother and confidant. Over the years, Arvizu and Kennedy had many discussions about Kennedy's intentions and desires concerning the Trust, and in light of those conversations, Arvizu believed that Kennedy expected her to look after Senez and pay for certain expenses if he was unable to pay for them himself. According to Arvizu, Kennedy repeatedly told her to take care of Senez, to help him keep the property up, and to pay for Senez's cremation and funeral using Trust assets. Based on their conversations, Arvizu also believed that her aunt wanted her to ensure that Senez (a Korean War veteran) was buried in a veterans' cemetery.

B. Senez's Last Few Years in the Residence

Kennedy died in 2007 at the age of 100. Arvizu, who was in her 70s by then and neither legally nor financially sophisticated,[3] became trustee. She retained the same attorney who had prepared the Trust to advise her in administering the Trust, and the attorney gave her instructions regarding her duties as trustee.

Senez was living in the Residence when Kennedy died (as he had been for decades), and unfortunately, he was not in a position to live by himself. He was elderly; he was also in failing health and displaying signs of dementia. Arvizu offered Senez a room in her house, but he became irate and replied that he would stay in the house where he had lived for 40 years until he died.

At some point, Arvizu's estranged daughter, Mary Ann, who was very close with Senez, moved into the Residence to help take care of him. She did so without permission from or even telling Arvizu, although Arvizu eventually learned that Mary Ann was living at the Residence. Mary Ann bathed and fed Senez, helped him with his medications, ran errands for him, monitored his medication, cleaned the house, and paid his bills. His dementia progressed to the point that if he was not monitored, he would wander off by himself, so Mary Ann prevented him from doing so.

Senez could not afford the expenses associated with living in the Residence. Thus, even though the Trust expressly required Senez to pay for certain expenses associated with the Residence, and even though Arvizu understood that the Trust required Senez to pay for those expenses, Arvizu paid Senez's bills using Trust assets. Arvizu testified that she "thought [she] was doing the right thing," that she "did what [her] aunt wanted [her] to do," and that in her mind, these payments were justified by the multiple statements Kennedy had made before her death that Arvizu should take care of Senez.

According to the Church, Arvizu spent $44,416 of Trust assets to pay expenses that should have been borne by Senez. The trial court found that these expenses fell into two main

---

[3] Arvizu has an 11th grade education, and she worked as a beautician for a few years and then as an assembler for TRW for many years.

categories: (1) expenses that clearly benefited the Residence, and (2) expenses that were personal to Senez. The first category of expenses, which totaled $40,208, included items such as property taxes and homeowners association dues; the trial court found that Arvizu credibly testified that she paid those expenses to avoid foreclosure.[4] The second category of expenses, which totaled $4,208, included items such as Senez's car payments, auto insurance, utilities, and (after his death) his funeral expenses, all of which the trial court found should *not* have been paid by the Trust.

C. Arvizu's Delay in Selling the Residence

Senez died in October 2012. On the day of his wake, Arvizu told Mary Ann that she needed to move out of the Residence. Mary Ann replied that she would do so but that she needed some time, and Arvizu believed her.

As it turned out, Mary Ann remained in the Residence for nearly two years after Senez's death, despite her mother's repeated requests that she move out. According to Mary Ann, it took her awhile to find a place to live. Arvizu did not act more decisively in evicting her daughter, in part because Arvizu was in and out of the hospital due to her own health problems (including breast cancer treatment and a knee surgery). Arvizu was also caring for her ill husband, who had a tumor.

During that two-year period, Arvizu did not collect rent from Mary Ann. According to the Church, the reasonable rental value of the Residence was about $2,900 per month (assuming the Residence was in average condition, which does not appear to have been the case). Thus, claimed the Church, the Trust lost about $70,000 in lost rent during that period.

Arvizu eventually involved her attorney, who wrote a letter to Mary Ann in July 2014 threatening her with legal action if she did not move out of the Residence. Mary Ann vacated the Residence the following month. By October, a realtor prepared a listing agreement for the Residence, which by then was in *extremely* poor condition and required extensive clean up and repairs. . . .

Despite the lost rent, Arvizu's two-year delay in putting the Residence on the market proved to be very beneficial to the Trust. It is undisputed that the market value of the Residence increased from $410,000 in November 2012 (the month after Senez died) to $546,000 in March 2015 (when the Residence was finally sold) as a result of the real estate market going up. . . .

D. Proceedings in the Trial Court

The Church filed a verified petition to remove and replace Arvizu and for damages for breach of trust and breach of fiduciary duty. After a two-day bench trial, the trial court issued an eight-page written decision denying the Church's petition. In its findings of fact, the court concluded

---

[4] Arvizu's attorney testified along similar lines: she said that paying those expenses (as opposed to filing a section 17200 petition for instructions and waiting months for an outcome) preserved Trust assets and benefited the Trust by avoiding additional penalties, liens, and foreclosure.

that Arvizu "plainly decided to act in a way that she believed carried out the wishes of her Aunt (Kennedy) notwithstanding the language of the Trust"; that in Arvizu's mind, the use of Trust funds to pay for various expenses was "justified by statements that had been made to her by Kennedy before her death" about the need to take care of Senez; and that "none of [Arvizu's] actions appear to have been taken to benefit her personally."

The court then reasoned as follows: "There is little question that Arvizu did not follow the exact requirements of the Trust in administering it after Kennedy's death. During the five years that Senez held a life estate in the Residence, she used Trust assets to pay both expenses that Senez was supposed to pay and some of his personal expenses. After his death in 2012, she failed to act promptly in selling the property and then turning the proceeds over to the Church. Further, during the two year period of delay, she did not rent the property, instead allowing her estranged daughter to remain there rent-free. This conduct falls below the standard of care required of a trustee by the Probate Code. *See* Probate Code §§ 16002, 16004, 16006, 16007.

"Balanced against these issues are the justifications offered by Arvizu for her actions. As to the payments of property taxes and homeowner association dues, Arvizu legitimately concluded that paying these expenses ultimately would benefit the Trust since possible foreclosure and penalties could be avoided. Other expenses that were plainly personal to Senez were paid not to benefit Arvizu, but to carry out what she believed were her Aunt's wishes.

"Considering these facts, it is difficult to fault Arvizu for her actions—at least up to the time of Senez's death. Thus, in response to the Court's questions at the conclusion of the trial as to what Arvizu should have done when it became clear to her that Senez could not make the payments required by the Trust, the attorney for the Church stated that Arvizu should have evicted Senez and sold the Residence (or simply deeded it over to the Church). While this statement may be technically correct, it strikes the Court as both unrealistic and not particularly charitable. How could Arvizu in good conscience boot out a man who essentially was a member of her family, had lived in the house for 40 years, was suffering from dementia and had minimal financial assets? Given his adamant refusal to move when asked to do so by Arvizu in 2007, her legal remedy would have been to institute an unlawful detainer action against him. Under the circumstances, it is hard to imagine that anyone would take that step.

"As to the two years of rent that Arvizu failed to charge for the Residence, she is somewhat more blameworthy. While it undoubtedly would have been uncomfortable to evict her daughter immediately after Senez's death, Arvizu, as the Trustee, was required to do whatever was reasonably necessary to preserve all Trust assets. Other than her own ill health and the obvious difficult dynamics of her relationship with Mary Ann, Arvizu presented no legitimate justification for her actions.

"That being said, the loss of $69,600 in rent is more than offset by the $136,000 increase in the value of the Residence as a result of the delayed sale. This increase in value also more than covers any of Senez's purportedly unauthorized expenses paid by the Trust. . . . Given this appreciation, the Church is hard-pressed to demonstrate any real losses attributable to Arvizu's actions.

". . . As set forth above, the evidence strongly supports the conclusion that Arvizu acted reasonably and in good faith under the unique circumstances of the case. Significantly, at no time did she take any actions designed to benefit herself personally. Further, although some of her actions were in contravention of the precise wording of the Trust, all of Arvizu's actions were, at least in her mind, consistent with the wishes of her aunt, the trustor."

For the above reasons, the trial court denied the Church's petition. It then entered a judgment denying the Church's petition, deeming the Trust fully distributed, and dissolving the Trust. The Church appealed the judgment, arguing (among other things) that the trial court erred in using its equitable powers to excuse Arvizu's breaches.

II. DISCUSSION

A. Standard of Review

We review the trial court's findings of fact, including its factual findings on witness credibility and whether Arvizu acted reasonably and in good faith, under the substantial evidence standard of review. . . . We review the trial court's exercise of its equitable powers—including its decision to excuse a trustee for breach of trust under section 16440(b)—for abuse of discretion. . . . We may reverse only if the trial court's decision " 'exceeds the bounds of reason, all of the circumstances before it being considered.' "

B. The Court's Equitable Powers Under Section 16440

"The remedies of a beneficiary against the trustee are exclusively in equity." (§ 16421 . . . .) This is significant, because it means that "wide play is reserved to the court's conscience in formulating its decrees." . . . Consistent with the equitable nature of a beneficiary's remedies, section 16440 gives trial courts wide latitude in deciding whether and what types of damages to impose on a trustee who commits a breach of trust. Subdivision (a) authorizes the trial court to determine which of three measures of liability provided in the statute "is appropriate under the circumstances," and subdivision (b) gives the court discretion to excuse the trustee from liability for any breach of trust that he or she committed reasonably and in good faith, if it would be equitable to do so. . . .

C. The Trial Court Did Not Abuse Its Discretion in Excusing Arvizu

Given the language of section 16440(b), a threshold question is whether there was substantial evidence to support the trial court's factual findings of reasonableness and good faith. We conclude there was. . . .

Given its findings of reasonableness and good faith, section 16440(b) afforded the trial court broad discretion to excuse Arvizu from liability, and we find no abuse of discretion in the trial court's decision to do so. (Contrast *Uzyel v. Kadisha, supra,* 188 Cal.App.4th at pp. 906-907, 116 Cal.Rptr.3d 244 [finding that subdivision (b) did not apply because the trustee had acted in bad faith by serving his own interests].) Since the determination of the appropriate relief in a trust dispute is exclusively a matter in equity (§ 16421), the relief afforded to the parties is properly left to the trial court for determination and generally should not be disturbed on appeal. . . .

The Church colorfully argues on appeal that the trial court could not use its equitable powers to excuse Arvizu's conduct because her treatment of Senez was "objectively despicable," "reprehensible," and amounted to "clear and patent elder abuse." More specifically, the Church asserts that Arvizu immorally abandoned a veteran with senile dementia by leaving him "to languish in filth" with Arvizu's dangerous and estranged daughter, rather than getting him the help he needed at "the V.A."

There are many problems with this argument. First, it is speculative and not supported by the record. Despite the Church's attempts at trial to paint Mary Ann as an unsavory individual, there was no evidence that Mary Ann ever physically mistreated or abused Senez; there was conflicting evidence at trial as to when exactly the Residence became so deteriorated to the point of being uninhabitable (i.e., whether that happened before or after Senez's death); and there was no evidence at trial concerning what veterans benefits, if any, Senez would have been entitled to had he applied, or how those benefits could have helped his situation. To the contrary, the evidence at trial overwhelmingly indicated that Arvizu was trying to do the right thing by letting Senez stay in the house he had lived in for over 40 years, and that Mary Ann generally *helped* Senez's situation. The Church's contention on appeal about Senez allegedly being mistreated is inconsistent with the position it took at trial, where the Church repeatedly advocated that Arvizu should have *evicted* Senez (in the words of the Church's counsel, "kick him out"), even though he was senile and destitute with no means to care for himself.

The Church also asserts on appeal that Arvizu "misappropriated money to be used for needy children and the elderly to help out her uncle," and that the trial court's ruling "came at a cost to the actual beneficiaries of the Kennedy's Trust Estate—the elderly and children to which she left it." This argument also falls flat. As noted above, the vast majority (over 90%) of expenses paid out of Trust assets during Senez's final years in the Residence benefitted the Residence (and hence the Trust, the Church, and the future recipients of any charity) by avoiding foreclosure, liens, and penalties. Further, the Trust sustained no damages as a result of Arvizu's delay in selling the Residence and her failure to rent it out; to the contrary, the Trust actually made money as a result of the Residence's $136,000 appreciation during the period of Arvizu's inaction. . . .

The Church also asserts that Arvizu should not have been rewarded for willfully breaching her fiduciary duties and for willfully disregarding the terms of the Trust. This argument misses the point of section 16440(b), the applicability of which does not turn on whether the trustee acted negligently or willfully. Section 16440(b) gives a trial court discretion to excuse a trustee from liability for *any* breach of trust committed reasonably and in good faith, if it would be equitable to do so. . . .

In affirming the judgment, we certainly do not mean to suggest the trial court was *required* to excuse Arvizu's conduct, or that a trustee who has acted reasonably and in good faith must *always* be relieved from liability for committing a breach of trust, or that a trustee *always* has free reign to ignore trust terms in the name of doing the "right thing." We hold only that the trial court had discretion to excuse Arvizu under section 16440(b), and given that substantial evidence supported the trial court's findings of good faith and reasonableness, we find no abuse of that discretion.

IV. DISPOSITION

The judgment is affirmed. Arvizu shall recover her costs on appeal.

WE CONCUR: O'LEARY, P.J., THOMPSON, J.

Section B. The Duty of Loyalty

CPC § 16002. Duty of Loyalty

(a) The trustee has a duty to administer the trust solely in the interest of the beneficiaries.

(b) It is not a violation of the duty provided in subdivision (a) for a trustee who administers two trusts to sell, exchange, or participate in the sale or exchange of trust property between the trusts, if both of the following requirements are met:

(1) The sale or exchange is fair and reasonable with respect to the beneficiaries of both trusts.

(2) The trustee gives to the beneficiaries of both trusts notice of all material facts related to the sale or exchange that the trustee knows or should know.

(Stats. 1990)

CPC § 16004. Conflicts of Interest

(a) The trustee has a duty not to use or deal with trust property for the trustee's own profit or for any other purpose unconnected with the trust, nor to take part in any transaction in which the trustee has an interest adverse to the beneficiary.

(b) The trustee may not enforce any claim against the trust property that the trustee purchased after or in contemplation of appointment as trustee, but the court may allow the trustee to be reimbursed from trust property the amount that the trustee paid in good faith for the claim.

(c) A transaction between the trustee and a beneficiary which occurs during the existence of the trust or while the trustee's influence with the beneficiary remains and by which the trustee obtains an advantage from the beneficiary is presumed to be a violation of the trustee's fiduciary duties. This presumption is a presumption affecting the burden of proof. This subdivision does not apply to the provisions of an agreement between a trustee and a beneficiary relating to the hiring or compensation of the trustee.

(Stats. 1990)

NOTE: Vance v. Bizek, 228 Cal. App. 4th 1155, 177 Cal. Rptr. 3d 167 (2014), held that only beneficiaries, not creditors of a beneficiary, can take advantage of CPC § 16004.

CPC § 16004.5. Trustee May Not Require Beneficiary to Relieve Trustee of Liability as Condition for Making Distribution

(a) A trustee may not require a beneficiary to relieve the trustee of liability as a condition for making a distribution or payment to, or for the benefit of, the beneficiary, if the distribution or payment is required by the trust instrument.

(b) This section may not be construed as affecting the trustee's right to:

(1) Maintain a reserve for reasonably anticipated expenses, including, but not limited to, taxes, debts, trustee and accounting fees, and costs and expenses of administration.

(2) Seek a voluntary release or discharge of a trustee's liability from the beneficiary.

(3) Require indemnification against a claim by a person or entity, other than a beneficiary referred to in subdivision (a), which may reasonably arise as a result of the distribution.

(4) Withhold any portion of an otherwise required distribution that is reasonably in dispute.

(5) Seek court or beneficiary approval of an accounting of trust activities.

(Stats. 2003)

NOTE: Bellows v. Bellows, 196 Cal. App.4th 505, 125 Cal. Rptr. 3d 401 (2011), held that Probate Code § 16004.5 overrides Commercial Code §3311 on accord and satisfaction. Trustee's statement that acceptance of check was acknowledgement of receipt of final distribution of the trust estate was not effective. Trustee not entitled to condition payment on release of other claimes or demands of trust beneficiary.

CPC § 16005. Adverse Trusts

The trustee of one trust has a duty not to knowingly become a trustee of another trust adverse in its nature to the interest of the beneficiary of the first trust, and a duty to eliminate the conflict or resign as trustee when the conflict is discovered.

(Stats. 1990)

Section C. The Duty of Prudence

CPC § 16040. Standard of Care; Modification by Trust Instrument

(a) The trustee shall administer the trust with reasonable care, skill, and caution under the circumstances then prevailing that a prudent person acting in a like capacity would use in the conduct of an enterprise of like character and with like aims to accomplish the purposes of the trust as determined from the trust instrument.

(b) The settlor may expand or restrict the standard provided in subdivision (a) by express provisions in the trust instrument. A trustee is not liable to a beneficiary for the trustee's good faith reliance on these express provisions.

(Stats. 1990, 1995)

CPC § 16041. Effect of Compensation

A trustee's standard of care and performance in administering the trust is not affected by whether or not the trustee receives any compensation.

(Stats. 1990)

CPC § 16014. Special Skills

(a) The trustee has a duty to apply the full extent of the trustee's skills.

(b) If the settlor, in selecting the trustee, has relied on the trustee's representation of having special skills, the trustee is held to the standard of the skills represented.

(Stats. 1990)

The Distribution Function

Discretionary Distributions

CPC § 16080. Discretionary Power Shall Be Exercised Reasonably

Except as provided in Section 16081, a discretionary power conferred upon a trustee is not left to the trustee's arbitrary discretion, but shall be exercised reasonably.

(Stats. 1990)

CPC § 16081. Trustee with Extended Discretion Subject to Fiduciary Principles

(a) Subject to the additional requirements of subdivisions (b), (c), and (d), if a trust instrument confers "absolute," "sole," or "uncontrolled" discretion on a trustee, the trustee shall act in accordance with fiduciary principles and shall not act in bad faith or in disregard of the purposes of the trust.

(b) Notwithstanding the use of terms like "absolute," "sole," or "uncontrolled" by a settlor or a testator, a person who is a beneficiary of a trust that permits the person, either individually or as trustee or cotrustee, to make discretionary distributions of income or principal to or for the benefit of himself or herself pursuant to a standard, shall exercise that power reasonably and in accordance with the standard. . . .

(Stats. 1990, 1996)

Exculpatory Clauses

CPC § 16461. Exculpation of Trustee

(a) Except as provided in subdivision (b), (c), or (d), the trustee can be relieved of liability for breach of trust by provisions in the trust instrument.

(b) A provision in the trust instrument is not effective to relieve the trustee of liability (1) for breach of trust committed intentionally, with gross negligence, in bad faith, or with reckless indifference to the interest of the beneficiary, or (2) for any profit that the trustee derives from a breach of trust.

(c) Subject to subdivision (b), a provision in a trust instrument that releases the trustee from liability if a beneficiary fails to object to an item in an interim or final account or other written report within a specified time period is effective only if all of the following conditions are met:

(1) The account or report sets forth the item.

(2) The period specified in the trust instrument for the beneficiary to object is not less than 180 days, or the trustee elects to follow the procedure provided in subdivision (d).

(3) Written notice in 12-point boldface type is provided to a beneficiary with the account or report in the following form: . . .

(Stats. 1990, 2004)

NOTE: Trust provisions that purport to allow former trustee to withhold communications with legal counsel from successor trustee violate public policy and are unenforceable. **Morgan v. Superior Court**, 23 Cal. App. 5th 1026, 233 Cal. Rptr. 3d 647 (2018).

The Investment Function

CPC § 16007. Productivity of Trust Property

The trustee has a duty to make the trust property productive under the circumstances and in furtherance of the purposes of the trust.

(Stats. 1990)

The Prudent Investor Rule

California's Uniform Prudent Investor Act is located at CPC §§ 16045-16054. Section 16047 is substantively the same as § (a)-(e) of the Uniform Prudent Investor Act. Subsection (f) was omitted because the subject is covered by CPC § 16014.

The Custodial and Administrative Functions

Duty to Collect and Protect Trust Property

CPC § 16006. Control and Preservation of Trust Property

The trustee has a duty to take reasonable steps under the circumstances to take and keep control of and to preserve the trust property.

(Stats. 1990)

Duty to Earmark Trust Property

CPC § 16009. Separation and Identification of Trust Property

The trustee has a duty to do the following:

(a) To keep the trust property separate from other property not subject to the trust.

(b) To see that the trust property is designated as property of the trust.

(Stats. 1990)

Duty to Bring and Defend Claims

CPC § 16010. Enforcement of Claims

The trustee has a duty to take reasonable steps to enforce claims that are part of the trust property.

(Stats. 1990)

CPC § 16011. Defense of Actions

The trustee has a duty to take reasonable steps to defend actions that may result in a loss to the trust.

(Stats. 1990)

Trustee Selection and Divided Trusteeship

Choosing a Trustee

CPC § 15680. Trustee Compensation; Variance from Terms of Trust

(a) Subject to subdivision (b), and except as provided in Section 15688,[36] if the trust instrument provides for the trustee's compensation, the trustee is entitled to be compensated in accordance with the trust instrument.

---

[36] Payment to public guardian or public administrator.—Ed.

(b) Upon proper showing, the court may fix or allow greater or lesser compensation than could be allowed under the terms of the trust in any of the following circumstances:

(1) Where the duties of the trustee are substantially different from those contemplated when the trust was created.

(2) Where the compensation in accordance with the terms of the trust would be inequitable or unreasonably low or high.

(3) In extraordinary circumstances calling for equitable relief.

(c) An order fixing or allowing greater or lesser compensation under subdivision (b) applies only prospectively to actions taken in administration of the trust after the order is made.

(Stats.1990, 2008)

NOTE: In **Thorpe v. Reed**, 211 Cal. App. 4th 1381, 150 Cal. Rptr. 3d 454 (2012) the court reversed an award of $51,285.63 for trustee and attorney fees to a temporary successor trustee of a special needs trust. The trust provided for reasonable compensation for the original trustee, but that no compensation should be paid to a special or successor trustee. The successor trustee did not obtain a court order under CPC § 15680(b) prior to undertaking administration of the trust.

Delegation by a Trustee

CPC § 16012. Duty Not to Delegate

(a) The trustee has a duty not to delegate to others the performance of acts that the trustee can reasonably be required personally to perform and may not transfer the office of trustee to another person nor delegate the entire administration of the trust to a cotrustee or other person.

(b) In a case where a trustee has properly delegated a matter to an agent, cotrustee, or other person, the trustee has a duty to exercise general supervision over the person performing the delegated matter.

(Stats. 1990, 1995)

Division by a Settlor

CPC § 15620. Cotrustees Must Act Unanimously

Unless otherwise provided in the trust instrument, a power vested in two or more trustees may only be exercised by their unanimous action.

(Stats. 1990)

CPC § 16013. Duties of Cotrustees

If a trust has more than one trustee, each trustee has a duty to do the following:

(a) To participate in the administration of the trust.

(b) To take reasonable steps to prevent a cotrustee from committing a breach of trust or to compel a cotrustee to redress a breach of trust.

(Stats. 1990)

Section D. The Duty of Impartiality

CPC § 16003. Duty of Impartiality

If a trust has two or more beneficiaries, the trustee has a duty to deal impartially with them and shall act impartially in investing and managing the trust property, taking into account any differing interests of the beneficiaries.

(Stats. 1990, 1995)

The Principal and Income Problem

California's Uniform Principal & Income Act is located at CPC §§ 16320-16375. Allocations and adjustments between principal and income are governed by §§ 16335 and 16336.

Section E. The Duty to Inform and Account

Duty to Inform

CPC § 16060. Duty to Inform Beneficiaries

The trustee has a duty to keep the beneficiaries of the trust reasonably informed of the trust and its administration.

(Stats. 1990)

NOTE: Williamson v. Brooks, 7 Cal. App. 5th 1294, 213 Cal. Rptr. 3d 388 (2017) agreed with trial court's conclusion that trustees did not breach their fiduciary duties to beneficiary by not informing her that she could withdraw funds from the trust. Beneficiary is entitled to be informed of trust's existence so that she can take action to gain more information, but absent request, trustees are not required to tell beneficiary about the details of the trust.

CPC § 16060.5. What "Terms of the Trust" Includes

As used in this article, "terms of the trust" means the written trust instrument of an irrevocable trust or those provisions of a written trust instrument in effect at the settlor's death that describe or affect that portion of a trust that has become irrevocable at the death of the settlor. In addition, "terms of the trust" includes, but is not limited to, signatures, amendments, disclaimers, and any directions or instructions to the trustee that affect the disposition of the trust. "Terms of the trust" does not include documents which were intended to affect disposition only while the trust was revocable. If a trust has been completely restated, "terms of the trust" does not include trust instruments or amendments which are superseded by the last restatement before the settlor's death, but it does include amendments executed after the restatement. "Terms of the trust" also includes any document irrevocably exercising a power of appointment over the trust or over any portion of the trust which has become irrevocable.

(Stats. 1997, 1998, 2000)

CPC § 16060.7. Duty to Provide Terms of Trust to Beneficiary

On the request of a beneficiary, the trustee shall provide the terms of the trust to the beneficiary unless the trustee is not required to provide the terms of the trust to the beneficiary in accordance with Section 16069.

(Stats. 2010)

CPC § 16061. Request by Beneficiary for Information

Except as provided in Section 16069, on reasonable request by a beneficiary, the trustee shall report to the beneficiary by providing requested information to the beneficiary relating to the administration of the trust relevant to the beneficiary's interest.

(Stats. 1990, 1998, 2010)

NOTE: Trustee not required to produce communications protected by attorney-client privilege, whether communications dealt with trust administration or allegations of misconduct; work product of co-trustee's counsel not subject to discovery by beneficiaries. **Wells Fargo Bank, N.A. v. Superior Court**, 22 Cal. 4th 201, 990 P.2d 591 (2000).

CPC § 16061.5. Duty to Provide Copy of Trust to Beneficiaries and Heirs When Revocable Trust Becomes Irrevocable

(a) A trustee shall provide a true and complete copy of the terms of the irrevocable trust, or irrevocable portion of the trust, to each of the following:

> (1) Any beneficiary of the trust who requests it, and to any heir of a deceased settlor who requests it, when a revocable trust or any portion of a revocable trust becomes irrevocable because of the death of one or more of the settlors of the trust, when a power of appointment is effective or lapses upon the death of a settlor under the circumstances

described in paragraph (3) of subdivision (a) of Section 16061.7,[37] or because, by the express terms of the trust, the trust becomes irrevocable within one year of the death of a settlor because of a contingency related to the death of one or more of the settlors of the trust.

(2) Any beneficiary of the trust who requests it, whenever there is a change of trustee of an irrevocable trust.

(3) If the trust is a charitable trust subject to the supervision of the Attorney General, to the Attorney General, if requested, when a revocable trust or any portion of a revocable trust becomes irrevocable because of the death of one or more of the settlors of the trust, when a power of appointment is effective or lapses upon the death of a settlor under the circumstances described in paragraph (3) of subdivision (a) of Section 16061.7, or because, by the express terms of the trust, the trust becomes irrevocable within one year of the death of a settlor because of a contingency related to the death of one or more of the settlors of the trust, and whenever there is a change of trustee of an irrevocable trust.

b) The trustee shall, for purposes of this section, rely upon any final judicial determination of heirship. However, the trustee shall have discretion to make a good faith determination by any reasonable means of the heirs of a deceased settlor in the absence of a final judicial determination of heirship known to the trustee.

(Stats. 1997, 1998, 2000, 2010)

NOTE: In addition to the circumstances described in footnote 37, CPC § 16061.7 requires a trustee to serve a notification that a revocable trust has become irrevocable or there has been a change of trustee of an irrevocable trust. If the trust has become irrevocable because of the death of one or more of the settlors, the notice must include a warning that an action to contest the trust must be brought within 120 days of the date the notification is served or 60 days from the date on which a copy of the terms of the trust is delivered during the 120-day period, whichever is later. A trustee who fails to serve the required notice may be liable for damages caused the failure to a beneficiary or heir under CPC § 16061.9.

Duty to Account

CPC § 16062. When Trustee Must Account

(a) Except as otherwise provided in this section and in Section 16064, the trustee shall account at least annually, at the termination of the trust, and upon a change of trustee, to each

---

[37] § 16061.7(a)(3) provides: "Whenever a power of appointment retained by a settlor is effective or lapses upon death of the settlor with respect to an inter vivos trust which was, or was purported to be, irrevocable upon its creation. This paragraph shall not apply to a charitable remainder trust. For purposes of this paragraph, "charitable remainder trust" means a charitable remainder annuity trust or charitable remainder unitrust as defined in Section 664(d) of the Internal Revenue Code."

beneficiary to whom income or principal is required or authorized in the trustee's discretion to be currently distributed.

(b) A trustee of a living trust created by an instrument executed before July 1, 1987, is not subject to the duty to account provided by subdivision (a). . . .

(e) Any limitation or waiver in a trust instrument of the obligation to account is against public policy and shall be void as to any sole trustee who is either of the following:

    (1) A disqualified person as defined in former Section 21350.5 (as repealed by Chapter 620 of the Statutes of 2010).

    (2) Described in subdivision (a) of Section 21380, but not described in Section 21382.

(Stats. 1990, 1993, 1998, 2001, 2010, 2016)

CPC § 16064. Exceptions to Accounting Requirement

The trustee is not required to account to a beneficiary as described in subdivision (a) of Section 16062, in any of the following circumstances:

(a) To the extent the trust instrument waives the account, except that no waiver described in subdivision (e) of Section 16062 shall be valid or enforceable. Regardless of a waiver of accounting in the trust instrument, upon a showing that it is reasonably likely that a material breach of the trust has occurred, the court may compel the trustee to account.

(b) As to a beneficiary who has waived in writing the right to an account. A waiver of rights under this subdivision may be withdrawn in writing at any time as to accounts for transactions occurring after the date of the written withdrawal. Regardless of a waiver of accounting by a beneficiary, upon a showing that is reasonably likely that a material breach of the trust has occurred, the court may compel the trustee to account.

(c) In any of the circumstances set forth in Section 16069.

(Stats. 1990, 1992, 1993, 2010)

CPC § 16069. Exceptions to Requirement to Provide Certain Information to Beneficiary

The trustee is not required to account to the beneficiary, provide the terms of the trust to a beneficiary, or provide requested information to the beneficiary pursuant to Section 16061, in any of the following circumstances:

(a) In the case of a beneficiary of a revocable trust, as provided in Section 15800, for the period when the trust may be revoked.

(b) If the beneficiary and the trustee are the same person.

(Stats. 2010)

CPC § 17200. Trustee or Beneficiary May Petition Court on Internal Affairs & Existence of Trust

(a) Except as provided in Section 15800, a trustee or beneficiary of a trust may petition the court under this chapter concerning the internal affairs of the trust or to determine the existence of the trust.

(b) Proceedings concerning the internal affairs of a trust include, but are not limited to, proceedings for any of the following purposes:

(1) Determining questions of construction of a trust instrument.

(2) Determining the existence or nonexistence of any immunity, power, privilege, duty, or right.

(3) Determining the validity of a trust provision.

(4) Ascertaining beneficiaries and determining to whom property shall pass or be delivered upon final or partial termination of the trust, to the extent the determination is not made by the trust instrument.

(5) Settling the accounts and passing upon the acts of the trustee, including the exercise of discretionary powers.

(6) Instructing the trustee.

(7) Compelling the trustee to do any of the following:

(A) Provide a copy of the terms of the trust.

(B) Provide information about the trust under Section 16061 if the trustee has failed to provide the requested information within 60 days after the beneficiary's reasonable written request, and the beneficiary has not received the requested information from the trustee within the six months preceding the request.

(C) Account to the beneficiary, subject to the provisions of Section 16064, if the trustee has failed to submit a requested account within 60 days after written request of the beneficiary and no account has been made within six months preceding the request.

(8) Granting powers to the trustee.

(9) Fixing or allowing payment of the trustee's compensation or reviewing the reasonableness of the trustee's compensation.

(10) Appointing or removing a trustee.

(11) Accepting the resignation of a trustee.

(12) Compelling redress of a breach of the trust by any available remedy.

(13) Approving or directing the modification or termination of the trust.

(14) Approving or directing the combination or division of trusts.

(15) Amending or conforming the trust instrument in the manner required to qualify a decedent's estate for the charitable estate tax deduction under federal law, including the addition of mandatory governing instrument requirements for a charitable remainder trust as required by final regulations and rulings of the United States Internal Revenue Service.

(16) Authorizing or directing transfer of a trust or trust property to or from another jurisdiction.

(17) Directing transfer of a testamentary trust subject to continuing court jurisdiction from one county to another.

(18) Approving removal of a testamentary trust from continuing court jurisdiction.

(19) Reforming or excusing compliance with the governing instrument of an organization pursuant to Section 16105.

(20) Determining the liability of the trust for any debts of a deceased settlor. However, nothing in this paragraph shall provide standing to bring an action concerning the internal affairs of the trust to a person whose only claim to the assets of the decedent is as a creditor.

(21) Determining petitions filed pursuant to Section 15687 and reviewing the reasonableness of compensation for legal services authorized under that section. In determining the reasonableness of compensation under this paragraph, the court may consider, together with all other relevant circumstances, whether prior approval was obtained pursuant to Section 15687.

* * *

(Stats. 1990, 1991, 1993, 1996, 1997, 1998, 1999, 2003, 2010)

NOTES:

1. Barefoot v. Jennings, 27 Cal. App. 5th 1, 237 Cal. Rptr. 3d 750 (2018), **_review granted Dec. 12, 2018_**, held that standing to petition under § 17200 is limited to current beneficiaries and trustees. Daughter who was expressly eliminated as beneficiary and removed as successor trustee by 17th through 24th amendments to her parents' trust, did not have standing to challenge validity of the amendments by petition under § 17200.

2. Graham-Sult v. Clainos, 756 F.3d 724 (9th Cir. 2013), held that trustee's statute of limitations defense may not prevail against trust beneficiaries because they were entitled to rely on statements and advice provided by the fiduciary.

3. Gaynor v. Bulen, 19 Cal. App. 5th 864, 228 Cal. Rptr. 3d 243 (2018) held that surcharge petition against de facto trustee for breach of fiduciary duty by actions designed to benefit cotrustees at the expense of other beneficiaries, including use of trust funds to file and defend probate petitions to modify trust terms to change trustee succession provisions to ensure their continued control of distributions, was not subect to anti-SLAPP statute. De facto trustee did not meet burden of showing that the surcharge claim arose out of his constitutionally protected litigation activity. His involvement in prior probate litigation was evidence of his alleged breaches of duty of loyalty—implementing a plan to benefit himself to the detriment of other trust beneficiaries. Probate court properly denied the anti-SLAPP motion without reaching the probability-of-prevailing issue.

Remainder Beneficiaries of Revocable Trust Have Standing to Sue Trustee for Breach of Duty to Settlor after Settlor's Death

ESTATE of GIRALDIN

Supreme Court of California
55 Cal. 4th 1058, 290 P.3d 199, 150 Cal. Rptr. 3d 205 (2012)

CHIN, J. . . . When the trustee of a revocable trust is someone other than the settlor, that trustee owes a fiduciary duty to the settlor, not to the beneficiaries, as long as the settlor is alive. . . . We must decide whether, after the settlor dies, the beneficiaries have standing to sue the trustee for breach of the fiduciary duty committed while the settlor was alive and the trust was still revocable. Because a trustee's breach of the fiduciary duty owed to the settlor can substantially harm the beneficiaries by reducing the trust's value against the settlor's wishes, we conclude the beneficiaries do have standing to sue for a breach of that duty after the settlor has died. We reverse the judgment of the Court of Appeal . . . .

In February 2002, William created . . . the William A. Giraldin [Revocable] Trust . . . , and made [son] Timothy the trustee. William was the sole beneficiary during his lifetime. The remainder beneficiaries were [wife] Mary, who was entitled to the benefits of the trust during her lifetime, and then . . . [their] nine children, who would share equally . . . .

The trust document . . . provided that "[d]uring [William's] lifetime, the trustee shall have no duty to provide any information regarding the trust to anyone other than [William]." After William's death, if Mary survived him, the trustee "shall have no duty to disclose to any beneficiary other than [Mary] the existence of this trust or any information about its terms or administration, except as required by law." The document also specified that William "waive[d] all statutory requirements . . . that the Trustee . . . render a report or account to the beneficiaries of the trust." . . .

[After William's death, four of his children] . . . sued Timothy in his capacity as trustee of the trust for breach of his fiduciary duties. They alleged, in effect, that Timothy had squandered William's life savings for his and [son] Patrick's benefit, depriving the other seven children of their benefits from the trust. . . . [They] sought to remove Timothy as trustee, . . . to compel him to account for his actions while acting as trustee, [and to S him] . . . for alleged breach of his fiduciary duties regarding . . . [a $4,000,000] investment and in making loans to himself and Patrick from trust assets. . . .

II. DISCUSSION

. . . Probate Code section 15800 provides: "Except to the extent that the trust instrument otherwise provides . . . , during the time that a trust is revocable and the person holding the power to revoke the trust is competent:

"(a) The person holding the power to revoke, and not the beneficiary, has the rights afforded beneficiaries under this division.

"(b) *The duties of the trustee are owed to the person holding the power to revoke.*" (Italics added.) . . .

The italicized language from section 15800, subdivision (b), makes clear that so long as the settlor is alive, the trustee owes a duty solely to the settlor and not to the   beneficiaries. . . .

The question we must decide is whether the plaintiffs had standing, after William's death, to allege Timothy's breach of fiduciary duty towards William. The Probate Code does not address this question directly. That is, no section expressly states that the beneficiaries of a revocable trust either have or do not have this standing. But the code, as a whole, implies that after the settlor has died, the beneficiaries of a revocable trust may challenge the trustee's breach of the fiduciary duty owed to the settlor to the extent that breach harmed the beneficiaries' interests. As the Law Revision Commission explained, section 15800 merely *postponed* the beneficiaries' enjoyment of their rights until after the settlor's death. . . .

As a general matter, the Probate Code affords beneficiaries broad remedies for breach of trust. Section 16420, subdivision (a), provides that "[i]f a trustee commits a breach of trust, or threatens to commit a breach of trust, *a beneficiary* . . . *may commence a proceeding* for any of the following purposes that is appropriate . . . ." (Italics added.) These purposes include "[t]o compel the trustee to redress a breach of trust by payment of money or otherwise." . . . The Law Revision Commission comment to this section states that the "reference to payment of money in paragraph (3) is comprehensive and includes liability that might be characterized as damages, restitution, *or surcharge.*" . . . Subdivision (b) of that section—which states that the "provision of remedies for breach of trust in subdivision (a) does not prevent resort to any other appropriate remedy provided by statute or the common law"—makes clear that the remedies the section affords beneficiaries are indeed broad.

Section 16462, subdivision (a), provides that "a trustee of a revocable trust is not liable *to a beneficiary* for any act performed or omitted pursuant to written directions from the person holding the power to revoke . . . ." (Italics added.) This provision is consistent with section 15800, which provides that the trustee's duties are owed to "the person holding the power to revoke," who in this case is the settlor. If the trustee's duty is to the settlor, and the trustee acts pursuant to the settlor's directions, the trustee has violated no duty. But section 16462, including the italicized language, "to a beneficiary," also implies that if the trustee does *not* act pursuant to the settlor's directions, the trustee *may* be liable to the beneficiaries. This implication would make no sense, and section 16462 would be meaningless, if the beneficiaries have no standing, ever, to bring an action challenging the trustee's actions while the settlor was still alive. We see no textual or other basis to support the dissent's argument section 16462 only governs actions taken after the settlor has died. . . .

Section 16069 (formerly part of section 16064) provides that the trustee need not account to the beneficiary "[i]n the case of a beneficiary of a revocable trust, as provided in Section 15800, for the period when the trust may be revoked." Timothy argues this means that he need not account to the beneficiaries ever for his actions while the trust could be revoked. The statutory language is somewhat ambiguous and may, indeed, be read as Timothy argues. But, as the cross-reference to section 15800 indicates, section 16069 must be read in context. Section 15800 provides that *during* the time the trust is revocable, the settlor has the rights afforded beneficiaries. We must read section 16069 to be consistent with section 15800. We do not read section 16069 to mean that the trustee never has to provide such an accounting, even after the trust becomes irrevocable, *i.e.*, after the settlor's death.

Section 17200 provides further support for this conclusion. Subdivision (a) of that section states: "Except as provided in Section 15800, a trustee or beneficiary of a trust may petition the court under this chapter concerning the internal affairs of the trust or to determine the existence of the trust." . . . Section 24, subdivision (c), states that "beneficiary," "[a]s it relates to a trust, means a person who has any present or future interest, vested *or contingent.*" (Italics added.) Thus, a contingent beneficiary may petition the court subject only to the limitations provided in section 15800. . . . Nothing in section 15800 limits the ability of beneficiaries to petition the court *after* the trust becomes irrevocable.

Other than the Court of Appeal in this case, no California court has held the beneficiaries have no standing in this situation. Indeed, we are aware of no statute, judicial decision, or other authority, from this or any other state, denying such standing. The only California case on point has found standing. (*Evangelho v. Presoto* (1998) 67 Cal. App. 4th 615, 79 Cal. Rptr. 2d 146 . . . .)

The Court of Appeal here found *Evangelho* . . . "unpersuasive, and decline[d] to follow it." It first "note[d] the *Evangelho* court did not have the benefit of the Supreme Court's opinion in *Steinhart [v. County of Los Angeles, supra,* 47 Cal. 4th 1298, 104 Cal. Rptr. 3d 195, 223 P.3d 57], with its clear explanation of the special nature of a revocable trust, to aid in its interpretation of Probate Code section 15800." But what we said in *Steinhart* about revocable trusts was merely background regarding the legal issue before us, which was a tax question. We said nothing about revocable trusts that was not already well established.

The Court of Appeal also stressed that the trustee's duties were owed to the settlor while he was still alive. It then stated: "And if the trustee's duties are not owed to the beneficiaries at the time of the acts in question, the death of the settlor cannot make them *retroactively* owed to the beneficiaries." This statement is correct, but it does not address the question whether the beneficiaries have standing to assert a breach of the duty towards the settlor after the settlor has died and can no longer do so personally.

The court provided a rather colorful hypothetical to illustrate its argument: "For example, if the settlor of a revocable trust learned he had a terminal disease, and was going to die within six months, he might decide that his last wish was to take his mistress on a deluxe, six-month cruise around the world—dissipating most of the assets held in his trust. The trustee, whose duties are owed to the settlor at that point, would have no basis to deny that last wish. However, if the trustee's duties were deemed to be retroactively owed to the trust beneficiaries—say, the settlor's widow and children—as soon as the settlor breathes his last breath on a beach in Bali, the trustee would find himself *liable* for having failed to sufficiently preserve *their interests* in the trust corpus prior to the settlor's death. . . . That is not—and cannot be—the law."

The court's argument, applied to its hypothetical facts, is correct. . . . But that is not the issue we are deciding. Let us change the hypothetical somewhat. Let us assume the *trustee* himself, unbeknownst to and against the wishes of the settlor (who wishes to leave behind a large trust for his beneficiaries), goes on the six-month cruise around the world with trust funds, dissipating most of the trust assets in the process. The acts do not come to light until the settlor has died and the beneficiaries discover the trust is devoid of assets. In that situation, the trustee *would* have violated his duty to the settlor, much to the beneficiaries' harm, and, as section 16462 implies, *would* be liable to the beneficiaries. The Court of Appeal is correct that the trustee owes no duty to the beneficiaries while the settlor is alive and competent, and this lack of a duty does not retroactively change after the settlor dies. But after the settlor has died and can no longer protect his own interests, the beneficiaries have standing to claim a violation of the trustee's duty *to the settlor* to the extent that violation harmed the beneficiaries' interests. A trustee . . . cannot loot a revocable trust against the settlor's wishes without the beneficiaries' having recourse after the settlor has died.

The case of *Johnson v. Kotyck, supra,* 76 Cal. App. 4th 83, 90 Cal. Rptr. 2d 99, illustrates the difference between the beneficiaries' standing before and after the settlor's death. . . . Other legal sources support finding standing after the settlor's death. . . .

Timothy argues that other remedies exist for the trustee's breach of the fiduciary duty owed to the settlor. . . . [But] . . . the existence of other possible remedies under other codes does not mean the beneficiaries lack standing under the Probate Code . . . to assert, after the settlor's death, a breach of the duty the trustee owed the settlor to the extent that breach harmed the beneficiaries. . . .

Finally, Timothy argues that even if vested beneficiaries have such standing, the actual plaintiffs' rights have still not vested. As long as Mary still lives, she is entitled to the benefits of the trust. . . . [T]he other beneficiaries will have to await her death to bring this action. We disagree. Section 17200 permits a "beneficiary" to petition the court concerning the trust's internal affairs except as section 15800 provides. . . . [S]ection 15800 merely postpones the beneficiaries' rights until the settlor's death. Section 24, subdivision (c), defines "beneficiary" to include a contingent beneficiary. The children need not wait for Mary's death to bring this action. . . .

III. CONCLUSION

We reverse the judgment of the Court of Appeal and remand the matter to that court for further proceedings consistent with our opinion.

WE CONCUR: CANTIL–SAKAUYE, C.J., BAXTER, CORRIGAN, and LIU, JJ.
Dissenting Opinion by KENNARD, J. . . . I CONCUR: WERDEGAR, J.

❧❧

NOTE:

1. Drake v. Pinkham, 217 Cal. App. 4th 400, 158 Cal. Rptr. 3d 115 (2013) held that beneficiary of contingent remainder in revocable trust had standing to petition under § 17200 while settlor still alive if petitioner alleged settlor's mental incompetency.

2. Babbitt v. Superior Court, 246 Cal. App. 4th 1135, 201 Cal. Rptr. 353 (2016) held that contingent beneficiary of revocable trust had standing to petition for an accounting after trust became irrevocable on death of one settlor, but probate court does not have authority to order trustee to account for period while trust was revocable where trustee and settlor were the same person and there is no claim that deceased settlor was incapacitated or subject to undue influence.

3. See Dibby Allan Green, *Giraldin Revisited: When Does a Trustee of a Revocable Trust Owe Duties to Remainder Beneficiaries?* 35 Est. Plan. & Calif. Prob. Reporter 5 (Aug. 2013).

❧❧

CPC § 17202. Dismissal of Petition if Proceeding Not Reasonably Necessary

The court may dismiss a petition if it appears that the proceeding is not reasonably necessary for the protection of the interests of the trustee or beneficiary.

(Stats. 1990)

NOTE: Gregge v. Hugill, 1 Cal. App. 5th 561, 204 Cal. Rptr. 3d 842 (2016) held that trial court abused its discretion in dismissing grandson's petition under § 17200 to determine validity of amendment to grandfather's trust alleging lack of capacity and undue influence. Even though grandson's pecuniary interest in pre-amendment trust was restored by other beneficiaries, grandson had interest in effectuating grandfather's intent and dissuading elder abuse.

❧❧

CPC § 17211. Award of Compensation & Litigation Expenses for Contesting or Defending Account Without Reasonable Cause & in Bad Faith

(a) If a beneficiary contests the trustee's account and the court determines that the contest was without reasonable cause and in bad faith, the court may award against the contestant the compensation and costs of the trustee and other expenses and costs of litigation, including attorney's fees, incurred to defend the account. The amount awarded shall be a charge against any interest of the beneficiary in the trust. The contestant shall be personally liable for any amount that remains unsatisfied.

(b) If a beneficiary contests the trustee's account and the court determines that the trustee's opposition to the contest was without reasonable cause and in bad faith, the court may award the contestant the costs of the contestant and other expenses and costs of litigation, including attorney's fees, incurred to contest the account. The amount awarded shall be a charge against the compensation or other interest of the trustee in the trust. The trustee shall be personally liable and on the bond, if any, for any amount that remains unsatisfied.

(Stats. 1996)

NOTES:

1. In Powell v. Tagami, 26 Cal. App. 5th 219, 236 Cal. Rptr. 3d 265 (2018), the court held that substantial evidence supported finding that beneficiary's objections to accounts were without reasonable cause and in bad faith and award of $42,115.38 in attorney fees and costs against objecting beneficiary was reasonable and not an abuse of discretion.

2. Leader v. Cords, 107 Cal. Rptr. 3d 505, 182 Cal. App. 4th 1588, rev. den. (4th Dist. 2010) held that a proceeding to compel a trustee to distribute trust funds wrongfully withheld is a contest of trustee's account within the meaning of §17211 even though the beneficiary did not challenge the amount of receipts or disbursements reported by the trustee.

3. Uzyel v. Kadisha, 116 Cal. Rptr. 3d 244, 188 Cal. App. 4th 866 rev. den. (2d Dist. 2010), held that an award of attorney fees under § 17211 was improper because, even though trustee had committed many breaches of trust and acted in bad faith, he successfully defended against some of the claims asserted by the beneficiaries. "Reasonable cause" to oppose a contest of an account requires an objectively reasonable belief, based on the facts then known to the trustee, either that the claims are legally or factually unfounded, or that the petitioner is not entitled to the requested remedies. Only if no reasonable attorney would have believed that opposition had no merit would there be no reasonable cause to oppose a contest of an account.

4. Chatard v. Oveross, 179 Cal. App. 4th 1098, 101 Cal. Rptr. 3d 883 (2009) rev. den. (2010) rejected an argument that § 17211 limits the amount that can be charged against a beneficiary's share to attorney's fees and costs: "nothing in the statute's legislative history supports appellant's argument that in enacting section 17211 the Legislature intended to exempt a beneficiary's interest in a spendthrift trust from being used to satisfy a surcharge based upon the beneficiary's wrongful conduct as a trustee."

NOTE: Litigation Expenses

1. In Smith v. Szeyller, 31 Cal. App. 5th 450, 242 Cal. Rptr. 3d 585 (2019), an award made over the objection of non-participating beneficiaries of $721,258.28 from trust assets for attorney and expert fees to the beneficiary who challenged the trustees' management, pursuant to stipulated settlement, was upheld on appeal. Payment from trust asssets is proper under "substantial benefit" exception to usual rule tht trust beneficiaries who challenge a trustee's conduct pay their own attorneys fees. Trial court may exercise its equitable discretion to award fees from the interests of those who receive a benefit to those who secured the benefit.

2. People ex rel. Harris v. Shine, 16 Cal. App. 5th 524, 224 Cal. Rptr. 3d 380 (2017) reversed an award of attorney fees pendente lite to former trustee for defense against petition for his removal and remanded for consideration whether he will be unduly prejudiced by having to bear his own attorney fees until resolution of the allegations of his breaches of trust and consideration of whether the charitable beneficiaries would be unduly prejudiced if the fees were advanced and not repaid if former trustee is found liable. Trust's indemnity provision is silent on question of advance fees and does not cover liability for willful misconduct or gross negligence.

3. Kasperbauer v. Fairfield, 171 Cal. App. 4th 229, 88 Cal. Rptr. 3d 494 (2009) held: attorneys hired by a removed trustee to aid in preparing accounting and responding to beneficiaries' objections are entitled to reasonable fees paid from trust estate; attorneys are not required to await final adjudication of claims against trustee to receive compensation; probate court had authority to order beneficiaries to return a portion of distributed trust assets to pay the attorneys in ongoing dispute over the accounting.

4. Donahue v. Donahue, 182 Cal. App. 4th 259, 105 Cal. Rptr. 3d 723 (4th Dist. Div. 3, 2010) reversed an order charging payment of $5,000,000 to the trust for attorneys retained by trustee to fight a beneficiary's $20,000,000 claim that trustee sold assets below market value. The case was remanded to determine the amount of fees reasonably incurred for the benefit of the trust as opposed to fees incurred for the benefit of the trustee. Fee awards must be reasonable in amount and reasonably necessary to the conduct of the litigation, and must also must be reasonable and appropriate for the benefit of the trust. During the 14-day trial, the trustee was represented by four lawyers and a paralegal from two major law firms.

5. Rudnick v. Rudnick, 179 Cal. App. 4th 1328, 102 Cal. Rptr. 3d 493 (2010) held that probate court had equitable power to charge attorney fees against trust distributions of beneficiaries who opposed trustee's petition to consummate sale of trust's principal assets pursuant to majority vote of beneficiaries where court found that opposition was primarily to cause unnecessary delay and was in bad faith. **Pizarro v. Reynoso**, 10 Cal. App. 5th 172, 215 Cal. Rptr. 3d 701 (2017) limited the court's power to ordering that fees and costs be paid out of beneficiaries' shares of trust assets; they could not be made personally liable.

6. Doolittle v. Exchange Bank, 241 Cal. App. 4th 529, 193 Cal. Rptr. 3d 818 (2015) held that direction in trust ordering trustee to defend against contests at expense of trust estate was not an element of trust's unenforceable no-contest clause and trustee could use trust funds to defend against contests before determination of the merits of the contests.

NOTES: Beneficiary Standing to Sue Persons Other Than Trustee for Breach of Trust

1. Estate of Bowles, 169 Cal. App. 4th 684, 87 Cal. Rptr. 3d 122 (2008), held that a remainderman had standing to sue another beneficiary and a third party for inducing the trustee to commit a breach of trust and to petition the Probate Court to surcharge a former trustee's estate under § 17200 even though a successor trustee had been appointed.

2. King v. Johnston, 178 Cal. App. 4th 1488, 101 Cal. Rptr. 3d 269 (4th Dist. Div. 1, 2009) held that although normally the trustee is the real party in interest with the exclusive right to sue third parties for recovery of trust property, a trust beneficiary may sue a third party without participation by the trustee when the third party actively participated in or knowingly benefited from a trustee's breach of trust.

Chapter 10. Trusts: Alienation and Modification

Section A. Alienation of the Beneficial Interest

Settlor's Creditors Have No Claim Against Assets of Irrevocable Trust if Settlor Is Not a Beneficiary

LAYCOCK v. HAMMER

Court of Appeal, Fourth District, Division 1
141 Cal. App. 4th 25, 44 Cal. Rptr. 3d 921 (2006)

BENKE, J. The decedent in this case, Spearl Ellison, purchased a substantial life insurance policy 13 years before his death and assigned all of his interest in the policy, including the right to any benefits, to an irrevocable life insurance trust he had established. When Ellison died the life insurance company paid $767,263.70 in death benefits to the trustee of the trust, Ellison's granddaughter, respondent Lynda Laycock.

Shortly before Ellison's death, appellants Leonard H. Hammer, Jr., Hammer Realty Group, Inc., and KanTex Hospitality, Inc. (collectively Hammer), had obtained a $4.65 million judgment against Ellison. Hammer asserted the proceeds of the life insurance policy were subject to its judgment. By way of a probate petition Laycock sought a declaration the proceeds of the life insurance policy were exempt from Hammer's claim. Laycock moved for summary judgment on her petition and the trial court granted the motion.

On appeal we affirm. By its terms the trust was irrevocable. Thus, under well established precedent, once Ellison transferred the policy to the trust, he no longer had any ownership interest in the policy and it was not subject to the claims of his creditors. . . .

DISCUSSION . . .

. . . [T]here is no serious dispute that in order to reach assets held by the trust Hammer must show that, notwithstanding the terms of the insurance trust, the trust was revocable. (See . . . *In re Barnes* (2002), 275 B.R. 889, 895-896 [settlor was not owner of assets of irrevocable trust and hence trust assets were not protected by exemptions available to settlor].)

The California cases which have considered the issue have looked to the express terms of the trust instrument in determining whether a trust is revocable or irrevocable. . . . There are no cases which permit the settlor of a trust to make an irrevocable trust revocable by way of conduct after the trust has been established. . . .

[Hammer produced evidence Ellison acted as a co-trustee of trust, that funds from the trust were distributed to his great-grandchildren, that he communicated about the insurance policy with his insurance agent and the insurance company, and borrowed funds from the policy. Hammer also presented evidence that Laycock used funds from the family trust to repay the amounts Ellison borrowed from the insurance policy because she believed the loans were

Ellison's debts. Finally, Hammer presented evidence that the other trust beneficiaries advised Laycock they believed Ellison should be permitted to do as he pleased with money he earned in his lifetime.][38]

Hammer contends that as a creditor it should be able to show Ellison treated the trust as his own property and thereby revoked the provisions of the trust. In the absence of the express language of Probate Code sections 18200 and 19001, Hammer's attempt to distinguish third party creditors from other trust claimants might have some currency. However, by expressly giving settlors' creditors the right to reach only the assets of revocable trusts, the Legislature . . . has clearly indicated an intention that creditors are to be bound by the terms of an irrevocable trust to the same extent settlors, beneficiaries and other claimants are bound by such an instrument.

In sum, contrary to Hammer's argument, a settlor's conduct after an irrevocable trust has been established will not alter the nature of such a trust. This conclusion is consistent with federal tax cases which, applying a broader incidents of ownership test, have found that breaches of the terms of a trust by a settlor will not make the settlor the owner of trust property for purposes of applying the federal estate tax. . . .

Code of Civil Procedure § 709.010. Enforcement of Money Judgment Against Interest in Trust

(a) As used in this section, "trust" has the meaning provided in Section 82 of the Probate Code.

(b) The judgment debtor's interest as a beneficiary of a trust is subject to enforcement of a money judgment only upon petition under this section by a judgment creditor to a court having jurisdiction over administration of the trust as prescribed in Part 5 (commencing with Section 17000) of Division 9 of the Probate Code. The judgment debtor's interest in the trust may be applied to the satisfaction of the money judgment by such means as the court, in its discretion, determines are proper, including but not limited to imposition of a lien on or sale of the judgment debtor's interest, collection of trust income, and liquidation and transfer of trust property by the trustee.

(c) Nothing in this section affects the limitations on the enforcement of a money judgment against the judgment debtor's interest in a trust under Chapter 2 (commencing with Section 15300) of Part 2 of Division 9 of the Probate Code, and the provisions of this section are subject to the limitations of that chapter.

(Stats. 1982, 1984, 1986)

---

[38] This paragraph has been moved from its original location in the opinion.—Ed.

NOTE: California Follows General Rules on Creditors' Rights but Limits Protection That May Be Given to Beneficiaries

California follows the general rule that vested interests of beneficiaries are available to creditors unless subject to a spendthrift clause or unless the trust is for the purpose of the beneficiary's education or support. CPC §§ 15300-15302 cover spendthrift and support trusts. California also follows the general rules that creditors may not reach assets in a discretionary trust until the trustee has exercised its discretion to make a payment to the beneficiary, CPC § 15303, and that neither a spendthrift clause, nor giving the trustee discretionary powers, protects the settlor with respect to any assets that could be distributed to the settlor, CPC § 15304. However, California imposes some special limits on the amount of protection provided to beneficiaries.

CPC § 15300. Restraint on Transfer of Income

Except as provided in Sections 15304 to 15307, inclusive, if the trust instrument provides that a beneficiary's interest in income is not subject to voluntary or involuntary transfer, the beneficiary's interest in income under the trust may not be transferred and is not subject to enforcement of a money judgment until paid to the beneficiary.

(Stats. 1990)

CPC § 15301. Restraint on Transfer of Principal

(a) Except as provided in subdivision (b) and in Sections 15304 to 15307, inclusive, if the trust instrument provides that a beneficiary's interest in principal is not subject to voluntary or involuntary transfer, the beneficiary's interest in principal may not be transferred and is not subject to enforcement of a money judgment until paid to the beneficiary.

(b) After an amount of principal has become due and payable to the beneficiary under the trust instrument, upon petition to the court under Section 709.010 of the Code of Civil Procedure by a judgment creditor, the court may make an order directing the trustee to satisfy the money judgment out of that principal amount. The court in its discretion may issue an order directing the trustee to satisfy all or part of the judgment out of that principal amount.

(Stats. 1990)

CPC § 15302. Trust for Support

Except as provided in Sections 15304 to 15307, inclusive, if the trust instrument provides that the trustee shall pay income or principal or both for the education or support of a beneficiary, the beneficiary's interest in income or principal or both under the trust, to the extent the income or principal or both is necessary for the education or support of the beneficiary, may not be transferred and is not subject to the enforcement of a money judgment until paid to the beneficiary.

(Stats. 1990)

CPC § 15305. Claims for Child and Spousal Support

(a) As used in this section, "support judgment" means a money judgment for support of the trust beneficiary's spouse or former spouse or minor child.

(b) If the beneficiary has the right under the trust to compel the trustee to pay income or principal or both to or for the benefit of the beneficiary, the court may, to the extent that the court determines it is equitable and reasonable under the circumstances of the particular case, order the trustee to satisfy all or part of the support judgment out of all or part of those payments as they become due and payable, presently or in the future.

(c) Whether or not the beneficiary has the right under the trust to compel the trustee to pay income or principal or both to or for the benefit of the beneficiary, the court may, to the extent that the court determines it is equitable and reasonable under the circumstances of the particular case, order the trustee to satisfy all or part of the support judgment out of all or part of future payments that the trustee, pursuant to the exercise of the trustee's discretion, determines to make to or for the benefit of the beneficiary.

(d) This section applies to a support judgment notwithstanding any provision in the trust instrument.

(Stats. 1990)

CPC § 15305.5. *Judgment Awarding Restitution or Damages for Felony*

(a) As used in this section, "restitution judgment" means a judgment awarding restitution for the commission of a felony or a money judgment for damages incurred as a result of conduct for which the defendant was convicted of a felony.

(b) If the beneficiary has the right under the trust to compel the trustee to pay income or principal or both to or for the benefit of the beneficiary, the court may, to the extent that the court determines it is equitable and reasonable under the circumstances of the particular case, order the trustee to satisfy all or part of the restitution judgment out of all or part of those payments as they become due and payable, presently or in the future.

(c) Whether or not the beneficiary has the right under the trust to compel the trustee to pay income or principal or both to or for the benefit of the beneficiary, the court may, to the extent that the court determines it is equitable and reasonable under the circumstances of the particular case, order the trustee to satisfy all or part of the restitution judgment out of all or part of future payments that the trustee, pursuant to the exercise of the trustee's discretion, determines to make to or for the benefit of the beneficiary.

(d) This section applies to a restitution judgment notwithstanding any provision in the trust instrument.

(Stats. 1991)

CPC § 15306. *Liability for Public Support of Beneficiary or Beneficiary's Spouse or Minor Child*

(a) Notwithstanding any provision in the trust instrument, if a statute of this state makes the beneficiary liable for reimbursement of this state or a local public entity in this state for public support furnished to the beneficiary or to the beneficiary's spouse or minor child, upon petition to the court under Section 709.010 of the Code of Civil Procedure by the appropriate state or local public entity or public official, to the extent the court determines it is equitable and reasonable under the circumstances of the particular case, the court may do the following:

(1) If the beneficiary has the right under the trust to compel the trustee to pay income or principal or both to or for the benefit of the beneficiary, order the trustee to satisfy all or part of the liability out of all or part of the payments as they become due, presently or in the future.

(2) Whether or not the beneficiary has the right under the trust to compel the trustee to pay income or principal or both to or for the benefit of the beneficiary, order the trustee to satisfy all or part of the liability out of all or part of the future payments that the trustee, pursuant to the exercise of the trustee's discretion, determines to make to or for the benefit of the beneficiary.

(3) If the beneficiary is a settlor or the spouse or minor child of the settlor and the beneficiary does not have the right under the trust to compel the trustee to pay income or principal or both to or for the benefit of the beneficiary, to the extent that the trustee has the right to make payments of income or principal or both to or for the beneficiary pursuant to the exercise of the trustee's discretion, order the trustee to satisfy all or part of the liability without regard to whether the trustee has then exercised or may thereafter exercise the discretion in favor of the beneficiary.

(b) Subdivision (a) does not apply to any trust that is established for the benefit of an individual who has a disability that substantially impairs the individual's ability to provide for his or her own care or custody and constitutes a substantial handicap. If, however, the trust results in the individual being ineligible for needed public social services under Division 9 (commencing with Section 10000) of the Welfare and Institutions Code, this subdivision is not applicable and the provisions of subdivision (a) are to be applied.

(Stats. 1990)

CPC § 15306.5. Subject to Limitations, Court May Order Trustee to Satisfy Judgment Despite Spendthrift Provision

(a) Notwithstanding a restraint on transfer of the beneficiary's interest in the trust under Section 15300 or 15301, and subject to the limitations of this section, upon a judgment creditor's petition under Section 709.010 of the Code of Civil Procedure, the court may make an order directing the trustee to satisfy all or part of the judgment out of the payments to which the beneficiary is entitled under the trust instrument or that the trustee, in the exercise of the trustee's discretion, has determined or determines in the future to pay to the beneficiary.

(b) An order under this section may not require that the trustee pay in satisfaction of the judgment an amount exceeding 25 percent of the payment that otherwise would be made to, or for the benefit of, the beneficiary.

(c) An order under this section may not require that the trustee pay in satisfaction of the judgment any amount that the court determines is necessary for the support of the beneficiary and all the persons the beneficiary is required to support.

(d) An order for satisfaction of a support judgment, as defined in Section 15305, has priority over an order to satisfy a judgment under this section. Any amount ordered to be applied to the satisfaction of a judgment under this section shall be reduced by the amount of an order for satisfaction of a support judgment under Section 15305, regardless of whether the order for satisfaction of the support judgment was made before or after the order under this section.

(e) If the trust gives the trustee discretion over the payment of either principal or income of a trust, or both, nothing in this section affects or limits that discretion in any manner. The trustee has no duty to oppose a petition to satisfy a judgment under this section or to make any claim for exemption on behalf of the beneficiary. The trustee is not liable for any action taken, or omitted to be taken, in compliance with any court order made under this section.

(f) Subject to subdivision (d), the aggregate of all orders for satisfaction of money judgments against the beneficiary's interest in the trust may not exceed 25 percent of the payment that otherwise would be made to, or for the benefit of, the beneficiary.

(Stats. 1990)

CPC § 15307. Amount in Excess of Beneficiary's Needs for Education and Support May Be Applied to Satisfy Money Judgment

Notwithstanding a restraint on transfer of a beneficiary's interest in the trust under Section 15300 or 15301, any amount to which the beneficiary is entitled under the trust instrument or that the trustee, in the exercise of the trustee's discretion, has determined to pay to the beneficiary in excess of the amount that is or will be necessary for the education and support of the beneficiary may be applied to the satisfaction of a money judgment against the beneficiary. Upon the judgment creditor's petition under Section 709.010 of the Code of Civil Procedure, the court may make an order directing the trustee to satisfy all or part of the judgment out of the beneficiary's interest in the trust.

(Stats. 1990)

CPC § 15309. Disclaimer Not Subject to Spendthrift Constraint

A disclaimer or renunciation by a beneficiary of all or part of his or her interest under a trust shall not be considered a transfer under Section 15300 or 15301.

(Stats. 1990)

NOTE: A spendthrift clause does not protect a trust's assets from enforcement of a federal lien. A federal restitution order is a lien on "all property and rights to property." The beneficiary of a discretionary support trust in California has a property right because under California law the beneficiary can petition the probate court to ensure that trustee's exercise of discretion is consistent with the trust's puposes. Issuance of writ of continuing garnishment on any current or future distributions from trust until restitution judgment satisfied affirmed. **United States v. Harris**, 854 F.3d 1053 (9th Cir. 2017).

25% Limit of § 15306.5 Does Not Apply to Amounts Due and Payable to Beneficiary Under § 15301(B)

CARMACK v. REYNOLDS

Supreme Court of California
2 Cal. 5th 844, 391 P.3d 625, 215 Cal. Rptr. 3d 749 (2017)

LIU, J. Under the terms of a spendthrift trust established by his parents, defendant Rick H. Reynolds is entitled to receive over a million dollars, all to be paid out of trust principal. Reynolds filed for bankruptcy before the trust's first payment, and the bankruptcy trustee seeks to determine what interest the bankruptcy estate has in the trust. The trust is governed by California law, and as the United States Court of Appeals for the Ninth Circuit observed, the relevant statutory provisions are "opaque." (*Frealy v. Reynolds* (9th Cir. 2015) 779 F.3d 1028, 1029.) Probate Code section 15306.5 appears to limit the bankruptcy estate to 25 percent of the beneficiary's interest; other provisions of the Probate Code suggest no such limitation. The Ninth Circuit asked us whether the Probate Code limits a bankruptcy estate's access to a spendthrift trust to 25 percent of the beneficiary's interest, where the trust pays the beneficiary entirely out of principal. We hold that the Probate Code does not impose such an absolute limit on a general creditor's access to the trust. With limited exceptions for distributions explicitly intended or actually required for the beneficiary's support, a general creditor may reach a sum up to the full amount of any distributions that are currently due and payable to the beneficiary even though they are still in the trustee's hands, and separately may reach a sum up to 25 percent of any payments that are anticipated to be made to the beneficiary.

I.

Reynolds's parents established the Reynolds Family Trust in 2005. The trust contains a spendthrift clause . . . . Reynolds's mother . . . died in 2007. Following her death, Reynolds's father Freddie received all the trust's distributions until . . . [he] died in 2009.

The trust provides that at Freddie's death, Reynolds is entitled to $250,000 from the trust if he survives Freddie by 30 days. In addition, Reynolds is entitled to receive $100,000 a year for 10 years and then one-third of the remainder. All payments are expected to be made from principal; the trust's assets are in undeveloped real estate [estimated to be worth several million dollars] that do not produce income. . . .

The day after his father died, Reynolds filed for voluntary bankruptcy under chapter 7 of the United States Bankruptcy Code. The trustees of the Reynolds Family Trust sought a declaratory judgment on the extent of the bankruptcy trustee's interest in the trust. The bankruptcy court held that under the California Probate Code, the bankruptcy trustee standing as a hypothetical lien creditor could reach 25 percent of Reynolds's interest in the trust. . . . The bankruptcy trustee appealed to the Ninth Circuit, which asked us to clarify if Probate Code section 15306.5 caps a bankruptcy estate's access to a spendthrift trust at 25 percent of the beneficiary's interest where the trust pays entirely from principal. We granted the Ninth Circuit's request.

II.

A spendthrift trust is a trust that provides that the beneficiary's interest cannot be alienated before it is distributed to the beneficiary. Creditors of the beneficiary generally cannot reach trust assets while those assets are in the hands of the trustee, even if they have secured a judgment against the beneficiary. Rather, creditors must wait until the trustee makes distributions to the beneficiary. The law permits such trusts because donors have "the right to choose the object of [their] bounty" and to protect their gifts from the donees' creditors. (*Canfield v. Security-First Nat. Bank* (1939) 13 Cal.2d 1, 11.) Providing donors some measure of control over their gifts encourages donors to make those gifts, to the benefit of the donor, the beneficiary, and ultimately the beneficiary's creditors.

Under the Probate Code, spendthrift provisions are generally valid as to both trust income and trust principal. . . . Yet creditors need not always wait for distributions to reach the debtor's hands. Spendthrift provisions are invalid when grantors name themselves beneficiaries. (§ 15304 (a).) When a trust includes a valid spendthrift provision, certain creditors may reach into the trust. Such creditors include those with claims for spousal or child support (§ 15305) and those with restitution judgments (§ 15305.5). In addition, a state or local public entity can reach trust assets when the beneficiary owes money for public support (§ 15306 (a)) unless distributions from the trust are required to care for a disabled beneficiary (§ 15306(b)).

Even general creditors, including a bankruptcy trustee standing as a hypothetical lien creditor, have some recourse under three provisions: section 15301(b), section 15306.5, and section 15307. The question here is how much access to trust principal a general creditor has under these provisions.

This is a question of statutory construction. . . . In construing the provisions at issue, we are mindful that the Reynolds Family Trust is distinctive in directing all disbursements to be made from principal. In other trusts, productive assets produce periodic income payments during the life of the trust, and preserving principal is one of the trustee's paramount duties. . . . It is common for trusts to specify that the principal may not be distributed for many years, and liquidating principal may signal that the trust's purpose has been fulfilled. We are also mindful that this case arises out of a bankruptcy proceeding. Ordinarily, a judgment creditor who is unable to satisfy all of the judgment out of the beneficiary's trust interest may continue to attempt to collect on the balance of the judgment from whatever other assets the beneficiary may have. Here, however, the amount Reynolds's creditors will receive depends on the reach of the bankruptcy trustee. Any remaining debts after the bankruptcy process will be extinguished, and any further distributions will be unencumbered. (11 U.S.C. § 541(c)(2).) That spendthrift provisions can work to beneficiaries' advantage in bankruptcy in this way has long been recognized . . . .

A.

We begin with section 15301(b), which provides in pertinent part: "After an amount of principal has become due and payable to the beneficiary under the trust instrument, upon petition to the court under Section 709.010 of the Code of Civil Procedure by a judgment creditor, the court may make an order directing the trustee to satisfy the money judgment out of that principal amount." . . .

As the Ninth Circuit observed, the statute does not define "due and payable." . . . The phrase is used in other provisions such as section 15305, which provides that creditors with judgments for child or spousal support may petition a court to satisfy their judgments out of disbursements of either income or principal "as they become due and payable, presently or in the future." . . . Any disbursement from the trust would appear to be due and payable in the sense the phrase is used in section 15305. But, as the Ninth Circuit recognized, applying such a reading to section 15301(b) could mean that creditors have "immediate access to all of a beneficiary's trust principal," which would eliminate spendthrift protections as to principal entirely.

We do not think the Legislature intended to remove all protections from trust principal immediately after specifying that spendthrift provisions are generally valid as applied to principal. Instead, the Legislature provided the limiting principle in the introductory clause of section 15301(b): "*After* an amount of principal *has become* due and payable . . . ." (Italics added.) This clause indicates that timing is critical: section 15301(b) reaches only those amounts which are presently set to be paid to the beneficiary. The provision thus requires an amount of principal to "ha[ve] become" due to the beneficiary, at which point upon a creditor's petition the court may enter an order "directing the trustee to satisfy the money judgment out of *that principal amount*." . . . [U]nder this provision creditors may reach the principal already set to be distributed and only up to the extent of that distribution. Such principal has served its trust purposes, and in many (but not all) cases, the distribution may signal that the trust is ending. Section 15301(b) makes these assets, and these assets only, fair game to creditors.

. . . [S]ection 15301(b) is properly viewed not as an exception to the general spendthrift protections but as a corollary. The general rule is that principal held in a spendthrift trust may not be touched by creditors until it is paid to the beneficiary. (§ 15301(a).) Section 15301(b) adds that once an amount of principal has become due and payable, the court can order the trustee to pay that amount directly to the beneficiary's creditors instead. . . . Because the beneficiary's interest in those assets has effectively vested, the law no longer has any interest in protecting them (except as provided in section 15302, as explained below).

The legislative history points the same way. . . .

Importantly, creditors' access under section 15301(b) is not unlimited. Section 15302 explains that where the trust instrument specifies that a distribution, whether from income or principal, is for the beneficiary's support or education, the amount the beneficiary actually needs for either purpose may not be reached by creditors until in the hands of the beneficiary. Section

15302 explicitly provides that it does not apply where creditors seek access under sections 15304 through 15307, but section 15302 does not exclude orders under section 15301(b). Section 15302 thus provides limited continued protection to former trust assets where the donor specifically intended the distribution to support the beneficiary. This protection encourages donors to provide for beneficiaries' support and helps to prevent beneficiaries from becoming public charges. (See *Canfield, supra.*)

B.

. . . [S]ections 15306.5 and 15307 . . . are exceptions to the general validity of spendthrift provisions as applied to trust principal . . . . Section 15306.5(a) provides that any judgment creditor can petition a court to order the trustee to satisfy the judgment out of payments to which the beneficiary is entitled. But those orders are limited to "25 percent of the payment that otherwise would be made to, or for the benefit of, the beneficiary" and they cannot cut into any amount required to support the beneficiary or the beneficiary's dependents. Section 15307 . . . provides: "Notwithstanding a restraint on transfer of a beneficiary's interest in the trust under Section 15300 or 15301, any amount to which the beneficiary is entitled under the trust instrument . . . in excess of the amount that is or will be necessary for the education and support of the beneficiary may be applied to the satisfaction of a money judgment against the beneficiary. . . ."

Section 15307 thus appears to allow any creditor to access all of a beneficiary's interest in a spendthrift trust besides what is necessary for the beneficiary's education and support, whereas section 15306.5 limits creditors to only 25 percent of the same interest. How are these two provisions to be reconciled?

One possibility is that section 15307 is only meant to apply to income, not principal. It is true that the Law Revision Commission titled this provision "Income in excess of amount for education and support subject to creditors' claims." (1986 Report, 18 Cal. Law Revision Com. Rep. at p. 1340 . . . . But this title was not part of the official legislative enactments . . . and therefore cannot have any bearing on the interpretation of the statute . . . . Moreover, section 15301(a), which applies only to principal, specifically refers to section 15307. . . [which] provides that it applies "[n]otwithstanding . . . [section] 15301." Both references would be unnecessary if section 15307 only applied to income. . . . In any event, excluding principal from section 15307 would not resolve the tension between sections 15306.5 and 15307 for income. We thus conclude that section 15307 applies to both income and principal, as its text plainly says.

The bankruptcy trustee suggests that section 15307 serves a different purpose from section 15306.5 by setting a higher bar for creditors . . . .

The bankruptcy trustee's theory might reflect sensible policy . . . . However, nothing in the statutes suggests that obtaining an order under section 15307 involves any different burden or standard of proof than obtaining an order under any other section. . . . The bankruptcy trustee does not cite any authority in support of its theory.

Instead, the more likely answer is that section 15307 reflects a drafting error. . . . [Lengthy discussion of statutory history omitted.—Ed.]

We conclude . . . that the ultimate enactment of section 15307 without apparent limitations on the reach of general creditors was inadvertent. The Legislature plainly intended general creditors to be limited to 25 percent of distributions from the trust.

C.

The final issue we must address is whether the 25 percent limitation of section 15306.5 applies to section 15301(b). Section 15306.5(f) provides: "Subject to subdivision (d), the aggregate of all orders for satisfaction of money judgments against the beneficiary's interest in the trust may not exceed 25 percent of the payment that otherwise would be made to, or for the benefit of, the beneficiary." Unlike section 15306.5(b)'s reference to "[a]n order under this section," the language of section 15306.5(f)—"all orders for satisfaction of money judgments"—is not limited to orders under section 15306.5. One possibility, therefore, is that section 15306.5(f)'s cap extends to all orders under any provision of the Probate Code.

We need not decide the full reach of the 25 percent cap under 15306.5(f) as this case involves only the scope of sections 15301(b) and 15306.5. Whatever other orders may be subject to section 15306.5(f)'s cap, we conclude that the cap does not apply to orders under section 15301(b). As explained above, section 15306.5 was modeled on the wage garnishment statute then in force . . . and provides creditors a limited exception to spendthrift protections on the beneficiary's continuing interest in the trust. As the use of the conditional in section 15306.5(f) suggests, "the payment that otherwise *would be* made to" the beneficiary is best understood as referring to ongoing payments the beneficiary stands to receive. (Italics added.) The cap thus operates to limit the sum of orders subject to section 15306.5(f)'s cap to 25 percent of any individual expected distribution.

By contrast, section 15301(b) makes clear that spendthrift protections do not apply to distributions of principal that have become due and payable. Where trust assets are not protected by a spendthrift provision, the default rule is that creditors may reach those assets. By crafting a specific rule for this narrow class of assets, the Legislature indicated its intent that those assets be treated differently. . . . Applying section 15306.5(f)'s cap to section 15301(b) assets would defeat the Legislature's specific intent to treat due and payable principal "in the hands of the trustee" on par with such principal "after payment to the beneficiary." (See 1986 Report, *supra*, 18 Cal. Law Revision Com. Rep. at pp. 1302–1303.)

In sum, after an amount of principal has become due and payable (but has not yet been distributed), a creditor can petition to have the trustee pay directly to the creditor a sum up to the full amount of that distribution unless the trust instrument specifies that the distribution is for the beneficiary's support or education and the beneficiary needs the distribution for those purposes (§ 15302). If no such distribution is pending or if the distribution is not adequate to satisfy a judgment, a general creditor can petition to levy up to 25 percent of the payments expected to be made to the beneficiary, reduced by the amount other creditors have already obtained and subject to the support needs of the beneficiary and any dependents. (§ 15306.5.)

As an illustration, suppose a trust instrument specified that a beneficiary was to receive distributions of principal of $10,000 on March 1 of each year for 10 years. Suppose further that a general creditor had a money judgment of $50,000 against the beneficiary and that the trust distributions are neither specifically intended nor required for the beneficiary's support. On March 1 of the first year, upon the creditor's petition a court could order the trustee to remit the full distribution of $10,000 for that year to the creditor directly if it has not already been paid to the beneficiary, as well as $2,500 from each of the nine anticipated payments (a total of $22,500) as they are paid out. If the creditor were not otherwise able to satisfy the remaining $17,500 balance on the judgment, then on March 1 of the following years, upon the general creditor's petition the court could order the trustee to pay directly to the creditor a sum up to the remainder of that year's principal distribution ($7,500), as the court in its discretion finds appropriate, until the judgment is satisfied.

CONCLUSION

We conclude that a bankruptcy trustee, standing as a hypothetical judgment creditor, can reach a beneficiary's interest in a trust that pays entirely out of principal in two ways. It may reach up to the full amount of any distributions of principal that are currently due and payable to the beneficiary, unless the trust instrument specifies that those distributions are for the beneficiary's support or education and the beneficiary needs those distributions for either purpose. Separately, the bankruptcy trustee can reach up to 25 percent of any anticipated payments made to, or for the benefit of, the beneficiary, reduced to the extent necessary by the support needs of the beneficiary and any dependents.

WE CONCUR: CANTIL-SAKAUYE, C. J.WERDEGAR, J., CHIN, J., CORRIGAN, J., CUÉLLAR, J.,KRUGER, J.

Creditors Entitled to Amount Allocated to Beneficiary of Discretionary Trust Above Needs for Support

CANFIELD v. SECURITY-FIRST NAT'L BANK OF LOS ANGELES

Supreme Court of California in Bank
13 Cal. 2d 1, 87 P.2d 830 (1939)

WASTE, Chief Justice. These three actions were brought by plaintiffs as judgment creditors of respondent Charles O. Canfield against Canfield and the respondent Security-First National Bank of Los Angeles. . . . By them plaintiffs-appellants seek to reach the claimed beneficial interest of respondent Canfield in a discretionary spendthrift trust created by [his father]

Charles A. Canfield, which trust is being administered by the respondent Security Bank as trustee. . . .

The trust here involved was created by the will of Charles A. Canfield . . . [which] disposed of an estate of several millions of dollars. To all of his children other than Charles the testator left outright a legacy of $1,000,000, and these other children were also made residuary legatees. In reference to Charles, the will bequeathed $900,000 to the Security Bank as trustee for the benefit of Charles and his two children by a prior marriage . . . . The trust thus created for the benefit of Charles was a spendthrift trust, discretionary in character. In the will the testator gave as his reason for thus creating this type of trust that the past conduct and life of his son had been "one of waste, dissipation and extravagance; and that his present associations, conduct and mode of living indicate no existing purpose of reform on his part; and that the probability of his reforming in the future, in my judgment, amounts to no more than a father's hope". . . .

The first question to be determined is whether the appellants as judgment creditors may reach any portion of the income allocated to Charles O. Canfield by the trustee in view of the spendthrift provisions of the trust and in view of the discretionary powers conferred upon the trustee. . . .

In California, prior to the adoption of the Codes in 1872, spendthrift trusts were recognized as valid without limitation. . . . Upon the adoption of the codes this type of trust was expressly authorized by the provisions of section 867 of the Civil Code . . . . But while this section authorized the creation of spendthrift trusts, section 859 of the Civil Code, also passed in 1872, placed a limitation thereon. That section as it read until its amendment in 1935 . . . provided that: "Where a trust is created to receive the rents and profits of real property, and no valid direction for accumulation is given, *the surplus of such rents and profits, beyond the sum that may be necessary for the education and support* of the person for whose benefit the trust is created, is *liable to the claims of the creditors of such person*, in the same manner as personal property which cannot be reached by execution."

It has been held that this section applies to spendthrift trusts . . . [and] to discretionary trusts. . . .

On the present trial, the court below found that $30,000 a year was necessary for the support of Charles O. Canfield in order to maintain him in the station in life to which he is and has been accustomed to live, and exempted this annual sum from the claims of appellants. All appellants challenge this finding. . . .

We . . . agree with appellants' contentions that the evidence is insufficient to support the $30,000 finding, and that the trial court adopted the wrong standards in fixing the amount that should be allowed to Canfield . . . .

Under section 859 of the Civil Code the trial court is required to fix the amount necessary for the "education and support" of the beneficiary. The statute fixes no standards by which the amounts necessary for these purposes are to be ascertained. . . . [I]n ascertaining the proper allowance, the courts of New York and of this state have held that the beneficiary is entitled to receive free from the claims of his creditors sufficient income to support himself and those dependent upon him, according to the mode of life to which they have been accustomed, and to care for any affliction from which he or his family may be suffering. No set sum can be fixed to apply to all cases. The amount varies according to the station in life of the beneficiary. This does not mean, however, that the needs of the beneficiary are to be measured by his extravagance or his ability to spend. It does not mean that an allowance is to be made for extravagant entertaining, and for unbridled luxuries. The manner of living of the beneficiary in the past, if such living was unreasonably extravagant and profuse, is no criterion of the reasonable amount necessary for support and maintenance. Evidence as to cost of living, wages of servants, medical expense and reasonable entertainment, and other reasonably necessary expenses, fixes the amount. . . . the manner in which the beneficiary has been reared, the number and health of his dependents, his own health, his entire background—all these and perhaps others should be considered. But cost of lavish entertaining, cost of betting on race horses and cost of obvious luxuries, etc.—these are all false factors. . . .

It is obvious that the . . . evidence does not sustain the finding that $30,000 per year is necessary for Charles O. Canfield's support. . . . He is entitled to support himself and family in reasonable comfort, but not in extravagant luxury. In determining the amount the trial court on the retrial will consider all of the factors heretofore mentioned in this opinion.

For the purposes of the retrial it is necessary to pass on the question of the personal liability of the trustee, and also on the question of the priority between appellants. The trial court held . . . that the trustee was not personally liable by reason of it having paid Charles all of the net income of the trust after service of process; that after date of entry of judgment appellants have equitable liens upon all income allocated to Charles in excess of $30,000 per year; that as between themselves appellants' liens have priority as follows . . . .

In so far as the trial court held that the equitable liens of appellants did not attach on the respective dates that summons in each action was served on the bank the trial court was clearly in error. The record discloses that after service of summons in each of the respective actions the trustee continued to pay to Charles O. Canfield large sums of money totalling to the date of judgment over $150,000. In so far as the sums so paid exceeded whatever sum may be determined to be the amount necessary for the reasonable needs of Charles O. Canfield, the trustee violated the rights of appellants and must be held personally liable therefor. The trustee could have protected itself by payment of the income allocated by it to Charles into court . . .

Respondent trustee urges that a creditor's bill will not lie, because the beneficiary of a discretionary trust has no enforceable interest in the income. This is so until such income has been allocated to the beneficiary. Neither the beneficiary nor the creditor can compel such allocation, but after it has been allocated the creditors can prevent its payment to the beneficiary . . . . After allocation of the income and after the trustee exercised its discretion,

Charles O. Canfield had the equitable right under this trust to have the payments made to him, and it is this equitable right to which the lien of appellants attached. . . .

. . . [W]e do not decide whether after payment to the appellants the trustee is entitled to reimbursement from the trust for such expenditures. That is a matter which will have to be determined in a proceeding between the beneficiary and trustee, and is not now involved. . . .

❧❧

Trustee of Discretionary Trust Ordered to Pay Child Support Judgments Under §§ 15305 & 15306

VENTURA COUNTY DEPARTMENT OF CHILD SUPPORT SERVICES v. BROWN

Court of Appeal, Second District, Division 6
117 Cal. App. 4th 144, 11 Cal. Rptr. 3d 489 (2004)

COFFEE, J. . . . [Kenneth Marinos had seven children from three different relationships. He failed to pay child support for approximately 15 years. After the death of his mother, the mother of two of his children and the Ventura County Department of Child Support Services (DCSS) obtained judgments against him for over $140,000 in past due support which they now seek to collect from a trust created by his mother, Helen, who died in 2002. They also seek $1,218 in ongoing monthly child support from the trust.

[The trust provided that on Helen's death, the trust should be divided equally between her two sons and maintained in trust to "provide for the proper support, care, maintenance and education of said child." There is a spendthrift provision and the trustee is given discretion to "distribute so much of the net income or principal, or both, of each trust . . . to or for the use and benefit of [the beneficiary], at any time and from time to time." Upon the death of either son, the trust estate is to be administered for the benefit of his children or spouse. The value of Kenneth's half of the trust is about $535,000.

[The trial court ordered the trustee to pay the judgments and ongoing monthly support to each of the mothers. The trustee appealed arguing that the trial court may not compel him to distribute trust funds for child support.—Ed.]

DISCUSSION

Appellant . . . acknowledges that the court is authorized to order payments from the Trust. He contends, however, that the court's authority is limited to those payments that the trustee has chosen to make in the exercise of his discretion. . . . It is undisputed that appellant alone has discretion to make payments from the Trust. Marinos has no right to compel such payments.

Newly Enacted Probate Code Sections 15300-15307

In 1986, the Law Revision Commission recommended enactment of new probate statutes to improve existing law relating to spendthrift trusts. . . . There were two objectives: 1) to reduce the ability of a general creditor to reach a beneficiary's interest in a trust; and 2) to give greater rights to support creditors. Child support creditors were elevated to the status of "preferred creditors" and permitted to reach a beneficiary's interest in the trust, despite the existence of a spendthrift clause. . . . [T]o effect these changes, the Legislature enacted sections 15300-15307 . . . .

Special Rights of Support Creditors (Probate Code Section 15305)

. . . Under section 15305, subdivision (b), when a trust instrument gives a beneficiary the right to compel the trustee to make payments to the beneficiary, the trial court may order the trustee to satisfy a support judgment from both present and future payments. Subdivision (b) makes no reference to a trustee's exercise of discretion. . . .

By contrast, section 15305, subdivision (c) contains language referring to a trustee's exercise of discretion: "Whether or not the beneficiary has the right under the trust to compel the trustee to pay income or principal or both to or for the benefit of the beneficiary, the court may, to the extent that the court determines it is equitable and reasonable under the circumstances of the particular case, order the trustee to satisfy all or part of the support judgment out of all or part of future payments that the trustee, *pursuant to the exercise of the trustee's discretion,* determines to make to or for the benefit of the beneficiary." (Italics added.) Appellant claims that under subdivision (c), the trial court must defer to the trustee's exercise of discretion when fashioning a support order. . . .

The question becomes: may a court order a trustee to exercise its discretion to make a payment to the beneficiary? . . . We acknowledge that existing law gives a trustee the discretion to determine whether payments are made and in what amount. However, in exercising its discretion to make or withhold payments, a trustee may not act in bad faith or with an improper motive.

"Where discretion is conferred upon the trustee with respect to the exercise of a power, its exercise is not subject to control by the court, except to prevent an abuse by the trustee of his discretion." (Rest. 2d Trusts, § 187, p. 402; 11 Witkin, Summary of Cal. Law, . . . Trusts, §97 . . . .) The court will not interfere with a trustee's exercise of discretion "unless the trustee, in exercising or failing to exercise the power acts dishonestly, or with an improper even though not a dishonest motive, or fails to use his judgment, or acts beyond the bounds of reasonable judgment." (Rest. 2d Trusts, § 157, com. *e* . . . .) When a trust instrument confers "absolute," "sole" or "uncontrolled" discretion, "the trustee shall act in accordance with fiduciary principles and shall not act in bad faith or in disregard of the purposes of the trust." (§16081, subd. (a).) To determine the extent of the trustee's discretion, we look to the intention of the trustor, as manifested in the trust instrument. . . .

According to the language of the Trust, Helen Marinos wished to provide for the "support, care, maintenance and education" of her sons. Upon the death of either son, the trust estate was to be administered for the benefit of his "children and/or to the spouse of a deceased child of the Grantor." Although neither son is deceased, the Trust instrument reflects Helen Marinos' intent to provide support to her grandchildren.

Public Policy Favoring Support

We next consider California's strong public policy in favor of the payment of support. . . . By enacting section 15305, the Legislature intended to allow a support creditor to satisfy court-ordered child support obligations where the parent is a trust beneficiary. The statute was crafted to preclude a beneficiary's efforts to avoid a support obligation. The fact that the statute refers to payments made by the trustee demonstrates legislative intent that the trustee make distributions from the trust. Although a trustee may be given broad discretion, it may not exercise its discretion with an improper motive.

Marinos has acted with patent disregard towards the support of his six children. . . . Appellant has refused to make any trust distributions to satisfy Marinos' child support obligation. In light of the statutory and public policy objectives in favor of the payment of support, we conclude appellant's exercise of his discretion was misdirected. To deny the trial court authority to compel the exercise of a trustee's discretion in this instance creates the very problem that the statute was enacted to remedy—avoiding the payment of child support. The statute cannot have been intended to allow a beneficiary to defraud support creditors by hiding behind the trustee's discretion. This is directly contrary to the legislative purpose behind section 15305.

. . . We conclude that, under section 15305, subdivision (c), a court may overcome the trustee's discretion under the narrow circumstances present here: when there is an enforceable child support judgment that the trustee refuses to satisfy. Under these circumstances, the trial court may order the trustee to satisfy past due and ongoing support obligations directly from the trust. There is no evidence of extenuating circumstances that would excuse Marinos from his statutory obligation to pay child support. . . .

Liability for Public Support (Section 15306)

Appellant points to a parallel statute, section 15306, governing reimbursement of public support. This statute allows the state to seek reimbursement for public support that has been furnished to a trust beneficiary, his spouse or minor child. . . . If the beneficiary is also the settlor (or the settlor's spouse or minor child), the court may order reimbursement "without regard to whether the trustee has then exercised or may thereafter exercise the discretion in favor of the beneficiary." . . . Appellant argues that since the Legislature expressly included this language in section 15306, it intended to exclude it under section 15305. He reasons that the court may only "override" the trustee's discretion in an action under section 15306.

There is ample reason for the differing language between the two statutes. Section 15306, subdivision (a)(3) echoes the statutory restriction in these trusts in which the settlor is also the beneficiary. (§ 15304.) Under section 15304, a settlor may not create a spendthrift trust in his own favor. The rationale is that a settlor may not enjoy his wealth while preventing his creditors from reaching it. . . . A spendthrift trust can be rendered invalid when the beneficiaries exercise excessive control. (*In re Moses* (9th Cir. 1999) 167 F.3d 470, 473 [construing a trust's spendthrift clause in bankruptcy proceeding].)

We observe that section 15306, subdivision (a)(3) provides that the court may overcome the trustee's discretion when the settlor and the beneficiary are the same person (or the settlor's spouse or minor child). Under such circumstances, the beneficiary is in a position to influence the actions of the trustee. This impropriety is particularly offensive because 1) the settlor has created a trust that shields his own assets; 2) although the settlor has the means to support his dependents, he has failed to do so; and 3) the state has had to step in to provide public support.

By contrast, section 15305, subdivision (c) applies when the settlor and beneficiary are different individuals. The settlor has expressed her wishes in the trust instrument and appointed the trustee to carry them out. It is presumed that the trustee will act in good faith to effectuate the settlor's intent. (§16081, subd. (a).) Under these circumstances, it is understandable that the Legislature did not include a provision allowing a court to overcome the trustee's discretion. It was not within their contemplation that the trustee, faced with an enforceable child support judgment, might act improperly and refuse to satisfy the support judgment altogether.

Appellant next contends that section 15303, subdivision (a) must be harmonized with section 15305 to effectuate legislative intent. We reject this argument without further analysis because section 15303 concerns the trustee's obligations to general creditors. It does not apply to enforcement of a support judgment. . . .

The judgment is affirmed. Appellant is ordered to satisfy the judgments for past due and future child support directly from trust income or principal. . . . Costs on appeal are awarded to respondents.

We concur: GILBERT, P.J., and PERREN, J.

Restitution Creditor Cannot Reach Assets of Discretionary Trust Unless Trustee Exercises Discretion to Make Payment to Beneficiary

YOUNG v. McCOY

Court of Appeal, Second District, Division 1
147 Cal. App. 4th 1078, 54 Cal. Rptr. 3d 847 (2007)

ROTHSCHILD, J. . . . Richard Young (Richard) . . . appeals from a final order denying his request, pursuant to Code of Civil Procedure section 709.010, that the court direct trustee Kathy Jayne McCoy (McCoy) to release funds from a discretionary trust created for the benefit of Richard's brother Steven Young (Steven) by their mother, Lucile A. Young (Lucile). Richard seeks to invade the trust's assets to enforce a restitution judgment against Steven arising from Steven's attempted murder of Richard. Although the trust allows McCoy to make payments of interest and principal as she deems necessary for Steven's health, support, maintenance, and education, it also allows her to refuse to make such payments if, in her discretion, she determines that Steven does not need them.

In this case, according to her uncontested declaration, McCoy believes, and Richard agrees, that such needs are being met by the state because Steven is serving a life prison term for attempting to kill Richard. As section 15305.5, subdivision (c) only permits the court to compel a trustee to pay income or principal to the creditor of a beneficiary if the trustee has, in the exercise of her discretion, determined to make payments to the beneficiary, and as McCoy's exercise of her discretion not to make such payments is not an abuse of her discretion, the court lacked the authority to compel McCoy to make any payment to Richard and properly denied his request. Accordingly, we affirm the trial court's order.

FACTS

On the morning of July 16, 1997, Richard was visiting Lucile at her home in Woodland Hills where Steven also lived. ... A family argument ensued and Steven shot Richard, who survived with injuries. Steven was convicted of premeditated attempted murder and was sentenced in January 1998 to life in prison plus 13 years. In July 1998, Richard filed a personal injury action against Steven, and in August 2001 he won a default judgment against Steven for $1,275,000.

On December 16, 1998, Lucile amended her testamentary trust, making McCoy her successor trustee and ordering the successor trustee to hold the entire trust for the benefit of Steven throughout his life, then distribute any remaining trust assets to the Christian Science Foundation of Boston, Massachusetts after Steven's death. The amended trust specified that Steven's interests were primary, the charitable remainder beneficiary's secondary. The trust stated, "The Trustee shall pay to or apply for the benefit of [Steven] . . . , so much of the income, and so much of the principal, of the Trust estate, up to the whole thereof, as the Trustee shall deem necessary for the health, support, maintenance, and education, of [Steven], taking into consideration all other sources available for such purposes."[5]

On May 14, 1999, Lucile again amended her trust. The newly amended version generally reaffirmed the original trust as previously amended, repeated the standard spendthrift clause, and reemphasized, "Upon the death of [Lucile], the primary purpose of this Trust is to care for [Steven], and the Trustee or Trustees shall give due concern to his needs and comfort, taking into consideration the needs that [Steven] will have for his support, health, maintenance, and education, for the rest of his life, and can use the income and principal, up to the whole thereof, pursuant to the terms of the Trust created for his benefit; the interest of the charitable remainder beneficiary is secondary to the purpose."

---

[5] The trust amendment included a standard spendthrift clause prohibiting a creditor's attachment or a beneficiary's alienation of trust assets, noted that Richard was one of Lucile's only two children, specified that the trustee not allow Richard into Lucile's home after her death, and granted Richard $5,000 after Lucile's death if he would release Lucile, Steven, and the trust from all claims known or unknown within 60 days of receiving notice of the clause. Richard never accepted this term.

Lucile died on March 4, 2005, survived only by Steven and Richard. . . .

DISCUSSION

. . . Richard contends that the trial court erred by not ordering McCoy to pay all or part of the restitution judgment from trust funds. Relying on his interpretation of legislative history and *Ventura County Dept. of Child Support Services v. Brown* (2004), 117 Cal. App. 4th 144, 11 Cal. Rptr. 3d 489 (*Ventura County DCSS*), he argues that once a restitution judgment exists, the court has authority to order the trustee to distribute funds from the trust regardless of how or why the trustee exercised her discretion. We disagree. . . .

Because we find the plain meaning of section 15305.5, subdivision (c) sufficiently clear, both in isolation and in its statutory context, we need not consider legislative history or other extrinsic indications of legislative intent. We note, however, that our interpretation is consistent with expressed legislative intent. The sponsor of the bill that became section 15305.5 stated, "I do not believe a beneficiary should be permitted to have the enjoyment of the interest under the trust while neglecting to pay restitution to the victim." (Assemblyman Tom Umberg, sponsor of Assem. Bill No. 534 (1991-1992 Reg. Sess.), letter to Governor Pete Wilson, July 12, 1991; . . . [L]ike the language of section 15305.5 itself and neighboring code provisions, the legislative history Richard provides does not indicate a legislative intent to eliminate a trustee's discretion.[9] . . .

A trustee's discretion is not unlimited, however. If a trustee abuses her discretion, a court may order that trustee to do things differently. But whether a trustee exercises her discretion appropriately or abusively is measured by how this exercise conforms to the trustor's intent. . . . As such, a trustee's determination not to make future payments cannot be an abuse of discretion if it is clearly in keeping with the trustor's intent. Moreover, the actions of a trustee are presumed to be in good faith . . . and the burden is on the party challenging the action to show otherwise. . . . Richard has not shown or even attempted to show that the trustee acted in bad faith. . . .

Richard, however, contends that *Ventura County DCSS,* in which Division Six of our district, under a closely parallel code provision, allowed a child support creditor to obtain payment from a discretionary trust, is precedent for his interpretation of section 15305.5.[12] We disagree. . . .

In *Ventura County DCSS*, the only apparent reason for nonpayment was to avoid paying child

---

[9] Notably, the case that provoked Assemblyman Umberg to propose his bill involved an incarcerated felon who was the beneficiary of a nondiscretionary spendthrift trust that released $300 to him monthly. (See Keaton, *Breach of Trusts* (Nov. 1990), Cal. Lawyer, p. 24.)

[12] Section 15305.5 clearly was derived from section 15305, which the court applied in *Ventura County DCSS*. Section 15305 was enacted in 1986 along with most of the other preferred creditor exceptions found in sections 15304-15307, but section 15305.5 was enacted in 1991. . . . The structure of the two statutes is identical, and the language is also identical but for the definition and use of "support judgment" in section 15305 as against "restitution judgment" in section 15305.5.

support. Indeed, the court in *Ventura County DCSS* found that the trustee had abused his discretion by frustrating the trustor's intent to provide support for her grandchildren. . . . Here, by contrast, McCoy explained why she did not deem any payments toward Steven's support to be necessary: given her obligation under the trust to consider alternate sources of support, she saw that the State of California was providing for Steven's needs. This explanation is reasonable and in keeping with Lucile's stated intent. . . .

DISPOSITION

The order is affirmed. Each side shall pay its own costs.

NOTES:

1. Pratt v. Ferguson, 3 Cal. App. 5th 102, 206 Cal. Rptr. 895 (2016) held that "shut down" clause ("all provisions for the payment of perioic installments of principal to any beneficiary shall become inoperative during any period when and to the extent that, if paid, they would become subject to the enforceable claims of creditors of the beneficiary") does not defeat right to enforce support judgment under § 15305. Nor does it prevent imposition of a judgment lien under CPC § 709.010.

2. In re Kuraishi, 237 B.R. 172, 3 Cal. Bankr. Ct. Rep. 106 (1999), a self-employed doctor's Keogh (non-ERISA) retirement plan trust with a spendthrift clause was held not exempt from creditors. The spendthrift clause did not shield the doctor who was treated as the settlor.

Purpose of Spendthrift Provision Not Frustrated by Enforcing Contract to Share Beneficiary's Interest in Trust

DeMILLE v. RAMSEY

California Court of Appeal, Sixth District
207 Cal. App. 3d 116, 254 Cal. Rptr. 573 review denied (1989)

BRAUER, Acting Presiding Justice. Two sisters [Margaret and Carla] agreed in writing that they would share equally any inheritance received from their mother [Margaret Kiebler], notwithstanding any unequal disposition her will might provide. The mother died and in her will left the bulk of the estate to one daughter in a spendthrift trust, with the remainder to a granddaughter [Michele]. . . . The trial court found that the agreement was enforceable and ordered that the daughter who was the trust beneficiary pay to her sister one-half of all monies she received.

BACKGROUND

During the times which concern us here, Margaret and Carla were loving sisters who maintained a close relationship, keeping in touch through the years by letters, phone calls and personal visits. They trusted and confided in each other. Their relationship with their mother was, on the other hand, somewhat strained. They both describe Kiebler as a difficult person, changeable and irritable, who would sometimes try to control the two daughters by playing one off against the other.

Carla was married to Ray Ramsey in 1970, and the two were separated in 1981. Ramsey had experienced a series of financial setbacks during the years of their marriage, to the extent that Carla became worried that her inheritance would be devoted to the benefit of Ramsey's creditors. Carla communicated these concerns to her mother and asked that measures be taken to protect her inheritance. Shortly thereafter, in 1980, Kiebler wrote a will which left Carla's one-third share of the estate in a spendthrift trust. The will provided that "This trust is created for the protection of my daughter from possible claims of creditors. If, in the trustee's discretion, there is no longer a need for such protection, the trustee may terminate this trust and distribute all of the trust estate to my daughter, CARLA BELGRANO RAMSEY." Margaret's husband, Richard DeMille, was named cotrustee with United California Bank. Both Carla and Margaret were sent copies of this will shortly after it was prepared.

Thereafter, the daughters became increasingly concerned about their mother's changing attitudes and unpredictable behavior. In Carla's words, "we both had problems with my mother, who tended to manipulate one against the other." In 1982, Carla called Margaret and suggested that the two of them make an agreement to share equally what was left to them when their mother died. This was entirely Carla's idea. According to her, "it just seemed a way to preserve our friendship."

An agreement was drafted by Margaret's husband, Richard DeMille, and sent to Carla. Carla consulted with her attorney, Eugene Epstein, who researched the matter and made some changes so that the language of the agreement conformed to established law. The agreement was signed in July of 1982 by both Carla and Margaret before notaries. It provides in pertinent part as follows: "[I]n consideration of our mutual love and affection and desire to avoid litigation over the estate of our MOTHER, we are entering into the following agreement: 3. That we shall inherit equally from our MOTHER, notwithstanding any changes she may make in her Will to leave us unequal shares." . . .

In 1985, Kiebler changed her will . . . [leaving] the bulk of the estate to the spendthrift trust created for Carla's benefit, with the explanation "that the difference in provision for my two living daughters is not due to lack of love or affection but is based on circumstances and need." Carla was to receive periodic payments of all of the net income from the trust estate. Moreover, if need be the trustee was authorized to invade the trust principal "up to the whole thereof," for Carla's maintenance and support, including the education of her daughter Michele.

The language creating the trust and the material terms of the trust were the same as in the 1980 will, with the exception that Carla's friend and attorney Eugene Epstein replaced Richard DeMille and United California Bank as trustee. . . .

Carla and Margaret did not learn of the terms of the new will until shortly after their mother's death in December of 1985. When they were told about the unequal distribution, Margaret asked Carla whether she would honor their agreement. Carla assured her she was "not the kind of person to go back on my word."

On or about March 18, 1986, attorney Epstein wrote to Margaret's attorney stating: "I think your analysis is correct that your client is entitled to receive one-half of the income received by Carla Ramsey during her lifetime." Soon after this, however, disagreements developed regarding Margaret's rights, if any, to one-half of the trust principal. Eventually, in June of 1986, Margaret filed this action for declaratory relief, asking for a determination that the sisters' agreement was valid and enforceable . . . .

Carla answered and cross-complained for rescission of the agreement on the basis of mutual mistake. She alleged that neither sister had known at the time they made their agreement that their mother's will would create a testamentary spendthrift trust, shielding Carla's share of the estate from claims of creditors, and that their agreement would therefore frustrate the intent of the testator and violate public policy. Carla's daughter Michele filed a separate answer, alleging that her rights as a remainder beneficiary of the trust would be impaired if the agreement were enforced. . . .

Judgment was entered May 1, 1987. It provided that Margaret was entitled to one-half of all monies Carla received from the spendthrift trust, and ordered that Carla convey to Margaret one-half of any funds received by her, whether distributed to her directly or spent on her behalf, and whether said funds were distributions of income or principal. The court retained jurisdiction to supervise enforcement of the judgment.

CONTENTIONS ON APPEAL

Carla and Michele have both appealed. They contend that the agreement between Carla and Margaret constitutes a prior assignment by Carla of her interest in the spendthrift trust. As such it is prohibited by the terms of the trust. . . . In addition, Michele challenges the court's ruling that Margaret's contractual rights take precedence over her rights as a trust beneficiary under Kiebler's will.

DISCUSSION

Enforceability of the Agreement

No one disputes the general rule that agreements such as that made by Carla and Margaret are enforceable. The case of *Spangenberg v. Spangenberg* (1912), 19 Cal. App. 439, 126 P. 379 settled that point. In *Spangenberg*, six siblings made a contract to pool and divide equally whatever their father might leave them in his will. The consideration for the contract was expressly stated to be "'their love and affection for one another'" and "being 'desirous of avoiding litigation over

297

the estate' of their father." The father died and his will left equal bequests to the siblings and the entire residue to two of them. One of the residuary beneficiaries objected to the enforcement of the contract. He contended that the agreement was void because the heirs apparent could not make a contract to divide property to which they might never have a right. And he argued that such an agreement to ignore the will provisions amounted to a fraud upon the testator and was against public policy. The court disagreed, finding that there was good consideration for the contract and that no policy or statute prohibited its enforcement . . . .

Carla and Margaret's agreement was fashioned with *Spangenberg* in mind. Attorney Epstein inserted the language of consideration quoted above from *Spangenberg*, and both sisters were provided with a copy of the case, which they read. Thus there is no doubt that the parties were aware their agreement was an enforceable contract.

Carla argues that the presence of the testamentary trust distinguishes our case from *Spangenberg*. In *Spangenberg* public policy considerations were resolved on the ground that the testator's intent was not frustrated by the heirs' agreement because the testator evidenced no intent to restrict the devisees' power to dispose of their share as they wished once they received it. The creation of a testamentary spendthrift trust, on the other hand, demonstrates a contrary intent, by providing certain restraints on the beneficiary's power to transfer or otherwise dispose of her interest. Carla argues that in such a case an agreement by the heirs to pool and share their interests in an estate is in conflict with the testamentary plan. Consequently its enforcement would run against the strong public policy to give effect to the testator's intent.

Margaret points out that the court's order does not purport to interfere with the administration of the trust; rather it is directed to Carla and pertains only to monies received by her out of trust, which she could presumably dispose of as she wishes. Even though the order does not directly affect property in trust, however, it has the effect of imposing a lien upon the proceeds received by Carla. Such a procedure was expressly disapproved by our Supreme Court in *Kelly v. Kelly* (1938), 11 Cal. 2d 356, 79 P.2d 1059, in the context of that case. . . .

Carla contends that *Kelly* is controlling authority and prohibits a judgment which orders her to pay Margaret one-half of any distribution she will receive from the trust. Under *Kelly*, Margaret would be required to bring suit to recover her one-half interest only *after* Carla received each payment.

We find *Kelly* to be distinguishable. In *Kelly* there was no question that the trustor intended to create a spendthrift trust. A stated purpose of the trust was to prevent any beneficiary from assigning his interest in the trust in anticipation of receiving it. It therefore follows that enforcement of the agreement as a lien on the proceeds clearly defeats the trustor's intent. In our case the court made a different finding, namely that the trust was not created by the trustor to curb the spendthrift tendencies of a beneficiary; rather it was Carla's idea, and its creation was for the sole purpose of protecting her inheritance from the creditors of her estranged husband. . . .

The trial court was entitled to determine, as it did, that in spite of the boilerplate provision, Kiebler's "was not a spendthrift trust." Her intent, as expressed in the language creating the trust, was not to keep money out of the hands of her daughter Carla but rather to keep creditors of Carla's husband at bay for as long as Carla needed this protection. This being so, the court's order enforcing the sisters' agreement from proceeds received by Carla did not frustrate the trust purpose, and is not inconsistent with the principles expressed in *Kelly*. . . .

Rights of the Remainder Beneficiary

. . . As a trust beneficiary, Michele has a right to enforce the trust in accordance with its terms. Her rights are violated only if the trust is administered in a way which violates its provisions or the trust purpose. Invasion of corpus is expressly authorized by the terms of the Kiebler trust. Article sixth, paragraph 2, provides that the trustee may invade principal if "in [his] absolute discretion" Carla needs money "*for any reason*" for her health, maintenance and support, over and above that provided by payments of net income. The trustee may "pay to or apply for [Carla's] benefit such amounts of the principal of the trust estate, *up to the whole thereof.*"

. . . [I]t cannot be said that the terms of Kiebler's trust are necessarily violated if sums from principal are applied to satisfy an obligation which Carla made freely and which she testified she "would like to uphold." . . .

We conclude that Carla's performance of her agreement with her sister can be accomplished without violating the trust created for Carla's benefit. Enforcement of the agreement therefore does not violate such limited rights as Michele has. . . .

CAPACCIOLI and PREMO, JJ., concur.

Spendthrift Clause Does Not Protect Trustee-Beneficiary's Share from Surcharge for Breach of Trust

CHATARD v. OVEROSS

California Court of Appeal, Second District, Division 4
179 Cal. App. 4th 1098, 101 Cal. Rptr. 3d 883 (2009) Review Denied (2010)

WILLHITE, J. . . .

DISCUSSION

. . . The issue here is whether the Trust's spendthrift provision precludes taking from appellant's distributive share of the Trust the amount that she was surcharged for breaching her duties as trustee. Section 257 of the Restatement Second of Trusts, entitled "Impounding Share of Trustee-beneficiary" and published in 1959, directly addresses this situation.[12] It

---

[12] California trust law is largely derived from the Restatement rules. . . .

provides: If a trustee who is also one of the beneficiaries commits a breach of trust, the other beneficiaries are entitled to a charge upon his beneficial interest to secure their claims against him for the breach of trust, unless the settlor manifested a different intention."[13]

Comment *f* to section 257 explains the section's applicability to a spendthrift trust. It provides: "Spendthrift trust. The rule stated in this Section is applicable although the interest of the trustee-beneficiary is not transferable by him or subject to the claims of his creditors, unless the settlor has manifested a different intention. . . . The settlor who has given the other beneficiaries their interests can restrict those interests by denying them power to reach the interest of the trustee-beneficiary to make good a breach of trust committed by him. . . . *The question is whether in view of all the circumstances the settlor would have desired to protect the trustee-beneficiary, not only as against the claims of ordinary creditors, but also against the claims of the other beneficiaries for breach of trust.*" (. . . italics added.)

In this case, nothing in the Trust document directly states that the settlors (appellant's parents) intended to insulate appellant's share of the Trust in the event that she became liable to the other beneficiaries (the settlors' children and grandchildren) because she breached her fiduciary duty as trustee. Appellant's multiple breaches of her fiduciary obligations resulted in significant financial loss to the Trust (more than $325,000). . . . If the surcharge is not taken from appellant's share before the assets are distributed on a pro rata basis, the other beneficiaries will be compelled to share in the reduction of value caused solely by appellant's misfeasance. Further, if the surcharge is not taken from appellant's share, it is reasonable to assume in light of appellant's misconduct as trustee that the beneficiaries would then be required to hire counsel and fund litigation to compel her (now apparently living in Florida) to comply with the trial court's surcharge order. Nothing in the Trust indicates that the settlors intended to protect appellant from the consequences of her misconduct to the detriment of the other beneficiaries. . . .

Trusts for the State Supported; Special Needs Trusts

Disabled Child Entitled to Inherit Balance of Special Needs Trust Remaining at Parent's Death Without Reimbursing State for Medical Payments.

SHEWRY v. ARNOLD

Court of Appeal, Second District, Division 5

---

[13] The American Law Institute is in the process of producing the Restatement Third of Trusts to supersede and replace the Second Restatement. . . . [C]omment a(2) to section 59 ("Spendthrift Trusts: Exceptions for Particular Types of Claims") of the Restatement Third of Trusts explains: "[T]he interest of a beneficiary . . . who—by breach of duty as trustee or otherwise—causes harm to the trust estate and the beneficial interests of others, may ordinarily be reached by set-off or impounding to satisfy the resulting obligation, *even in the case of a spendthrift trust*. . . . " [Italics added.]

125 Cal. App. 4th 186, 22 Cal. Rptr. 3d 488 (2004)

GRIGNON, J. . . . Etoria Hatcher was born on March 5, 1935. Her sole living child is Arnold, who is permanently and totally disabled. Arnold has received disability benefits from Social Security since 1986 and is a disabled person . . . . Arnold was appointed as conservator of Hatcher's person and estate.

Hatcher intended to apply for Medi-Cal benefits. . . . Hatcher became entitled to receive proceeds from the settlement of a lawsuit. If the settlement proceeds became part of the conservatorship estate, Hatcher would not be eligible for Medi-Cal benefits. Therefore, Arnold, as Hatcher's conservator, petitioned the probate court for approval to create a special needs trust pursuant to Probate Code section 3600 et seq. . . . On December 22, 1997, the probate court approved the creation of the trust to be funded with $450,000. The probate court concluded that an irrevocable special needs trust was in Hatcher's best interest and approved Arnold as the settlor and trustee of the trust. The stated intent of the trust was to supplement any benefits that Hatcher might be eligible to receive through government assistance programs. . . . The trust provided that it would terminate upon the depletion of the assets or the death of the beneficiary. If terminated on the death of the beneficiary, the remaining principal and income was to be distributed to Arnold as the only living child of the beneficiary. "However, pursuant to Probate Code section 3604, at the time of termination of the Trust, either by death or depletion of assets, the Trustee shall give notice to the State Department of Health Services, the State Department of Mental Health, the State Department of Developmental Services, and any county or city in this state. All valid liens in favor of these agencies shall first be satisfied before any distribution of remaining [principal] or income is made, even to the extent of exhausting any remaining [principal] or income."

In January 1999, Hatcher applied for the Medi-Cal program. The Department approved the application based on the understanding that the trust would reimburse the Department from the remaining trust assets after Hatcher's death or the trust's termination. The Department provided retroactive coverage to July 1997. . . . [T]he Department paid $90,043.70 through the Medi-Cal program for health care services provided to Hatcher. Hatcher died on September 20, 1999. Arnold withdrew $183,000 from the trust assets on December 13, 1999, and $101,727.23 from the trust assets on October 16, 2000, leaving a balance of $2.31. Arnold did not notify the Department of Hatcher's death.

The Department discovered Hatcher's death as a result of a routine periodic check of the Medi-Cal Eligibility Data System on October 9, 2001. On November 9, 2001, the Department wrote to Arnold and demanded $90,043.70 from the remainder of the trust. Arnold wrote to the Department and explained that she was Hatcher's sole surviving child and was disabled, and therefore, any property distributed to her was exempt from reimbursement claims. She refused to pay the Department's claim.

On December 23, 2002, the Department filed a complaint against Arnold, as the recipient of property from a Medi-Cal beneficiary, to enforce and collect money due on a Medi-Cal creditor's claim pursuant to Probate Code section 3605. . . . On December 15, 2003, the trial court entered judgment in favor of the Department and ordered Arnold to pay $90,043.70, plus interest and costs, to the Department. Arnold filed a timely notice of appeal.

DISCUSSION
. . .

Medicaid

"Medicaid (42 U.S.C., § 1396 et seq. [tit. XIX of the Social Security Act; . . .)" is a federal program that enables states to provide medical assistance to impoverished individuals who are aged, blind, disabled, or families with dependent children. . . . "The program is optional, but once a state decides to participate it must comply with the federal government's requirements . . . ." . . . "As a Medicaid program, California's Medi-Cal program must . . . conform to federal Medicaid statutes and regulations. . . . " . . .

. . . Title 42 of the United States Code section 1396p(d)(1) governs the treatment of trust assets for purposes of determining an individual's eligibility for benefits under a state plan. In general, trust assets are considered in determining an individual's income and asset eligibility for benefits. However, this eligibility subsection does not apply to a trust established for the benefit of a disabled individual under age 65, such as a special needs trust, "if the State will receive all amounts remaining in the trust upon the death of such individual up to an amount equal to the total medical assistance paid on behalf of the individual under a State plan . . . ." . . . [S]ection 1396p(b)(1) provides that the state must seek adjustment or recovery of any medical assistance paid on behalf of certain individuals from the individual's estate. . . . However, section 1396p(b)(2)(A) provides that any adjustment or recovery under subparagraph (1) may be made only after the death of the individual's surviving spouse, if any, and only at a time when he has no surviving child who is under age 21 or is blind or permanently and totally disabled.

Special Needs Trust

. . . Under California law, when a court approves a settlement of an action to which an incompetent person is a party, the conservator may petition the court for an order that money owed to the incompetent person pursuant to the settlement not become part of the conservatorship estate, but instead be paid to a special needs trust established under Probate Code section 3604 for the benefit of the incompetent person. (Prob. Code § 3602.) . . . Under Probate Code section 3604, subdivision (b), a special needs trust may be established and continued only if the court determines that the incompetent person has a disability that substantially impairs the individual's ability to care for himself or herself and constitutes a substantial handicap, the incompetent person is likely to have special needs that will not be met without the trust, and the money to be paid to the trust does not exceed the amount that appears reasonably necessary to meet the special needs of the incompetent person.

Probate Code section 3605 provides in pertinent part: ". . . Notwithstanding any provision in the trust instrument, at the death of the special needs trust beneficiary or on termination of the trust, the trust property is subject to claims of the State Department of Health Services . . . to the extent authorized by law as if the trust property is owned by the beneficiary or is part of the beneficiary's estate." . . .

[Reimbursement]

. . . Welfare and Institutions Code section 14009.5 provides for Medi-Cal reimbursement from decedents' estates . . . [but] "(b) The department may not claim in any of the following circumstances: . . . (2) Where there is any of the following: . . . (C) A surviving child who is blind or permanently and totally disabled . . . ."

. . . This case involves the interplay of the federal and state statutory provisions relating to special needs trusts and those relating to Medi-Cal reimbursement. Arnold contends that after Hatcher's death, the remaining assets of the special needs trust were treated as part of Hatcher's estate, and the property of an estate that is distributed to a decedent's adult disabled child is exempt from Medi-Cal reimbursement claims. The Department responds that Medi-Cal is required to comply with the federal Medicaid provisions that require a state to be reimbursed from the remaining assets of a decedent's special needs trust. The Department argues that the assets of a special needs trust may be disregarded for purposes of Medi-Cal eligibility only if the state is assured of reimbursement from any remaining assets. . . .

The Department argues that subdivision (d) of title 42 United States Code section 1396p governs reimbursement from special needs trust assets. The Department argues further that subdivision (d) includes no express provisions exempting from reimbursement distributions to adult disabled children of a beneficiary. Accordingly, the Department asserts that the exemption for assets distributed to an adult disabled child in subdivision (b) is not applicable to special needs trust assets.

This argument is not persuasive. . . . The Department has put forth no persuasive argument that reimbursement from special needs trusts should be treated differently than other reimbursements. We conclude such trusts should not be treated differently. Thus, qualification of a state plan for medical assistance under the federal Medicaid provisions does not require reimbursement from special needs trust assets distributed to an adult disabled child. . . .

. . . This construction of the statutes . . . comports with sound public policy. Special needs trusts cannot be used to shelter excessive assets, because the probate court will approve only the amount that appears reasonably necessary to meet the special needs of the incompetent person. Both the federal and state Legislatures have determined that distributions from estates to adult disabled children should be exempt from Medi-Cal reimbursement claims because enforcement of such claims would likely result in hardship. We can discern no reason that the remaining assets of a court-approved special needs trust should be treated differently than any other assets of an estate. . . .

DISPOSITION

The judgment is reversed. The trial court is ordered to enter judgment in favor of defendant and appellant Brenda Arnold. Defendant and appellant Brenda Arnold is awarded her costs on appeal.

We concur: TURNER, P.J., and ARMSTRONG, J.

NOTE: State's claim for reimbursement of Medi-Cal payments under Welfare & Institutions Code § 14009.5, after recipient has died, is subject to 3-year statute of limitations in Code of Civil Procedure §338(a), not 1-year statute in § 366.3. **Maxwell-Jolly v. Martin**, 198 Cal. App. 4th 347, 129 Cal. Rptr. 3d 278 (2011).

Section B. Modification and Termination

Consent of the Beneficiaries

The *Claflin* Doctrine

CPC § 15403. Modification or Termination by Beneficiaries (Claflin Doctrine)

(a) Except as provided in subdivision (b), if all beneficiaries of an irrevocable trust consent, they may petition the court for modification or termination of the trust upon petition to the court.

(b) If the continuance of the trust is necessary to carry out a material purpose of the trust, the trust cannot be modified or terminated unless the court, in its discretion, determines that the reason for doing so under the circumstances outweighs the interest in accomplishing a material purpose of the trust. If the trust subject to a valid restraint on the transfer of the beneficiary's interest as provided in Chapter 2 (commencing with Section 15300), the trust may not be terminated unless the court determines there is good cause to do so.

(c) If the trust provides for the disposition of principal to a class of persons described only as "heirs" or "next of kin" of the settlor, or using other words that describe the class of all persons who would take under the rules of intestacy, the court may limit the class of beneficiaries whose consent is necessary to modify or terminate a trust to the beneficiaries who are reasonably likely to take under the circumstances.

(Stats. 1990, 2017)

§ CPC § 15404. Modification or Termination by Settlor and All Beneficiaries

(a) A trust may be modified or terminated by the written consent of the settlor and all beneficiaries without court approval of the modification or termination.

(b) If any beneficiary does not consent to the modification or termination of the trust, the court may modify or partially terminate the trust upon petition to the court by the other beneficiaries, with the consent of the settlor, if the interests of the beneficiaries who do not consent are not substantially impaired.

(c) If the trust provides for the disposition of principal to a class of persons described only as "heirs" or "next of kin" of the settlor, or using other words that describe the class of all persons who would take under the rules of intestacy, the court may limit the class of beneficiaries whose consent is necessary to modify or terminate a trust to the beneficiaries who are reasonably likely to take under the circumstances.

(Stats. 1990, 2017)

CPC § 15405. *Guardian ad Litem Can Give Consent*

For the purposes of Sections 15403 and 15404, the consent of a beneficiary who lacks legal capacity, including a minor, or who is an unascertained or unborn person may be given in proceedings before the court by a guardian ad litem, if it would be appropriate to do so. In determining whether to give consent, the guardian ad litem may rely on general family benefit accruing to living members of the beneficiary's family as a basis for approving a modification or termination of the trust.

(Stats. 1990)

CPC § 15406. *Presumption of Fertility Rebuttable in Determining Consent Required*

In determining the class of beneficiaries whose consent is necessary to modify or terminate a trust pursuant to Section 15403 or 15404, the presumption of fertility is rebuttable.

(Stats. 1990)

Deviation and Changed Circumstances

Creating a Special Needs Trust

Probate Court Can Establish Special Needs Trust with Conservatee's Inheritance

CONSERVATORSHIP of KANE

Court of Appeal, First District, Division 5
137 Cal. App. 4th 400, 40 Cal. Rptr. 3d 378 (2006)

JONES, P.J. Barbara Simon, the court-appointed conservator of Kevin Kane, appeals the probate court's denial of a petition for a substituted judgment to establish a special needs trust under the authority of Probate Code section 2580. We reverse the probate court's order denying the petition, and remand for further proceedings.

I. FACTS AND PROCEDURAL HISTORY

Kevin Kane (Kane) is a developmentally disabled adult who lived with his mother until her death in March, 1999. Upon his mother's death, Kane became entitled to an inheritance of approximately $65,000. Kane is unable to live safely independently, or to manage his prospective inheritance. Accordingly, the court established a limited conservatorship of Kane's estate and appointed Barbara Simon as conservator on December 8, 2003. Kane resides in a group living facility, which is suitable for his special needs, and attends a day program in another city nearby. Kane receives Supplemental Security Income (SSI) and Medi-Cal benefits, which pay for much of his care and medical treatment.

The estate planning previously undertaken for Kane's mother did not, unfortunately, include any special provisions for Kane, such as the establishment of a special needs trust for him. In particular, such a special needs trust is desirable for Kane, because if he were to receive his inheritance directly, he would be ineligible for SSI and Medi-Cal benefits, and would likely deplete the inheritance relatively quickly to pay for ordinary living expenses and medical care. However, if the legacy was placed in a special needs trust, he could use the trust proceeds for his special needs, such as various types of therapy, while he is still receiving public benefits.

The conservator set forth these circumstances in her petition, seeking court authority to create such a trust for Kane pursuant to Probate Code section 2580, *et seq.* . . . An investigator employed by the court in conservatorship matters conducted an investigation, including an interview with Kane. The investigator recommended that the petition be granted, because it was in the best interests of Kane, the conservatee.

The court expressed some sympathy for the petition, but questioned whether it had statutory authority to order the creation of such a special needs trust in these circumstances, under the substituted judgment procedure set forth in section 2580. The lower court reasoned that under the substituted judgment procedure, the court would essentially be only a substitute for Kane himself, and the court questioned whether Kane could have been the grantor of such a trust. Lacking relevant authority for the creation of such a special needs trust for Kane in these circumstances, the court denied the petition.

II. DISCUSSION

A. The Substituted Judgment Procedure

. . . The Legislature has generally authorized a probate court to substitute its judgment for that of a conservatee. (§ 2580 *et seq.*) As the court explained in *Conservatorship of Hart* (1991), 228 Cal. App. 3d 1244, 279 Cal. Rptr. 249 (*Hart*): "The doctrine underlying the substituted-judgment statute was first recognized in California in *Estate of Christiansen* (1967), 248 Cal. App. 2d 398[, 56 Cal. Rptr. 505 (*Christiansen*)] . . . . *Christiansen* declared 'that the courts of this state, in probate proceedings for the administration of the estates of insane or incompetent persons, have power and authority to determine whether to authorize transfers of the property of the incompetent for the purpose of avoiding unnecessary estate or inheritance taxes or expenses of administration, and to authorize such action where it appears from all the circumstances that the ward, if sane, as a reasonably prudent man, would so plan his estate, there being no substantial evidence of a contrary intent.' . . . Significantly, *Christiansen* did not require that a court find the ward would have acted as proposed; instead it adopted an essentially objective prudent-person standard. Thus *Christiansen* contemplated substitution of the court's judgment for that of the incompetent person." . . .

Further, in *Christiansen* as in the present case, the authority of the probate court was being invoked in order to conform the conservatee's estate to federal and state law provisions designed to minimize the extent to which those assets would be acquired by the federal and state government, a goal that was deemed legitimate and in the interests of the conservatee.

In accordance with the relevant case law, section 2580 now generally provides that the court may make an order for the purpose of (1) benefiting the conservatee or the estate; (2) minimizing current or prospective taxes; or (3) providing gifts to persons or charities which would be likely beneficiaries of gifts from the conservatee . . . .

Other sections of the Probate Code set forth a procedure and standards for deciding such petitions. Section 2582 provides that the court may make an order for substituted judgment only if it determines that the conservatee either is not opposed to the order or, if opposed, lacks legal capacity. Section 2582 also provides that the court must determine either that the action will have no adverse effect upon the estate, or that the remaining estate will be adequate for the needs of the conservatee. Section 2583 provides that, in deciding a motion for substituted judgment, the court should consider all other relevant circumstances, including but not limited to various enumerated circumstances. One such consideration is "[t]he minimization of current or prospective income, estate, inheritance, or other taxes. . . ." . . . Finally, section 2584 states: "After hearing, the court, in its discretion, may approve, modify and approve, or disapprove the proposed action and may authorize or direct the conservator to transfer or dispose of assets or take other action as provided in the court's order."

B. The Showing of the Desirability of a Special Needs Trust for Kane

. . . [A] special needs trust is desirable for Kane, because he is presently receiving federal social security benefits, and state Medi-Cal benefits. . . . [I]f he were to receive the inherited legacy from his mother outright, he could no longer receive such benefits. However, if the legacy was placed in a special needs trust, he could use the trust proceeds for his specialized care, while he is still receiving public benefits.

C. The Probate Court Had Jurisdiction and Authority to Establish a Special Needs Trust for Kane.

. . . Both federal and California statutes are relevant on the subject of the creation of a special needs trust.

Pursuant to relevant provisions of federal law, particularly provisions of the Omnibus Budget Reconciliation Act of 1993 (OBRA) now generally codified at title 42 United States Code section 1396d, such a special needs trust may be created for a person such as Kane. In particular, title 42 United States Code section 1396p, subsection (d)(4)(A), provides a definition of such a special needs trust, as follows: "A trust containing the assets of an individual under age 65 who is disabled (as defined in section 1382c(a)(3) of this title) and which is established for the benefit of such individual by a parent, grandparent, legal guardian of the individual, *or a court*. . . ." . . . (Italics added.) Assets held in such a trust must be used for the special medical and therapeutic needs of the beneficiary, but these assets will be excluded when considering whether a person qualifies for public benefits such as Medi-Cal coverage.

California law also authorizes the establishment of special needs trusts to preserve the availability of public benefits to the conservatee, under the same circumstance. The California Code of Regulations, title 22, section 50489.9, subsections (a)(3)(B) and (a)(4), contain state law provisions parallel to federal law, allowing the use of a special needs trust to hold certain assets, without losing eligibility for public benefits such as Medi-Cal.

The issue confronting the trial court here was whether the substituted judgment doctrine, codified in section 2580, is available to establish the special needs trust in the circumstance presented by Kane's conservator: a disabled beneficiary, who has no living parents or grandparents, but who faces substantial living and medical care expenses over a relatively long life expectancy.

Section 2580, subdivision (b), provides authority for any order that "may include, but is not limited to" a variety of enumerated actions. Among the enumerated actions, subsection (b)(5), provides for an order for the creation of trusts, including certain types of special needs trusts for the benefit of persons with special medical or health needs: "Creating for the benefit of the conservatee or others, revocable or irrevocable trusts of the property of the estate, which trusts may extend beyond the conservatee's disability or life. A special needs trust for money paid pursuant to a compromise or judgment for a conservatee may be established only under Chapter 4 (commencing with Section 3600) of Part 8, and not under this article." The cross-reference in section 2580, subdivision (b)(5), to Chapter 4, for the creation of litigation special needs trusts (LSNT's) as a result of a compromise or judgment in litigation, is inapposite here, because the trust to be established for Kane is not being funded by a compromise or judgment in litigation. . . . As section 3600 is unavailable to Kane, the statutory authority to create such a special needs trust in the present circumstances is solely conferred by section 2580, subdivision (b)(5).

In our view, it is inconsistent with federal legislation to allow a special needs trust for litigation beneficiaries, but not to beneficiaries of an inheritance in these circumstances. The relevant federal and state statutes provide that upon the creation of such a special needs trust by a court, a conservatee in Kane's circumstance may continue to receive public benefits, and may use the proceeds of the special needs trust for his unique medical and therapeutic needs. A proper purpose for application of the substituted judgment doctrine is the avoidance of taxes or other governmental assessments. . . . We conclude the provisions of section 2580 are available to establish such a trust for his benefit.

. . . Of course, it is for the probate court, in the first instance, to exercise its discretion as to whether such a trust should be created, based upon the facts placed in the record. We simply hold here that the probate court had jurisdiction and authority to order the establishment of such a special needs trust, and the lower court should reconsider the matter, in light of this legal conclusion. . . .

CPC § 15409. Modification or Termination in Changed Circumstances

(a) On petition by a trustee or beneficiary, the court may modify the administrative or dispositive provisions of the trust or terminate the trust if, owing to circumstances not known to the settlor and not anticipated by the settlor, the continuation of the trust under its terms would defeat or substantially impair the accomplishment of the purposes of the trust. In this case, if necessary to carry out the purposes of the trust, the court may order the trustee to do acts that are not authorized or are forbidden by the trust instrument.

(b) The court shall consider a trust provision restraining transfer of the beneficiary's interest as a factor in making its decision whether to modify or terminate the trust, but the court is not precluded from exercising its discretion to modify or terminate the trust solely because of a restraint on transfer.

(Stats. 1990)

NOTE: CPC § 15409 and Reformation of Trusts

In **Bilafer v. Bilafer**, 161 Cal. App. 4th 363, 73 Cal. Rptr. 3d 880 (2008), the court held that § 15409 does not prevent a court from reforming an irrevocable trust if a drafting error defeats the trustor's intentions. Although § 15409 was part of a "comprehensive" set of rules for modifying trusts, it did not displace the common law rules allowing reformation.

NOTE: Reformation and Modification to Achieve Tax Objectives

The need to reform instruments to achieve tax objectives is limited to some extent by Probate Code Division 11, Part 5, §§ 21500-21541 which allow various provisions to be construed to comply with the Internal Revenue Code.

✥

CPC § 15408. Trust with Uneconomically Low Principal

(a) On petition by a trustee or beneficiary, if the court determines that the fair market value of the principal of a trust has become so low in relation to the cost of administration that continuation of the trust under its existing terms will defeat or substantially impair the accomplishment of its purposes, the court may, in its discretion and in a manner that conforms as nearly as possible to the intention of the settlor, order any of the following:

    (1) Termination of the trust.

    (2) Modification of the trust.

    (3) Appointment of a new trustee.

(b) Notwithstanding subdivision (a), if the trust principal does not exceed fifty thousand dollars ($50,000) in value, the trustee has the power to terminate the trust.

(c) The existence of a trust provision restraining transfer of the beneficiary's interest does not prevent application of this section.

(Stats. 1990, 2010, 2018)

Disposition of Trust Property on Termination of Trust

CPC § 15410. Disposition of Property upon Termination

At the termination of a trust, the trust property shall be disposed of as follows:

(a) In the case of a trust that is revoked by the settlor, the trust property shall be disposed of in the following order of priority:

    (1) As directed by the settlor.

    (2) As provided in the trust instrument.

    (3) To the extent that there is no direction by the settlor or in the trust instrument, to the settlor, or his or her estate, as the case may be.

(b) In the case of a trust that is revoked by any person holding a power of revocation other than the settlor, the trust property shall be disposed of in the following order of priority:

    (1) As provided in the trust instrument.

    (2) As directed by the person exercising the power of revocation.

    (3) To the extent that there is no direction in the trust instrument or by the person exercising the power of revocation, to the person exercising the power of revocation, or his or her estate, as the case may be.

(c) In the case of a trust that is terminated by the consent of the settlor and all beneficiaries, as agreed by the settlor and all beneficiaries.

(d) In any other case, as provided in the trust instrument or in a manner directed by the court that conforms as nearly as possible to the intention of the settlor as expressed in the trust instrument.

(e) If a trust is terminated by the trustee pursuant to subdivision (b) of Section 15408, the trust property may be distributed as determined by the trustee pursuant to the standard provided in subdivision (d) without the need for a court order. If the trust instrument does not provide a manner of distribution at termination and the settlor's intent is not adequately expressed in the trust instrument, the trustee may distribute the trust property to the living beneficiaries on an actuarial basis.

(Stats. 1990, 2012)

NOTE: Trolan v. Trolan, 2019 WL 365977, held that trial court exceeded its authority when it ordered immediate liquidation of the trust assets and substituted its judgment regarding the method of distribution for that of the trustees. The court should have deferred to trustees' determination under trust provision giving trustees the power "to partition, allot and distribute the Trust Estate in undivided interests or in kind, at valuations determined by the Trustee, and to sell such property as the Trustee may deem necessary to make division or distribution."

CPC § 15413. Termination After Perpetuities Period Has Expired

A trust provision, express or implied, that the trust may not be terminated is ineffective insofar as it purports to be applicable after the expiration of the longer of the periods provided by the statutory rule against perpetuities, Article 2 (commencing with Section 21205) of Chapter 1 of Part 2 of Division 11.

(Stats. 1991)

Trust Decanting

California adopted the Uniform Trust Decanting Act effective Jan. 1, 2019. It is codified at CPC §§ 19501-19530.

Section C. Trustee Removal

CPC § 15642. Removal of Trustee: Grounds, Costs, Surrender of Property or Suspension of Powers

(a) A trustee may be removed in accordance with the trust instrument, by the court on its own motion, or on petition of a settlor, cotrustee, or beneficiary under Section 17200.

(b) The grounds for removal of a trustee by the court include the following:

(1) Where the trustee has committed a breach of the trust.

(2) Where the trustee is insolvent or otherwise unfit to administer the trust.

(3) Where hostility or lack of cooperation among cotrustees impairs the administration of the trust.

(4) Where the trustee fails or declines to act.

(5) Where the trustee's compensation is excessive under the circumstances.

(6) Where the sole trustee is a person described in subdivision (a) of Section 21350 or subdivision (a) of Section 21380, whether or not the person is the transferee of a donative transfer by the transferor, unless, based upon any evidence of the intent of the settlor and all other facts and circumstances, which shall be made known to the court, the court finds that it is consistent with the settlor's intent that the trustee continue to serve and that this intent was not the product of fraud or undue influence. Any waiver by the settlor of this provision is against public policy and shall be void. This paragraph shall not apply to instruments that became irrevocable on or before January 1, 1994. This paragraph shall not apply if any of the following conditions are met:

(A) The settlor is related by blood or marriage to, or is a cohabitant with, any one or more of the trustees, the person who drafted or transcribed the instrument, or the person who caused the instrument to be transcribed.

(B) The instrument is reviewed by an independent attorney who (1) counsels the settlor about the nature of his or her intended trustee designation and (2) signs and delivers to the settlor and the designated trustee a certificate in substantially the following form: . . . [form is the same as required under § 21384 reproduced in Chapter 3 above].

This independent review and certification may occur either before or after the instrument has been executed, and if it occurs after the date of execution, the named trustee shall not be subject to removal under this paragraph. Any attorney whose written engagement signed by the client is expressly limited to the preparation of a certificate under this subdivision, including the prior counseling, shall not be considered to otherwise represent the client.

(C) After full disclosure of the relationships of the persons involved, the instrument is approved pursuant to an order under Article 10 (commencing with Section 2580) of Chapter 6 of Part 4 of Division 4.

(7) If, as determined under Part 17 (commencing with Section 810) of Division 2, the trustee is substantially unable to manage the trust's financial resources or is otherwise substantially unable to execute properly the duties of the office. When the trustee holds the power to revoke the trust, substantial inability to manage the trust's financial resources or otherwise execute properly the duties of the office may not be proved solely by isolated incidents of negligence or improvidence.

(8) If the trustee is substantially unable to resist fraud or undue influence. When the trustee holds the power to revoke the trust, substantial inability to resist fraud or undue influence may not be proved solely by isolated incidents of negligence or improvidence.

(9) For other good cause.

(c) If, pursuant to paragraph (6) of subdivision (b), the court finds that the designation of the trustee was not consistent with the intent of the settlor or was the product of fraud or undue influence, the person being removed as trustee shall bear all costs of the proceeding, including reasonable attorney's fees.

(d) If the court finds that the petition for removal of the trustee was filed in bad faith and that removal would be contrary to the settlor's intent, the court may order that the person or persons seeking the removal of the trustee bear all or any part of the costs of the proceeding, including reasonable attorney's fees.

(e) If it appears to the court that trust property or the interests of a beneficiary may suffer loss or injury pending a decision on a petition for removal of a trustee and any appellate review, the court may, on its own motion or on petition of a cotrustee or beneficiary, compel the trustee whose removal is sought to surrender trust property to a cotrustee or to a receiver or temporary trustee. The court may also suspend the powers of the trustee to the extent the court deems necessary.

(f) For purposes of this section, the term "related by blood or marriage" shall include persons within the seventh degree.

(Stats. 1990, 1993, 1995, 2006, 2010)

NOTES:

1. Sterling v. Sterling, 242 Cal. App. 4th 185, 194 Cal. Rptr. 3d 867 (2015) held that husband, Donald Stirling, was properly removed as cotrustee, pursuant to terms of the trust, after two physicians who regularly determine capacity determined that cognitive impairments consistent with Alzheimer's disease meant he was no longer competent to act as trustee. Remaining cotrustee became sole trustee with power to sell the Los Angeles Clippers and wind up the trust under § 15407 which provides that, on termination or revocation of a trust, the trustee continues to have the powers reasonably necessary to wind up the affairs of the trust.

2. NOTE: Trolan v. Trolan, 2019 WL 365977, held trial court abused its discretion when it removed trustees based on its erroneous finding that trust required liquidation of the assets on termination (which trustees had failed to do) and there was hostility between cotrustees. There was no evidence that hostility between the trustees impaired administration of the trust under its clear and unambiguous terms.

Chapter 12. Trusts: Powers of Appointment

California's Powers of Appointment statutes were originally enacted in 1969. They were moved from the Civil Code to the Probate Code in 1992 and are located in Division 2, Part 14, §§ 600-695. Several sections were amended and a few new ones added in 2016 in reaction to promulgation of the Uniform Powers of Appointment Act by the Uniform Law Commission in 2013. The principal change was substituting the term "powerholder" for "donee," but there are also a few substantive changes. See R. Denham, *RUFADAA is not a Root Vegetable: California's 2016 Legislative Harvest*, 38 Est. Plan. & Calif. Prob. Rptr. 68 (2016).

In the sections that follow, enactment/amendment dates are included only for those sections enacted or amended after 1992. The sections reproduced here are a selection and do not include all of Division 2, Part 14. Not included are sections 612 (definition of testamentary powers, powers presently and not presently exercisable and postponed powers); 625 (capacity of powerholder to transfer interest in property); 633 (consent of donor or other person to exercise power); 634 (exercise by two or more powerholders); 635 (defective exercise of imperative power, remedy); 642 (exercise by will executed before creation of power); 662 (release on behalf of minority powerholder); and 681 (property covered by special power).

CPC § 600. Common Law Governs Powers Except as Modified by Statute

Except to the extent that the common law rules governing powers of appointment are modified by statute, the common law as to powers of appointment is the law of this state.

Section A. Purposes, Terminology, and Types of Powers

Terminology and Relationships

CPC § 610. Definitions

As used in this part:

(a) "Appointee" means the person in whose favor a power of appointment is exercised.

(b) "Appointive property" means the property or interest in property that is the subject of the power of appointment.

(c) "Creating instrument" means the deed, will, trust or other writing or document that creates or reserves the power of appointment.

(d) "Donor" means the person who creates or reserves the power of appointment.

(e) "Permissible appointee" means a person in whose favor a power of appointment can be exercised.

(f) "Power of appointment" means a power that enables a powerholder acting in a nonfiduciary capacity to designate a recipient of an ownership interest in or another power of appointment over the appointive property. The term does not include a power of attorney.

(g) "Powerholder" means the person to whom a power of appointment is given or in whose favor a power of appointment is reserved.

(Stats. 1992, 2016)

Creation of Power

CPC § 620. Capacity to Create Power of Appointment

A power of appointment can be created only by a donor having the capacity to transfer the interest in property to which the power relates.

CPC § 621. Creation of Power of Appointment

(a) A power of appointment is created only if all of the following are satisfied:

(1) There is a creating instrument.

(2) The creating instrument is valid under applicable law.

(3) Except as provided in subdivision (b), the creating instrument transfers the appointive property.

(4) The terms of the creating instrument manifest the donor's intent to create in a powerholder a power of appointment over the appointive property exercisable in favor of a permissible appointee.

(b) Paragraph (3) of subdivision (a) does not apply to the creation of a power of appointment by the exercise of a power of appointment.

(Stats. 2016)

CPC § 695. Authority to Revoke a Power

(a) Unless the power to revoke is in the creating instrument or exists pursuant to Section 15400,[39] the creation of a power of appointment is irrevocable.

***

---

[39] Section 15400 is set forth in Chapter 7, *supra.*—Ed.

General and Nongeneral Powers

CPC § 611. General and Special Powers

(a) A power of appointment is "general" only to the extent that it is exercisable in favor of the powerholder, the powerholder's estate, the powerholder's creditors, or creditors of the powerholder's estate, whether or not it is exercisable in favor of others.

(b) A power to consume, invade, or appropriate property for the benefit of a person in discharge of the powerholder's obligation of support that is limited by an ascertainable standard relating to the person's health, education, support, or maintenance is not a general power of appointment.

(c) A power exercisable by the powerholder only in conjunction with a person having a substantial interest in the appointive property that is adverse to the exercise of the power in favor of the powerholder, the powerholder's estate, the powerholder's creditors, or creditors of the powerholder's estate is not a general power of appointment.

(d) A power of appointment that is not "general" is "special."

(e) A power of appointment may be general as to some appointive property, or an interest in or a specific portion of appointive property, and be special as to other appointive property.
(Stats. 1992, 2016)

Creditor Rights

CPC § 680. Donor Cannot Nullify or Alter Rights of Creditors

The donor of a power of appointment cannot nullify or alter the rights given creditors of the powerholder by Sections 682, 683, and 684 by any language in the instrument creating the power.
(Stats. 1992, 2016)

CPC § 682. When Powerholder's Creditors May Reach Property Subject to General Power

(a) To the extent that the property owned by the powerholder is inadequate to satisfy the claims of the powerholder's creditors, property subject to a general power of appointment that is presently exercisable is subject to the claims to the same extent that it would be subject to the claims if the property were owned by the powerholder.

(b) Upon the death of the powerholder, to the extent that the powerholder's estate is inadequate to satisfy the claims of creditors of the estate and the expenses of administration of the estate, property subject to a general testamentary power of appointment or to a general power of appointment that was presently exercisable at the time of the powerholder's death is subject to the claims and expenses to the same extent that it would be subject to the claims and expenses if the property had been owned by the powerholder.

(c) This section applies whether or not the power of appointment has been exercised.

(Stats. 1992, 2016)

CPC § 683. When Donor's Creditors May Reach Property Subject to General Power

Property subject to a general power of appointment created by the donor in the donor's favor, whether or not presently exercisable, is subject to the claims of the donor's creditors or the donor's estate and to the expenses of the administration of the donor's estate, except to the extent the donor effectively irrevocably appointed the property subject to the general power of appointment in favor of a person other than the donor or the donor's estate.

(Stats. 1992, 2016)

CPC § 684. Creditor Includes Person to Whom Legal Obligation of Support Is Owed

For the purposes of Sections 682 and 683, a person to whom the powerholder owes an obligation of support shall be considered a creditor of the powerholder to the extent that a legal obligation exists for the powerholder to provide the support.

(Stats. 1992, 2016)

Section B. Exercise of a Power of Appointment

Manifestation of Intent

CPC § 640. Manifestation of Intent to Exercise Power

(a) The exercise of a power of appointment requires a manifestation of the powerholder's intent to exercise the power.

(b) A manifestation of the powerholder's intent to exercise a power of appointment exists in any of the following circumstances:

    (1) The powerholder declares, in substance, that the powerholder exercises specific powers or all the powers the powerholder has.

    (2) The powerholder purports to transfer an interest in the appointive property that the powerholder would have no power to transfer except by virtue of the power.

    (3) The powerholder makes a disposition that, when considered with reference to the property owned and the circumstances existing at the time of the disposition, manifests

the powerholder's understanding that the powerholder was disposing of the appointive property.

(c) The circumstances described in subdivision (b) are illustrative, not exclusive.

(Stats. 1992, 2016)

CPC § 641. General Residuary Clause Does Not Exercise Power

(a) A general residuary clause in a will, or a will making general disposition of all the testator's property, does not exercise a power of appointment held by the testator unless specific reference is made to the power or there is some other indication of intent to exercise the power.

(b) This section applies in a case where the powerholder dies on or after July 1, 1982.

(Stats. 1992, 2016)

CPC § 695. Revocability of Exercise

***

(b) Unless made expressly irrevocable by the creating instrument or the instrument of exercise, an exercise of a power of appointment is revocable if the power to revoke exists pursuant to Section 15400 or so long as the interest in the appointive property, whether present or future, has not been transferred or become distributable pursuant to the appointment.

***

⋰⋱

Formal Requirements Imposed by the Donor

CPC § 630. Compliance with Specified Requirements for Exercise of Power

(a) Except as otherwise provided in this part, if the creating instrument specifies requirements as to the manner, time, and conditions of the exercise of a power of appointment, the power can be exercised only by complying with those requirements.

(b) Unless expressly prohibited by the creating instrument, a power stated to be exercisable by an inter vivos instrument is also exercisable by a written will.

CPC § 631. Judicial Relief from Formalities Specified in Creating Instrument

(a) Where an appointment does not satisfy the formal requirements specified in the creating instrument as provided in subdivision (a) of Section 630, the court may excuse compliance with the formal requirements and determine that exercise of the appointment was effective if both of the following requirements are satisfied:

(1) The appointment approximates the manner of appointment prescribed by the donor.

(2) The failure to satisfy the formal requirements does not defeat the accomplishment of a significant purpose of the donor.

(b) This section does not permit a court to excuse compliance with a specific reference requirement under Section 632.

CPC § 632. Specific Reference Requirement

If the creating instrument expressly directs that a power of appointment be exercised by an instrument that makes a specific reference to the power or to the instrument that created the power, the power can be exercised only by an instrument containing the required reference.

NOTE: Estate of John O'Connor, 26 Cal. App. 5th 871, 237 Cal. Rptr. 3d 519 (2018), held that "I exercise any Power of Appointment which I may have over that portion of the trust or trusts established by my parents for my benefit or any other trusts for which I have Power of Appointment" in decedent's will was sufficient to exercise a power granted in a trust established by his parents that gave him a power exercisable by "a will specifically referring to and exercising this general testamentary power of appointment." The trust only required reference to the power, not to to the trust or to the instrument creating the power. John's will contained enough detail that it is reasonable to conclude that he made an intentional and deliberate exercise of the power granted by his parents.

Permissible Exercise of the Power

Permissible Appointees and the Problem of Lapse

CPC § 673. Issue Substituted for Permissible Appointees Who Predecease Powerholder

(a) Except as provided in subdivision (b), if an appointment by will or by instrument effective only at the death of the powerholder is ineffective because of the death of an appointee before the appointment becomes effective and the appointee leaves issue surviving the powerholder, the surviving issue of the appointee take the appointed property in the same manner as the appointee would have taken had the appointee survived the powerholder, except that the property passes only to persons who are permissible appointees, including appointees permitted under Section 674. If the surviving issue are all of the same degree of kinship to the deceased appointee, they take equally, but if of unequal degree, then those of more remote degree take in the manner provided in Section 240.

(b) This section does not apply if either the donor or powerholder manifests an intent that some other disposition of the appointive property shall be made.
(Stats. 1992, 2016)

CPC § 674. Appointment May Be Made to Issue of Predeceased Permissible Appointee

(a) Unless the creating instrument expressly provides otherwise, if a permissible appointee dies before the exercise of a special power of appointment, the powerholder has the power to appoint to the issue of the deceased permissible appointee, whether or not the issue was included within the description of the permissible appointees, if the deceased permissible appointee was alive at the time of the execution of the creating instrument or was born thereafter.

(b) This section applies whether the special power of appointment is exercisable by inter vivos instrument, by will, or otherwise.

(c) This section applies to a case where the power of appointment is exercised on or after July 1, 1982, but does not affect the validity of any exercise of a power of appointment made before July 1, 1982.

(Stats. 1992, 2016)

❧❧

Permissible Appointments

CPC § 650. Permissible Appointments of Property Subject to General Power

(a) The powerholder of a general power of appointment may make an appointment:

(1) Of all of the appointive property at one time, or several partial appointments at different times, where the power is exercisable inter vivos.

(2) Of present or future interests or both.

(3) Subject to conditions or charges.

(4) Subject to otherwise lawful restraints on the alienation of the appointed interest.

(5) In trust.

(6) Creating a new power of appointment.

(b) The listing in subdivision (a) is illustrative, not exclusive.

(Stats. 1992, 2016)

CPC § 651. Permissible Appointments of Property Subject to Special Power

Subject to the limitations imposed by the creating instrument, the powerholder of a special power may make any of the types of appointment permissible for the powerholder of a general power under Section 650.

(Stats. 1992, 2016)

CPC § 670. Validity of Exercise that Exceeds Scope of Power

An exercise of a power of appointment is not void solely because it is more extensive than authorized by the power, but is valid to the extent that the exercise was permissible under the terms of the power.

Exclusive and Nonexclusive Powers

CPC § 652. Special Power Is Exclusive Unless Minimum or Maximum Share Is Specified

(a) Except as provided in subdivision (b), the powerholder of a special power of appointment may appoint the whole or any part of the appointive property to any one or more of the permissible appointees and exclude others.

(b) If the donor specifies either a minimum or maximum share or amount to be appointed to one or more of the permissible appointees, the exercise of the power must conform to the specification.

(Stats. 1992, 2016)

NOTE: Sefton v. Sefton, 206 Cal. App. 4th 875, 142 Cal. Rptr. 3d 174 (rev. den. 2012), held that a power of appointment created by will executed in 1955 by testator who died in 1966 was governed by prior law, not by CPC § 652, which was in effect when power was exercised. Thus, power to appoint to donee's "then living issue" was not exclusive and donee could not exclude one of his children from "at least a substantial portion" of the estate.

On appeal after remand, **Sefton v. Sefton (II)**, 236 Cal. App. 4th 159, 187 Cal. Rptr. 3d 421 (2015) held that donee's attempted appointment was void to the extent it excluded one of his children and that child took the share he was entitled to in default of appointment, rather than a "substantial share" as determined by the court.

Takers in Default and Salvage Doctrines: Allocation and Capture

CPC § 672. Taker in Default, Reversion, or Implied Alternative Appointment to Powerholder's Estate When Powerholder Fails to Make Effective Appointment (Capture Doctrine)

(a) Except as provided in subdivision (b), if the powerholder of a discretionary power of appointment fails to appoint the property, releases the entire power, or makes an ineffective appointment, in whole or in part, the appointive property not effectively appointed passes to the person named by the donor as taker in default or, if there is none, reverts to the donor.

(b) If the powerholder of a general power of appointment makes an ineffective appointment, an implied alternative appointment to the powerholder's estate may be found if the powerholder has manifested an intent that the appointive property be disposed of as property of the powerholder rather than as in default of appointment.

(Stats. 1992, 2016)

CPC § 675. *Allocation of Appointive and Owned Property*

If a powerholder exercises a power of appointment in a disposition that also disposes of property the powerholder owns, the owned property and the appointive property shall be allocated in the permissible manner in accordance with the terms of the creating instrument and that best carries out the powerholder's intent.

(Stats. 2016)

CPC 676. *Partial Appointment to Taker in Default*

Unless the terms of the instrument creating or exercising a power of appointment manifest a contrary intent, if the powerholder makes a valid partial appointment to a taker in default of appointment, the taker in default of appointment may share fully in unappointed property.

(Stats. 2016)

Disclaimer, Release, and Contract

CPC § 660. *Contract to Exercise Power*

(a) The powerholder of a power of appointment that is presently exercisable, whether general or special, can contract to make an appointment to the same extent that the powerholder could make an effective appointment.

(b) The powerholder of a power of appointment cannot contract to make an appointment while the power of appointment is not presently exercisable. If a promise to make an appointment under such a power is not performed, the promisee cannot obtain either specific performance or damages, but the promisee is not prevented from obtaining restitution of the value given by the promisee for the promise.

(c) Unless the creating instrument expressly provides that the powerholder may not contract to make an appointment while the power of appointment is not presently exercisable, subdivision (b) does not apply to the case where the donor and the powerholder are the same person. In this case, the powerholder can contract to make an appointment to the same extent that the powerholder could make an effective appointment if the power of appointment were presently exercisable.

(Stats. 1992, 2016)

CPC § 661. Release of Discretionary Power

(a) Unless the creating instrument otherwise provides, a general or special power of appointment that is a discretionary power, whether testamentary or otherwise, may be released, either with or without consideration, by a written instrument signed by the powerholder and delivered as provided in subdivision (c).

(b) A releasable power may be released with respect to the whole or any part of the appointive property and may also be released in such manner as to reduce or limit the permissible appointees. No partial release of a power shall be deemed to make imperative the remaining power that was not imperative before the release unless the instrument of release expressly so provides. No release of a power that is not presently exercisable is permissible where the donor designated persons or a class to take in default of the powerholder's exercise of the power unless the release serves to benefit all persons designated as provided by the donor. . . .

(Stats. 1992, 2016)

CPC § 695. Absent Reserved Power, Release is Irrevocable

***

(c) Unless the power to revoke is reserved in the instrument releasing the power, a release of a power of appointment is irrevocable.

Section C. Failure to Exercise a Power of Appointment

General Power

See §§ 672 and 676 above.

Special Power

CPC § 613. Meaning of "Imperative" Power

A power of appointment is "imperative" where the creating instrument manifests an intent that the permissible appointees be benefited even if the powerholder fails to exercise the power. An imperative power can exist even though the powerholder has the privilege of selecting some and excluding others of the designated permissible appointees. All other powers of appointment are "discretionary." The powerholder of a discretionary power is privileged to exercise, or not to exercise, the power as the powerholder chooses.

(Stats. 1992, 2016)

CPC § 671. *Permissible Appointees Take Property When Powerholder Fails to Exercise Imperative Power*

(a) Unless the creating instrument or the powerholder, in writing, manifests a contrary intent, where the powerholder dies without having exercised an imperative power of appointment either in whole or in part, the persons designated as permissible appointees take equally of the property not already appointed. Where the creating instrument establishes a minimum distribution requirement that is not satisfied by an equal division of the property not already appointed, the appointees who have received a partial appointment are required to return a pro rata portion of the property they would otherwise be entitled to receive in an amount sufficient to meet the minimum distribution requirement.

(b) Where an imperative power of appointment has been exercised defectively, either in whole or in part, its proper execution may be adjudged in favor of the person intended to be benefited by the defective exercise.

(c) Where an imperative power of appointment has been created so that it confers on a person a right to have the power exercised in the person's favor, the proper exercise of the power can be compelled in favor of the person, or the person's assigns, creditors, guardian, or conservator.

(Stats. 1992, 2016)

Applicable Rule Against Perpetuities

CPC § 690. *USRAP Applies to Powers of Appointment*

The statutory rule against perpetuities provided by Part 2 (commencing with Section 21200) of Division 11 applies to powers of appointment governed by this part.

Chapter 13. Trusts: Construction and Future Interests

Section B. Construction of Trust Instruments

Division 11, Part 1 of the Probate Code, Rules for Interpretation of Instruments, §§ 21101-21135, apply to wills, trusts, deeds and other instruments unless the provision of context otherwise requires. Pertinent sections are set forth in Chapter 5, Wills: Construction.

Requiring Survival to Time of Possession

See CPC §§ 21104 and 21109-21111, set forth in Chapter 5, which apply to a transferee who fails to survive the transferor of a revocable trust or until any future time required by the instrument.

❧❧

Claimant Bears Burden to Show That Trustee Unreasonably Delayed Distribution Until After Death of Beneficiary

EDWARDS v. GILLIS

Court of Appeal, Fourth District, Division 2
208 Cal. App. 4th 1318, 146 Cal. Rptr. 3d 256, Review Denied (2012)

MILLER, J. . . . On December 8, 1988, Eileen P. Gillis (decedent) executed the Eileen Gillis 1988 Trust . . . which named her daughter, Beverly Sims ("Sims"), as successor trustee and distributed the entire contents of the trust equally between her children Sharyn . . . , Barbara . . . , Wayne . . . , Kim . . . , and . . . Sims, upon decedent's death. The Trust provided that the beneficiaries must survive distribution of the assets of the Trust to inherit or their shares would be distributed equally among the surviving beneficiaries. On December 30, 1991, decedent executed a "First Amendment to Declaration of Trust of Eileen Gillis 1988 Trust" . . . which removed Sims as both a beneficiary and successor trustee; the First Amendment named Kim . . . as successor trustee.

On September 5, 2001, decedent executed a "Second Amendment to Declaration of Trust of Eileen Gillis 1988 Trust" . . . , which removed Kim as the successor trustee and replaced her with defendant and respondent John T. Gillis, decedent's husband from whom she was legally separated. The Second Amendment provided, "Under no circumstances do I wish my eldest daughter, Beverly Sims, a.k.a., Beverly Edwards, to receive anything whatsoever from my estate or to have any control or influence over the administration or distribution of the estate."

Decedent died on February 22, 2007. On June 29, 2007, Sims filed a petition to void the trust amendments claiming decedent was ill and in a weakened physical and mental condition when she executed the amendments, and defendant used undue influence and unfair advantage to induce her to amend the Trust. Sims died on May 11, 2008. Defendant made a preliminary distribution to the beneficiaries of $24,000 each on July 22, 2008. Plaintiff and appellant Rex Edwards was substituted in as the special administrator and executor of Sims's estate. Defendant successfully moved for bifurcation of the trial to separately consider first whether plaintiff had standing to challenge the amendments because she predeceased distribution. After a bench trial, the court ruled plaintiff failed to demonstrate defendant had unreasonably delayed distribution of the Trust assets; therefore, plaintiff lacked standing to challenge the amendments because even if invalidated, she would not have stood to inherit from the trust. The court entered judgment for defendant.

On appeal, plaintiff maintains the court applied an incorrect rule of law in requiring plaintiff to bear the burden of proving defendant unreasonably delayed distribution of the trust assets. Instead, plaintiff contends the court should have applied a rule that would only have required plaintiff prove defendant could and should reasonably have made preliminary distributions of the Trust assets prior to Sims's death. We affirm the judgment.

FACTUAL AND PROCEDURAL HISTORY

. . . Sims testified at an expedited deposition due to her poor health that she received an anonymously sent letter from England after her mother's death, in which her mother wrote that she was "forced to remove you from my trust. I am writing this to let you know it was not my intention to take you out of my original trust and will. . . . Please don't feel that I did not appreciate all the work you did for me, and then for me to take you out of my will, that is not what I wanted."

Sims testified she later found another letter addressed to her from her mother behind a picture of her grandmother. In that letter, decedent wrote she "was forced by [defendant] to sign papers saying that if I should die, you are on notice to immediately demand through your attorney to rescind any written agreements. I was very ill at the time and not able to read the papers that [defendant] was forcing me to sign. I had a previous encounter years ago and was forced to sign something and was knocked to the ground which is on Police records as it was reported to them." Petitioner prayed for enforcement of the terms of the Trust as of the date it was originally executed on December 8, 1988.

At trial, Nora Teasley, the CPA hired by defendant on March 8, 2007, to conduct accounting and tax preparation for the Trust testified she had worked as a CPA since 1978 . . . and was an expert in trust administration. . . . Defendant sought Teasley's advice regarding the making of preliminary distributions of the Trust assets . . . Teasley testified that in her experience, her advice "to trustees in the past and present had been not to do any significant distribution until after receipt of the U.S. closing document because the personal liability falls totally on the fiduciary. [Defendant] is personally liable." "[M]y recommendation always is to delay any distribution to the beneficiaries until after receipt of the closing letter." She told defendant there was personal risk to him if he made any distributions too early. . . .

Nevertheless, defendant made a distribution from the trust to the beneficiaries on July 22, 2008, of $24,000 each for a total amount of $96,000. Teasley apparently acquiesced because "there was a strong feeling that it was a small dollar amount" relative to the entire estate. . . .

The closing letter from the IRS was received on February 19, 2009. On May 20, 2009, defendant made another preliminary distribution from the Trust totaling $750,000. Teasley opined it was not unreasonable for defendant to have made no distribution prior to May 11, 2008, because there was no requirement that such a distribution be made, there was no such request from the beneficiaries, and they had yet to receive the U.S. Estate Tax Closing Letter. She concluded it would have been reasonable and prudent for defendant to wait until after receipt of the letter before making any distributions. . . .

Eric Gronroos, a CPA with 24 years of experience and a Master's degree in tax, testified on behalf of plaintiff . . . [that] distributions from trust assets can be made prior to receipt of a closing letter from the IRS: "It is done all the time." He testified that . . . "Typically what we do is we will estimate the potential tax liability that we feel that there is exposure on the estate, if any, and recommend, based on that calculation, what amount should be withheld for potential disputes with the IRS."

In his opinion, preliminary distributions could have been made "without unreasonably exposing the trustee or the beneficiaries to any tax liability." . . .

Defendant testified he did not learn Sims was terminally ill until her deposition in 2008. He made the preliminary distribution on July 22, 2008, at the behest of one of the beneficiaries; he did so over Teasley's objection: "I felt that that small amount of $24,000 would not have a direct impact upon the trust." He also set aside an additional $24,000 should the court determine Sims was entitled to inherit. . . .

After the court heard testimony, plaintiff argued the standard by which the court should resolve the matter was whether defendant reasonably could and should have made a preliminary distribution. Defendant countered that "[t]he test, which [plaintiff] urges the Court to use, would render virtually every distribution survivorship clause found in any trust completely meaningless. It is almost always the case that some small distribution can be made almost immediately after the trustor's death." The court stated, "the trust document itself provided for the reality that you can't just close an estate right after death. There's some properties that you're going to have to manage while you're closing. And when I look at the trust instrument and the cases, the issue really isn't whether it could have been done, it's whether it was unreasonable to not make a distribution. [T]he issue is whether, based on all of the circumstances, it was unreasonable to not make a distribution prior to the first distribution date. Based on the evidence submitted, I can't find that it was unreasonable to wait, based on the CPA's testimony saying 'I always consider it imprudent to distribute prior to a closing letter.' " "I can't say that it was unreasonable to wait for distribution to occur, especially when we have a trustee who's not a beneficiary of this trust, and he's the one personally liable if he messes up."

DISCUSSION

A. *UNREASONABLE DELAY* . . .

In *Taylor*,[40] the decedent died testate providing in her will that one of the beneficiaries, Ellen Catherine Glasky, would take a third share of the estate if she survived distribution; if not, her share would be distributed equally among the remaining two designated beneficiaries.... "The will was admitted to probate on November 26, 1963, and letters testamentary were issued to ... the executor of the estate, on December 2, 1963. The petition for final distribution was filed March 4, 1965, requesting that one-third of the residue of the estate be distributed to [Glasky]. Hearing on the petition was set for March 29, 1965. [Glasky] died March 15, 1965." One of the remaining beneficiaries then filed a petition requesting that the portion of the estate bequeathed to Glasky be distributed among the remaining beneficiaries.... Glasky's legatees filed an objection to the petition. "The court sustained the objections to the petition for final distribution and decreed that [Glasky's] interest vested in her before her death. The court found that the estate could have been distributed in September of 1964 and should have been distributed before the death of [Glasky] in March of 1965."

On appeal, the court framed the issue as "whether a clause requiring survivorship should be interpreted to mean survivorship to distribution or survivorship to the time distribution should have occurred, or, as an alternative, whether survivorship to the earlier date constitutes substantial compliance with the condition." ... The appellate court cited the rule that "vesting cannot be postponed by unreasonable delay in preparing an estate for distribution and that when there is such delay contingent interests vest at the time distribution should have been made. [Citation.]" The court held, "[t]he trial court was ... justified in concluding that the overall delay was unreasonable and in finding that the estate should have been distributed before [Glasky's] death." "[U]nreasonable delay cannot defeat the beneficiary's interest. This conclusion promotes the established policy favoring prompt distribution of estates [citations] and carries out the presumed intent of the testatrix. In the absence of any indication to the contrary a testator contemplates prompt distribution. His intention is substantially complied with if a beneficiary who is alive at the time distribution could and should have occurred is allowed to take under the will. [Citation.]" ...

In *Germond*,[41] decedent died testate on June 9, 1962, leaving all her property to her sister Jessie Nulsen so long as Nulsen lived until distribution of the estate. If not, the whole estate would be divided and distributed between 10 charities. Nulsen died more than 22 months after decedent's death.... "The trial court found that the ... estate could and should have been distributed to ... Nulsen prior to her death and, more specifically, that the estate 'could and should have been distributed to ... Nulsen not later than September 19, 1963.'" ...

On appeal, the reviewing court noted that "[t]he court applied the rule that vesting of interests which are contingent on surviving distribution cannot be postponed by unreasonable delay in distribution and that when there is such delay contingent interests vest at the time distribution should have been made. [Citation.]" ... "The law, however, does not require an executor to proceed 'as quickly as possible'; it requires him to proceed without 'unreasonable delay.' [Citation.]" ...

---

[40] In re Taylor's Estate (1967) 66 Cal. 2d 855, 59 Cal. Rptr. 437, 428 P.2d 301.—Ed.

[41] Estate of Germond (1971) 4 Cal. 3d 573, 94 Cal. Rptr. 153, 483 P.2d 769.—Ed.

The appellate court reversed the judgment, holding that although the executor's delay in filing the estate tax return was unreasonable, speedier liquidation of other assets would not have enabled him to close the estate prior to Nulsen's death. . . . Thus, "[i]n the actual circumstances of this case . . . a preliminary distribution would have been unreasonable, to say the least, because it would have burdened the California realty with a federal tax lien and imposed personal liability on the executor for the amount of that lien, and the . . . estate would never have been able to obtain enough cash to clear the lien." . . . The court reasoned that although "[i]n some circumstances a reasonable executor might be required to make prompt preliminary distribution" . . . the court could not hold "that because there was a survival of distribution clause in the . . . will the executor was required to administer the estate in a manner different from that required by generally accepted reasonable probate practice." . . .

[T]he rule that has developed is that any contingent beneficiary who petitions the court contending a preliminary distribution of the assets of an estate or trust could or should have been made at an earlier date has the burden of establishing that the executor or trustee unreasonably delayed such distribution.

This is because any other rule would, as defendant noted below, "render virtually every distribution survivorship clause found in any trust completely meaningless. It is almost always the case that some small distribution can be made almost immediately after the trustor's death." . . .

If a trustor wishes all beneficiaries to take immediately upon her death, she can so provide in the trust. However, where she includes a provision that allows the beneficiaries to take only upon survivorship of distribution, we hold any contingent beneficiary's interest vests only when she meets the contingency, distribution actually occurs, or when that beneficiary, or her heirs, can prove a time, before the her death, beyond which any distribution was unreasonably delayed.

For sure, in determining whether distribution was unreasonably delayed, a court should examine the assets of the trust, the health and financial condition of the contingent beneficiaries, and any personal interest the trustee might have in delaying distribution. However, none of these considerations should change the underlying rule that the contingent beneficiary prove the trustee unreasonably delayed distribution. Thus, the trial court applied the correct rule of law. . . .

Here, sufficient evidence supported the trial court's determination defendant did not unreasonably delay distribution of the Trust's assets. First, defendant had no personal, financial interest in the assets of the trust; thus, he did not stand to gain by delaying distribution. Second, Sims had not been a beneficiary of the Trust since execution of the First Amendment on December 30, 1991; over 15 years by the time decedent died on February 22, 2007. Thus, defendant could hardly be said to have unreasonably delayed distribution so as to disinherit someone who did not, from his perspective, have any claim on the Trust. Third, defendant testified he did not learn of Sims's ovarian cancer until her deposition on March 18, 2008, only three months before her death, but more than a year after decedent's death. It is simply untenable to contend defendant should have issued a distribution in the three months between learning of Sims's fatal illness, and her death, when he did not issue one in the preceding 13 months, and Sims had no standing at that time to benefit from such a distribution. . . .

DISPOSITION

The judgment is affirmed. Responded is awarded his costs on appeal.

Gifts to Classes

Gifts to Children, Issue, or Descendants

See CPC §§ 245-247 for the manner of distributing gifts to issue or descendants in trusts and CPC § 21115 for determining whether halfbloods, adopted persons, persons born out of wedlock, stepchildren, foster children, and their issue are included in class gifts. These sections are set forth in Chapter 2.

Gifts to Heirs

CPC § 21114. Meaning of Gift to Heirs

(a) If a statute or an instrument provides for transfer of a present or future interest to, or creates a present or future interest in, a designated person's "heirs," "heirs at law," "next of kin," "relatives," or "family," or words of similar import, the transfer is to the persons, including the state under Section 6800, and in the shares that would succeed to the designated person's intestate estate under the intestate succession law of the transferor's domicile, if the designated person died when the transfer is to take effect in enjoyment. If the designated person's surviving spouse is living but is remarried at the time the transfer is to take effect in enjoyment, the surviving spouse is not an heir of the designated person for purposes of this section.

(b) As used in this section, "designated person" includes the transferor.

(Stats. 1994, 2002)

CPC § 21108. Doctrine of Worthier Title Does Not Apply

The law of this state does not include (a) the common law rule of worthier title that a transferor cannot devise an interest to his or her own heirs or (b) a presumption or rule of interpretation that a transferor does not intend, by a transfer to his or her own heirs or next of kin, to transfer an interest to them. The meaning of a transfer of a legal or equitable interest to a transferor's own heirs or next of kin, however designated, shall be determined by the general rules applicable to the interpretation of instruments.

(Stats. 1994, 2002)

Civil Code § 779. Rule in Shelley's Case Does Not Apply

When a remainder is limited to the heirs, or heirs of the body, of a person to whom a life estate in the same property is given, the persons who, on the termination of the life estate, are the successors or heirs of the body of the owner for life, are entitled to take by virtue of the remainder so limited to them, and not as mere successors of the owner for life.

(Stats. 1872)

Chapter 14. The Rule Against Perpetuities and Trust Duration

USRAP

California adopted the Uniform Statutory Rule Against Perpetuities in 1991. It is codified at CPC §§ 21200-21231.

Duration of Trusts

CPC § 15413. Termination After Perpetuities Period Has Expired

A trust provision, express or implied, that the trust may not be terminated is ineffective insofar as it purports to be applicable after the expiration of the longer of the periods provided by the statutory rule against perpetuities, Article 2 (commencing with Section 21205) of Chapter 1 of Part 2 of Division 11.

Chapter 14 The Rule Against Perpetuities and Trust Duration

Table of Cases

Principal cases are in upper case, note cases are in lower case.

Table of Statutes

California Bar Statutes

California Probate Code Non-Bar Statutes

California Family Code

California Civil Code

California Code of Civil Procedure

California Welfare & Institutions Code